Contemporary Theology: An Introduction will assuredly—and quickly—become an indispensable addition to the required reading list for undergraduate and graduate courses on Christian theology and Christian ethics. As in all his publications, Professor MacGregor combines comprehensive and context-driven historical analysis with superlative writing skills. Difficult concepts are presented in a clearly-written, crisp, and engaging style. For the general reader interested in the positive impact of Christian ethics on our fragmented and contentious world, your understanding of the ongoing cultural struggle for ethical assurances, drawn from the long history of Christian theology, will be exponentially enhanced. Highly recommended!

JOHN K. SIMMONS, professor emeritus of religious studies,
Western Illinois University

With *Contemporary Theology: An Introduction* Professor MacGregor presents the theological community a highly readable, cogent, and insightful inventory of two centuries of modern theological thought. Scholars will appreciate the comprehensive overview, students will love the easy access of thirty-eight nearly standalone chapters, and the generally educated layperson will value the contextualization of their own experiences which this volume offers. Additionally, the extensive critical apparatus helpfully lays out both pivotal primary texts and useful secondary sources, thus ensuring that *Contemporary Theology* shall soon become a sought after college and seminary textbook as well as a frequently consulted theological handbook.

ROMWALD MACZKA, professor emeritus of religion,
Carthage College

In *Contemporary Theology* Kirk MacGregor skillfully acquaints readers with the principal thinkers and schools of thought in Christian theology over the past two hundred years, both inside and outside evangelicalism. MacGregor beautifully discloses how the renaissance in philosophy of religion over the past half-century has shaped many of the most creative and constructive strides in theology today. I heartily recommend this book.

WILLIAM LANE CRAIG, research professor of philosophy,
Talbot School of Theology, and professor of philosophy,
Houston Baptist University

When traveling through new and unfamiliar terrain, having a knowledgeable guide is essential. But if that guide is also an excellent communicator, then so much the better. MacGregor demonstrates that he is both. In *Contemporary Theology: An Introduction*, MacGregor gives the reader a clear and balanced tour through the modern theological landscape.

> **KENNETH D. KEATHLEY**, senior professor of theology,
> Jesse Hendley Endowed Chair of Biblical Theology,
> and director of the L. Russ Bush Center for Faith and Culture,
> Southeastern Baptist Theological Seminary

Kirk MacGregor has given to us an accessible, wide-ranging overview of the contemporary theological scene. It is not only a valuable resource, but it rightly recognizes the important contributions of philosophy of religion and analytic theology in helping to shape and guide much of today's theological discourse.

> **PAUL COPAN**, the Pledger Family Chair of Philosophy and Ethics,
> Palm Beach Atlantic University, and author of *A Little Book for New Philosophers*

textbook*plus*⁺

Equipping Instructors and Students with
FREE RESOURCES *for Core Zondervan Textbooks*

Available Resources for
Contemporary Theology: An Introduction

Instructor Resources

- Instructor's manual
- Presentation slides
- Chapter quizzes
- Midterm and final exams
- Sample syllabus
- Image/map library

Student Resources

- Videos
- Flashcards
- Exam study guide

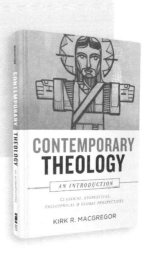

CONTEMPORARY
THEOLOGY
AN INTRODUCTION

CLASSICAL, EVANGELICAL,
PHILOSPHICAL & GLOBAL PERSPECTIVES

KIRK R. MACGREGOR

*How To Access Resources

- Go to www.ZondervanAcademic.com
- Click "Sign Up" button and complete registration process
- Find books using search field or browse using discipline categories
- Click "Teaching Resources" or "Study Resources" tab once you get to book page to access resources

▶ *www.ZondervanAcademic.com*

CONTEMPORARY
THEOLOGY

An *INTRODUCTION*

CLASSICAL, EVANGELICAL, PHILOSOPHICAL,
AND GLOBAL PERSPECTIVES

KIRK R. MACGREGOR

ZONDERVAN

Contemporary Theology: An Introduction
Copyright © 2019 by Kirk R. MacGregor

This title is also available as a Zondervan ebook.

Requests for information should be addressed to:
Zondervan, *3900 Sparks Dr. SE, Grand Rapids, Michigan 49546*

ISBN 978-0-310-53453-2

Cover design: Brian Bobel
Cover photo: Shutterstock, Getty Images
Interior design: Kait Lamphere

Printed in the United States of America

18 19 20 21 22 23 24 25 26 27 28 /DHV/ 15 14 13 12 11 10 9 8 7 6 5 4 3 2 1

To my colleagues at McPherson College

CONTENTS

ACKNOWLEDGMENTS

I would like to thank my colleagues at McPherson College, who have all shown me tremendous support and encouragement as I have worked on this book. I am especially grateful to Dr. Michael Schneider, president, and Dr. Bruce Clary, vice president for Academic Affairs, who care deeply about me as a teacher-scholar and have created an optimal work environment for me to thrive and flourish. I am also especially grateful to Dr. Herb Smith and Dr. Tom Hurst, my peers in the Department of Philosophy and Religion, whose warmth, invaluable friendship, and terrific sense of humor make every day at work quite enjoyable. Special thanks to Dr. Kerry Dobbins in the Department of History and Politics for taking good care of my wife and son while they were ill and I was out of town filming the video lectures that form a companion to the textbook. Thanks also to Professor Kyle Hopkins in the Department of Music for allowing me to experience spirituality through trumpet performance as a community member of the McPherson College band. Kyle was my motivation for including chapter 34 on theology and the arts.

I owe a debt of gratitude to Madison Trammel, my editor at Zondervan, for his backing and assistance from the start of this project and for his outstanding suggestions regarding the content of the book. I wish to extend a special note of appreciation to Dr. Michael Wittmer at Grand Rapids Theological Seminary, Cornerstone University, and Matthew Estel at Zondervan for reviewing the manuscript in its entirety and providing extremely valuable feedback. Accordingly, I bear sole responsibility for interpretations of all doubtful points and decisions on what material to include and exclude. Any defects that remain in the book are therefore entirely my own.

Last but certainly not least, I would like to thank my wife, Lara, and my son, Dwiane. My regular theological conversations with Lara greatly enhance my scholarship, and the energy and *joie de vivre* constantly exhibited by Dwiane inspire me.

TO THE READER

This book will acquaint you with the major thinkers and schools of thought in Christian theology from the nineteenth century to the present, both inside and outside the scope of the evangelical tradition, in roughly chronological order. As a result, you will understand how today's evangelical, mainline, and radical perspectives have achieved their current shape. Your tour through the last two centuries will commence with the birth of modern liberal theology and existentialism together with such contemporaneous evangelical developments as dispensationalism and Princeton theology. You will see the contributions to contemporary theology made by the great preacher Charles Haddon Spurgeon and revivalist theologians like D. L. Moody. Starting in the twentieth century, you will encounter significant evangelical theological innovations in global Christianity. Latin American pneumatology, African Christology viewing Jesus as healer and ancestor, and Chinese eschatology reflect the reality that the more than two-thirds of the world's evangelical Christians who live in the global South and Asia have much to teach their Western counterparts.

Alongside such twentieth-century theological heavyweights as Karl Barth, Rudolf Bultmann, and Paul Tillich, you will witness the emergence of contemporary evangelicalism and fresh developments in the Roman Catholic world. You will encounter Jürgen Moltmann's theology of hope, liberation theology, feminist theology, and evangelical complementarianism and egalitarianism, all phenomena that are vitally important in the church today. You will discover the evangelical renaissance in philosophy of religion that has taken place over the past half century. This philosophical renaissance has arguably resulted in the most creative and constructive strides in evangelical theology, as evidenced by the formation of the Evangelical Philosophical Society and the Society of Christian Philosophers. You will witness groundbreaking recent developments in exegetical theology, including the new perspective on Paul, the theological interpretation of Scripture, and evolutionary creation. You will learn about new directions in Christian ethics, as evinced by current Anabaptist theology, and new directions in worship, as evinced by Jeremy Begbie's theology of the arts.

As far as I am able, I hope to provide a clear and unbiased perception of the theological landscape of the past two centuries and furnish you a springboard for your own theological explorations. Enjoy the journey!

CHAPTER 1

PHILOSOPHICAL BACKGROUNDS

The aim of this opening chapter is to briefly sketch the philosophical backdrop of the modern period. In examining contemporary theology, one realizes that much of contemporary theology has appropriated various ideas and methods from modern philosophy and conjoined them to biblical language and concepts. Hence to understand the contemporary era of theology, it is imperative that we gain a handle on the philosophy that underlies the modern period. Many intellectual historians have justifiably quipped that modern philosophy began with the thought of French philosopher and mathematician René Descartes (1596–1650), for he introduced major changes in philosophical thinking and method that have profoundly shaped the course of philosophy since his time. The most monumental of all these changes was the removal of God from the center of the philosophical enterprise. Accordingly, we need to survey these changes and note their ramifications in the history of philosophy from Descartes onward.

PRE-CARTESIAN RELATIONSHIP BETWEEN PHILOSOPHY AND THEOLOGY

Prior to Descartes in the medieval period (and stretching back in some degree to the ancient period), all philosophers were by definition theologians, and all theologians were by definition philosophers. The medieval period regarded theology as the queen of the sciences, such that those who endeavored for ecclesiastical careers studied the fields of logic, mathematics, language, literature, and philosophy as the indispensable preliminaries for laboring in the most important field, theology. Conversely, perceiving theology as the queen of the sciences meant that all other disciplines must in some fashion be related to theology. Thus medieval philosophers, while treating many of the same broad topics treated in modern philosophy (such as metaphysics, epistemology, and ethics), would view these topics through the *Vorhabe*, or presuppositional lens, of God's existence and ultimate significance as the *summum bonum*, or highest good. In short, God was the starting point of medieval philosophy, and all philosophical work saw God playing a significant role.

For instance, the Franciscan philosopher-theologian Bonaventure (1221–74) held that God has ideas in his mind about all the possible objects he could create. Patterned after these ideas, God created various objects in the physical and spiritual world. All physical and spiritual objects therefore conform to the ideas in God's mind, and the ideas would conform to the objects that God created. Knowledge requires access to the ideas in God's mind. If someone, then, wanted to gain knowledge of any particular object, such as a cat, God would need to bestow illumination upon the human mind. Although contemporary Christians usually take illumination to be a theological doctrine whereby God enables the human mind to accurately understand Scripture, Bonaventure posited illumination as the basis of his epistemology. Here God, after creating the cat on the pattern of his idea, would illumine the human mind so that as it looked out into the world, it would be able to perceive that it was seeing a cat. Likewise, for any human to know any object of knowledge, God would need to illumine the mind. Following suit with Bonaventure, it can be generally stated that, for medieval philosophers, without divine illumination all human knowledge is impossible. Hence epistemology and perception simply could not be discussed in the medieval period sans God.

DESCARTES'S NEW METHODOLOGICAL APPROACH

Descartes, however, championed a new way of doing philosophy based on a radically different epistemology. His motivation was to secure an indubitable foundation upon which to erect the edifices of faith and knowledge, thereby refuting skepticism. He held that the proper starting point for philosophical reflection was not God but rather that which the human mind could know beyond any doubt. Thus his 1641 *Meditations on First Philosophy* commences by calling into question everything he thought he knew to test whether he, in fact, actually knew it. Descartes resolved to maintain only those elements in his thinking which he was indubitably sure he truly did know. Systematically questioning one element after another that he formerly held as knowledge, Descartes found reasonable doubt that he really knew these elements. Even for elements that seemed certain, such as the existence of the external world, Descartes concluded that they were doubtable, since it was logically possible for there to be an evil demon who was tampering with his sensory perceptors!

As a result of this method of calling into question everything he seemingly knew to find out what he did know beyond all doubt, Descartes arrived at one certain truth that he said must serve as the starting point of philosophy. Without such a truth, Descartes held, there would be no way to attain knowledge at all. At this juncture, I remind the reader that it was not Descartes's purpose to undermine faith; rather, he wished to ground faith on a sure foundation that could be definitely proved and could not reasonably be doubted. Descartes's one certain truth turned out to be his own existence, summed up in the Latin phrase *cogito ergo sum* ("I think/doubt, therefore I am"). For Descartes found that even when he doubted his own existence, there was someone—he himself—who did the doubting, thus proving his existence absolutely. This certain truth, often styled the *cogito*, gained almost unanimous assent in the subsequent history of philosophy as its new epistemological starting point. Hence the starting point of philosophy was no longer God but rather one's own consciousness, the certainty of oneself as a thinking being. God, if posited at all in philosophical discussion, would now be posited as a consequence of previous arguments or an afterthought, usually at some late stage in a philosophical system. With Descartes, then, we observe the new significance placed on consciousness and in particular self-consciousness of one's own person.

This specific trend of making humanity, and humanity's own consciousness, the initial focus (and even emphasis) of philosophy would roll through later philosophy like a tidal wave and grow increasingly important in contemporary theology. Hence post-Cartesian philosophy and theology alike repeatedly emphasize the standing of the individual knower, with his own consciousness and own self, as subject rather than as object. Upon discovering the indubitable *cogito*, Descartes felt he needed to establish some criterion for truth so that he would have a method of being able to discover what other things he might know. This criterion deemed true only those items of which he possessed a clear and distinct idea. If he possessed the clear and distinct idea of a cat standing before him, then he would conclude that there truly was a cat standing before him.

But observing the principle of radical doubt, Descartes realized that one could doubt even those things of which one possessed a clear and distinct idea (e.g., one could be having an illusion or be overcome by an evil demon) unless some greater reality existed that ensured the reality or veridicality of one's perceptions.

For Descartes, this greater reality was God. Consequently, his third and fifth *Meditations* set out to prove God's existence not as a starting point of philosophy but as the being who guarantees that a person cannot be mistaken when he thinks he is having a clear and distinct idea. For if God exists, then God would protect the person from anything that might tamper with reason or sense perception. Here we see the paradigm that prompted the later inclination to invoke God only when needed to secure a specific point in a philosopher's epistemology.

RATIONALISM VERSUS EMPIRICISM

If knowledge must start with the self rather than God, then how does the self acquire truth? Two different answers to this question were furnished by rationalism and empiricism. Descartes spearheaded the movement known as rationalism, which proceeded to encompass Baruch Spinoza (1632–77) and Gottfried Wilhelm von Leibniz (1646–1716). Rationalism is a theory of philosophy in which the criterion of truth is primarily intellectual and deductive (and which, only secondarily, may appeal to the senses when first grounded upon an intellectual and deductive basis). Rationalists believe in innate or intuitable knowledge—namely, knowledge that is self-contained within the intellect, lacking any reference to the external world beyond the mind. Such knowledge is deductive and noncontradictory. Frequently appealing to the law of noncontradiction (that a statement cannot be both true and false at the same time and in the same sense), rationalism introduced mathematical models into philosophy. Rationalists often maintained that the noncontradictory character of a possible entity was sufficient to guarantee its actual existence; for instance, if no contradiction was to be found in the notion of humans having an immortal soul, then humans must have an immortal soul. In contrast to rationalism, the movement of empiricism, represented by John Locke (1632–1704), George Berkeley (1685–1753), and David Hume (1711–76), maintained sensory experience as its criterion of truth. Postulating that nothing is in the mind that is not first in the senses, empiricists argued that sensory experience was the sole source of knowledge, such that knowledge could only be acquired via sensory contact with the external world.

KANT AND THE COPERNICAN REVOLUTION IN PHILOSOPHY

Combining the opposing traditions of rationalism and empiricism was the epochal German philosopher Immanuel Kant (1724–1804). Before the time of

Kant, philosophers viewed the mind as quite passive in its acquisition of knowledge, whereby data would inundate the senses and imprint themselves on the mind as though the mind were a tabula rasa, or blank slate. Kant asserted that such a view, dubbed retrospectively as "naive realism," proved fundamentally inaccurate, as the mind interacted with the world logically prior to the world's impacting the mind. Kant postulated that there are certain basic concepts inherent in the mind that allow the mind to interact with the world and to make judgments about what is and is not actually occurring in the world. One such concept is causality. While humans do not actually see causal connections in the world, they frequently see one event occur and then another event occur and conclude, based on the idea of causation intrinsic to the mind, that the first event caused the second event. This, along with other mentally intrinsic categories like disjunction (perceiving various things as alternatives), particularity, and universality, allow us to evaluate and understand reality.

Kant termed these categories transcendental because, although located in experience as an interconnected whole, they transcend and are separate from the sensuous materials found in the world. Hence Kant's system is a priori in that the categories logically precede the material objects that they relate. Through these categories, the mind interacts with data in the external world and makes judgments about them, such as their relation to each other and their respective sizes. The sensuous materials in the world Kant denominated percepts (things we can perceive). Through the understanding, reason furnishes the concepts that synthesize the percepts into meaningful judgments about the natural order. Kant's twofold change in the understanding of the knowing relation and the understanding of how the mind functions in knowing was so monumental that it is recognized as his Copernican Revolution in philosophy. Just as Copernicus made the pivotal cosmological shift from Ptolemaically viewing the earth as the center of the galaxy to heliocentrically viewing the sun as the center of the galaxy, so Kant's epistemology made the pivotal philosophical shift from viewing the mind as passive to viewing the mind and the world as synergistically involved in the knowing process.

Perception

Kant's Copernican Revolution in philosophy had profound repercussions for the theory of sense perception. While agreeing with empiricism that our knowledge of the world comes to us via our senses, Kant held with rationalism that the mind itself contributes to our perception. Prior to Hume, the dominant theory of perception was naive realism, such that the mind passively and precisely mirrors reality. Upon their bombardment by objects of experience, the sensory organs would imprint this data on the mind, giving the mind a perception of objects as they are in themselves. During Hume's time, however, philosophers recognized that perception could be partially distorted by the sensory organs, leading to a sort of tempered realism. To illustrate, looking at a pencil partially submerged in a glass of water yields perception that the pencil is bent, while looking at the pencil out of water furnishes perception that the pencil is straight. Moreover, people looking at the same object from different positions may see that object differently. So the sensory organs were now seen as impressing generally reliable, but not infallible, data upon the mind, such that the mind passively but somewhat imprecisely mirrors reality.

A more sophisticated theory of sensory perception than either naive realism or "tempered" realism was furnished by Kant. Kant reasoned that if the mind is as active and significant in the gaining of knowledge as the data of sense, distortion of reality may occur not only through the sensory organs but also through the mind itself. Consequently, Kant insisted that for any given thing, we must distinguish between the thing in itself and the thing for us (or as it appears to us). Due to possible distortion by sensory organs and the mind alike, no one is ever in a position to see a thing in itself but may only see a thing as it appears to the observer. The accuracy of this sight is proportional to the proper working of our sensory organs, the function of concepts in our mind, and the degree to which those concepts integrate the data from the external world. Accordingly, if one's mind possesses the concept of a cat but lacks the concept of a dog and one sees a dog, one may well misidentify the dog as a large cat. Hence perception is not simply a matter of the world being mirrored by the mind, but the mind must possess an adequate range of intrinsic concepts to make an accurate judgment as to what is being seen. The Kantian view of perception generated an increasing philosophical consensus that humans lack the ability to have direct and immediate contact with the external world; they only possess the ability to have direct and immediate contact with the basic thoughts and ideas in their own consciousness.

Metaphysics

Related to epistemology is metaphysics, which deals with the nature and structure of reality; this field encountered far more radical change from the time of Descartes to Kant than did epistemology. In short, the Kantian change in epistemology produced even greater change in metaphysics. Such change proved immensely important to subsequent philosophy and theology alike. Before Kant, philosophers regularly discussed topics like God, the soul, immortality, and the world as a whole. On the one hand, rationalists would attempt to reason in favor of the existence of these realities, even though they would not employ these topics as starting points for their reflection in the fashion of medieval philosophy. On the other hand, empiricists questioned how much humans could know about these realities, which stand at least partially if not completely beyond our sensory experience. Thus even Hume, an avowed skeptic, argued in his *Dialogues Concerning Natural Religion* (1750–76) not so much concerning whether God exists but how much humans could truly know about God if God exists. But in either the case of rationalism or empiricism, discourse about God and spiritual matters were possible.

Exhibiting a far more negative assessment than any of his precursors, Kant boldly asserted that he put an end to metaphysics altogether. We recall that, for any object experienced through sense perception, Kantian epistemology averred that while we cannot know the object in itself, we can at least know the object as it appears to us. Kant claimed that the objects of experience that we can know for us exist in the phenomenal realm, namely, the realm of appearances. However, Kant proceeded to insist that there are a number of things, including God, the soul, immortality, and the world as a whole, that lie utterly beyond our experience. These things transcend our experience and are not things for us at all, for Kant deemed that in no way can the mind apply the categories of thought to a nonsensuous thing. All of the objects not available to us via the senses Kant placed in the noumenal realm. Kant then contended that anything in the noumenal realm is ipso facto not an object of knowledge. Thus with Kant, the notion of metaphysics turns full circle, as God goes from being the starting point of philosophy and the foundation of knowledge in medieval thought to no longer being considered even an object of knowledge. So according to Kant, things like God, the immortal soul, and the world in its entirety are not objects of knowledge. This does not mean that such entities do not exist, but it does mean that even if they do exist, there is no way to prove that they exist. And Kant maintained the premise that knowledge requires proof, a premise that has become foundational to modernity.

Here I quote from Kant's *Critique of Pure Reason* (1781) on the noumenal and phenomenal realms, such that the things in the noumenal realm are not objects of knowledge:

> At the very outset, however, we come upon an ambiguity which may occasion serious misapprehension. The understanding, when it entitles an object in a

[certain] relation mere phenomenon, at the same time forms, apart from that relation, a representation of an *object in itself*, and so comes to represent itself as also being able to form *concepts* of such objects. And since the understanding yields no concepts additional to the categories, it also supposes that the object in itself must at least be *thought* through these pure concepts, and so is misled into treating the entirely *indeterminate* concept of an intelligible entity, namely, of a something in general outside our sensibility, as being a *determinate* concept of an entity that allows of being known in a certain [purely intelligible] manner by means of the understanding.[1]

Essentially, what Kant suggested here is that the object in itself does not belong to our phenomenal realm and so is not an object of knowledge. In the same section, Kant proceeded to say that although we can intellectually discern that the things in the noumenal realm *may* exist, we cannot know that they *actually* exist.

Further, the concept of a noumenon is necessary, to prevent sensible intuition from being extended to things in themselves, and thus to limit the objective validity of sensible knowledge. The remaining things, to which it does not apply, are entitled noumena, in order to show that this knowledge cannot extend its domain over everything which the understanding thinks.[2]

This noumenon includes things that we simply are not able to know through experience. For Kant, positing in a rationalist vein that we do know some such things because their concepts are not self-contradictory is insufficient.

The possibility of a thing can never be proved merely from the fact that its concept is not self-contradictory, but only through its being supported by some corresponding intuition. If, therefore, we should attempt to apply the categories to objects which are not viewed as being appearances, we should have to postulate an intuition other than the sensible, and the object would thus be a noumenon in the positive sense. Since, however, such a type of intuition, intellectual intuition, forms no part whatsoever of our faculty of knowledge, it follows that the employment of the categories can never extend further than to the objects of experience.[3]

Because we need to possess and use the categories of knowledge to know anything about the world, we extend those categories that are in the mind to the sensible data of the world. But if there are no sensory data in regard to some-thing we hope to know, then that thing cannot be an object of knowledge. For Kant, knowledge required both rational concepts and empirical percepts. Thus knowledge must be experiential, and it must conform to our a priori mental categories.

THE PURPOSE OF RELIGION

From Kant's perspective, therefore, there may be a God, but there is nothing we can really say about him as to his being an object of our knowledge. So surely, Kant argued, we cannot produce any argument, much less demonstrative proof, that God exists. While Kant did believe in the existence of God, he averred that God must be a postulate of practical rather than pure reason (that is, ethics rather than epistemology). Kant was an ethicist, and he believed he needed the existence of God to ensure the moral governance of the world. If there is no God, then everyone might live as they please without fear of a final judgment. Kant believed that religion had one main purpose: to furnish moral foundations and education for society. In his most significant book on religion, *Religion within the Limits of Reason Alone*, Kant relegated religion to the ethical realm. Authentic religion, including true Christianity, amounted to living a life in harmony with rationally discernible duty.

Given the indispensability of genuine moral accountability in the universe, Kant claimed that there had to be a God. However, we cannot prove this because God lies in the noumenal realm, far beyond what our experience can know. As a result, God is effectively taken out of metaphysics and thus debarred from demonstration, knowability, and meaningful discourse. Ironically, Kant viewed this as a major step forward for Christianity: "I have therefore found it necessary to deny knowledge, in order to make room for faith."[4] So although Christians can never know God and other realities beyond the human senses, they can still believe in them. Hence Kant instigated the infamous distinction between knowledge and faith. This Kantian maneuver unwittingly paved the way for what we will encounter in chapter 19, namely, the death of God theologies. For suppose the best theists can do is to postulate that God exists because they need God to ensure the moral governance of the world. Then it will not be long before God is seen as even more transcendent to the point where theologians will claim that God is totally beyond our knowledge and our being able to say anything about him. And if this is the case, we might as well say that there is no God or, at least, that God as we thought of him certainly must not exist.

CONCLUSION

This chapter has presented some of the key concepts that form the background of modern theology and philosophy. We may summarize the main elements of modernity in three convictions. First is the autonomy of self, where the self is the starting point. Second is the notion that knowledge requires proof. Third is the reduction of God and religion to morality. The major Enlightenment developments occurring from Descartes to Kant form the thematic springboard for the work of several contemporary theologians and philosophers discussed in this book, who were spurred to react to these developments in both positive and negative ways. These reactions will begin to surface in the next chapter, where we will explore the theology of Schleiermacher.

FOR FURTHER READING

Primary Sources

Descartes, René. *A Discourse on Method*. Trans. John Veitsh. London: J. M. Dent, 1912.
———. *Meditations on First Philosophy*. Trans. Laurence J. Lafleur. New York: Liberal Arts Press, 1951.
Kant, Immanuel. *Critique of Practical Reason*. Trans. Lewis White Beck. Indianapolis: Bobbs-Merrill, 1956.
———. *Critique of Pure Reason*. Trans. Norman Kemp Smith. New York: St. Martin's, 1965.
———. *Religion within the Limits of Reason Alone*. Trans. Theodore M. Greene and Hoyt H. Hudson. New York: Harper, 1960.

Secondary Sources

Beck, Lewis W. *A Commentary on Kant's "Critique of Pure Reason."* Chicago: University of Chicago Press, 1966.
———, ed. *Kant Studies Today*. LaSalle, IL: Open Court, 1969.
Butler, R. J., ed. *Cartesian Studies*. Oxford: Blackwell, 1972.
Carus, Paul, ed. *Kant's Prolegomena to Any Future Metaphysics*. Chicago: Open Court, 1949.
England, Frederick E. *Kant's Conception of God*. London: Allen and Unwin, 1929.
Flesher, Paul V. "Structure and Argument: A Study of Immanuel Kant's Religion within the Limits of Reason Alone." *Journal of Religious Studies* 15 (1989): 115–30.
Mahony, Michael J. *Cartesianism*. New York: Fordham University Press, 1925.
Palmquist, Stephen R. "Immanuel Kant: A Christian Philosopher?" *Faith and Philosophy* 6, no. 1 (1989): 65–75.
Popkin, Richard H. *The History of Scepticism from Erasmus to Spinoza*. Berkeley: University of California Press, 1979.
Schoenborn, Alexander von. "Kant's Philosophy of Religion Reconsidered: Reason, Religion, and the Unfinished Business of the Enlightenment." *Philosophy and Theology* 6, no. 4 (1991): 101–16.

CHAPTER 2

FRIEDRICH SCHLEIERMACHER

Founder of Modern Liberal Theology

Friedrich Schleiermacher (1768–1834) was the first professional Protestant theologian to propose across-the-board revisions of traditional Protestant beliefs reconcilable with the *Zeitgeist* of modernity. Schleiermacher is the first modern theologian because he starts with the autonomous self and what she can grasp or prove of God. The result marked the birth of modern liberal theology, a style of theology that locates piety within the individual as the *Gefühl*—the feeling of being totally dependent on something infinite that manifests itself in and through finite things.

SCHLEIERMACHER'S PERSONAL BACKGROUND

Schleiermacher was born in the German state of Prussia to devout Pietist parents who held traditional Protestant beliefs. They sent the young Friedrich first to a Pietist-operated boarding school and then to a Pietist secondary school focused on the training of future church leaders. Upon pursuit of higher education at the University of Halle (also founded by Pietists), Schleiermacher embraced Enlightenment thought, especially the philosophy of Kant. As a result, Schleiermacher began articulating doubts about the veracity of some orthodox Christian doctrines in letters to his father, creating a schism between the two that was gradually bridged. Nonetheless, Schleiermacher continued to grapple with his father's traditional Christianity, years later expressing in a letter to his sister his own perspective of always remaining a Pietist of a "higher order." After earning his doctorate, Schleiermacher became a minister of the Reformed Church and served as a chaplain at a hospital in Berlin. In 1804 Schleiermacher returned to the University of Halle as professor of theology and university preacher. When Napoleon closed the university two years later, Schleiermacher moved back to Berlin, pastoring the city's prominent Trinity Church and cofounding the University of Berlin. While serving as dean of Berlin's theology faculty, Schleiermacher amassed a reputation as a national hero, powerful preacher, and towering intellectual throughout Germany. At his death, the people of Berlin lined the streets in mourning as the funeral procession came through the city.

ON RELIGION: ADDRESSES IN RESPONSE TO ITS CULTURED DESPISERS

While Schleiermacher authored several books throughout his career, two stand out as foundational to the formation of liberal Protestantism. The first is his 1799 *On Religion: Addresses in Response to Its Cultured Despisers*, which Schleiermacher's future adherents would recognize as a classic apologetic of theological liberalism. Taking part in the salon culture of Berlin, Schleiermacher queried how to reach Christianity's "cultured critics" and convince them of the truth of Christianity as a positive, or historically situated, religion based on divine revelation. Moreover, in his work as a pastor and hospital chaplain, Schleiermacher experienced the popular cultural fascination with Romanticism, an affective reaction to the Enlightenment's overemphasis on objective reason. Accordingly, the Romantics embraced "feelings," by which they denoted not irrational emotions but profound human longings and appreciation for beauty in the natural world. In an age that valued hard, scientific data and intellectualism, the Romantic movement birthed new flowerings of the arts, including the literature of Goethe and the music of Beethoven. Hence Schleiermacher desired to locate a point of contact for Christianity in his circle of friends, most of whom were highly skeptical of traditional religion. For them he wrote *On Religion*, which postulated that the essence of religion does not lie in anything supernatural, dogmatic, churchly, or ritualistic. Rather, the essence of religion is a "fundamental, distinct, and integrative element of human life and culture," namely, the *Gefühl*.[1] This innate and distinctively human faculty of deep inner experiential awareness is each person's "religious a priori"—a religious sense that everyone brings to their experience. This religious sense is a "feeling of absolute dependence" in which each person recognizes she or he utterly depends on something infinite beyond the self.

For Schleiermacher, authoritative and objective revelation did not stand at the center of religion. Instead, the center of both religion in general and Christianity in particular comprised a universal human faculty and the experience it affords. According to Schleiermacher's account, Christianity offered the highest form of this experience. This vision of the faith appealed to the Romantics and proponents of the Enlightenment who desired a spirituality free from blind faith in church doctrines. Schleiermacher opened a way for them to be religious without abandoning any of what they perceived as the Enlightenment enhancement of their true humanity. His path of Christian liberalism encouraged Romantics to cultivate the universal human religiosity within themselves (which Schleiermacher defined as "piety") and discover their link with the infinite to a higher degree than could be experienced elsewhere.

THE CHRISTIAN FAITH

Schleiermacher's second major work was *The Christian Faith*, a liberal Protestant systematic theology first published in 1821 and updated and revised in 1830. Most scholars of contemporary theology would concur with Keith W. Clements's verdict that "nothing on such a scale, and so systematic, had appeared in Protestantism since John Calvin's *Institutes of the Christian Religion* nearly three centuries earlier."[2] *The Christian Faith* was commissioned in 1817 by the Lutheran and Reformed churches of Germany, having decided for the three-hundred-year anniversary of the Reformation that they would resolve their long-standing differences and form the Prussian Union of Churches. Schleiermacher successfully devised a construction that made distinctly Reformed doctrines palatable to Lutherans and made distinctly Lutheran doctrines palatable to the Reformed, but at a very stiff price indeed. This price amounted to deliteralizing distinctly Reformed and Lutheran doctrines alike as well as deliteralizing all supernatural elements of the Christian faith. While retaining the terms (or linguistic handles) of traditional Christian theology, *The Christian Faith* proved to be a comprehensive new lexicon that radically redefined these terms along naturalistic lines in the context of human religious experience. Thus "all attributes which we ascribe to God are to be taken as denoting not something special in God, but only something special in the manner in which the feeling of absolute dependence is to be related to Him."[3] In other words, talk about God is, following Kant, simply talk about human experience of God that does not describe God-in-himself.

God

So who, or what, is God? Here Schleiermacher reacts against Kant's banishment of God into a realm beyond the reach of human knowledge. But if the transcendent realm is indeed off-limits to human rationality, then God must, it seems, be construed as entirely immanent. And one could legitimately, though not without dissent, charge Schleiermacher with making such a move. For Schleiermacher located God within the realm of human experience and even within the human consciousness. The closest Schleiermacher came to a literal definition of God is the *Geist*, or world spirit that pervades everything. One therefore wonders whether Schleiermacher's God exists outside the time-space universe at all or exists entirely within the universe as its underlying spirituality or depth dimension of meaning, value, and being. If the latter, then Schleiermacher offers a panentheistic conception of God, whereby God is in all things and, so to speak, nowhere else. This differs from a classical theistic conception of God as both transcendent (existing by himself outside space and time) and immanent (at all points within space and time).

In *The Christian Faith*, Schleiermacher expanded the meaning of *Gefühl* along panentheistic lines as "God-consciousness." He held that there is a universal God-consciousness in humanity, such that being in relationship with God comes through intuition. It does not come through the Bible, the church, morality, or religion, but "it is a universal element of life" to grow self-consciously aware of being dependent on God, the universal being.[4] Since the intuitive feeling of absolute dependence on God is a universal experience, it provides all persons everywhere with the reality of God, such that no further proof of God's existence is necessary. So how is Christian faith, at its core, different from this generic experience or from other religious faiths? Schleiermacher held that Christianity possessed a higher intuition than other faiths. For example, Schleiermacher compared Christianity with Judaism. Unlike Judaism, which in Schleiermacher's assessment expresses its feeling of absolute dependence with the intuition of retribution, Christianity expresses its feeling of absolute dependence with the intuition of "mediation" or redemption. Schleiermacher proceeded to maintain that what distinguished Christianity from generic God-consciousness and other particular religions—the "essence of Christianity"—was a deep awareness of Jesus Christ as one's link to the God on whom one was totally dependent. This particularly Christian brand of *Gefühl* constituted the authoritative source and norm for Schleiermacher's theology, by which Christian tradition and even Scripture itself would be interpreted and judged. No doctrine, however traditional or biblical, would be sacrosanct.

Only those compatible with the specifically Christian *Gefühl* would be accepted by Schleiermacher.

Distancing himself from abstract Christian dogmas, Schleiermacher proclaimed that the doctrine of the Trinity was not essential to the Christian faith since it does not comport well with the experience of God-consciousness. Since it is impossible to infer the Trinity from a general feeling of dependence, Schleiermacher did not have much room for the doctrine. While never formally denying the Trinity, Schleiermacher admitted to doubts about it and pronounced it as virtually useless for Christian theology: "The assumption of an eternal distinction in the Supreme Being is not an utterance concerning the religious consciousness, for there it never could emerge."[5] For this reason, Schleiermacher treated the Trinity as incidental to Christianity, only briefly discussing it in the appendix of his systematic theology.

The Bible

Schleiermacher was pivotal in bringing a revised concept of biblical inspiration into Protestantism. He declared that the Bible is not an absolute authority but a collection of reports about the religious experiences of persons throughout antiquity. It is neither supernaturally inspired nor infallible, such that it could be wrong at any point and would necessarily be mistaken if it contradicted the generic or Christian *Gefühl*. Indeed, the New Testament, which simply contains the apostles' reflections on their faith in Christ, "contained much in detail that had been misinterpreted, or inaccurately grasped, or set in a wrong light owing to confusions of memory."[6] However, by providing a record of the religious experiences of the earliest Christian communities, the New Testament possesses a certain "normative dignity" in furnishing a model for contemporary attempts to interpret the significance of Jesus Christ in various historical circumstances.[7] Rejecting the "God-breathed" notion of inspiration (2 Tim. 3:16), Schleiermacher reinterpreted 2 Peter 1:21 to mean that inspiration is simply to be carried along by *Geist*, the universal spirit. Such a wide-ranging inspiration extends to art, music, poetry, and other creative endeavors of all times and places. It cannot be confined to the process of writing Scripture: "The peculiar inspiration of the apostles is not something that belongs exclusively to the books of the New Testament."[8]

Unlike the perceived dignity of the New Testament, Schleiermacher relegated the Old Testament to a virtually irrelevant, secondary status. Observing the common consensus among Christians that a major difference exists between the Old and New Testaments, Schleiermacher insisted that when Christians take the Old Testament seriously, their Christianity becomes infected with legalism and offers negligible support for Christian doctrines. Schleiermacher rejected the notion that Jesus and the apostles set a precedent for Christians to observe by utilizing the Old Testament; to the contrary, he pronounced the "gradual retirement" of the Old Testament on the emergence of the New Testament and claimed that "the real meaning of the facts would be clearer if the Old Testament followed the New as an appendix."[9] Dividing the Old Testament into Law, History, and Prophets, Schleiermacher explicitly denied that the Holy Spirit inspired Law, History, and the legal and historical portions of the Prophets. With apparent reticence, Schleiermacher entertained the possibility that the prophets' messianic prophecies were inspired by the world *Geist*.

Miracles, Science, and Christianity

Abandoning the distinction between the natural and the supernatural, Schleiermacher contended that Christian God-consciousness forces believers to regard absolutely everything that occurs in nature and history as the activity of God. This redefinition of divine providence fits well with Schleiermacher's panentheistic understanding of God as the all-pervasive world spirit. Since Schleiermacher's God seems part of the natural world and totally immanent (such that there appears to be no personal being outside nature to intervene in nature), the possibility of miracles becomes highly suspect. Hence Schleiermacher averred, "As regards the miraculous, the general interests of science, more particularly of natural science, and the interests of religion seem to meet at the same point, i.e., that we should abandon the idea of the absolutely supernatural because no single instance of it can be known by us, and we are nowhere required to recognize it."[10] For Schleiermacher, then, science and Christianity in principle cannot conflict: science deals exclusively with proximate causes, whereas Christianity deals with the ultimate cause of everything. While Schleiermacher never explicitly denied Jesus's bodily resurrection, he did raise the suggestion in *The Christian Faith* that the disciples could have mistaken an internal, psychological event for an external, physical event. He elsewhere toyed with the hypothesis that Jesus had only appeared to have died. Perhaps Jesus was not completely dead when he was taken down from the cross, and later he revived in the coolness of the tomb and escaped to convince his disciples that he had risen from the dead.

Christology

Schleiermacher's theological liberalism is exemplified in his Christology. He replaced the traditional Christology regarding the two ontological natures of

Christ with a functional Christology based entirely on Jesus's experience of God-consciousness. Possessing only a human nature, Jesus differed from the rest of humanity in just one respect: the absolute potency of his God-consciousness. As Schleiermacher put it, "The Redeemer, then, is like all men in virtue of the identity of human nature, but distinguished from them all in the constant potency of his God-consciousness, which was a veritable existence of God in him."[11] Schleiermacher therefore exegeted Colossians 2:9 ("For in Christ all the fullness of the Deity lives in bodily form") as follows: "To ascribe to Christ an absolutely powerful God-consciousness, and to attribute to him an existence of God in him, are exactly the same thing."[12] In other words, Christ fully experienced the *schlechthin Abhängigkeit*, or absolute dependence on God-consciousness, and this reality was what made him unique from yet similar to all other human beings in pursuit of such consciousness. From Jesus's birth on, he lived in total dependence on God, his heavenly Father, and never violated that relationship of dependence by asserting his autonomy over against God. Accordingly, Schleiermacher conceived the sinlessness of Christ as the gradual yet complete submission of his self-consciousness into his God-consciousness: "No impression was taken up merely sensuously into the innermost consciousness and elaborated apart from God-consciousness into an element of life, nor did any action . . . ever proceed solely from the sense-nature and not from God-consciousness."[13] Schleiermacher's functional Christology influenced many later theologians, who further modified the doctrine.

Not surprisingly, Schleiermacher presented Jesus as the ideal human being in whom God-consciousness reached its zenith: "His particular spiritual content cannot . . . be explained by the content of the human environment to which he belonged, but only by the universal source of spiritual life in virtue of a creative divine act in which, as an absolute maximum, the conception of man as the subject of the God-consciousness comes to completion."[14] Schleiermacher proceeded to offer a new, subjective theory of the atonement, far removed from the satisfaction and substitution models and somewhat similar but not identical to the moral influence model. Unlike earlier models, the subjective theory sees atonement as taking place through Jesus's life and not necessarily through his death. Jesus's redemptive work lay in his ability to communicate the potency of his God-consciousness in some measure to others, nurturing in them the intuitive awareness of being dependent on and united with the world spirit that pervades everything. This ability is evidenced in the community he founded known as the church. Although Jesus's death indeed drew believers into the depth of his spirituality, Jesus would still be the Savior of the world even if he had never been crucified; the crucifixion was simply a continuation of the salvific work in which he had previously engaged. Through his life essentially and his death incidentally, "the Redeemer assumes believers into the power of his God-consciousness, and this is his redemptive activity."[15] As a result, the event of justification is not an objective reality, but a subjective reality in the human consciousness whereby one recognizes one's radical contingency while internally sensing one's dependence on the Ultimate, thus finding an inner state of peace.

The Church

For Schleiermacher, full human dependence on the Ultimate can only be actualized in church, in which the bond with God is celebrated. This solidarity is now defined as the body of Christ in the world. The church works toward the perfection of the human spirit in unity with the divine spirit through Christ. In this way the church advances God's governance of the world, which Schleiermacher defined as predestination and foreordination. God's quest for unity with the perfected human spirit is the sole unified goal for all that exists, and all that exists must be pondered in relation to that unified goal. As a result, Schleiermacher found meaningless the idea of God's external, physical transformation of this present world into a perfected universe where the redeemed would enjoy body-soul immortality. On this score, Schleiermacher wrote, "We therefore always remain uncertain how the state which is the church's highest consummation can be gained or possessed in this form by individual personalities emerging into immortality."[16] Rather, the church is the key to eschatology, for it is the place where the specifically Christian *Gefühl* may be obtained in the present and future alike.

Angels and Demons

Exhibiting a bias against supernatural matters, Schleiermacher treated the doctrine of angels and demons with detachment at best and derision at worst. He viewed the notion of angels as having neither a positive nor a negative value: "It can, therefore, continue to have its place in Christian language without laying on us the duty of arriving at any conclusion with regard to its truth."[17] Regarding the many biblical passages about angels, Schleiermacher mused that "Christ and the apostles might have said all these things without having had any real conviction of the existence of such beings or any desire to communicate it."[18] In this vein, Schleiermacher found the literal existence of angels a puerile belief beyond which the church has largely evolved. Likewise, Schleiermacher criticized the doctrine of the devil as "so unstable that we cannot expect anyone to be convinced of its truth."[19] In an enlightened world, the church has no need to assert the existence of the devil, a belief that could prove quite hazardous: "It would be bad enough if anyone neglected due care for himself and others because of his trust in the protection of angels. But it would certainly be more dangerous if at will, in place of self-examination, he attributed his growing wickedness to the influence of Satan."[20] In spite of this threat, Schleiermacher considered it appropriate to use the devil as a metaphor of the "godlessness of evil in itself, or to emphasize the fact that it is only in a higher protection that we can find help against an evil the source of whose power our will and intelligence seem unable to reach."[21]

Eternal Punishment and Last Judgment

Consistent with his stress on the Christian *Gefühl*, Schleiermacher rejected the doctrine of eternal punishment. Schleiermacher argued via *reductio ad absurdum* that punishment "cannot be ordained by God as reformative," since if it could be so ordained, then "a system of divine penalties as perfect as possible could have been made to serve instead of redemption."[22] Nor could punishment be "merely vengeful or retributive," as this would make God an evil returner of an eye for an eye and destroy the impassibility of God: "Divine penalties of such a type . . . could be believed in only at a very primitive stage of development—a stage at which the Deity is still thought of as susceptible to irritation, and as not above feeling an injury or having other passive states."[23] Accordingly, God's punishment could only be interpreted as his prevention or deterrence of evil by not allowing those who commit it to experience the height of God-consciousness. For if evildoers did experience the height of God-consciousness, they would lack any existential motivation to stop performing evil. But when evildoers sense that, by performing evil, they deprive themselves of something necessary to their fulfillment as human beings, they are driven to repent and become righteous.

In line with this framework, Schleiermacher dispensed with the concept of a last judgment. Seeing no purpose for a final separation between believers and unbelievers, Schleiermacher attempted to confute the idea by eliciting the example of Jesus, who "partook in the common life shared by sinners."[24] But in view of the virtually universal prevalence of the last judgment in Christendom, Schleiermacher felt driven to discern a deeper meaning that the idea figuratively expressed. This meaning, for Schleiermacher, amounted to complete freedom from evil, such that the last judgment pointed to the hope that ultimately all persons would experience the feeling of absolute dependence on God through Christ. Hence Schleiermacher held that the doctrine of eternal damnation was unsupportable by the teachings of Christ on the matter because such teachings were metaphorical in nature. Philosophically, Schleiermacher rejected eternal damnation because he envisioned that any type of eternal punishment involving misery could not help but result in less and less misery as time went on. Moreover, Schleiermacher deduced that if the punishment of the wicked was spiritual, then it would effectuate a "quickened conscience" that issues in some good, making the wicked "better by far in their damnation than they were in this life."[25] Schleiermacher felt that the proverbial nail in the coffin of eternal damnation was the pathos that the blessed in heaven would experience for their fellow beings who suffer eternal misery in hell, thus negating the former's blessedness. Due to the deep-rooted nature of the historical position of the church on eternal damnation, Schleiermacher called for a softening rather than a total dismissal of that view. This softening constituted a return to the third-century church father Origen's doctrine of *apokatastasis panton* (restitution of all things), namely, the view "that through the power of redemption, there will one day be a universal restoration of all souls."[26]

CONCLUSION

In *On Religion* and *The Christian Faith*, Schleiermacher's intention was to furnish a theology that was both thoroughly modern and thoroughly Christian. In his judgment, this theology would require no beliefs essentially contrary to modern thought and would discard no beliefs essential to Christianity. To accomplish this task, Schleiermacher systematically redefined all of the core Christian theological categories to make them more palatable to cultured, enlightened humanity. Such a project was incredibly controversial. Schleiermacher's critics, past and present, denounced his work as so radically revisioning Christian faith that it was no longer Christian faith. Far from discarding no core Christian beliefs, Schleiermacher's critics accused him of discarding them all. Further, his critics charged him with making theology entirely subjective by construing it as reflection on religious experience rather than as analysis of objective, historical revelation in Scripture. However, Schleiermacher's allies, past and present, lauded his work as successfully translating the timeless message of Christianity into the contemporary world. They praised Schleiermacher for his emphasis on feeling and its dynamic influence, which had largely become lost in the coolly intellectual climate of the Enlightenment. In either case, Schleiermacher erected the pillars of a liberal Christianity that would gradually extend to many theologians and mainline denominations in Europe and America.

FOR FURTHER READING

Primary Sources

Schleiermacher, Friedrich. *The Christian Faith*. Ed. H. R. Mackintosh and J. S. Stewart. Edinburgh: T&T Clark, 1928, repr. 1960.

———. *Hermeneutics and Criticism and Other Writings*. Ed. Andrew Bowie. Cambridge Texts in the History of Philosophy. Cambridge: Cambridge University Press, 1998.

———. *On Religion: Addresses in Response to Its Cultured Critics*. Trans. Terrence N. Tice. Richmond: John Knox, 1969.

Secondary Sources

Clements, Keith W. *Friedrich Schleiermacher: Pioneer of Modern Theology*. London: Collins, 1987.

Gerrish, B. A. *A Prince of the Church: Schleiermacher and the Beginnings of Modern Theology*. Minneapolis: Fortress, 1984.

Kelsey, Catherine L. *Thinking about Christ with Schleiermacher*. Louisville: Westminster John Knox, 2003.

Mariña, Jacqueline, ed. *The Cambridge Companion to Friedrich Schleiermacher*. Cambridge Companions to Religion. Cambridge: Cambridge University Press, 2005.

Olson, Roger E. *The Story of Christian Theology: Twenty Centuries of Tradition and Reform*. Downers Grove, IL: IVP, 1999.

Vial, Theodore. *Schleiermacher: A Guide for the Perplexed*. London: Bloomsbury T&T Clark, 2013.

CHAPTER 3

G. W. F. HEGEL

Dialectical Theology

P
hilosopher Georg Wilhelm Friedrich Hegel (1770–1831) exerted a major impact on modern theology and modern philosophy, much of which derived from reactions in one way or another to his thought. The overarching goal of Hegel's thought was to explain the movement of world history. Hegel wondered why history often proceeds cyclically from stability to conflict to a new stability. Seeing the manifestation of God in history, Hegel believed that history is the narrative of the development and realization of the divine spirit. Since giving a conceptual account of world history entails giving a conceptual account of everything, Hegel aspired to formulate a philosophy that met this lofty aspiration.

This chapter will deal with three broad areas. First, we shall define several key terms in Hegel's philosophical system. Second, we shall discuss Hegel's dialectical method, seeing in the process that the way the dialectical method is often presented in contemporary thinking is a caricature of what Hegel meant. Finally, we shall unfold the dominant concepts in Hegel's philosophy, which would prove extremely important for theology. It should be noted at the outset that Hegel's thought is quite dense—indeed, arguably the densest we will encounter in this book. Hence this chapter attempts to present Hegel's philosophy in as simple a manner as possible while still remaining true to Hegel's own thought.

KEY TERMS

Hegel employed a somewhat limited vocabulary in his most influential work, *The Phenomenology of Spirit* (*Phänomenologie des Geistes*), focusing especially on three terms. While these terms seem familiar to us, Hegel attached specific and distinctive meanings to them that are quite different from their usual meanings.

The first term is *absolute*. By calling an entity absolute, Hegel meant that the entity is unconditioned by any object outside of it. The entity is all-comprehensive. Thus to say that someone's knowledge is absolute means that there is not anything outside of what that person knows that could be known. Indeed, Hegel spoke about absoluteness largely in relation to knowledge. For Hegel, absolute knowledge is one of many shapes of consciousness. A shape of consciousness is a set of ideas about the sort of thing the knower is, the sort of thing the object of knowledge is, and the sort of thing the relation between the two is. Absolute knowledge is the ultimate or final shape of consciousness, as there is nothing outside it to condition or determine it.

In the preface to *Phenomenology*, Hegel proclaimed that everything depends on regarding the absolute "not only as *Substance*, but equally as *Subject*."[1] By this Hegel meant that the true, or absolute, is not just an entity out there in the world but is also a subject, possessing the ability to act and to move. Far from any static thing, the absolute is a process that continues to unfold itself. As the self-reflexive manifestation or revelation of itself, the absolute exhibits the paradox of not really being something until it is fully manifested and yet always being a something working itself out in the process of manifesting itself fully. Hence the absolute is a something in one sense and not a something in another sense. Hegel regarded his own philosophy as absolute, as opposed to others that were merely relative. In his philosophy, Hegel sought to grasp a reality that lives in particular things by means of a thought that passes through and encompasses them. Hegel claimed that his philosophy was not a theory beside practical life but an activity that moves through both theory and practice, thus in a sense neither and in a sense both. For Hegel, the difference between philosophy and the whole remainder of life is one of standpoint. All other human activities are truly in contact with reality but reach partial truths only because they are limited to finite standpoints. The true or final philosophy—which Hegel judged to be his own—rises to an infinite or absolute standpoint, thereby encompassing and transfiguring the partial truths of the finite standpoints into an ultimate truth.

The second term is *faith*. In contrast to Schleiermacher, Hegel denied that faith is the recognition of one's own powerlessness, the response to the wholly other, or the throwing of oneself on the mercy of an omnipotent God whom one cannot hope to please by any works. Nor is faith a mere feeling that one might have toward God. Instead, Hegel held that the ground of faith is spirit and the recognition of spirit in another. Faith is the recognition of what is like or similar in another. As a result, faith is the whole inward-outward life of the human being in his relation to the divine infinity: the inward life of the human is his feeling, and the outward life of the human is his affirmation. Hegel asserted that faith cannot be initiated by external things like miracles, divine threats or promises, or the Holy Scriptures. For Hegel, what produces faith is not something external to the divine-human relationship but something inside that relationship—spirit and the recognition of spirit by spirit.

Accordingly, the final term is *spirit* (Ger., *Geist*). Hegel asserted, "Reason is Spirit when its certainty of being all reality has been raised to truth, and it is conscious of itself as its own world, and of the world as itself."[2] In Hegel, *Geist* is a complex notion, working as both a thing and an activity. As a thing, *Geist* is some sort of general consciousness, a single mind common to all people that extends over all reality, material as well as otherwise. As an activity, *Geist* is a free, internal self-development of that consciousness that gradually develops reality. Hegel proposed that reality—both material reality and all else that encompasses existence—is spirit. So spirit, for Hegel, is not opposed to matter. Hegel proceeds to refine the concept of spirit by explaining what it is not and then what it is. Spirit is not a transcendent entity (e.g., God, the soul) nor a set of common thoughts in each of our individual minds nor an abstract entity that includes the common properties of all individuals, such as "the average German citizen." Instead, spirit is the underlying principle of consciousness and the underlying rational will behind all practical reason and action. It is a doubling of self-consciousness whereby each individual self-consciousness recognizes other self-consciousnesses and the unification or unity of all self-consciousnesses. As a force of universal consciousness, spirit enables us to see that to exist is to exist in relation to other things, causing each person to move from "I" to "we." Any given individual's assertion, "I exist," is only possible through another individual's assertion, "I exist." Spirit is therefore found to be that activity that relates particular things to each other and unifies them into an intersubjective whole. Spirit unites all things without obliterating the individuality of anything it unites. Circling back to the concept of faith, spirit performs the monumental task of unifying two particular self-consciousnesses: the individual human being and God.

HEGEL'S DIALECTICAL METHOD

With these basic terms in view, Hegel delineated his dialectical method, a method that is not argumentative but demonstrative. Unlike a philosophical argument, Hegel's method does not move from premises to conclusion. Instead, Hegel shows the movement of a concept or idea and then tries to demonstrate the necessity in the development of the concept. The goal of the dialectical method is to explain the cyclical process of world history. The only type of argument appearing in Hegel is the positing of the conceptual motion from stage x to stage y, a motion that Hegel took to be necessary and self-evident. This kind of demonstration occurs through what Hegel styled the immanent unfolding of a concept. Three important German words help us understand Hegel's method: *Aufheben*, *Aufgehoben*, and *Aufhebung*. *Aufheben* carries the root meaning of canceling or eliminating. That which is canceled or eliminated is *Aufgehoben*. The cancellation or elimination is *Aufhebung*. But these terms mean more than simply cancellation or elimination of things contradictory. They also imply the preservation and sublimation of that which is negated. According to Hegel, for a philosophical system to be absolute, anything it cancels needs to be preserved and sublimated in a higher-order reality.

The dialectical method begins with a particular concept, where the thinker working with the concept reflects on everything the concept means and implies and therefore sees how that concept unfolds. This process of reflecting on a concept is the immanent unfolding of the concept. It is immanent in the sense that what the thinker employs in considering the concept is not other concepts external to it, but rather the various facets of the concept itself. In perceiving these different facets, the thinker moves, so to speak, to a greater understanding of that concept. Hegel also states that this process of analyzing and understanding a concept is immanently formative, as the concept forms itself out of itself. An example will assist us in grasping Hegel's point. Suppose we were trying to understand the concept of freedom. We then think about different aspects of freedom, including the things it inherently involves and does not inherently involve. So whatever we reflect on to understand the notion of freedom needs to be suggested by the concept of freedom itself. If there were some other concept we knew about that was in no way related to freedom, it would be inappropriate to import that concept into the discussion of freedom to better understand the notion of freedom.

We now turn to the three essential elements of the dialectical method, namely, what must happen in thought for this immanent movement to unfold. When examining a concept, the first element is to think of one facet, or determination, of that concept as thoroughly as we can. This facet is known as the *thesis*. By thinking in terms of one determination of a concept, Hegel notes that we think abstractly, isolating one item from the rest. The second element is to consider the contradictory of this facet. The contradictory is known as the *antithesis*. For Hegel, it is important not just to think of the contradictory in utter abstraction, but rather to think of the facet and its contradiction simultaneously. In doing so, we heighten the contradictoriness between the two determinations before moving on to a resolution. The third element is to unify the determinations by sublimating and preserving the two contradictory ideas in a higher-order concept, known as the *synthesis*. Paradoxically, we must not straightforwardly cancel out the contradictions, but we must instead cancel them in such a way that we preserve them at the same time. Then and only then, Hegel insisted, we arrive at the truth concerning the original facet.

At this juncture, we repeat the process by using this synthesis as the next determination we thoroughly reflect upon, consider its antithesis, and then resolve it and its contradiction in an even higher-order synthesis. We continue to repeat the process until each determination in the entire concept is mediated or related to other determinations in the concept, such that the truth about the total concept now emerges. We then move to a new concept, starting with a thesis and recursively progressing through the dialectical method until we arrive at the truth about that concept. We repeat with another concept, and then another, and so forth, only coming to a stop when each concept in all of reality is completely mediated. This fully mediated reality is the realm of spirit, where the absolute is what is thought. Notice that the absolute is totally unbounded, totally comprehensive, and complete in itself. There is nothing outside absolute knowledge because all has been mediated or related; everything is incorporated in this all-encompassing philosophy.

Hegel's dialectical method stands in contrast to the typical understanding, and in fact caricature, of that method. Since Hegel, many philosophers and theologians have adapted the method to their own needs, thereby simplifying it. Often when people explain the method, they picture the thesis as one idea or concept or phase, possessing certain characteristics. They then picture the antithesis as simply another (not the contradictory) idea or concept or phase, possessing its own set of characteristics. To form the synthesis, they propose that we join the characteristics identical in both ideas or concepts or phases, where the characteristics of the thesis that do not match the antithesis drop out altogether. In short, the synthesis is just the blending together of all the common ideas in the thesis and antithesis. Now, if this were indeed the way Hegel's dialectical method moved, many elements of the thesis and antithesis would not get incorporated into the synthesis, which runs contrary to Hegel's project of building an all-encompassing philosophy that leaves out nothing. Hence any portrayal of a dialectical method that leaves out various things is unsatisfactory. Rather, an accurate portrayal considers the thesis and all it entails, its literal antithesis (its contradictory) and all it entails, and the paradoxical conjunction of everything in the thesis with everything in the antithesis. This conjunction is accomplished by subliming the contradictions up to a higher plane of reality. As a higher-order concept, the synthesis includes common items and contradictory items, uniting them at the same time as it maintains their distinctiveness.

I shall illustrate the dialectical method in action through Hegel's dialectics of master and slave. Our initial reflection on this relationship yields the thesis, namely, the pure dominance of the master over the slave. But when we undertake further reflection on this relationship, the reality is the antithesis—the dominance of the slave over the master. The basic concept here is that the master is related to the world mediately through the slave who works on the world for the master. The master does not go out and do anything in the world, like tilling a garden or planting a field; the slave does that for him. As a result, the master is not actually related to anything in the world immediately. The only way he can be related to anything in the world is through his slave, because he gave up the world and being tied to it to gain his freedom and his dominance over the slave. Moreover, the master relates himself to the slave through the world since the master's power over the slave ties the slave to the world in bondage. In all of this, Hegel alleged, the slave is better off than the master. For the slave, on his own, relinquished his independence before the master but, in return for that, he gained recognition as the master's slave. So the slave has asserted his self-certainty in two ways. He has asserted it by the act of relinquishing; one cannot relinquish a self if there is no self that is actually there and of which one is certain. The slave has also asserted it by getting the master's recognition. Further, the master depends exclusively on the slave for recognition, having no content in the world because the master is detached from it. But the slave can point to things in the world he has made and say, "This is what *I* have done." So the slave, not the master, can be free in the world. But this freedom is contradicted by the reason the slave puts form on the world: he does it out of bondage to the master. So, in a sense, the slave is free, and in a sense, the slave is not free. How, then, are the contradictory dynamics of the master-slave relationship to be unified? If neither the master nor the slave can be free in the world, where can they be free? Hegel now proceeds to the synthesis: Stoicism. According to Hegel, both the master and the slave can be free in thought. Thinking is free because it is not foreign; it is one's own thoughts that one is thinking, not someone else's. Thinking is also free in the sense that the mind can relate immediately to itself without any mediation through a slave (if a master) or through a master and world (if a slave). Thus the inherent reality of independent consciousness is mental. The necessary move in the dialectics is to Stoicism, as the essence of humanity is seen to be thinking, in spite of other external relations that pertain to the master and the slave.

The dialectical method is extremely important in contemporary theology and philosophy. Whether or not later thinkers accepted Hegel, most of them incorporated the dialectical method into their own research programs.

DOMINANT CONCEPTS IN HEGEL'S PHILOSOPHY

We now explore the dominant concepts in Hegel's philosophy, beginning with his concept of philosophy itself. For Hegel, philosophy is a rise to absoluteness or divinity. Any philosophy that fails to recognize itself as this rise is only a phase of a rise. Therefore the purpose of philosophy is to be all-comprehensive. The true philosophy is one that rises to absoluteness without destroying that from which it arises. In other words, it does not reject any partial standpoints as exemplified by one philosophy as opposed to another, but instead encompasses and transfigures all finite standpoints. The true philosophy must not be set over against reality as fleeing from it, as Hegel charged Greek philosophy with doing. Hegel alleged that Greek philosophy rose to a divine standpoint at the cost of abandoning the world. While true philosophy must rise to divinity, it must also unite the knowledge of God with the wisdom of the world and indeed with the world itself. On Hegel's view, reality or life is the merger of union and nonunion. Only the philosophy that recognizes and preserves this feature of life has reached the absolute standpoint. Hegel charged that philosophical thought stood superior to scientific thought. Because scientific thought is finite, it requires external, empirical confirmation. On the other hand, philosophical thought is infinite and has internalized all external verification, thus making it incapable of external refutation. Accordingly, when we judge Hegel's own system, Hegel insisted that the question is not whether the system meets external standards, because there are none. Rather, we must ask whether the system meets its own standards.

The next major concept in Hegel's philosophy is religion. Hegel stipulated that in every genuine religion, the human is inwardly related to the divine and remains other than the divine. In no genuine religion is the divinity simply present as something other than the human being but unrelated to that human being. Further, in no genuine religion is the distinction blurred between the divine and the human being, a blurring that Hegel found in Spinoza's pantheism. By contrast, Hegel regarded mysticism and Hinduism as forms of genuine religion because the dual features of human inward relation to the divine and human otherness than the divine could be found within them. Although in mysticism and Hinduism divinity is radically incommensurate with everything finite and the radically infinite dissolves the radically finite, the self recognizes itself being dissolved and willfully surrenders itself, thus paradoxically gaining itself even as it is dissolved. At this juncture Hegel defined religion as human inward receptivity of the divine other without obliteration of the individual human.

Hegel maintained that three traits existed in every genuine religion: feeling, religious representation, and cult. For Hegel, feeling is to be geared to a real object that is felt. Due to the fact that the object is real, religious feeling cannot be totally subjective and self-enclosed. This real object cannot be an empty mystery but must have content, for it is difficult to feel something toward that which we know nothing about. The object must be absolutely higher than the human, such that we can legitimately worship it. We do not worship it as an idol but for what it really is, the infinite. All these characteristics are united and contained in what Hegel calls religious representation.

Religious representation is the human use of limited language and thought to point to an infinite object. Hegel demanded that the represented object must be other than the act of representing it, as God is not a psychological projection but is actually something different than our act of thinking about him. The represented thing must in its divine infinity be radically other than the representing individual in his human finiteness, or the relation would not be genuinely religious. But the infinite cannot be so wholly other as to be totally inaccessible, in which case there would be no possible way for the human to enjoy relationship with it. Hence religious representation requires a symbol that points to the divine infinity while itself being finite. Hegel characterizes a religious representation by the following six features. First, it refers to the infinite in contrast to the merely finite picture. Second, it refers to the infinite in a finite way, using analogies from natural life and employing externally connecting terms like "and" and "also," while taking the infinite as external to the human person who does the referring. Third, the represented object is accepted by the representing person as given. One therefore does not try to prove that there is a thing that one is actually representing. Assuming its reality, the representation tries to link the person with the object the person is representing. Fourth, even while this representation remains a representation, it is capable of expressing its fundamental inadequacy. Anything finite is in some respect inadequate in referring to the infinite. At the same time as the symbol points us toward the infinite, it dialectically points to its own inadequacy. Fifth, even though the represented object is taken as given, both the represented object and the representation itself are part of a spiritual God-human relation in which mere external givenness is transcended. Sixth, a religious representation moves toward but fails to reach the universality of speculative thought.

Cult is the labor of acting out the relationship between the divine and the human, thereby binding together feeling and religious representation. This labor must thoroughly permeate the length and breadth of one's existence so as to cause one not merely to feel transformed but also to be transformed. In Christianity the aspects of the cultic life that best unite the divine and the human are baptism and Holy Communion. In Hegel's estimation, these are not mere external observances, but they are inward rites in which the human is inwardly related to the divine. For Hegel, the key to religion is neither objective events in history nor an objective book like the Bible nor an objective set of propositions (such as a theology or a set of dogmatics). Instead, religion is subjectivity, the subjective relation of the divine and the human.

Hegel then turned to the relation of religion and philosophy. In short, Hegel contended that religion can exist without philosophy, but philosophy cannot exist without religion, for it encompasses religion. Since true philosophy, by definition, is all-encompassing of every reality there is, it has to incorporate religious reality. A key idea for Hegel is that the true religion already is the true content of the all-encompassing philosophy. All that needs to be added to true religion to get true philosophy is the true form of speculative thought. These notions led Hegel to the following dilemma. The true content of absolute philosophy already exists in religion. Philosophy then needs to reenact the content and transfigure it, giving it the right form. But philosophy cannot shed the religious forms of symbols and myths without also losing the content that they embody. So either the representational form of religion is essential to its content or philosophy achieves its unprecedented feat of rising to divinity apart from the content and the form of religion. Both horns of the dilemma imply that religious content cannot, by the nature of the case, be expressed in philosophy, leaving philosophy incomplete and thus not true philosophy. To split the horns of the dilemma, Hegel sought a religion that would allow him to rise to a divine perspective and incorporate all the entities of that religion without having to strip away the particulars of that religion and thus lose the religion in the process. Hegel concluded that Christianity in particular was the right religion for this procedure. Why?

Negatively, Hegel determined that other religions failed in one of two respects. First, some religions never really got off the ground, so to speak; they did not rise to an infinite standpoint. The gods conceived in those religions were quite embroiled in finitude. Greek and Roman religions fell prey to this failure. Second, other religions rose to divinity but became so transcendent in understanding God that there was no longer any authentic relationship with the real world. Criticizing Judaism on this score, Hegel averred that in Judaism there is indeed a rise to the infinite Lord but that Judaism just leaves the Lord in his otherworldly transcendence. There is no real union between the infinite and the finite.

Positively, Christianity posited an infinite God who bridged the gap between the finite and the infinite. For Christ, as the God-man, unites both the finite and the infinite in his one person. Neither the finite nor the infinite obliterates the other, but what transcends each part without obliterating either is the person Jesus Christ. But there exist two further respects in which Christianity is, Hegel claimed, the right religion for philosophy. First, in Christianity, Christ as the God-man is an actual person external to any human representation of him. He really does exist outside of our minds. In that sense, he is transcendent to us; he is other than the worshiper. But Jesus is the same as the worshiper in their common humanity. Second, Christ is appropriated by the worshiper through a free act. But the human freedom used in appropriating Christ is itself an act of divine grace. So we have a double activity in this appropriation of God for humanity. One activity is from the human side; the other is from the divine side. The human moves to unite the finite with the infinite by means of freedom, but the divine moves to unite the finite to the infinite through grace. While other religions have two separate activities with an emphasis on one or the other, Christianity equally focuses on both. So in Christianity, the relationship between God and humanity is all-comprehensive because it unites the finite with the infinite without obliterating or de-emphasizing either the finite or the infinite in this union.

Hegel brought these insights together with a distinctively four-faceted concept of God. These facets in one way or another have been incorporated into most contemporary thinkers. While it is rare for any contemporary theologian to incorporate all four Hegelian facets, various theologians incorporate and adapt to their own purposes one or more of these divine facets.

First is the facet of God as Spirit. Here God is understood to be a force or general consciousness uniting all finite consciousnesses. Spirit is absolute, so God is absolute, and extremely immanent, as Spirit.

Second is the facet of God as equivalent to the Infinite. When Hegel spoke of philosophy as rising to infinity, he often stated that it rises to God or a divine viewpoint. Here the term *God* is equivalent to transcendent, all-encompassing thought. With this facet, God is portrayed as transcendent but not necessarily personal at all.

Third is the facet of God as the object toward which religious representation points symbolically. This God is the wholly other and does not really act in the world at all. This God may be personal (in dialectical tension with the previous facet), but he is so totally transcendent that it is impossible for us to know exactly what he is like.

Fourth is the facet of God as Christ. Christ represents for Hegel the union of transcendence and immanence. For Christ is God and man united. Moreover, in Christ a person other than us (transcendent) is to be worshiped and is simultaneously the same as us (immanent).

CONCLUSION

Hegel saw God manifested in the world in many ways. For Hegel, history itself is a study of divine providence. Through divine action, contradictions between antithetical movements are repeatedly resolved into higher syntheses. God expressed himself fully in the incarnation, for here his presence was not restricted beyond the world. God is love, so that while negation and opposition are historically necessary between theses and antitheses, reconciliation and synthesis are always essential. Hegel interpreted the dialectical movements of history as expressions of God's providence throughout time. The importance of Hegel's dialectical method for later theologians and philosophers, as well as many social historians and political scientists, cannot be overemphasized.

FOR FURTHER READING

Primary Sources
Hegel, G. W. F. *Lectures on the Philosophy of Religion: The Lectures of 1827*. Ed. Peter C. Hodgson. Rev. ed. Oxford: Oxford University Press, 2006.
———. *Phenomenology of Spirit*. Trans. A. V. Miller. Analysis and foreword by J. N. Findlay. Oxford: Oxford University Press, 1977.

Secondary Sources
Beiser, Frederick. *Hegel*. The Routledge Philosophers. New York: Routledge, 2005.
Hyppolite, Jean. *Genesis and Structure of Hegel's Phenomenology of Spirit*. Evanston, IL: Northwestern University Press, 1979.
Lewis, Thomas A. *Freedom and Tradition in Hegel: Reconsidering Anthropology, Ethics, and Religion*. Notre Dame, IN: University of Notre Dame Press, 2005.
———. *Religion, Modernity, and Politics in Hegel*. Oxford: Oxford University Press, 2014.
Pippin, Robert B. *Hegel on Self-Consciousness: Desire and Death in the Phenomenology of Spirit*. Princeton, NJ: Princeton University Press, 2014.
Singer, Peter. *Hegel: A Very Short Introduction*. Oxford: Oxford University Press, 2001.
Taylor, Charles. *Hegel*. Cambridge: Cambridge University Press, 1977.

CHAPTER 4

SØREN KIERKEGAARD

Existentialism

Søren Kierkegaard (1813–55) was the father of existentialism, a philosophy that focuses primarily on the individual and rejects pure abstract thought in favor of subjective thought and subjective truth. Kierkegaard vehemently opposed the abstract thought of Hegel, which he judged as destructive of true Christianity. Six themes characterize Kierkegaard's existentialism. First is anti-essentialism, which emphasizes the individual in the act of existing over against the detached reflection on ideal forms or essences of things found in Plato and Hegel. Kierkegaard said Hegel had built a brilliant rational system with no intrinsic flaws, but that it simply did not correspond to reality. Second, emphasis is placed on the individual instead of the crowd, as each individual thing has meaning independently of anything else. Third, existence is viewed as becoming, for existence precedes essence. We make choices in life that shape who we eventually become. Unlike a bookshelf, whose essence exists in the mind of the craftsman before it is made, human persons exist first and then craft the essence they will become. Existence is therefore dynamic, not static. Fourth, freedom is the basis for human becoming. A good part of what it means to be human is to be free. Radical freedom to become whatever is possible within the range of humanity is a great value, but it also includes risk. Still, it is better to choose than not choose, for at least one then exists. Fifth, estrangement, anguish, and death constitute the stimuli for becoming. By estrangement Kierkegaard meant that each person is thrown into the world by being born and is involuntarily estranged from the world. We are estranged from the natural order (as no harmony exists in this order) and from other human beings (as we do not naturally form relationships). Thus we must courageously use freedom to overcome estrangement. For Kierkegaard, anguish is the irrational and unexplainable feeling caused when the human being confronts nothingness, coming face-to-face with finitude, death, and potentially ceasing to exist. While anguish is very stressful, it has creative significance. Death is the final step into potential nothingness, and each person must consider the way she lives in terms of her upcoming death. One must take death seriously to be an authentic human being. Sixth, truth is relational rather than cognitive or pure; for example, rational, scientific, or mathematical thought, as pure thinking (like that of Hegel) tells an individual nothing about her individual existence and provides no personal relationship with the facts known.

MAJOR EVENTS IN KIERKEGAARD'S LIFE

Kierkegaard was born on May 5, 1813, in Copenhagen. From 1830 to 1834, Kierkegaard's mother, brother, and two of his sisters died, thus provoking a pessimism and melancholy with which he would approach life. In 1835 Kierkegaard experienced what he described in his journal as the "Great Earthquake." This earthquake comprised Kierkegaard's breach with his father when he learned of his father's deep, dark secrets down the path to perdition. Despite being raised by his father in a strict moral home with the harshest requirements of Christianity, Kierkegaard discovered that his father was prone to sensuality, as his mother was already pregnant at the time of their marriage. Moreover, early in life his father cursed God for letting him suffer as a shepherd and thus may have committed the unforgivable sin against the Holy Spirit. Kierkegaard feared that God had cursed his family for the acts of his father, which would explain the deaths of his family members and his sustained melancholy. But in 1838 Kierkegaard experienced what he dubbed the "Indescribable Joy," a profound conversion experience to personally become a disciple of Christ. From 1840 to 1841, Kierkegaard experienced a tempestuous relationship with Regina Olsen that strongly colored his theology. Kierkegaard was deeply in love with and became engaged to Regina, but he broke the engagement so that he would not burden her with his melancholy or cause her to be cursed with the sins of his family. Displaying deep introspection, Kierkegaard viewed his separation from Regina as renouncing marriage in terms of the greater good.

In 1846 Kierkegaard was lampooned for his appearance, voice, and habits in *The Corsair*, a weekly satirical paper that ridiculed people of repute and was therefore read surreptitiously by many. The so-called Corsair Affair began on

December 22, 1845, when P. L. Møller published a careless yet opportunis-
tic critique of Kierkegaard's *Stages on Life's Way*. Møller's opportunism was a
double-sided coin. He was seeking a chair at the University of Copenhagen even
while secretly editing *The Corsair*. In response to Møller, Kierkegaard wrote
two small pieces, *The Activity of a Traveling Esthetician* and *Dialectical Result
of a Literary Police Action*. Kierkegaard's *Activity* exposed Møller's hypocrisy
by publicly revealing him to be the editor of *The Corsair*, and Kierkegaard's
Dialectical Result denounced the low, tabloid-like journalistic standards of *The
Corsair*. Not surprisingly, *The Corsair* retaliated with illustrated cartoons car-
icaturing Kierkegaard, causing this very public individual to become a laugh-
ingstock among his countrymen. But in the 1848 "Metamorphosis" entry of
his journal, Kierkegaard declared that he had found peace with himself and
could therefore do exactly what God wanted. But what did God want from
Kierkegaard? Kierkegaard believed that God wanted him to attack the state
church of Denmark because biblical Christianity no longer existed in the
church. Most people believed they were Christians merely because they had been
baptized as infants and raised in a nominally Christian nation. From 1849 to
1855, Kierkegaard launched his literary attack on the Danish established church
in an attempt to restore biblical Christianity and salvation to Denmark. Amid
this controversy with the established church, Kierkegaard died on November
11, 1855.

KEY IDEAS IN KIERKEGAARD'S MAJOR WORKS

Kierkegaard's first major work was *Either/Or* (1843), a repudiation of the
Hegelian dialectical method and a presentation of the three stages of human lifestyle. Kierkegaard's basic complaint against Hegelian philosophy was that this
allegedly all-comprehensive system left out the two most important ingredients
of metaphysics, namely, human existence and authenticity. These ingredients
never received consideration because each emerged only from an "either/or"
choice between one of two contradictory notions, namely, "to be" or "not to be"
and "authenticity" or "inauthenticity." Such a choice was ruled out by Hegel's
"both/and" synthesis of two contradictory notions into a higher sphere of reality
that preserves their full contradictoriness.

   Kierkegaard illustrates the human journey toward authenticity by explaining that there are three distinct stages along the way. These three stages of
lifestyle are the aesthetic, the ethical, and the religious. The aesthetic stage is
the level of pleasure and perdition, where one merely feels rather than decides.

The individual operates from her instincts for new and pleasurable sensations but makes only insignificant choices. Kierkegaard poignantly disclosed the futility of living at the aesthetic level through his so-called rotation method, which shows how to get the most out of the aesthetic life while minimizing boredom. As the name suggests, if people slightly rotate what they do, eat, listen to, and so forth each day, then the possibilities are almost limitless. For example, a person could eat pepperoni pizza one night, pepperoni and ham pizza the next night, pepperoni and sausage pizza the next night, and so forth, just as a farmer rotates crops from one field to another. The rotation method avoids hope and cultivates an inappropriate type of remembering and forgetting, the key to which is having many experiences rather than intense experiences. By demonstrating that living at the aesthetic level is ultimately bankrupt and meaningless, Kierkegaard hoped to cause readers to jump to the ethical level, where they can make significant choices and thus exist.

The ethical stage is the level of deciding, where one is controlled by rules and universal norms. One creates an authentic self by confronting and making significant decisions in matters of good and evil. But mere rules cannot empower a person to do the right thing, as they furnish no motivation or incentive for action. Therefore the only way to act out one's choices and so possess a personal identity is by making a paradoxical leap of faith to the religious level. While repentance from sin does not save, it brings a person to the end of her rope so that she will make the leap of faith that saves. Displaying anti-Hegelianism, Kierkegaard refused to view faith as a facet in our system of thought to be negated and transcended, but rather as the highest good that could never be transcended.

The religious stage is the level of most authentic existence, where one is living for God rather than deciding to follow commands. This stage is God-centered, not rule-centered. Thus, if the universal norm commands one thing and God says another, one must follow God. However, if God tells one to follow the rule, one does it for the sake of obeying God rather than simply out of ethical rule keeping. Kierkegaard asserted that the way to live most authentically is to choose the Judeo-Christian God.

Kierkegaard further distinguished between life lived at the ethical stage and life lived at the religious stage in his next major work, *Fear and Trembling* (1843). Here Kierkegaard told the surface story of Abraham and Isaac at Mount Moriah, where Abraham's experience is paradigmatic of life at the religious stage and of conflict between the ethical and religious stages. Sometimes the moral law will contradict the moral Lawgiver, God, which is part of what it means to live at the religious level instead of merely the ethical level. Abraham was commanded by God to sacrifice Isaac on the altar, while the moral law commanded him not to murder his own son. Because Abraham lived at the religious level, he chose to obey God by sacrificing Isaac, even though it violated the very law God gave to humanity.

Kierkegaard explained that living by faith is the highest life one could possibly obtain, and most people never come to real Christian faith. Thus he compared the knight of resignation, that is, the moral or tragic hero, with the knight of faith, who attaches directly to God. Kierkegaard related the narrative of Abraham and Isaac to his experience with Regina, for to serve the higher principle, he had to give up Regina just as Abraham had to give up Isaac. Ironically, Kierkegaard depicted himself as only the knight of resignation and not the knight of faith, because he did not hold his wish fast after giving it up like Abraham did. According to Kierkegaard, the knight of resignation is a person who sees his duty, is resigned to it, and gives up what he has to give up, never expecting it back. However, the knight of faith sees his duty, is resigned to it, gives up what he has to give up, and trusts that God will give him back what he has resigned not to have. Such trust, Kierkegaard observed, is totally irrational, but the knight of faith trusts God anyway. Consequently, Kierkegaard defined the movement from resignation to faith as believing in the absurd.

Kierkegaard explored the above issues in further detail in the section titled "Panegyric on Abraham." For Kierkegaard, Abraham was such a great man because he both gave up his wish to have Isaac alive and held fast his wish after giving it up. Kierkegaard claimed that it is great to give up one's wish, but greater to hold it fast after giving it up; likewise, it is great to hold fast the eternal but greater to hold fast to the temporal after giving it up. Hence Abraham was great in proportion to his expectation, for he expected the impossible (i.e., Isaac alive after he was sacrificed), which is greater than all, rather than the possible, which is great, or the eternal, which is greater. Abraham never abandoned his wish; if he had, he would have saved many, but since he did not, he became the father of faith, which otherwise would have been impossible.

Following the "Panegyric on Abraham," Kierkegaard raised three "Problemata" raised by the account of Abraham's near-sacrifice of Isaac. First, Kierkegaard asked if there is such a thing as a teleological suspension of the ethical. In other words, can the universal ethical norm be suspended for God's purposes? Kierkegaard's answer is yes, since a suspension of the ethical rule is allowable for a person to exercise faith. This yields the paradox that the particular is higher than the universal, by which Kierkegaard can assert that the person in relationship to God is higher than the universal rule. Second, Kierkegaard queried if there is such a thing as an absolute duty toward God. His answer is yes, for this absolute duty is the religious duty, not the ethical, which can be suspended and is not absolute. The absolute duty is relationship to God and always obeying what God says. For example, one who lives at the religious level follows the rule "You shall not murder" because God tells him to obey it, while one who lives at the ethical level obeys this rule since the rule itself imposes force on the person's consciousness. Third, Kierkegaard inquired whether Abraham was ethically defensible in keeping silent about his purpose to sacrifice Isaac before Sarah, Eleazar, and Isaac. He answered that from an ethical standpoint, Abraham was indefensible. But if Abraham had told Sarah, Eleazar, and Isaac that God had commanded him to slay Isaac, the commandment would no longer have been particular, but a universal rule to obey God against the moral law. From a religious standpoint, not only was Abraham justified in keeping silent, but he had to keep silent for the commandment to be a test of personal faith that was not turned into a universal rule.

Strongly influenced by the dissolution of his engagement to Regina Olsen, Kierkegaard's *Stages on Life's Way* (1845) employs his three stages of lifestyle to evaluate love and marriage. In part one, "The Banquet, Aesthetic Perspectives on Love," five different fictional characters at a banquet make speeches giving their aesthetic opinions on love, from a higher to a lower level. First, a young man expresses his indecision concerning womanhood. Second, Constantine gives an experience-hardened understanding of womanhood. Third, Victor claims that love is an ironic experience. Fourth, Taylor evinces a demonic despair toward love. Fifth, Johannes the Seducer shows a cold-blooded and evil approach to love. By their obsession with meaningless relations with women, all five men avoid living at the ethical level. The basic point of this parody of Plato's *Symposium* is that aesthetic perspectives on love all avoid ethical choices by wrongfully focusing on relations with women. In part 2, "The Judge Williams Part," Kierkegaard discussed ethical reflections on marriage through the character of a judge seated with his wife at breakfast. Strongly protesting against the banquet speeches, Judge Williams proffers a positive view of marriage, exalting it as a vehicle for bringing the infinite into the temporal since the bride and groom pledge themselves to one another for infinity. Judge Williams concludes that marriage should be the rule or norm for most people, except for those who live fully at the religious level for God. They should not marry but still respect marriage as an institution. Part 3, "Quidam's Diary," is a chronicle of Kierkegaard's personal struggle, which asks if a melancholy person should marry and thus inflict melancholy on his or her spouse. Kierkegaard compared this quandary to a soldier who marries but dies in war. Kierkegaard explained his own thinking as to why he did not marry Regina by presenting three alternatives to the quandary: the melancholy person should tell his fiancée about his melancholy, the melancholy person should marry his fiancée anyway with the hope of absolving the melancholy, or the melancholy person should so humiliate himself that his fiancée would reject him. Kierkegaard posited that the third alternative is the correct one.

In 1846 Kierkegaard published his *Philosophical Fragments* and its sequel, *Concluding Unscientific Postscript*. Here Kierkegaard asserted that any genuine Christian must become a contemporaneous disciple of Christ. This meant gaining spiritual contemporaneity, not historical contemporaneity, with Christ. It occurs in the instant of personal encounter, when Christ discloses himself and the individual responds to Christ by making a subjective leap of faith. For Kierkegaard, there are no secondhand disciples. The only advantages possessed by Jesus's first-century disciples were historical in nature: the ability to know more facts about Jesus, the opportunity to obtain better Socratic self-knowledge, and the direct transmission of information with little chance for the message to be distorted. But they possessed no spiritual advantage over today's disciples, for discipleship is based solely on a relationship with God through Christ received in personal encounter and not on historical facts. Kierkegaard asserted that knowledge of historical truths about Christ, even if one had been an eyewitness, would not make one a disciple, and even that learning all of Christ's doctrine would not make one a disciple. Historicity only gives temporal significance, not eternal consequence. The Bible only provides an occasion for one to encounter God and to respond to God through the faith that he gives. According to Kierkegaard, the Scriptures are historical documents that contain the historical record of what Christ said and did, and provide only an approximation of these facts. Thus they can never be the basis for eternal happiness, and neither defending nor attacking the accuracy of the Bible has any bearing on eternal happiness, for inerrancy is unimportant. He maintained that no one has ever acquired faith by having the Bible defended, and that no one with faith will ever be bothered by an errant Bible, since genuine faith does not rest on historicity anyway. Christianity is inward and subjective, while Scripture is external and objective and hence gives no basis for faith.

Even more radical was Kierkegaard's position on faith and reason. Kierkegaard alleged that the role of reason in coming to genuine faith is to show people that reason cannot get them to God. Reason shows people just how irrational the leap of faith is that they must make to encounter God. Kierkegaard defined faith as "the objective uncertainty due to the repulsion of the absurd held fast by the passion of inwardness, which in this instance is intensified to the utmost degree."[1] However, Christianity is neither logically inconsistent nor according to reason nor against reason. But it is above and beyond reason, for the point where reason can go no further is where Christian truth resides. Thus reason distinguishes between nonsense and paradox, as Christianity is not nonsense but paradoxical, and it prepares one for the point where God breaks through. Kierkegaard identified Jesus as the ultimate paradox, as both God and man, the revealer and hider of God at the same time. Since Christ's humanity was real, it is paradoxical to think of Christ as the God-man. On Kierkegaard's reckoning, faith in God cannot be rationally or empirically grounded, as God by nature is transempirical. Moreover, the evidence at best shows Jesus to be a virtuous and honorable man but not a God-man. Reason comprehends that this paradox cannot be comprehended. At this point, there are three ways that one's intellect can respond to Christianity: by being offended; by not being offended at all, in which case there is no chance of becoming a Christian; and by knowing the possibility of offense but not being offended, in which case one becomes a Christian.

Not surprisingly, Kierkegaard stipulated that "truth is subjectivity,"[2] by which he meant that subjectivity is a condition for religious truth and that objective truth cannot make one a Christian. Christian truth is not in the mind but appropriated by the will, for "truth as subjectivity" is the truth that comes through committing one's will rather than logical contemplation. All theological truth is subjective, but objective truth can be found in other disciplines like the natural and physical sciences (e.g., mathematics, biology, chemistry, and physics) and the social sciences (e.g., history, political science, and sociology). Hence genuine disciples have no objective grounds for believing what they do. It is indeed absurd to be a Christian—there is no evidence to support it, and evidence may very well refute it. Faith therefore demands a leap that is based not on anything objective but on the passion of inwardness that God gives to a person. For Kierkegaard, there are four steps in gaining subjective truth. First, one must reject an outward, objective orientation to things and therefore move beyond the aesthetic level. Second, one must develop a responsible inwardness of duty and so embrace the ethical level. Third, one must cultivate a passionate concern for eternal blessedness that surpasses anything else in life, thus approaching the religious level. Fourth, one must receive the paradoxical revelation of God in Christ, which is disturbingly subjective, and consequently live at the religious level.

At the height of his attack on the Danish established church, Kierkegaard wrote *Training in Christianity* (1850). Kierkegaard protested bitterly against basing one's faith on "the upshot,"[3] by which he meant the tangible results of Jesus's earthly life throughout eighteen hundred years of church history. Kierkegaard's complaint is that one who tries to become a Christian due to the upshot is basing her belief on evidence, which is only approximate to the truth and can never bring eternal happiness. Thus one cannot even become a Christian through rationality, while the genuine Christian becomes spiritually contemporaneous with Christ by grasping faith beyond reason and experiencing the divine encounter. Kierkegaard asserted that we can know nothing about Christ from history, which is extremely radical since he did not make the distinction between the Jesus of history and the Christ of faith. Displaying amazing historical skepticism, Kierkegaard literally taught that history tells us nothing about either Christ as a man or Christ as God. Because the life of Christ is more important than the historical results of his life, any purported historical evidence is meaningless, for one must become a contemporary of Christ spiritually to find salvation. Kierkegaard illustrated his point with the illustration of six first-century figures—a wise and prudent man, a clergyman, a philosopher, a statesman, a solid citizen, and a mocker—who all became offended at Christ. Accordingly, historical contemporaneity with Jesus does nothing to make someone his disciple.

CONCLUSION

We conclude by reflecting on Kierkegaard's theological program in its historical context. Kierkegaard was horrified at what he considered an utter subversion of biblical Christianity to cultural Christendom in his native Denmark. Kierkegaard blamed this predicament on Hegel's enormously influential philosophy, which he regarded as a counterfeit of true Christianity that threatened to destroy it. For Kierkegaard, Christianity is not a philosophy—much less an objective and speculative one like Hegel's—and existence is not amenable to total rational comprehension. Truth, especially about God and the divine-human relationship, is not objective correspondence between thought and reality. Due to the "infinite qualitative difference"[4] between the infinite God and finite, fallen humans, truth itself must be embraced in passionate inwardness through decision, a leap of faith that cannot be reduced to logical contemplation. In short, knowing God entails faith, and faith entails risk. Apart from that risk, an individual can have an ethical religion but not biblical Christianity. Kierkegaard's understanding of faith has been embraced by a sizable number of theologians and laypeople since his day. His existentialism would resonate profoundly with Karl Barth and Paul Tillich, as we shall witness in later chapters.

FOR FURTHER READING

Primary Sources

Kierkegaard, Søren. *Concluding Unscientific Postscript*. Ed. and trans. Howard and Edna Hong. Princeton, NJ: Princeton University Press, 1992.

———. *Either/Or*. Ed. Victor Eremita, trans. Alastair Hannay. Rev. ed. New York: Penguin, 1992.

———. *Fear and Trembling*. Trans. Alastair Hannay. Princeton, NJ: Princeton University Press, 1983.

———. *Philosophical Fragments*. Ed. and trans. Howard and Edna Hong. Princeton, NJ: Princeton University Press, 1985.

———. *Stages along Life's Way*. Trans. Walter Lowrie. New York: Schocken, 1967.

———. *Training in Christianity and the Edifying Discourse Which "Accompanied" It*. Trans. Walter Lowrie. Princeton, NJ: Princeton University Press, 1944.

Secondary Sources

Backhouse, Stephen. *Kierkegaard: A Single Life*. Grand Rapids: Zondervan, 2016.

Berry, Wanda Warren. "Kierkegaard's Existential Dialectic: The Temporal Becoming of the Self." *Journal of Religious Thought* 38 (Spring/Summer 1981): 20–41.

Collins, James D. *The Existentialists: A Critical Study*. Chicago: Regnery, 1952.

———. *The Mind of Kierkegaard*. Princeton, NJ: Princeton University Press, 1983.

Deede, Kristen K. "The Infinite Qualitative Difference: Sin, the Self, and Revelation in the Thought of Søren Kierkegaard." *International Journal for Philosophy of Religion* 53, no. 1 (2003): 25–48.

Dunning, Stephen N. "The Dialectic of Contradiction in Kierkegaard's Aesthetic Stage." *Journal of the American Academy of Religion* 49 (1981): 383–408.

Evans, C. Stephen. "Kierkegaard's Attack on Apologetics." *Christian Scholar's Review* 10 (1981): 322–32.

Perkins, Robert L., ed. *Kierkegaard's Fear and Trembling: Critical Appraisals*. Tuscaloosa, AL: University of Alabama Press, 1981.

Pojman, Louis P. "Kierkegaard on Faith and History." *International Journal for Philosophy of Religion* 13 (1982): 57–68.

CHAPTER 5

EARLY DISPENSATIONALISM

While Kierkegaard was emphasizing the subjectivity of personal faith over the objectivity of Scripture, a movement in the British Isles sought to recover the objective truth of Scripture with its new interpretation. John Nelson Darby (1800–1882) was an Anglo-Irish biblical exegete and translator and onetime curate in the Church of Ireland. He resigned his curacy upon coming to the conviction that the very notion of a clergyperson violated the recognition that the Holy Spirit could speak through any member of the church. In 1831 Darby joined an interdenominational meeting of believers in Dublin who "broke bread" together as a symbol of their unity in Christ. As this group traveled and started new assemblies in Ireland and England, they formed a movement dubbed the "Plymouth Brethren." Fascinated with biblical prophecy and applying a rigidly "literal" reading to the scriptural text, Darby formulated a novel type of premillennial eschatology called *dispensational theology*. For Darby, biblical prophecies should be interpreted "literally where possible" and symbolically only when a literal reading proves impossible. Since it is possible for every Old Testament prophecy to be literally fulfilled, every promise and prediction concerning Israel that had not yet been fulfilled completely must apply to the future. Participating in the 1831–33 Powerscourt Conference, an annual meeting of Bible students, Darby first propounded his eschatological views. In 1840 Darby delivered eleven significant lectures in Geneva, *L'attente actuelle de l'église* (The Actual Expectation of the Church), which established his reputation as a leading interpreter of biblical prophecy.

THE SEVEN DISPENSATIONS, ISRAEL, AND THE CHURCH

Darby divided Bible history into dispensations, or eras, in which God dealt with his people in distinctive ways. These dispensations are seven in number. First is innocency, the state of Adam in Eden. Second is conscience (from Adam to Noah), during which dispensation obedience to the dictates of conscience constituted humanity's principal responsibility. Third is civil government (from Noah to Abraham), where humanity's responsibility lay in obedience to human government. Fourth is patriarchal rule (from Abraham to Moses), where one family was set apart and given the responsibility of believing and serving God. Fifth is the age of the Law (from Moses to Jesus), during which dispensation the Israelites were held responsible to obey God's law. Sixth is the church age (from the first coming to the second coming of Christ), where humans are responsible to accept God's free gift of righteousness. Seventh is the millennium—Jesus's thousand-year reign (Rev. 20:4–5)—when humanity will be responsible to obey Christ the King and his laws.

While such distinctions were not in themselves unusual, Darby's division of Israel and the church into two peoples of God was novel. Darby insisted that the church had not replaced Israel as the people of God; rather, the two are distinct groups, each with its own history, destiny, and hope. Israel was depicted in the Old Testament, would endure the great tribulation, and was promised earthly blessings in the promised land. The church was not present in the Old Testament, came into being at Pentecost, and was promised heavenly blessings. Moreover, law is the rule of life for Israel; grace is the rule of life for the church. For Darby, "two great subjects present themselves to us in Scripture: the church, that sovereign grace that gives us a place along with Christ himself in glory and blessing; and God's government of the world, of which Israel forms the center and the immediate sphere."[1] Darby came to this conclusion based on the many prophecies made concerning Israel in the Old Testament that had not yet been literally fulfilled. While Darby's contemporaries saw these prophecies as spiritually fulfilled in the church, Darby felt that this spiritualization did violence to the biblical text. If God could not be trusted to literally fulfill his promises in the Old Testament, how could God be trusted to literally fulfill his promises to Christians today? Moreover, a significant feature of prophecies about Israel, Darby emphasized, is that they have a track record of being fulfilled literally. Exactly as prophesied, Israel went to Egypt and returned, and Israel was taken captive by Babylon and returned. So when Scripture prophesies that Israel would be scattered and then regathered in the land at the time of Jesus's return, and the diaspora occurred in the first Christian century, the final regathering of Israel at the second coming must also be fulfilled literally.

Darby dismissed out of hand the suggestion that New Testament statements about the church as the true Israel could have contradicted or even abrogated Old Testament statements about physical Israel, as this undermined the plenary inspiration of Scripture. But Darby also dismissed out of hand the suggestion that perhaps individual prophecies or the sum total of prophecy was mysterious and so beyond human ability to unfold. As Ernest R. Sandeen put it, "Too traditional to admit that biblical authors might have contradicted each other, and too rationalist to admit that the prophetic maze defied penetration, Darby attempted a resolution of his exegetical dilemma by distinguishing between Scripture intended for the Church and Scripture intended for Israel. . . . The task of the expositor was, in a phrase that became the hallmark of dispensationalism, 'rightly dividing the word of truth.'"[2] Proposing that the dispensation from the time of Christ to his second coming (the "church age") was a parenthesis in the prophetic unfolding of God's plan for Israel, Darby conceived of a "rapture" (from the Latin *rapturo*, "caught up" or "carried away") of the church. When Israel rejected Jesus, God turned temporarily to work with the church. God's attention will return to his primary program with Israel when he raptures the church at the start of the tribulation. Thus, according to Darby, Christ's second coming will occur in two stages: a momentary return to earth to rapture the church before the seven-year great tribulation and the final return of Christ to establish the millennial kingdom, from which he will rule over the earth and dispense the last judgment.

FROM THE RAPTURE TO THE MILLENNIUM

On Darby's view, at some point during the church age—abruptly, unpredictably, and clandestinely—Jesus will return to earth, coming on the clouds, and will call believers up to himself. Believers who have died will be instantly resurrected from the dead in glorified, immortal bodies free from the effects of sin, and living believers on the earth will experience an immediate transformation from their present bodies to glorified, immortal bodies free from the effects of sin. With resurrection bodies like Jesus's resurrected body, believers ascend from earth to the sky to meet Jesus and then exit this world for heaven. Darby found the proof of this scenario in 1 Thessalonians 4:16–17—"For the Lord himself will come down from heaven, with a loud command, with the voice of the archangel and with the trumpet call of God, and the dead in Christ will rise first. After that, we who are still alive and are left will be caught up together with them in the clouds to meet the Lord in the air. And so we will be with the Lord forever." In the Vulgate, the historic Latin translation of the Bible, "caught up" (Gk., *harpazō*) is translated *rapturo*. Jesus will then return to heaven along with the believers who have been raptured out of the earth. According to Darby, the church's hope is not Jesus's coming to earth but being carried up to heaven in the rapture: "The thing [the church] has to expect for itself is not—though sure of that also—Christ's appearing, but her being taken up where he is. We go to meet Christ in the air. Nothing clearer, then, than that we are to go up to meet him, and not await his coming to earth."[3]

Darby accentuated two points about the rapture. First, "as to the time of this rapture, no one, of course, knows it"[4]—it will occur without warning and could occur at any moment. Second, the rapture will happen immediately prior to the start of the great tribulation. This claim was based on Darby's interpretation of two key passages in Revelation. Regarding Jesus's words to the church in Philadelphia—"Since you have kept my command to endure patiently, I will also keep you from the hour of trial that is going to come on the whole world to test the inhabitants of the earth" (Rev. 3:10)—Darby took this promise as applicable to the church as a whole and saw the hour of trial as the great tribulation. In Revelation 12:10–12, Darby observed that certain individuals triumphed over the devil by the blood of the Lamb and the word of their testimony, that those who dwell in the heavens are told to rejoice, and that woe is cast on earth because the devil had gone down to it. Darby identified the triumphant individuals as all true believers and reasoned that since they had defeated the devil, they could not still be on earth to face the devil's wrath; hence they must be in heaven. These passages "show our exemption from the tribulation predicted."[5]

Once the church is in heaven, the "judgment seat" of Christ will transpire there (Rom. 14:10–12; 2 Cor. 5:10). At this judgment, believers will be assessed regarding the quality of their lives and their suitability for rewards. For Darby, the issue at this judgment is not salvation, as everyone in heaven is saved. Nor will this be a judgment pertaining to sin, because believers are justified by faith and stand in Christ's perfect righteousness. Rather, the issue will be what believers have accomplished for God and how they have utilized the opportunities for service God has furnished them. At this judgment, each believer will give an account to God, just as stewards or trustees are accountable for what has been entrusted to them. Concerning 1 Corinthians 3:10–15, Darby held that the gold, silver, and costly stones refer to deeds in a believer's life that are eternal in value, and the wood, hay, and straw consumed by fire and reduced to ashes refer to deeds in a believer's life not counted worthy of eternal recognition.

Darby interpreted the rewards that believers will receive in heaven as forms of privileged service. Throughout eternity, believers who have served God well on earth will be assigned tasks for further heavenly service in keeping with what they have accomplished. Sharply distinguishing between heaven and earth, Darby emphasized that the church would never return to earth, as the notion of the church possessing an ultimate earthly destiny robs the church of all significance: "There are indeed the called from among the nations (namely the church) but it is for the heavens they are called. The calling of God for the earth is never transferred to the nations; it remains with the Jews. If I want an earthly religion, I ought to be a Jew. From the instant that the church loses sight of its heavenly calling, it loses, humanly speaking, all."[6]

Following the rapture, Darby claimed that there will be a great tribulation on the earth for a period of seven years. During this period expressing "the fury of the wrath of God Almighty" (Rev. 19:15), many signs of Christ's final return will be fulfilled. The signs include the preaching of the gospel to all nations (Matt. 24:14; Mark 13:10), false prophets performing miracles (Matt. 24:23–24; Mark 13:22), signs in the heavens (Matt. 24:29–30; Mark 13:24–25; Luke 21:25–27), the coming of the man of sin (i.e., the beast or Antichrist) and the rebellion (2 Thess. 2:1–10; Rev. 13:1–8), and the salvation of Israel (Rom. 11:12, 25–26). Thus the great harvest of the fullness of the Jewish people will transpire, as "144,000 from all the tribes of Israel" (Rev. 7:1–8; 14:1–5) trust in Jesus as their Messiah. Amid tremendous suffering there will also be much powerful evangelism, especially carried out by the new Jewish Christians. God will protect these Jewish Christians during the seven trumpet judgments (Rev. 8–11) and the seven bowl judgments (Rev. 16), whose plagues will reduce the earth's population by at least half. During this period, many persons will be saved, and many of the saved persons will be killed due to either their refusal to worship the Antichrist or the worldwide catastrophes. Persecution of Israel by the Antichrist will commence in the middle of the seven years, as the Antichrist breaks his peace agreement with Israel and desecrates the temple with an "abomination that causes desolation" (Dan. 9:27; 11:31; 12:11; Mark 13:14). For Darby, this desecration implied that the Islamic Dome of the Rock, which currently stands on the foundation of the First and Second Temples in Jerusalem, would someday be destroyed and a third temple constructed in its place, where the animal sacrifices of the Old Testament would again be offered. After the Antichrist's desecration of the third temple and halting of the sacrifices, Israel will suffer greatly (Jer. 30:5–7) and be scattered, fleeing to the mountains (Matt. 24:15–21). But God will save Israel out of this time of trouble.

At the final return of Christ, the people of Israel will be reassembled in the promised land to serve him. Coming to earth to establish a millennial kingdom, Jesus will resurrect the tribulation martyrs, who will be his priests and reign with him for a thousand years (Rev. 20:5). According to Darby, Israel will be gathered from all over the world, as God stated through Jeremiah: "See, I will bring them from the land of the north and gather them from the ends of the earth.... A great throng will return. They will come with weeping; they will pray as I bring them back. I will lead them beside streams of water on a level path where they will not stumble, because I am Israel's father, and Ephraim is my firstborn son" (Jer. 31:8–9). This gathering includes the resurrection of all Old Testament saints (Isa. 26:19; Ezek. 37:1–14). In defense of this view, Darby pointed to the many Old Testament prophecies that Israel would permanently receive the land from the Wadi of Egypt to the Euphrates River (Gen. 12:7; 13:14–17; 15:18–21; 26:3–5; 28:13–15). This promise of the land, Darby insisted, will ultimately be fulfilled in the millennial kingdom. Moreover, Darby turned to the Davidic covenant, in which God assured David that his descendant—whom Darby identified as Christ—would reign over the house of Israel forever (2 Sam. 7:12–16; Ps. 89:3–4, 29–37; cf. 1 Kings 9:3–5). As Darby argued, the relevant passages clearly indicate that David's kingdom is a political kingdom, not the spiritual kingdom of God. David's kingdom reflects Christ's political rule over Israel, which is not the same as the spiritual kingdom concerning salvation and an individual's relationship to Christ as Lord and Savior. In the millennium, Christ will "rule from sea to sea and from the River to the ends of the earth. May the desert tribes bow before him and his enemies lick the dust.... May all kings bow down to him and all nations serve him" (Ps. 72:8–9, 11). Interestingly, Darby maintained that the 144,000 and all living Gentiles who converted during the tribulation will enter the millennium in mortal bodies, such that marriage and childbearing continues throughout the millennium. Darby was silent on the question of how God will deal with saints who die during the millennium or with saints living on earth at the end of the millennium.

Darby bolstered his view of the millennium with an innovative approach to the new covenant delineated in Jeremiah and Ezekiel. For Darby, this new covenant is related to God's purpose to regather Israel in its land and assures Israel that it will again be a prominent people (Jer. 30:1–11, 18–21; 31:8–14, 23–28). Accordingly, the church shares in a different new covenant than the one described in the Old Testament. Hence Ezekiel quoted God's statement to Israel: "For I will take you out of the nations; I will gather you from all the countries and bring you back into your own land.... Then you will live in the land I gave your ancestors; you will be my people, and I will be your God" (36:24, 28).

At Jesus's return, Israel will be spiritually cleansed, David will be resurrected as a prince to rule over Israel with Christ the King, and Israel will enjoy God's peace (Ezek. 37:25–28). The Jews will remain God's primary instrument of rule on earth during the millennium, with all Gentile nations subordinate to them. Many peoples will travel to Jerusalem to learn God's ways and his word (Isa. 2:3). Christ's millennial kingdom will be characterized by righteousness and the complete absence of violence: "He will judge between the nations and will settle disputes for many peoples. They will beat their swords into plowshares and their spears into pruning hooks. Nation will not take up sword against nation, nor will they train for war anymore" (Isa. 2:4; cf. Joel 3:10; Mic. 4:3). This state of peace is due jointly to Christ's perfectly just reign and to his binding of Satan in the bottomless pit so that he cannot deceive the nations.

For Darby, one of the major features of the millennium is the Third Temple, which will be the center of worship in the enlarged Jerusalem. God provided Ezekiel detailed architectural features of this temple (Ezek. 40:1–46:24), which does not correspond to the First Temple or the Second Temple as constructed by Zerubbabel or refurbished by Herod. Animal sacrifices, alleged Darby, will continue in the Third Temple as a memorial of Jesus's death on the cross, just as the Lord's Supper currently functions for the church. These sacrifices do not furnish expiation for sin and are no more expiatory than the sacrifices in the Old Testament. But any attempt to spiritualize the animal sacrifices neglects the specific mention of sacrifices, including rooms in the Third Temple to prepare animals for sacrifice (Ezek. 40:38–43) and an altar for offering the sacrifices (Ezek. 43:13–17).

At the end of the millennium, Darby posited that Satan will be released from the pit and deceive all persons who only externally submitted to Christ's earthly authority but did not internally submit to him or love him as Lord. These persons will form an army and attempt an attack on Jerusalem. This attempt will prove futile, as Jesus will bring fire down from heaven to consume them. Jesus will then throw Satan into the lake of fire, from which he will never escape (Rev. 20:7–10). Immediately afterward, the wicked dead throughout all time (both before and during the millennium) will be resurrected to face judgment at the great white throne. When it is found that their names are not written in the Lamb's Book of Life, the wicked will be judged by their works and henceforth cast into the lake of fire (Rev. 20:11–15). Following the eternal condemnation of the wicked, God will create a new heaven for the church and a new earth for Israel. Darby insisted that the new heaven is kept distinct from the new earth: the Israelites, along with the believing tribulation and millennial Gentiles, will never enter the new heaven, and members of the church will never enter the new earth. However, the inhabitants of the new earth will walk by the light of the heavenly Jerusalem, both under the rule of the omnipresent Christ.

INFLUENCE OF DISPENSATIONALISM

Spreading his views in conservative Christian circles, in the 1850s Darby started to make frequent trips to North America and throughout the United Kingdom and Europe. Dispensationalism made its greatest impact in North America, where Darby spent a total of more than six years. Darby influenced numerous prominent pastors in cities such as St. Louis, Chicago, New York, and Boston. The Presbyterian pastors James H. Brookes (1830–97) and W. J. Erdman (1834–1903) became American propagators of dispensationalism. Dispensationalism was expounded at the Niagara Bible conferences (beginning in 1875) and the numerous Bible and prophetic conferences stemming from them. These conferences kindled an interest in biblical prophecy and the doctrine of a "secret rapture." Significantly, the conferences used dispensationalism as the key to unlocking Scripture, thereby combating theologically liberal perspectives, which they believed did not take the Bible seriously. Darby's message was effectively communicated in popular form in the books of Charles Henry Mackintosh (1820–96) and William E. Blackstone (1841–1935), with a circulation of more than one million copies in more than thirty languages. Even more significant were the works of Cyrus I. Scofield (1843–1921), whose *Rightly Dividing the Word of Truth* (1885) and *Scofield Reference Bible* (1909) transported dispensationalism across the globe. Because of its acceptance by D. L. Moody (1837–99), Lyman Stewart (1840–1923), and Lewis Sperry Chafer (1871–1952), dispensationalism was taught in the Bible schools these figures respectively founded, namely, Moody Bible Institute (1889), the Bible Institute of Los Angeles (1907; now Biola University), and Dallas Theological Seminary (1925). And because of the popularity of these schools and the fame of their graduates, dispensationalism has enjoyed a sizable influence in contemporary evangelicalism.

FOR FURTHER READING

Primary Sources

Blackstone, William E. *Jesus Is Coming*. 3rd rev. ed. Chicago: Revell, 1908.
Darby, John Nelson. *The Collected Writings of J. N. Darby*. Ed. William Kelly. 34 vols. Repr. ed. Sunbury, PA: Believers Bookshelf, 1972.

Mackintosh, Charles Henry. *The Mackintosh Treasury*. Neptune, NJ: Loizeaux Brothers, 1987.

Scofield, Cyrus I. *Rightly Dividing the Word of Truth, Being Ten Outline Studies of the More Important Divisions of Scripture*. Chicago: Bible Institute, 1885.

———. *The Scofield Reference Bible*. Oxford: Oxford University Press, 1909.

Secondary Sources

Bingham, D. Jeffrey, and Glenn R. Kreider, *Dispensationalism and the History of Redemption: A Developing and Diverse Tradition*. Chicago: Moody, 2015.

Callahan, James Patrick. *Primitivist Piety: The Ecclesiology of the Early Plymouth Brethren*. Lanham, MD: Scarecrow, 1996.

Rowdon, Harold H. *The Origins of the Brethren, 1825–1850*. London: Pickering & Inglis, 1967.

Sandeen, Ernest R. *The Roots of Fundamentalism: British and American Millenarianism, 1800–1930*. Chicago: University of Chicago Press, 1970.

Sauer, Erich. *From Eternity to Eternity: An Outline of the Divine Purposes*. London: Paternoster, 1954.

Weremchuk, Max S. *John Nelson Darby*. Neptune, NJ: Loizeaux Brothers, 1992.

CHAPTER 6

PRINCETON
THEOLOGY

From 1812 to 1921, an enormously influential movement arose at Princeton Theological Seminary that aimed to reclaim theology as the queen of the sciences against Kantian skepticism, to establish the total authority and reliability of Scripture against speculative methods in biblical scholarship, and to defend the historic doctrines of Christianity in general and the Reformed tradition in particular against the doctrinal revisionism of Schleiermacher. Known as Princeton theology or the Princeton school of theology (sometimes "Old Princeton" in distinction to post-1921 Princeton, which does not share its views), this dynasty of theological scholarship remains a stronghold for many contemporary evangelicals. While dispensationalism endeavored to promote and defend conservative theology on the popular level, Princeton theology endeavored to promote and defend conservative theology on the academic level. To understand Princeton theology, we must first look at its precursor movement, Protestant orthodoxy.

PROTESTANT ORTHODOXY

Following the first generation of sixteenth-century Protestant reformers, an influential movement known as Protestant orthodoxy arose that dominated seventeenth-century theology. The movement's hallmarks included a reclamation and application of a scholastic method of theology—characteristic of the tightly logically reasoned systems of medieval theologians Anselm and Aquinas—in Protestant thought and an unwavering commitment to Scripture as verbally inspired, propositionally infallible, and even without error. An outstanding and arguably extreme representative of Protestant orthodox theology is the influential

Italian-Swiss Reformed systematic theologian Francis Turretin (1623–87), whose three-volume *Institutes of Elenctic Theology* constitutes, in the assessment of historian of Christian thought Justo González, "the most systematic and thorough treatise on doctrinal theology in the Reformed camp after Calvin's *Institutes*."[1] According to González, Turretin was a "typical exponent of Protestant orthodoxy . . . in his scholastic style and methodology" since "here again we find the endless and subtle distinctions, the rigid outlines, the strict systematization, and the propositional approach that had been characteristic of late medieval scholasticism. Therefore, there is ample reason to call Turretin and his contemporaries 'Protestant scholastics.'"[2] Turretin powerfully asserted the verbal inspiration of all Scripture in a form that came close to, but did not assert, dictation by the Holy Spirit. Thus Turretin averred that even the vowel points of the Hebrew text of the Old Testament were divinely inspired and therefore exactly right. Now scholars of Turretin's day were cognizant that the autographs of the Hebrew Bible contained no vowel points, which had been added by sixth-century AD Jewish scholars known as the Masoretes. To protect the Bible from ambiguity as to its precise content and meaning, Turretin insisted that the Masoretic text of the Old Testament is inspired and error-free and cannot be corrected by earlier Hebrew manuscripts.

Turretin's scholastic Protestant orthodoxy constituted the basis for theological study and ministerial preparation at the flagship Princeton Theological Seminary, where most American Presbyterian pastors trained in the nineteenth century. Turretin's systematic theology served as required reading there until late in that century, and for many professors and students it furnished not simply one possible view of true theology but the only correct view of Protestant doctrine. In this way, Princeton theology arose from Turretin's teaching.

THE GREAT PRINCETON THEOLOGIANS

Princeton theology was epitomized by Archibald Alexander (1772–1851), the father-and-son duo of Presbyterian theologians Charles Hodge (1797–1878) and Archibald Alexander Hodge (1823–86), and their successor Benjamin Breckinridge Warfield (1851–1921). Throughout more than a century of influence at Princeton, the Alexander-Hodge-Warfield dynasty of Princeton theology mediated Turretin-style Protestant scholasticism and orthodoxy into a nineteenth-century American context and constituted the theological bastion of conservative Protestantism.

Of the four great Princeton theologians, the foremost was undoubtedly Charles Hodge, who was born into a very conservative Presbyterian family where the Westminster Confession of Faith and Shorter Catechism were honored second only to the Bible itself. Hodge prepared for the Presbyterian ministry under Archibald Alexander at Princeton Seminary, and his principal textbook was Turretin's *Institutes of Elenctic Theology*. Following seminary, the newly ordained Presbyterian pastor furthered his education at various European universities. Upon attending the lectures of Schleiermacher at Berlin and of Hegel at Tübingen, Hodge became convinced of the weaknesses of the new, liberal approach to Protestant theology and the strengths of his own heritage in Protestant orthodoxy. Seeking an appropriate philosophical foundation for his own theology, Hodge embraced the Scottish commonsense realism of Thomas Reid (1710–96). Contrary to his more prominent fellow Scotsman David Hume (1711–76), Reid propagated a nonidealistic and nonskeptical version of John Locke's empiricism. Reid's epistemology posited that all normal human beings are endowed by God with various reliable cognitive faculties, which yield sound observations and ideas about the world. Accordingly, people need only to gather and classify evidence and accept the "facts" that emerge from its careful generalization. Hodge embraced Reid's epistemology and rejected the prevailing and more skeptical epistemologies of Hume and Kant as well as the more speculative and rationalistic epistemology of Hegel. By way of Hodge, Reid's Scottish commonsense realism became the "orthodox" philosophy of Princeton theology.

Utilizing Reid's epistemology as the foundation of systematic theology, Hodge endeavored to revive the tradition of theology as a rational science. In his three-volume magnum opus, *Systematic Theology* (1871–73), Hodge proposed theology's proper method as phenomenological in nature. In other words, theology gathers and organizes the phenomena or data of divine revelation from Scripture to yield doctrinal facts just as natural science gathers and organizes the data of nature to yield the facts of biology or chemistry. In Hodge's words, "The Bible is to the theologian what nature is to the man of science. It is his store-house of facts; and his method of ascertaining what the Bible teaches, is the same as that which the natural philosopher adopts to ascertain what nature teaches."[3] Accordingly, Hodge formulated a tightly coherent system of conservative Reformed theology based on the plenary, verbal inspiration of the Bible, which he viewed as a collection of divinely revealed propositions waiting to be organized by rational human beings guided by the Holy Spirit.

While he denied that the human authors of the Bible were nothing more than machines who wrote mechanically under divine dictation, Hodge maintained that inspiration and infallibility extend to the very words and not simply to the ideas of Scripture. Exalting the Bible's divine qualities and minimizing its human qualities, Hodge mused that "it is enough to impress any mind with awe, when it contemplates the Sacred Scriptures filled with the highest truths, speaking with authority in the name of God, and so miraculously free from the soiling touch of human fingers."[4] Hence Hodge refused to seriously entertain objections to biblical inspiration or the error-free quality of the Bible based on various apparent discrepancies that cannot be easily answered. Though implicitly conceding their existence, Hodge proclaimed that "they furnish no rational ground for denying [biblical] infallibility. . . . A Christian may be allowed to tread such objections under his feet."[5] Unquestionably, Hodge proffered one of the highest views of the sole authority of Scripture in the history of Christian theology. Reacting against what he saw as liberal Protestant theology's denigration of that authority in favor of reason and experience, Hodge expanded bibliology, or the doctrine of Scripture, to a level of prominence unparalleled before his day. A corollary to Hodge's bibliology was his rejection of the Roman Catholic doctrine that church tradition stood alongside Scripture as an equal stream of divine revelation. Hence Hodge argued against the two-source notion of divine revelation as follows:

> If there are two standards of doctrine of equal authority, the one the explana-
> tory, and infallible interpreter of the other, it is of necessity the interpretation
> that determines the faith of the people. Instead, therefore, of our faith resting
> on the testimony of God as recorded in his Word, it rests on what poor,
> fallible, often fanciful, prejudiced, benighted men, tell us is the meaning of
> that Word. Man and his authority take the place of God.[6]

Accordingly, human tradition can never trump the plain meanings of the propo-sitions of Holy Scripture, a text that serves as its own interpreter.

Not surprisingly, Hodge deplored liberal theology as a malevolent and incapacitating influence on Christianity. Focusing his critique on its principal architect, Hodge condemned Schleiermacher for emptying Christianity of its doctrinal content and reducing it to a subjective mystical feeling:

> Christianity has always been regarded as a system of doctrine. Those who
> believe these doctrines are Christians; those who reject them, are, in the
> judgment of the Church, infidels or heretics. If our faith be formal or specu-
> lative, so is our Christianity; if it be spiritual and living, so is our religion.
> But no mistake can be greater than to divorce religion from truth, and make
> Christianity a spirit or a life distinct from the doctrines which the Scriptures
> present as the objects of faith.[7]

Indeed, Hodge's denunciation of Schleiermacher and his theology drove him to treat Christianity primarily as intellectual assent to a system of supernaturally disclosed truths without significant ambiguity or need of correction.

Hodge's actual theological system is a manifestation of classical Protestant orthodoxy and is delineated in such a way as to cast any significant departure from it in whole or in part as heresy if not apostasy. In his doctrine of God, Hodge stressed God's transcendent sovereignty and majesty. God is totally unchangeable and sovereignly controls the courses of nature and history down to their last details. Concerning predestination, Hodge stipulated a strongly Calvinistic view, opting for infralapsarianism over supralapsarianism. As a result, Hodge denounced Arminianism as an accommodation to humanism and thus a halfway house to theological liberalism. Eschewing Schleiermacher's propensity to address sin more as a social phenomenon than an individual problem, Hodge defended a traditional doctrine of sin, stressing both the natural headship of Adam as the physical head of all humanity and the federal headship invested in Adam: "Over and beyond this natural relation which exists between a man and his posterity, there was a special divine constitution by which he was appointed the head and representative of his whole race."[8] By virtue of this divine constitution, all persons were seminally present in the loins of Adam and unanimously chose to sin against God simultaneous with Adam's sin, thus rendering the doctrine of original sin as just.

Hodge stood as one of the most exceptional defenders of the penal substitutionary theory of the atonement in the history of Christian thought. He encapsulated the doctrine as follows:

> It is the plain doctrine of Scripture that . . . Christ saves us neither by the mere exercise of power, nor by his doctrine, nor by his example, nor by the moral influence which he exerted, nor by any subjective influence on his people, whether natural or mystical, but as a satisfaction to divine justice, as an expiation for sin and as a ransom from the curse and authority of the law, they reconciling us to God, by making it consistent with his perfections to exercise mercy toward sinners, and then renewing them after his own image, and finally exalting them to all the dignity, excellence, and blessedness of the sons of God.[9]

Hodge aimed to refute two objections frequently offered against penal substitutionary atonement. According to the first objection, love is the defining principle of God's actions toward humanity, such that there is no antagonism in God with an impulse to punish and a countervailing impulse not to punish. Thus God's plan to save sinners can only be viewed as an exhibition of love, not of justice in any kind. Granting that God is love, Hodge responded that love in God is not a weakness that impels God to fail to do what ought to be done. So if sin ought to be punished, a fact on which conscience and Scripture concur, then there is nothing in God that impels him to leave it unpunished. The harmony of God's nature, which equally includes love and justice, is the harmony of moral excellence. According to the second objection, it is unjust that the innocent suffer on behalf of the guilty, and it is pagan to suppose that God could be propitiated in this way. Hodge countered by declaring that no one has the right to make personal taste or feelings the test for truth: "That a doctrine is disagreeable is no sufficient evidence of its untruth."[10] Moreover, the fact that the concept of expiation forms part of many religions proves that it is not revolting to the vast majority of humankind but rather loved and exulted in as the only hope of the guilty.

While Hodge was theologically conservative, he differed from theologically conservative dispensationalists in that he opposed their pretribulational premillennialism with amillennialism, in which there is no future millennium yet to come. The only biblical description of the thousand-year reign of Christ is in the most apocalyptic book of the Bible (Rev. 20:1–10) replete with symbolism, and "a thousand years" is used elsewhere in nonapocalyptic portions of Scripture to symbolically denote a long period of time (Ps. 90:4; Eccl. 6:6; 2 Peter 3:8). To be consistent, then, the thousand years of Revelation refers to an indefinitely long time period. That period is the present church age, in which Satan's influence over the nations has been greatly reduced so that the gospel can be preached to the whole world. Those who are described as reigning with Christ for the thousand years are Christians who have died and are already reigning with Christ in heaven. The present church age will continue until the time of Christ's second coming, which occurs all at once and not in stages. When Christ returns, there will be one general resurrection of both believers and unbelievers. On the one hand, the souls of believers will be reinfused into their newly transformed, glorified physical bodies, and believers, body and soul, will live forever with God in the new heavens and new earth, which Hodge interpreted as the renovated and perfected physical universe. On the other hand, unbelievers are raised to face the final judgment and eternal condemnation. Hodge regarded amillennialism as the historic view of the church and accused pretribulational premillennialism as a Jewish doctrine that disparaged the gospel.

In sum, Hodge's theology is a philosophically refurbished augmentation of seventeenth- and eighteenth-century Protestant scholasticism. The whole thrust of

Hodge's approach to theology—followed by the other Princeton theologians—was to secure and defend what they regarded as the "truth once and for all delivered" in Protestant orthodoxy and to forestall theological novelty or experimentation.

Hodge's successor as professor of didactic and polemic theology at Princeton Seminary was B. B. Warfield, a Princeton graduate and student of Hodge's. Warfield perpetuated and expanded his mentor's accentuation of the divine inspiration and inerrancy of Scripture as the doctrinal bedrock of orthodox theology. Warfield defined inspiration as "that particular operation of God in the production of Scripture . . . with the effect of giving to the resultant Scripture a specifically supernatural character, and constituting it a Divine, as well as human, book."[11] Warfield argued, based on 2 Peter 1:19–21, that inspiration was confluent, meaning that Scripture was the product of both a divine author and various human authors. However, Warfield did not believe that part of Scripture was composed by God and another part was composed by the human authors. Rather, "the Spirit of God, flowing confluently in with the providentially and graciously determined work of men, spontaneously producing under the Divine directions the writings appointed to them, gives the product a Divine quality unattainable by human powers alone."[12] As a result, the inspiration by which Scripture is produced guarantees its complete authoritativeness and trustworthiness. Warfield insisted that his view was no novelty but represented the position of Jesus himself and the writers of the New Testament: "This is the doctrine of inspiration which was held by the writers of the New Testament and by Jesus as reported in the Gospels. It is this simple fact that has commended it to the church of all ages as the true doctrine. . . . This church-doctrine of inspiration was the Bible doctrine before it was the church-doctrine, and is the church-doctrine only because it is the Bible doctrine."[13]

During Warfield's time at Princeton (1887–1921), the Northern Presbyterian denomination suffered a lengthy, fractious controversy over the nature of Scripture. The newer methods of biblical scholarship termed "higher criticism" endeavored to evaluate Scripture using allegedly objective literary and historical methods and frequently yielded conclusions that denied traditional views of authorship, date, and composition of biblical books. No question existed as to where Warfield stood—staunchly opposed to higher criticism and any diminution of Princeton theology's high view of Scripture. In several articles and books, Warfield repeated and defended Princeton bibliology and claimed that anything short of belief in the complete errorlessness of the autographs of Scripture would result in theology's descending down the slippery slope into liberalism and utter relativism. Thus Warfield declared, "We cannot modify the doctrine of plenary inspiration in any of its essential elements without undermining our confidence in the authority of the apostles as teachers of doctrine."[14]

That neither Hodge nor Warfield found Darwin's theory of evolution threatening to Christian faith may be surprising. As a matter of fact, Warfield had earned his undergraduate degree in biology and always subscribed to evolution. Thus Warfield was "sure that the old faith will be able not merely to live with, but assimilate to itself all facts [of evolution]. . . . I am free to say, for myself, that I do not think that there is any general statement in the Bible or any part of the account of creation, either as given in Genesis 1 and 2 or elsewhere alluded to, that need be opposed to evolution."[15] However, Hodge and Warfield opposed the combination of philosophical naturalism and evolution and viewed evolution as a means God employed in creation. Dismissing the young-earth view, which utilized the genealogies of Genesis 5 and 11 to formulate a recent chronology of the earth's primitive period, Warfield wrote: "It is precarious in the extreme to drawn chronological inferences from these genealogies. The genealogies of Scripture were not constructed for a chronological purpose, and any appearance they present of affording materials for chronological inferences is accidental and illusory."[16]

In response to the emergence of the Pentecostal movement at the beginning of the twentieth century, Warfield advocated cessationism, according to which the Holy Spirit no longer gives believers miraculous spiritual gifts as a normative Christian experience as it was for the apostles. Warfield presented seven lines of support for cessationism. First, the primary purpose of miracles has always been to establish the credibility of persons who had been given words directly by God. Hence God enabled Moses to perform miracles so as to validate his claim to speak for God. Elijah and Elisha were given miraculous gifts to demonstrate that they spoke authoritatively and infallibly for God. The central reason for Jesus's miracles was to confirm his credentials as God's final and ultimate messenger. Likewise, the Holy Spirit empowered the apostles to do miracles to confirm that they spoke the words of God. Based on this scriptural pattern, it is most reasonable to conclude that miracles ceased with the death of the apostles, just as they ceased when Moses died and Elijah and Elisha died. Second, the gift of apostleship has come to an end, as the prerequisites for apostleship included being an eyewitness of Jesus's life and resurrection, being personally appointed by Jesus, and being authorized by Jesus to work miracles (Matt. 10:1–2). Obviously no one in the twentieth century could meet these conditions, implying that they could not perform the signs of an apostle. Third, the New Testament identifies the apostles and prophets as the foundation of the church (Eph. 2:20–22), where the context necessitates that Paul referred here to New Testament and not Old

Testament prophets. Once the apostles and prophets finished their role in laying the foundation of the church, their gifts were completed.

Fourth, the nature of the New Testament miraculous gifts differs markedly from purported manifestations of those gifts today. Regarding the gift of tongues, the languages spoken at Pentecost were preexisting, understandable languages, not ecstatic languages characteristic of Pentecostalism. Regarding the gift of prophecy, the New Testament prophets spoke direct, infallible revelation from God, while contemporary prophets may and often do err. Fifth, the testimony of church history bears witness to cessationism. The practice of apostolic gifts declined even during the lifetimes of the apostles. In the books of the New Testament, the miraculous gifts are mentioned less as the date of their writing gets later. After the New Testament era, we see the miraculous gifts cease, as attested by John Chrysostom and Augustine. Sixth, a continuation of the miraculous gifts, such as prophecy, would compromise the sufficiency of Scripture. The Spirit speaks only in and through the inspired Word, not through subjective personal messages. Seventh, the rules accompanying the exercise of New Testament gifts are no longer followed.

PRINCETON THEOLOGY AND LATER FUNDAMENTALISM

Comparing and contrasting Princeton theology with twentieth-century fundamentalism, a movement with which Princeton theology is often uncritically identified, would be instructive. Princeton theology both differed from fundamentalism in various respects and in other respects paved the way for it. Unlike many of the later fundamentalists, the Princeton theologians were highly educated intellectuals with broad appreciation of culture and deep knowledge of philosophy, biblical languages, and historical theology. They self-consciously viewed themselves as churchmen who comprised part of the Great Tradition of catholic, orthodox Christianity throughout the centuries. Thus Charles Hodge asserted that the Protestant doctrine of the sufficiency of Scripture does not abolish tradition of a certain type, namely, "a common faith of the church, which no man is at liberty to reject, and which no man can reject and be a Christian,"[17] which has been handed down from generation to generation. This is because Christ promised that the Holy Spirit would guide the people of God into the knowledge of the truth, meaning that classic Christian doctrines that, under the teaching of the Spirit, Christians have historically agreed in accepting must be true.

By contrast, fundamentalists would essentially renounce much of that tradition and instead posit an apostasy immediately following the death of the apostles coupled with the rediscovery of the true gospel in their ranks. However, Princeton theology prefigured fundamentalism in its identification of Christianity as accurate doctrine, its stress on revelation as propositional truths transmitted by divine inspiration in an inerrant Bible, and its polemical reactions to liberal Protestant theology and higher-critical methods of biblical scholarship. All in all, Princeton theology would prove a closer precursor to certain sectors of contemporary Reformed evangelical scholarship than to fundamentalism. In its own day, Princeton theology helped spark the neo-Calvinist revival in the Dutch Reformed Church led by Abraham Kuyper (1837–1920) and Herman Bavinck (1854–1921). A Dutch statesman, Kuyper emphasized the sovereignty of God over all spheres of life, including the social and political spheres, and contended that the function of the state amounted to preserving God's justice in society. Bavinck encouraged his students at the Free University of Amsterdam to take up, from a conservative perspective, the problems raised by higher biblical criticism.

FOR FURTHER READING

Primary Sources

Hodge, Charles. *Systematic Theology*. 3 vols. Grand Rapids: Eerdmans, 1973.

Turretin, Francis. *Institutes of Elenctic Theology*. Trans. George Musgrave Giger. Ed. James T. Dennison Jr. 3 vols. Philipsburg, NJ: Presbyterian and Reformed, 1997.

Warfield, Benjamin Breckinridge. *Counterfeit Miracles*. London: Banner of Truth, 1918.

———. *The Inspiration and Authority of the Bible*. Ed. Samuel G. Craig. Philadelphia: Presbyterian and Reformed, 1948.

———. Various writings and lectures on evolution. In *Evolution, Scripture, and Science*. Ed. Mark A. Noll and Daniel N. Livingstone. Grand Rapids: Baker, 2000.

Secondary Sources

González, Justo. *A History of Christian Thought*. Vol. 3, *From the Protestant Reformation to the Twentieth Century*. Rev. ed. Nashville: Abingdon, 1987.

Hoffecker, W. Andrew. *Piety and the Princeton Theologians*. Philipsburg, NJ: Presbyterian and Reformed, 1981.

Noll, Mark A., ed. *The Princeton Theology, 1812–1921: Scripture, Science, and Theological Method from Archibald Alexander to Benjamin Warfield*. Grand Rapids: Baker, 1983.

Olson, Roger E. *The Story of Christian Theology: Twenty Centuries of Tradition and Reform*. Downers Grove, IL: IVP, 1999.

Smylie, James H. "Defining Orthodoxy: Charles Hodge (1797–1878)." In *Makers of Christian Theology in America*, ed. Mark G. Toulouse and James O. Duke, 153–60. Nashville: Abingdon, 1997.

CHAPTER 7

CHARLES HADDON
SPURGEON

Practical Biblical Theology

K nown as the Victorian prince of preachers, Charles Haddon Spurgeon (1834–92) was a Particular (i.e., inclined toward Calvinism) Baptist who pastored the New Park Street Chapel (later the Metropolitan Tabernacle) in London for thirty-eight years. With spellbinding oratorical talents, Spurgeon offered to congregations of several thousand weekly a conservative biblical theology that they could put into practical effect in their public and private lives. In his day, Spurgeon's New Park Street Chapel was the world's largest Protestant megachurch. Many of Spurgeon's sermons were transcribed as he spoke and quickly translated into various languages. A prolific author of several genres, Spurgeon wrote commentaries, books on prayer, devotionals, magazines, poetry, hymns, and an autobiography, comprising a total of nearly 150 books. In fifty-seven years, Spurgeon accomplished three lifetimes of work by following a rigorous weekly schedule. Each week he preached four to ten times, read six substantial books, lectured, and edited a monthly magazine. Spurgeon also directed a theological college, ran an orphanage, and oversaw sixty-six Christian charities. Despite his Calvinistic belief that God only intends particular individuals to be saved rather than all humanity, Spurgeon regularly offered "gospel invitations" for all sinners to commit their lives to Jesus and thereby find salvation. The following invitation is characteristic of Spurgeon's ministry:

> Notice the breadth of the Gospel invitation. "Let him who thirsts come. And whoever will, let him take the water of life freely." . . . "Oh, I am willing

enough," says one, "but perhaps, after all, I am not one of those persons who are invited!" Oh, but it says, "Whoever will." I am very fond of that word, "whoever." . . . There is no limit to the mercy of God to all who trust His dear Son! And there is no limit to you but that which your own will imposes. If you nil it, that is, make nothing of it, then it shall be nil, that is, nothing, to you. But if you will it, it is God's will that you should have it! When your will is brought to accept the Savior, then, depend upon it, it is God's will that you should have Him! "Whoever will." "Whoever." I cannot conceive, in any language, a wider sweep of word than that, so come along, poor troubled Sinner, come to Jesus Christ! Accept Him and you shall be saved here and now![1]

Spurgeon found no way to comprehend how his Calvinistic doctrine of election and God's universal salvific will could both be true, though he firmly believed that both were plainly taught in Scripture. Hence he embraced the paradox that both were somehow true in a way transcending his understanding, in the process sacrificing the possibility of a theology that attempted to connect all the dots of Scripture. Due to its unsystematic character, Spurgeon's theology was radically biblical, as he expressed in a famous sermon on election:

It has been my earnest endeavor ever since I have preached the Word, never to keep back a single doctrine which I believe to be taught of God. It is time that we had done with the old and rusty systems that have so long curbed the freeness of religious speech. The Arminian trembles to go an inch beyond Arminius or Wesley, and many a Calvinist refers to John Gill or John Calvin as any ultimate authority. It is time that the systems were broken up, and that there was sufficient grace in all our hearts to believe everything taught in God's Word, whether it was taught by either of these men or not. . . . If God teaches it, it is enough. If it is not in the Word, away with it! Away with it! But if it be in the Word, agreeable or disagreeable, systematic or disorderly, I believe it.[2]

The twin organizing principles of Spurgeon's theology were biblicality and practicality, which henceforth became hallmarks of the Baptist movement. As Spurgeon biographer Tom Nettles points out: "Whatever else he was, Spurgeon was a Christian theologian, and, preeminently as a 'Pastor/Theologian,' he must covet the rightness of both the head and the heart of his people."[3] This chapter will explore the doctrinal legacy Spurgeon bequeathed to Baptist thought.

APPLIED THEOLOGY

In his "Battlements" sermon on Deuteronomy 22:8, Spurgeon delineated his view of the expositor's task in deriving practical theological ideas from the Bible. Battlements were erected around the roofs of homes to protect children and careless adults from falling off the roof to their death. This implies that expositors not overstep designated boundaries for the eternal safety of their own souls and the souls of others. For Spurgeon, none need fear the "most high and sublime doctrines" of divine revelation, since God had "battlemented" them. To illustrate, Spurgeon deemed it a truth of clear revelation that "God hath from the beginning chosen his people unto salvation through sanctification of the Spirit and the belief of the truth."[4] However, many simpleminded people corrupted this doctrine into antinomianism, jumping over the battlements God placed around it. Not only does God possess a chosen people, but this people will be recognized by the fruits of holiness and their zeal for good works; they will be not only forgiven of sin but also purged from sin. Similar divine safeguards surround the doctrine of the perseverance of the saints. Spurgeon cited Hebrews 6:4–12 and 2 Peter 2:20–22 as applicable to Christians in order to disclose that "if the first salvation could have spent itself unavailingly, there would be no alternative, but a certain looking for of judgment and of fiery indignation." Nonetheless, the doctrine of justification stipulates that justifying faith is absent if no sanctification follows: "Where faith is genuine, through the Holy Spirit's power, it works a cleansing from sin, a hatred of evil, an anxious desire after holiness, and it leads the soul to aspire after the image of God."[5] Therefore Paul and James work as a team in ensuring that both the tower of predestination and the battlement of perseverance are in place.

Together the tower of predestination and the battlement of perseverance entail Spurgeon's doctrine of providence. Regarding providence, Spurgeon asserted that "every particle of dust that dances in the sunbeam does not move an atom more or less than God wishes." But there is a colossal difference between such governance and fate, since fate is blind but providence is full of sight. While fate functions without any personal purpose of either mercy or justice, providence emerges from the wisdom of God who "never ordains anything without a purpose."[6] The believer's involvement in ministry of all forms—extending to all occupations, which are equally vocations before God—should rely on the omnipotence and purposes of God without ever degenerating into fatalism. Using God's purposes as an excuse to do nothing is to indulge a frightful piece of mischief. It does not follow from the fixity of God's decrees and the certainty of their fulfillment that one need do nothing toward the conversion of others; one may as well conclude that it is unnecessary to eat, drink, breathe, and labor.

Spurgeon's deep theological understanding is equally visible in the tension between hating and loving the world. The biblical admonition, "Do not love the world," reverberates with the believer's love of holiness and the glory of Jesus, and the believer experiences the truth that "If anyone loves the world, the love of the Father is not in him" (1 John 2:15 ESV). Not surprisingly, the natural Christian response is a visceral loathing of the world's decaying mass of evil. In spite of this, Jesus came to precisely this world and told believers, "You are the salt of the earth" (Matt. 5:13). Thus we are unusable to God if we do not give succor to the world just as a nurse does to the baby placed in her arms: "Unless you feed it, it will die; unless you clothe it, it will starve with cold; unless you bear it in your bosom, there is no shelter for it. The Lord has committed this poor world into the tender hand of His Church; and the very miseries of the world make us pity it; and love it in the next degree."[7] By "next degree" Spurgeon indicated that believers could not love the immoral world with a love of complacency but with a love of benevolence. The deliberate pursuit of this love comprised the imitation of Christ in his cries of concern for the hardness, blindness, and hostility of Jerusalem's response to his deeds of mercy and doctrines of true righteousness. So Spurgeon declared: "We shake our heads at the world, and as a sinful world we can only loathe it; but as a world of men with immortal souls, as a world of men that shall yet be washed clean, if God's Spirit go forth with us to the blessed work, we feel that we do not hate the world, after all, in that wrong sense."[8] If we are indeed friends of God, we must be friends of humanity, made in the image of God.

To properly hate the world while loving it, Spurgeon emphasized that the Christian must be engaged in the process of sanctification, in particular, the rooting out of "cant, hypocrisy, pride, and those secret bosom-sins which so easily beset a man in daily life."[9] Spurgeon understood sanctification as a progressive work of God and the believer that makes the believer more and more free from sin and like Jesus in his daily life. With a clear beginning at regeneration, sanctification affects the whole person, including intellect, emotions, will, soul, and body. The role the believer plays in sanctification is double-sided, both passive and active. Passively, the believer yields fully to God and displays dependence on the Holy Spirit's work to grow in sanctification (Rom. 6:13; 8:13; 12:1). Actively, the believer is to use the power of the Spirit to put to death the deeds of the body. Commenting on Romans 8:13, "If by the Spirit you put to death the misdeeds of the body, you will live," Spurgeon pointed out that although it is by the Spirit that the believer is able to mortify the flesh, it is believers who must actually do it, working out their salvation (Phil. 2:12–13). It is not the Spirit who is exhorted to mortify the flesh, but Christians themselves. There are several aspects to the active role believers are to play in sanctification. Believers must strive for holiness (Heb. 12:14), abstain from immorality (1 Thess. 4:3), work at purification (1 John 3:3), and refuse to have partnership with unbelievers (2 Cor. 6:14). Consequently, a believer can never say, for example, "I've been prideful for thirty years, and I will be until the day I die, and the church is going to have to put up with me just the way I am." For anyone who maintains this has allowed sin to gain dominion over themselves, which contradicts the mark of a Christian that "sin shall no longer be your master" (Rom. 6:14).

What made Spurgeon's doctrine of sanctification distinctive was not the issue itself, as sanctification has always been a Baptist belief. It was rather the centrality that Spurgeon gave to sanctification, his interweaving into a common fabric many if not all of the scriptural threads on sanctification, and the translatability of his concept of the double-sided nature of sanctification to the lives of everyday people that rendered sanctification a special legacy of his thought to the church thereafter. Spurgeon underlined the need for believers to grow both in their passive trust in God to sanctify them and in their active striving for holiness and increased obedience in their lives. If believers ignore the passive role, they become proud and overly confident in themselves. If believers ignore the active role, they become lazy and spiritually stunted. However, it should be emphasized that Spurgeon did not confuse sanctification with religious legalism, for Spurgeon was no legalist. He loved smoking fine cigars, telling his congregation that he did not consider smoking a sin and that he would "continue to smoke to the glory of God." Likewise, Spurgeon regularly drank alcoholic beverages in moderation. He judged absolute prohibitions on smoking and drinking "a Pharisaic system which adds to the commands of God the precepts of men," and stated that "to that system I will not yield for an hour. The preservation of my liberty may bring upon me the upbraidings of many good men, and the sneers of the self-righteous; but I shall endure both with serenity so long as I feel clear in my conscience before God."[10] This stood in contrast to the views of Seventh-Day Adventist Church founder Ellen G. White (1827–1915), who was at the same time warning Christians against the dangers of tobacco and alcohol.

HIGH VIEW OF THE LORD'S SUPPER

Unique to Spurgeon among Baptists was his doctrine of the Lord's Supper, in which Jesus was really present—in fact, allegedly more present than he was purported to be in Roman Catholic transubstantiation and Lutheran consubstantiation. Spurgeon disagreed with transubstantiation and consubstantiation on the Calvinistic ground that it is logically impossible for Jesus's human body to be present in the Supper. However, Spurgeon disagreed with many of his fellow Baptists in concluding that the Lord's Supper was merely symbolic or a memorial of Christ's passion. Here Spurgeon emphasized that it is entirely logically possible for Jesus's divinity, naturally endowed with omnipresence, to be present in the Supper, and that such a divine presence may manifest itself in any possible way, as there are by definition no logical constraints on this presence.

Spurgeon stipulated that in the Supper, the soul of the believer literally feeds on the omnipresent divinity of Jesus in the same way and at the same time that the body feeds on the bread and wine. Spurgeon wrote, "At this table Jesus feeds us with His body and His blood. His corporeal presence we have not, but His real spiritual presence we perceive."[11] Thus a genuine eating and drinking of Jesus's infinite divine spirit by the finite human spirit transpires in the Lord's Supper, which consumption Spurgeon defended from Jesus's twofold description of his spirit as "the bread of life" (John 6:35, 51) and the wellspring of "living water" (John 4:10, 14; 7:37–38). That these passages refer to Jesus's spirit and not his body is evident by their depiction of the living bread and living water as "coming down from heaven" (see John 6:33, 38), a portrayal that could apply only to Jesus's eternally preexistent divinity and not to the humanity he acquired on earth in the womb of Mary. As Spurgeon explained, "I can bear my own witness that, many and many a Sabbath, when I have found but little food for my soul elsewhere, I have found it at the communion table. We believe that Jesus Christ spiritually comes to us and refreshes us, and in that sense we eat his flesh and drink his blood."[12]

Spurgeon argued that his model actually mediated the highest possible form of real presence. What separates Spurgeon's model from transubstantiation, consubstantiation, and the standard Baptist sacramentarianism is that the soul of the believer literally eats and drinks the infinite divine spirit of Jesus, thus respectively satisfying the soul's literal hunger and quenching the soul's literal thirst. Since the spirit of Jesus possesses an ontological value not merely higher than but infinitely higher than the humanity of Jesus, Jesus's divine spirit is infinitely more real than his human body. Hence Spurgeon explained that his theology of the Lord's Supper features an even more real presence than that proposed in Roman Catholicism.

> The priest who celebrates mass tells us that he believes in the real presence, but we reply, "Nay, you believe in knowing Christ after the flesh, and in that sense the only real presence is in heaven; but we firmly believe in the real presence of Christ which is spiritual, and yet certain." By spiritual we do not mean unreal;

in fact, the spiritual takes the lead in real-ness to spiritual men. I believe in the true and real presence of Jesus with His people, such presence has been real to my spirit. Lord Jesus, Thou Thyself hast visited me. As surely as the Lord Jesus came really as to His flesh to Bethlehem and Calvary, so surely does He come really by His Spirit to His people in the hours of their communion with Him.[13]

This ultimate presence of Jesus renders the Supper of utmost importance in the Christian life and, in Spurgeon's view, remedies the low view of the Supper that plagued most Baptists. Spurgeon compared Jesus's presence at the Lord's Table with the reflection on Jesus that occurs in believers' devotional lives: "To know that Jesus loves me is one thing. But to be visited by Him in love is more. Nor is it simply a close contemplation of Christ; for we can picture Him as exceedingly fair and majestic, and yet not have Him consciously near us. Delightful and instructive as it is to behold the likeness of Christ by meditation, yet the enjoyment of His actual presence is something more."[14] Accordingly, Spurgeon insisted on the weekly celebration of the Lord's Supper, since "the moments we are nearest to heaven are those we spend at the Lord's table."[15]

SALVATION OF INFANTS

In addition to the Lord's Supper, a hotly contested issue of Spurgeon's day was whether infants are necessarily saved. This question became even more pressing for Calvinistic Baptists, who conjoined a belief in individual predestination with the conviction that only persons who understood saving faith and gave a sincere profession of commitment to Jesus could be baptized. In Calvinistic fashion, Spurgeon insisted that native and total depravity did not exclude children, as Adam represented all his posterity, adult and infant alike, and when he fell he fell for them all. Thus any qualification that a child had for heaven was not through its sinlessness, for it had none. Based on Psalm 51:5, Spurgeon depicted the infant as "born in iniquity; in sin did his mother conceive him. He has an evil heart; he knows not God." Infants do not have good seed in them, waiting to sprout acts of love and righteousness. Nor are infants morally neutral and spiritually receptive to the earliest religious influences, but they have evil seed within their hearts. The infant's mind is a carnal mind, filled with "enmity against God."[16] Against those who alleged that sin enters human experience through bad example, Spurgeon submitted a dramatically different situation. Spurgeon invited his hearers to imagine a child who from its first day lived under carefully controlled Christian influences, so that "the very air it breathes be purified by piety; let it constantly drink in draughts of holiness. Its ears hear nothing but the voice of prayer and praise and notes of sacred song." Contrary to all environmental factors, that child "may still become one of the grossest of transgressors" and "if not directed by divine grace, march downward to the pit."[17] Children are therefore evil not by example but by nature.

However, mitigating circumstances allow parents to hope and take action accordingly. Parents may be used by God to plant the good seed of the Word of God in children's minds, and divine grace may cause the teaching to be effectual. Moreover, Spurgeon proposed the concept of an age of accountability, defined as the point when a child became capable of sinning. Though its heart harbors enmity against God, that enmity is not developed. Until the age of accountability, Spurgeon viewed children as under some gracious provision that guaranteed their salvation: "No doubt, in some mysterious manner the Spirit of God regenerates the infant soul, and it enters into glory made meet to be a partaker of the inheritance of the saints in light."[18] Accordingly, when he spoke to parents who had lost children in infancy, Spurgeon comforted them that they would yet "know those dear Babes of yours. . . . Ye shall hear those loved voices again: ye shall hear those sweet voices once more; ye shall yet know that those whom ye loved have been loved by God."[19] Spurgeon emphasized that he had never "at any time in my life, said, believed, or imagined that any infant under any circumstances would be cast into hell," going so far as to declare: "I do not believe that on earth there is a professing Christian holding the damnation of infants, or if there be, he must be insane or utterly ignorant of Christianity."[20] Dying infants therefore proved a powerful means of evangelism, as they roused desires for heaven in the parents: "How many a mother has had her first desires for heaven kindled by the flight of her little cherub up to the bosom of Christ."[21]

Remarkably, Spurgeon believed that the salvation of infants was the means by which God guaranteed that, in the end, the number of the saved would exceed the number of the lost. The majority of believers could not come from the realm of adults since in the world, even in the nominally Christian world, so few were truly Christ-followers. Spurgeon therefore deduced, "I do not see how it is possible that so vast a number should enter heaven, unless it be on the supposition that infant souls constitute the great majority."[22]

THE DOWNGRADE CONTROVERSY

The Downgrade Controversy of 1887–88 amounted to the most intense episode of Spurgeon's career and the gravest existential crisis that ever faced the Baptist

Union, the denomination to which Spurgeon belonged. Prior to the controversy, Spurgeon had grown tremendously popular in the Baptist Union and was regularly invited to perform the central preaching role at Union meetings. But starting in 1887, Spurgeon attacked the Baptist Union as beating and scourging the historic Christian faith in the person of some of its ministers. In Spurgeon's words, "The case is mournful. Certain ministers are making infidels. Avowed atheists are not a tenth as dangerous as those preachers who scatter doubt and stab at faith."[23] Accordingly, Spurgeon endeavored to warn against the rise of theological liberalism among the Nonconformists (groups not conforming to the Anglican Church, that is, Presbyterians, Independents or Congregationalists, Baptists, Quakers, and Methodists). Spurgeon charged that three essential doctrines were being abandoned: biblical infallibility, substitutionary atonement, and the condemnation of those who died without faith in Christ. This "downgrade" of Christian faith could, for Spurgeon, lead to nothing but disaster: "We have had enough of 'The Down-Grade' for ourselves when we have looked down upon it. What havoc false doctrine is making, no tongue can tell. Assuredly the New Theology can do no good towards God or man; it has no adaptation for it. If it were preached for a thousand years by all the most earnest men of the school, it would never renew a soul, nor overcome pride in a single human heart."[24]

Perhaps the decisive factor in launching a protracted debate was Spurgeon's adverse comparison between the Nonconformists and the Church of England. When the Baptist Union met in October 1887, the "downgrade" was the major subject of conversation, though fear of troubling the theological waters kept the topic off the official program. As a result of the Union's diversity of theological opinion, Spurgeon lamented: "Believers in Holy Scripture are in confederacy with those who deny plenary inspiration; those who hold evangelical doctrine are in open alliance with those who call the fall a fable, who deny the personality of the Holy Ghost, who call justification by faith immoral, and hold that there is another probation after death, and a future restitution for the lost."[25] Not surprisingly, Spurgeon proceeded to withdraw from the Baptist Union in November 1887.

Spurgeon intended for the controversy to end at this point, but its intensity redoubled, for Spurgeon's fame caused his resignation to deal a devastating blow to the standing of the Baptist Union. The Council of the Baptist Union met in December 1887 to reflect on the crisis. Furious at the harm Spurgeon had inflicted on the Union's reputation, Spurgeon's hardline opponents repudiated his claims to have done all he could to eliminate the evils he lamented before withdrawing. They anticipated that their next aim—to force Spurgeon to renounce his charges or proffer evidence against named individuals—could be achieved if Spurgeon met with a delegation from the Union. Nevertheless, Spurgeon was determined not to name anyone, as he was highly cognizant of the repercussions of creating martyrs. Before meeting with the delegation, Spurgeon carefully negotiated the meeting's terms to prevent any discussion of his withdrawal. The meeting would exclusively discuss what the Union could do to put its house in order. Accordingly, Spurgeon was shocked when his charges and withdrawal were raised at the January 1888 meeting, followed by a successful vote to officially censure him for making charges without providing names and supporting evidence.

The third and concluding phase of the controversy surrounded rival declarations of the Union's faith. The council passed a resolution with the fragile twofold aim of upholding the evangelical credentials of the Union while not violating the consciences of its more liberal members. At the same time, supporters of Spurgeon's protest finally started to make an impact under the leadership of Spurgeon's brother James. They campaigned for the adoption of theological declarations that would restore the Baptist Union to an unambiguously evangelical alliance. Although Spurgeon was pessimistic about the possibility of their success, he encouraged his supporters because he thought it only right that they should try to do something about the "downgrade" before submitting their resignation from the Union. At a council meeting immediately preceding the annual assembly, endeavors were made to bridge the gap between two sets of theological declarations, one definitively more evangelical than the other. Negotiations were finally successful only five minutes before the crucial session was set to open on April 23, 1888. But these negotiations did not favor the more evangelical declarations, which left Spurgeon devastated and cast a dark shadow over his last few years. As a result of the controversy, Spurgeon's health declined, such that his wife, Susannah, reported following his death in 1892 that "his fight for the faith . . . cost him his life."[26]

CONCLUSION

The threads of Spurgeon's theological convictions may well be drawn together in his doctrine of assurance. Due to his perceptions of the ubiquitous heavy-handedness of the Anglican state church and the nominalist Christianity endemic within it, Spurgeon often issued warnings about the danger of salvific presumption. It was trivial for the nominalistic outlook to permeate all denominations and every English citizen, for in the end, was not England a

Christian nation? Thus Spurgeon observed many who "have concluded that they were saved when they were not, have fancied they believed when as yet they were total strangers to the experience which always attends true faith."[27] On the other hand, both the testimony of Scripture and Spurgeon's personal experience convinced him that some people possessed such a strong sense of assurance coupled with an equally strong love of holiness that the Holy Spirit had made their salvation as clear to them as a geometrical proof demonstrated by Euclid. For Spurgeon, "such a man could as soon doubt his own existence as suspect his possession of eternal life."[28] But Spurgeon was not naive about the vacillation of confidence in even the strongest believer, who had no objective reason to doubt. He knew of seasons in which even he had sung with John Newton, "'Tis a point I long to know, oft it causes anxious thought. Do I love the Lord or no? Am I his or am I not?"[29] But Spurgeon counseled that, although the believer may sing it, it should be short meter and not sung too long. Assurance of pardon and therefore all the blessings of the new covenant can and should be solid for those who hope in Christ.

FOR FURTHER READING

Primary Sources

Spurgeon, Charles Haddon. *The Autobiography of Charles H. Spurgeon.* 2 vols. Chicago: Revell, 1899.

———. *The Complete Works of C. H. Spurgeon.* Harrington, DE: Delmarva, 2013.

———. *Metropolitan Tabernacle Pulpit.* London: Passmore & Alabaster, 1861–92.

———. *Sermons of Rev. C. H. Spurgeon.* 20 vols. New York: Funk & Wagnalls, 1857–92.

———. *Spurgeon's Expository Encyclopedia.* 15 vols. Grand Rapids: Baker, 1977.

———. *The Sword and the Trowel.* London: Passmore & Alabaster, 1865–92.

———. *"Till He Come": Communion Meditations and Addresses.* London: Passmore & Alabaster, 1896.

Secondary Sources

Carlile, J. C. *Charles H. Spurgeon: An Interpretative Biography.* London: Religious Tract Society, 1933.

Drummond, Lewis. *Spurgeon: Prince of Preachers.* Grand Rapids: Kregel, 1992.

Hopkins, Mark. "The Down-Grade Controversy." *Christian History* 29 (1991): 29–30.

Kruppa, Patricia Stallings. *Charles Haddon Spurgeon: A Preacher's Progress.* New York: Garland, 1982.

Nettles, Tom. *Living by Revealed Truth: The Life and Pastoral Theology of Charles Haddon Spurgeon.* Fearn, Scotland: Mentor, 2013.

CHAPTER 8

VATICAN I AND NEO-THOMISM

Due to the influence of Romanticism, the seventeenth and eighteenth centuries saw the flourishing of a creative impulse within the Roman Catholic tradition. Composers, artists, and architects joined forces to engulf worshipers with a sense of God's mystery and power and the presence of the church within culture. Intense devotion flourished in the mysticism of Margaret Mary Alacoque (1647–90) and Jeanne Marie Bouvier de la Mothe Guyon (1648–1717). New missionary religious orders including the Lazarist Fathers, the Sisters of Charity, and the Redemptorists promoted revival and renewal within the Catholic Church. Nevertheless, despite these improvements in the church, external developments in the eighteenth and nineteenth centuries drove the church and society further apart. Threats to the authority of the Catholic Church were posed by the American and especially the French revolutions of the late eighteenth century, the rise of industrialism in the early nineteenth century, and the Revolutions of 1848 (a series of republican revolts against European monarchies beginning in Sicily and spreading to France, Germany, Italy, and the Austrian Empire). The Catholic response was typically defensive and divisive. Declaring itself opposed to many modern and progressive ideas, the Roman Catholic Church identified the "errors" of the time, including secular political philosophies, ethics, and views of sexuality as well as Eastern Orthodoxy and all forms of Protestantism. At the same time, however, a philosophical revolution was underfoot in Catholic theology that aimed to fully engage with late nineteenth-century secular thought.

POPE PIUS IX

Born Giovanni Mastai-Ferretti, Pope Pius IX (1792–1878; r. 1846–78) proved to be the towering figure of nineteenth-century Catholicism as well as a highly controversial one. For conservative Catholics, he was the shepherd who led the Roman Church through a tumultuous phase of the modern era. For liberals within and outside the church, he was the pope who opposed modernity with edicts that seem as obstinate and muddle-headed as the flat-earth stance of the medieval period. At the start of his pontificate, Pius IX strove to maintain control of the Papal States in the face of the efforts of such revolutionaries as Giuseppe Mazzini (1805–72) and Giuseppe Garibaldi (1807–82) to unite the various Italian territories into an independent nation. In effect, the papacy constituted a monarchy, an endangered species in an age that saw claims to a divinely privileged order as aristocratic fictions. Furthermore, the papacy was a source of religious teachings at a time when such teachings were being resentfully dismissed by many cultured people as pernicious fables. Following his distant predecessor Pius VII, Pius IX believed that true democracy was compatible with Christianity, such that any democracy that expelled Christianity was a false one. As for the papacy, it possessed structural distinctiveness from secular states. The mandate given to Peter (Matt. 16:18–19) needed to be upheld by Peter's successors, and neither divided nor delegated. But by the end of 1870, the Papal States, Rome included, formed a small part of the new state of Italy. During the last eight years of his life, Pius was relegated to the Vatican, ruling like a monarch but regarding himself a prisoner. His reactionary perspectives toward the secular world must be interpreted as the result of his embattled political life. Assessing Pius's pontificate as objectively as possible, it marks a valiant yet somewhat vain effort to safeguard the Catholic tradition amid a flood of political, economic, and scientific change.

The initial sign that Pius's pontificate would be a stormy one came with the bull *Ineffabilis Deus* on December 8, 1854. In this pronouncement, Pius IX elevated to official dogma the belief, maintained for several centuries, that the Virgin Mary had herself been born without original sin, so rendering her an exception to the human condition. Dubbed the "immaculate conception," this doctrine placed Mary in a unique category, further from the general lot of humanity and closer than ever before to the Trinity. Obviously this bull underscored differences between the Roman Church and the various denominations of Protestantism. As if this were not divisive enough, on the next day (December 9, 1854) Pius gave an allocution, or papal address to a secret consistory, that salvation was impossible outside the Roman Church. This allocution explicitly anathematized every form of Protestantism as well as Eastern Orthodoxy. Such words had not been uttered by any church official since the Council of Trent (1545–63). Similarly, the 1863 encyclical *Quanto conficiamur moerore* condemned perceived heresy with the same if not more stridency as the condemnations issued during the Reformation era. Such harshness is best understood as the pope's attempt to protect the revealed and transcendent verities of Christianity against the inclination of popular theological liberalism to reduce Christianity to the merely human and cultural.

Antagonism to the secularization of culture reached its zenith in 1864 with Pius's famous *Syllabus of Errors*, repudiating most of the dominant schools of modern thought. Sparking a furor in liberal circles, the *Syllabus* identified the "errors" of the time in political and social life, in ethics, concerning Christian marriage, concerning the primacy of the Roman pope, and in other matters of dissent. In sum, there were eighty assumptions or attitudes that fell under condemnation. Many of the ideas Pius assaulted had already become common throughout the Western world (e.g., the separation of church and state, freedom of religion, and state-controlled public education), and many others were well on their way to virtually universal acknowledgment. All were equally denied. It seemed to many that the Roman Church had set itself as the opponent of all modern and progressive thought. The Catholic faithful, who had to live in the secular world while remaining good Catholics, found themselves in the highly difficult position of having to opt for the church or for secular progress.

THE FIRST VATICAN COUNCIL

Pius IX was not satisfied with declaring war against materialistic ideas or Protestant doctrines. He perceived himself as the defender of the faith in an age of chaos. The last great challenge to the Roman Church had been faced by the Council of Trent (1545–63), and Pius was determined to meet the next such challenge with a similar council. Meeting at the Vatican, it thus became known as the Vatican Council, later as the First Vatican Council to differentiate it from the one convened between 1962 and 1965. Unlike Trent, it was a brief council, lasting only from 1869 to 1870, but it exerted a monumental effect on the thought of the Roman Church. In its tenor, the council did not significantly depart from Pius's work of the prior thirty years. A majority of the cardinals in attendance had been appointed during his papacy and embraced several of his views. It appeared that all shared a skepticism toward the advance of materialism in culture and politics, and most felt that conservation of the tradition, not adaptation, was the way to uphold the faith.

But Vatican I differs from its predecessor, Trent, in the political slant of its deliberations and edicts. Many of its conversations would have been baseless in any century before the nineteenth, and a number of its assertions would have been needless in an era when divine ordering of the cosmos went unchallenged. Questions about the meaning of the council started from the moment it was summoned. Did the calling of a council signify that the Roman Church was now also a parliamentary democracy, with bishops as the regional representatives contributing to policy? Was Pius going to build constructive alliances with the rapidly changing secular society? This would continue the process begun in 1851 when Pius forged a concordat with Spain, the first of many strategic alliances that strengthened the church's power just as its geographical territory was diminishing. Or would the meeting serve to solidify an already entrenched resistance to modernity and secularism, which had also been firmly in place since the 1850s? Hopes and fears alike ran high on the eve of the first meeting on December 8, 1869. Debates about procedure and the initial drafting of a statement of faith occupied the first month, but matters got no easier when substantive issues came to the table. The statement of faith mirrors in style but not in content the *Syllabus of Errors*, listing the ideas that the church deemed heretical to deny, such as the creation of the world for God's glory and the Bible's inspiration by God. Other early documents debated at the council included disciplinary and regulatory measures, some of which sparked major disagreement. One argument surrounded the proposal that the Catechism of the Council of Trent be standardized throughout the church; German bishops blocked this motion because the catechism of the Jesuit Peter Canisius had been normative in their dioceses since the sixteenth century. A Hungarian bishop came to the Germans' rescue by depicting the slippery slope the motion could create: What would then prevent sermons from eventually being dictated by Rome? Hence no action was taken on this issue. However, a much larger issue appeared that would take up the rest of the council's effort.

This issue was papal infallibility, which would amount to one of the most controversial issues for the rest of the nineteenth century and most of the twentieth. It was not simply about whether a pope could err, for in some respects all popes had erred. The question was whether the pope, under certain circumstances, had the power to make statements that could not be challenged or reformed over time. The qualifications for infallible pronouncements were as follows: the pope needed to be speaking *ex cathedra*, "from the bishop's chair" as the heir of

Saint Peter; and he needed to be defining matters of faith or morals. Under those conditions, the Holy Spirit supernaturally protected the statements of the pope from error, making them permanently binding and incapable of improvement. If the *Syllabus of Errors* proved a declaration of war against modernism and secularism, the doctrine of infallibility proved a declaration of war against dissenters within the church. Instead of putting an end to controversy, the doctrine fanned controversy into flame. Proponents of the measure successfully placed it at the top of the council's agenda, which elicited criticism even from their allies for putting excessive importance on the issue. These wary advocates maintained that it was inopportune to push the question so hard. The outright opposition was based on several arguments, most importantly the lack of historical precedent and the negative effect such a definition would have on non-Catholic churches. Additional reservations about the definition came in the form of suggested alternate wording, as a total of two hundred changes were proposed.

More campaigning and debating followed until the final votes were cast on July 18, 1870, while a violent thunderstorm raged so greatly that additional lamps were needed in the chamber and some voices were difficult to hear. In the end, all but two bishops approved the definition. The others who opposed the definition conveyed their views privately but voted with the majority for the unity of the church. The definition read:

> We, adhering faithfully to the tradition received from the beginning of the Christian faith—with a view to the glory of our Divine Saviour, the exaltation of the Catholic religion, and the safety of Christian peoples (the Sacred Council approving), teach and define as a dogma divinely revealed: That the Roman Pontiff, when he speaks *ex cathedra* (that is, when—fulfilling the office of Pastor and Teacher of all Christians—on his supreme Apostolical authority, he defines a doctrine concerning faith or morals to be held by the Universal Church), through the divine assistance promised him in blessed Peter, is endowed with that infallibility, with which the Divine Redeemer has willed that His church—in defining doctrine concerning faith or morals—should be equipped: And therefore, that such definitions of the Roman Pontiff of themselves—and not by virtue of the consent of the church—are irreformable. If anyone shall presume (which God forbid!) to contradict this our definition; let him be anathema.[1]

The staunchest opponents to the new dogma formed a schismatic church dubbed the "Old Catholics," which took hold in Switzerland, Germany, and Austria for a few decades but never drew large numbers away from the Roman Church. For most Catholic laypeople, the doctrine of papal infallibility may have been a welcome event in the face of the change and doubt that rocked the secular world. Historian of Christianity Ralph Keen comments: "Regardless of the implications for the clergy, a strengthening of the authority of the papacy was seen as a strengthening of the church generally. This was one 'monarchy' that was not going to change or topple."[2]

Nonetheless, the papacy remained susceptible to political affairs. The same month, July 1870, saw the beginning of the Franco-Prussian War, in which Italy was embroiled from the outset. Italian king Victor Emmanuel I (r. 1861–78) desired to keep the peninsula as unified as possible and thus requested papal support. Pius refused, but such resistance was futile absent the continued backing of French troops, now engaged in battling Prussia. For a brief period, the Vatican functioned as a fortress for its papal monarch, entrenched until, amid cannon fire, the flag of surrender was elevated above the dome of St. Peter's Basilica.

THE RECOVERY OF SCHOLASTIC THEOLOGY

After Pius died on February 8, 1878, he was succeeded by Leo XIII (r. 1878–1903), born Vincenzo Gioacchino Pecci. An ardent student of the theology of Thomas Aquinas, Pecci was regarded a moderate when elected pope, and as Leo XIII he was on much friendlier terms with the secular world than Pius had been. However, Leo was resolved not to diminish the authority of the papacy, leading some of his early decretals against political and ideological threats to prove just as conservative as his predecessor's. Notwithstanding this fact, Leo's approach to these threats was more intellectual. In his encyclical *Aeterni Patris* of August 4, 1879, Leo proclaimed that Aquinas far surpassed all other Scholastic theologians, thus essentially declaring Aquinas the official theologian of the Roman Church: "Reason can scarcely rise higher, while faith could scarcely expect more or stronger aids from reason than those which she has already obtained through Thomas. . . . But the chief and special glory of Thomas, one which he has shared with none of the Catholic Doctors, is . . . to lay upon the altar, together with sacred Scripture and the decrees of the supreme Pontiffs, the 'Summa' of Thomas Aquinas, whence to seek counsel, reason, and inspiration."[3]

The pope appointed Thomas as the church's official theologian in order to encourage others to follow his example in combating liberalism and secularism. Just as Thomas used the world's Aristotelian philosophy in service of the church, so the church in the late nineteenth century needed new theologians to engage the culture. Leo founded an academy in Rome for Thomistic studies, the first of a number of pontifical institutes (others may be found in, for example, Louvain and Toronto) dedicated to research on scholasticism generally. From these institutes, there emerged a philosophy known as neo-Thomism or neo-scholasticism.

This revived attention on Thomas temporarily averted attention away from the infallibility controversy, since infallibility was not recognized in the thirteenth century. But the larger impact of neo-Thomism was to position the Catholic Church as the extension of Christ by which God draws everything that is separate and finite back to its absolute source. Recognizing the Aristotelian difference between actuality (what is) and potentiality (what any given entity is ultimately capable of being), neo-Thomism ascribes a higher state of being (or ontological value) to potentialities than actualities. The highest ontological value belongs to God, who perfectly unifies potentialities with actualities and thus transcends the separation between essence and existence. God's essence is his existence, and vice versa. Further, neo-Thomism views the plurality of things in the actual world as subordinate to a unity of all things in the world of potentiality. This unity is the being of God, the exclusive source of all matter and its ultimate end. Accordingly, the world is like a huge jigsaw puzzle, each piece of which has its meaning only in reference to the whole. Presently God is cosmically putting all the unfree pieces (nonhuman animals, plants, and inanimate objects) back together. However, humans, being free, must will to be restored to the Divine One and need a model to which to conform. For neo-Thomism, the model is Christ, and the means of achieving restoration is the Roman Church. Known as *exitus-reditus* (emanation and return), this understanding of the relationship between God and the world aims to reconcile secular thought with Christian belief in God as the origin and end of all matter. Moreover, the *exitus-reditus* doctrine carries powerful moral implications. No individual is morally permitted to do anything that diminishes the larger whole, such as committing murder, adultery, theft, and so forth. As the standard of objective moral values, God has implanted in rational persons an innate sense of good and evil that guides actions even in the absence of explicit commands issued by authorities. This view of a divine moral governance of all human society, termed *natural law*, dominated Western religious thought into the twentieth century.

Neo-Thomism featured a more optimistic view of human nature than that furnished by existentialism or Princeton theology. Neo-Thomist anthropology held that the fall partially compromised but neither thoroughly infected nor destroyed the image of God in humanity. As a result, grace was not a thorough-going reconstitution of a fatally flawed human nature but an indispensable aid toward achieving salvation. Due to natural human goodness, God might regard the works of the baptized Christian with some, but not complete, favor; grace was the necessary supplementary gift (*donum superadditum*) that made one just, or righteous, before God. Likewise, revelation proved an auxiliary to reason. Theologically, there indeed are things humans can understand, and there are also things that humans must simply believe. But in a fascinating parallel with Princeton theology, neo-Thomism maintained that such beliefs are not incompatible with understanding. Rather, these beliefs illuminate the understanding, furnishing insights and explanations that provide certainty and completeness to our awareness of the world. Hence, in neo-Thomism (as in Princeton theology), understanding and belief are mutually necessary and complementary.

In addition, the neo-Thomist revival of Scholastic theology enabled the Catholic Church to systematize and structure its teachings. Catholic theological faculties could operate on a common foundation, and philosophical rigor served as a standard for good theological arguments. Divisions of theology into separate areas such as fundamental, moral, and sacramental theology ensured that clergy grasped the current doctrinal questions, had traditional sources available for their own study, and understood the connections between various issues. It also spurred academic theologians in seminaries and universities to seriously engage with Scholastic materials for answers to urgent contemporary problems. In several respects, the intellectual tradition of Catholic theology reached its current plateau in the last two decades of the nineteenth century.

CONCLUSION

Called by Pius IX, Vatican I attempted to stem the tide of materialism in society and establish itself as the authoritative source of truth in an uncertain world. This establishment was apparent in its promulgation of the doctrine of papal infallibility. Seeking to bring the medieval philosophical worldview into full engagement with the late nineteenth century, Pope Leo XIII, Pius's successor, declared Thomas Aquinas to be the official theologian of the Roman Catholic Church. Since Thomas granted a great deal of power to human rationality yet insisted that this faculty was insufficient for understanding the world and God completely, his theology was understood as making the best use of modern science while reminding the modern world of science's limitations.

FOR FURTHER READING

Primary Sources

Leo XIII. *Aeterni Patris*. Papal Encyclicals Online. http://www.papalencyclicals.net/Leo13/ L13cph.htm.

Vatican Council, Session IV. In *Documents of the Christian Church*, 4th ed., ed. Henry Bettenson and Chris Maunder, 277. Oxford: Oxford University Press, 2011.

Secondary Sources

Burton, Katherine. *Leo XIII: The First Modern Pope*. Philadelphia: David McKay, 1962.

Costigan, Richard F. *The Consensus of the Church and Papal Infallibility: A Study in the Background of Vatican I*. Washington, DC: Catholic University of America Press, 2005.

Hasler, August Bernhard. *How the Pope Became Infallible: Pius IX and the Politics of Persuasion*. New York: Doubleday, 1981.

Hudson, Deal W., and Dennis W. Moran, eds. *The Future of Thomism*. Notre Dame, IN: University of Notre Dame Press, 1992.

Keen, Ralph. *The Christian Tradition*. Lanham, MD: Rowman and Littlefield, 2008.

McCool, Gerald. *The Neo-Thomists*. Marquette Studies in Philosophy 3. Milwaukee: Marquette University Press, 1994.

CHAPTER 9

REVIVALIST THEOLOGY

The Roman Catholic Church responded to liberalism with a council and Neo-Thomism. Evangelicals such as Dwight L. Moody (1837–99) responded with revivalist sermons. Epitomized by the thought of Moody, this chapter surveys the distinctive three-pronged theology embraced by nineteenth-century revivalists, which would continue to influence the framing of the gospel message to this day. For them, the gospel message started with the fact that humankind was ruined by the fall: Adam's sin made everyone absolutely helpless and morally corrupt. At its center, however, the gospel message proceeded to affirm that humankind is redeemed by the blood: God's love provides a remedy for human ruin in that the shed blood of the crucified Jesus redeems from sin. The gospel message concluded with the work of regeneration by the Holy Spirit. Due to their profound awareness that regeneration was the Spirit's work, Moody and his colleagues, such as Holiness movement founder and evangelist Phoebe Palmer (1807–74), refused to scare people into heaven by preaching hellfire. Nor did they conclude their sermons with high-pressure invitations. Persons concerned for their soul's well-being were directed to the inquiry room, a calm, sober place where seekers were encouraged to respond to the Spirit's movement. The Spirit was responsible for conviction, conversion, repentance, and faith. The chapter concludes with reflection on Moody's theological hallmark that while what one believes is important, in whom one believes is of ultimate importance.

THE ORIGINS OF MOODY'S THEOLOGY

Although a world-renowned evangelist, Moody never had any formal theological training, and the sum of his formal academic training did not exceed a fifth-grade education. However, Moody read the works of the practical biblical theologian Charles Haddon Spurgeon and often asked ministers questions about the Bible and theology. On one of these occasions, Henry Moorhouse (1840–80), the prominent British Bible teacher dubbed the "boy preacher," counseled, "If you will stop preaching your own words and preach God's Word, he will make you a power for good."[1] From that point onward, Moody resolved to be a preacher of the Word. He fervently studied the Bible and mastered its historical and doctrinal contents. Moody's biblicism is evident in the fact that many of his sermons comprised a retelling of scriptural narratives in the vernacular of the common people attending his meetings. The major themes of his sermons were the themes he discovered in the Bible. For Moody, if something was not in the Bible, it was not worth believing. But if something was in the Bible, there could exist no dispute about believing it. When preaching on heaven, for instance, Moody began his sermon with a question and response that characterized his theological epistemology: "On this important matter how are we to gain reliable information? Simply by Scripture. Here then is our guidebook, our textbook— the Word. If I utter a syllable that is not justified by the Scriptures, don't believe me. The Bible is the only rule. Walk by it and it alone."[2]

Moody perceived a deleterious effect of liberal theology on American and British churches. He maligned liberal pastors for using a "penknife on the Bible, clipping out this and that part because it contains the supernatural or something he cannot understand."[3] Moody exhorted laypeople to protest against all preachers who regarded it as a mark of scholarship to accept the conclusions of higher criticism: "I tell you the time has come for the laity to speak out, and if a minister begins to pick the Bible to pieces, get up and go out. I have said it the length and breadth of this country, and I am going to say it. I believe that a minister that gets a white cravat on and goes into the pulpit and picks the Bible to pieces is doing the devil's business better than he could do it himself; and I think the time has come for the laity to speak right out and give no uncertain sound."[4]

Moody exhibited no patience with any scholarly theory that threatened to undermine the Bible, the source of Christian belief that contained the gospel as its heart. Moody was highly cognizant that a particular biblical theology was central to his preaching. This theology can be summarized in three overarching doctrines, which Moody dubbed the "three Rs" of the Bible: ruined by the fall; redeemed by the blood; and regenerated by the Spirit. According to W. H. Daniels, compiler of a volume of Moody's sermons, Moody did not enter into theological speculation beyond these three biblical themes. Eschewing innovative doctrinal constructs, Moody gladly boasted in his sermons that his theology was the same as that of Abel: "Some people in Minneapolis the other day declared that Moody's theology is thirty years old. Well, if I was sure it wasn't six thousand years old, I'd pitch it into the Mississippi. I believe that sin is the same today as then and that its remedy is the same. I'm an Abelite. If I could go back behind Abel for my theology, I'd do it, but I can't."[5]

RUINED BY THE FALL

According to Moody's anthropology, each human being was both sinful and a sinner, with this condition descending from Adam. This anthropology was of course not unique to Moody, but the homespun flair by which he explained it proved quite distinctive. By the inherited sinful nature from Adam (the Adam nature) and by works springing from this nature, individuals are exceptionlessly marked by sin. Moody summarized the human condition in his famous sermon on the "brazen serpent," which analyzed Nicodemus's encounter with Jesus. Although Nicodemus was a noble teacher, aristocrat, and member of the Sanhedrin whose integrity could not be surpassed, he still needed to be born again, since "that which is born of the flesh is flesh. . . . We may try to patch up our old Adam nature, but it is of no use."[6] Even regeneration does not restore the Adam nature; rather, it creates a new nature, thus launching a battle between the flesh and the Spirit in the regenerated person. This new nature is necessary because of the total depravity—and so irreparability—of the Adam nature, a doctrine Moody deemed as empirically verified by the history of the world: "The first man born into the world became a murderer; he became the killer of his own brother; and all the way down through the ages man had been piling up sins against God and against himself. It didn't take the Bible to prove that man was entirely depraved. All experience of every age proved it. There was nothing good in man."[7] When expounding the sinfulness of humanity, Moody commonly spoke of such deeds of sin as ungratefulness to parents, drunkenness, sexual immorality, partaking of worldly entertainments, and violating the Sabbath. However, these deeds amounted to the fruits of a bad tree; with or without the fruits, the tree is still bad. Hence Moody argued, "If you don't actually do any sin, yet if you neglect Christ, and neglect salvation as a gift from God, you must perish."[8] Moody therefore conceived of the earth as a vast hospital where everyone is wounded and needs the Great Physician.

Moody engaged in apologetics to defend his conception of the fall from perennial attacks. Regarding the problem of evil, Moody conceded that he did not understand why God would permit evil but argued that it was an even greater mystery how God came to bear the brunt of evil himself. Since the objector concedes the possibility that God could take our sins on himself, it follows from the greater to the lesser that God may well be justified in permitting evil. To the objection that God would be unjust in condemning and punishing us because someone else—namely, Adam—sinned six thousand years ago, Moody replied that we are not guilty for having the Adamic nature or even for how the Adamic nature behaves. Instead, we are guilty solely because we reject the cure God has graciously provided: "If you men and women are lost it is because we have spurned the remedy, not because we are the sons of Adam and have inherited his nature."[9] Thus God is absolved of any charge of injustice in holding us accountable for the Adam nature and its actions because he furnished the remedy that is available to everyone. Moody did not take up the question of the salvific status of persons who never hear the gospel. But to the objection that some people cannot believe since they are not elect, Moody retorted that each person has the ability to accept the remedy on his or her own. It is unclear whether Moody grounded this ability in prevenient grace dispensed to all humans before coming to faith or in the notion that humans, still bearing the *imago Dei* after the fall, retained as an essential and ineffaceable part of that image the inherent ability to believe apart from grace. But in either case, persons have only themselves to blame if they find themselves in hell.

Nevertheless, Moody rarely preached on hell, doing so only when necessary to prove his orthodoxy. Preaching on Luke 16:25, Moody recounted, "A man came to me the other day and said, 'I like your preaching because you don't preach hell. I suppose you don't believe in that doctrine?' I don't want any man to rise up in judgment and say that I was not faithful while here—that I preached only one side of the truth. If a man is a messenger of God he must tell His truth as He gives it to him; he must not pick out some passages and say they are true, and pick out others and say they are not true. Now, the same Bible that pictures to me Heaven, with all its beauty and glory, tells me of hell."[10] In light of the extant evidence, it appears that Moody never preached a single sermon dedicated exclusively to the dreadful subject of hell. Hence the question arises, why this unusual silence, especially when other revivalists of the eighteenth and nineteenth centuries graphically depicted the torments of hell as an essential tool of their trade? Moody's reply was strikingly profound: God desires to draw children to himself by love, not to draw slaves to himself by fear. Moody perceived that to manipulate crowds through fear of hellfire and damnation did not conform to the nature of God and did not yield the fruit of repentance God desired. Moody explained himself as follows:

Now, my friends, repentance is not fear. A great many people say I don't preach up the terrors of religion. I don't want to—don't want to scare men into the kingdom of God. I don't believe in preaching that way. If I did get some in that way they would soon get out. If I wanted to scare men into heaven, I would just hold the terrors of hell over their heads and say, "Go right in." But that is not the way to win men. They don't have any slaves in heaven; they are all sons, and they must accept salvation voluntarily. Terror never brought in a man yet. Look at a vessel tossed upon the billows, and sailors think it is going to the bottom and death is upon them. They fall down on their knees, and you would think they were all converted. They ain't converted, they're only scared. There's no repentance there, and as soon as the storm is over, and they get on shore, they are the same as ever.[11]

Although helpless sinners ruined by the fall are destined for eternal torment, fear of that torment does nothing to produce conversion. Only the love and goodness of God break the rebellious heart and yield repentance. As a result, Moody consistently preached the love of God.

REDEEMED BY THE BLOOD

For Moody, the center of the gospel proclaims that God's love furnishes a remedy for human ruin: the redeeming blood of Jesus. As Moody exclaimed, "There is nothing, my friends, that brings out the love of God like the cross of Christ; it tells of the breadth, the length, and the height of his love. If you want to know how much God loves you, you must go to Calvary to find out."[12] In his famous sermon "Tracing the Scarlet Thread," Moody delineated a cruciform hermeneutic in which the entire Bible must be interpreted in the light of Calvary. All the Old Testament instances of shedding blood foreshadow the death of Jesus, and the New Testament employed "blood" as a linguistic handle denoting Jesus's death and its saving benefits. Following the New Testament, Moody attributed saving powers to the blood, including justification (Rom. 5:9), redemption (Eph. 1:7; 1 Peter 1:18–19), forgiveness of sins (Heb. 9:22), and purification (1 John 1:7–9; Rev. 7:14). Moody went to great lengths in unfolding how this hermeneutic disclosed the fullest meaning of Scripture. He began with primal humanity's violating the prohibition against eating from the Tree of Knowledge of Good and Evil. Since a penalty is a necessary component of every law, death resulted from the transgression of Adam and Eve. But treating Adam and Eve with grace, God fashioned for them coats of animal skin before their banishment from

Eden, where animals had to be killed and hence their blood shed to make the skins. This served as a precursor to Christ's sacrifice: "Here we find the first glimpse of the doctrine of substitution—the substitution of the just for the unjust—the great doctrine of the atonement and substitution foreshadowed in Genesis."[13]

Moody found this same principle in the sacrifices that Cain and Abel offered to God. Because Cain's sacrifice was bloodless, it proved unacceptable to God. From this fact, Moody made the contemporary application that all churches that disregarded the blood by preaching salvation through human good works were similarly unacceptable to God. But because Abel's sacrifice necessitated the shedding of blood, it proved acceptable to God. Moody continued this theme with Noah, who offered God an animal sacrifice when he emerged from the ark. A *locus classicus* of this theme for Moody was Abraham's near-sacrifice of Isaac, where Isaac was spared through the shedding of blood of the ram. Here Abraham's response to God's command so delighted God that "He showed Him the grace of heaven and lifted the curtain of time to let him look down into the future and see the Son of God offered bearing the sins of the world."[14] Hence Moody concluded from Genesis that all the patriarchs went to heaven through the blood atonement. Turning to the Exodus institution of the Passover, Moody emphasized that to be safe within the house, the blood of the Passover lamb—representing Jesus, the ultimate Lamb of God—needed to be on the front door; natural birth in the house did not suffice.

> When the hour came you could see them all slaying their lamb, and not only that, but putting the blood on the door-posts. To those Egyptians, or to the men of the world, how absurd it looked. . . . This blood was to be a substitution for death. . . . It was death that kept death out of the dwelling. . . . And the question ought to come to every one tonight, "Are we sheltered behind the blood?" If not, death will come by and by, and you will be separated from God for eternity. If you have not a substitute you will die. Death is passed on all of us. Why? Because of our sin. If we have not a substitute we have no hope.[15]

Likewise, the entire system of animal sacrifices in Leviticus pointed to the blood of Jesus. Moody concluded his survey of the Old Testament with Isaiah 53, which he viewed as a transparent prophecy of the passion of Jesus.

For Moody, the scarlet thread bound the Old and New Testaments together. Responding to Unitarians and Universalists who detested the notion of a God propitiated by blood, Moody quoted the words of institution of the Lord's Supper to show that Jesus—the paradigm of love—taught and grounded this very doctrine. Surveying the Pauline texts referring to the blood, Moody deduced, "The law had been broken and the penalty of death had come upon us, and it required life to redeem us. . . . Christ has bought me by His blood. I am no longer my own. I am His. He has ransomed me."[16] Finally, Moody launched into an extended exposition of the book of Hebrews, stressing the role of Jesus's high priesthood as making one infinitely valuable sacrifice—the sacrifice of the God-man—to atone for the sins of the world.

REGENERATED BY THE SPIRIT

Another reason why Moody declined to frighten people into heaven by portraying the fires of hell is his acute recognition that regeneration was entirely the work of the Holy Spirit. On the same score, Moody did not end his sermons with high-pressure invitations. Anyone concerned for the well-being of their soul was guided to an inquiry room, a peaceful, serious place where seekers were urged to respond to the movement of the Holy Spirit. For Moody, the Spirit was responsible for conviction and repentance or conversion (Moody used the latter two terms interchangeably). So while individuals could freely choose to believe in the gospel, the Spirit infallibly responds to their faith by producing conviction of sin and repentance. Since conviction and repentance are prerequisites to salvation, Moody contended that persons are not saved by their own free choice, but by the Spirit's response to their free choice. Upon conviction and repentance, the Holy Spirit regenerates a person. Moody insisted that regeneration was not something that could be accomplished by human effort, such as attending church, getting baptized, being confirmed, praying, reading the Bible, doing one's best, or turning over a new leaf. Just as no one can cause himself to born the first time, so no one can cause himself to be born the second time. Hence Moody declared:

> The trouble with people is that they are trying to make that stream good while the fountain is bad. And that is why I am so opposed to all the work being put on the old man, trying to straighten out the old man and make him upright when he is bad from the crown of his head to the sole of his foot. It isn't patching up the old man, but it is hewing down that tree and putting a new graft in. It is entirely changed, a new creation. I have heard of reform, reform, until I am tired and sick of the whole thing. It is regeneration by the power of the Holy Ghost that we need.[17]

In regeneration, the Spirit renders one elect from before the foundation of the world and gives the individual a kind of soul operation by which his Adamic nature is expunged and his new nature is created and instilled. Moody held that it was logically impossible for someone with the new nature to reject Christ or otherwise invalidate his salvation by living a life dominated by unrepented sin. For a good tree, or someone with the new nature, cannot habitually bear bad fruit. This middle ground between Arminian synergism and Calvinist monergism exemplified the tension in which Moody perpetually held these doctrines. As a result, both Arminians and Calvinists collaborated with Moody in his evangelistic meetings, although neither camp was fully comfortable with his theology. While Calvinists were disturbed by Moody's stress on human responsibility and the universal provision and offer of salvation, Arminians were disturbed by Moody's endorsement of divine election and perseverance of the saints.

Moody preached his famous "New Birth" sermon more often than any other. To illustrate, between October 1881 and November 1899 Moody preached it 183 times almost verbatim, from Savannah and Scranton to Oxford and Cambridge. Nonetheless, Moody felt that something more than regeneration was crucial to effective Christian labor. This "something more" was the "Holy Spirit upon us for service,"[18] which he used synonymously with a filling, a baptism, or an anointing. But Moody denied that this experience brought about entire sanctification, elimination of the desires of the flesh, or perfection.

CONCLUSION

While Moody believed we are ruined by the fall, redeemed by the blood, and regenerated by the Sprit, he underscored that this theology is valuable only insofar as it serves as a signpost to Jesus. In other words, while what a person believes is significant, in whom a person believes is of ultimate significance. Theological statements, doctrines, and creeds are not the objects of saving faith. For Moody, possessing a correct theology is as important as taking the correct road home, but it holds no value if one refuses to enter the door of the house: "Doctrines are all right in their places, but when you put them in the place of faith or salvation, they become sin. If a man should ask me to his house to dinner tomorrow, the street would be a very good thing to take me to his house, but if I didn't get into the house, I wouldn't get any dinner. Now a creed is a road or a street. It is very good as far as it goes, but if it doesn't take us to Christ, it is worthless."[19] Faith is in a person, namely, Jesus, not in any description of him. So Moody would ask us not simply whether we have located the correct road and the house, but also whether we have entered into the house.

FOR FURTHER READING

Primary Sources

Moody, Dwight L. *Moody's Great Sermons*. Chicago: Laird & Lee, 1900.

———. *Moody's Latest Sermons*. Chicago: BICA, 1900.

———. *New Sermons, Addresses and Prayers*. St. Louis, MO: N. D. Thompson, 1877.

Needham, George. *Recollections of Henry Moorhouse, Evangelist*. Chicago: Revell, 1881.

Secondary Sources

Bebbington, David W. *The Dominance of Evangelicalism: The Age of Spurgeon and Moody*. Downers Grove, IL: IVP, 2005.

Dorsett, Lyle. *A Passion for Souls: The Life of D. L. Moody*. Chicago: Moody, 2003.

Findlay, James F., Jr. *Dwight L. Moody: American Evangelist, 1837–1899*. Chicago: University of Chicago Press, 1969.

Gundry, Stanley N. *Love Them In: The Life and Theology of D. L. Moody*. Chicago: Moody, 1999.

———. "The Three Rs of Moody's Theology." *Christian History* 25 (1990): 16–19.

Pollock, John. *Moody: A Biography*. 3rd ed. Grand Rapids: Baker, 1997.

CHAPTER 10

THE SOCIAL GOSPEL

The same modern progressivism that frightened Spurgeon, Moody, and Vatican I Roman Catholicism found sympathetic ears in theological liberalism and its social gospel. Conceptualized à la Schleiermacher as historical rather than eschatological, the kingdom of God became a powerful image for social change during the final decades of the nineteenth century. Given the palpable notions of progress and evolution, the kingdom of God was increasingly seen as a realizable goal. On this score, the liberal German Protestant theologian Albrecht Ritschl (1822–89) developed an innovative doctrine of justification centered on the kingdom of God. Ritschl began by defining Christianity as an ellipse with two foci—Jesus, who reveals God's love for us and reconciles us, and the church, which is the spiritual and ethical community Jesus founded that aims to transform human society into the kingdom of God. In justification, God assigns a person to a particular place in the kingdom where she engages in virtuous activity and, with God's help, overcomes the contradictions pervading human existence.

This chapter explicates the ways in which the liberal Baptist minister Walter Rauschenbusch (1861–1918) interpreted the New Testament message as a command to heal society's ills through a socially committed theology and socially engaged clergy. This "social gospel" centered on the prevailing social and economic crises and the responses contained within the Bible and Christian history.

DEFINING MOMENTS IN RAUSCHENBUSCH'S LIFE

The father of the social gospel, Rauschenbusch became the pastor of New York City's largely immigrant Second German Baptist Church, located on the

Lower East Side in an area fittingly dubbed Hell's Kitchen, in 1886. There Rauschenbusch observed firsthand the immigrants' wretched living conditions, labor exploitation by industrial powers, and governmental apathy for the suffering of the poor. These experiences led Rauschenbusch to rethink his theological categories, to undertake a fresh study of the Bible, and to study the positions of social critics like economist Henry George (1839–97) and urban planner Jacob Riis (1849–1914). When Rauschenbusch took a professorial position in 1897 at Rochester Theological Seminary, he did not forget his New York encounters. In 1892 Rauschenbusch, along with two other Baptist ministers, formed a society called the "Brotherhood of the Kingdom." This group, which drew many followers, met to discuss ways of implementing the kingdom of God, which Rauschenbusch deemed the most splendid idea that has ever enriched human thought. Opposing the dominant laissez-faire capitalism in economic life and its promotion of unrestricted competition, the social gospelers urged brotherhood that included cooperation between management and labor. They found in the Old Testament prophets' condemnation of injustice, in the life and teachings of Jesus, and in the immanence of a God of love the foundations of a distinct human order. This order would be actualized in the kingdom of God, a kingdom in which God's will would be done as humans expressed his love across the range of their relationships and of society's institutions. The work of the social gospelers received wide public attention with Rauschenbusch's publication of *Christianity and the Social Crisis* (1907) and *Christianizing the Social Order* (1912).

Delivered as a series of lectures at Yale, Rauschenbusch's monumental 1917 work, *A Theology for the Social Gospel*, endeavored to furnish the theological substance necessary for sustaining the social program. In the book's opening words, "We have a social gospel. We need a systematic theology large enough to match it and vital enough to back it."[1] Calling for a socially committed theology, the book's underlying subtext maintained that the work of the brotherhood and the activities of the socially engaged clergy, who saw Jesus's kingdom proclamation as a mandate to eliminate the problems of society, cannot be written off as something tangential to theology. This is manifested in Rauschenbusch's description of the kingdom of God:

> The Kingdom of God, therefore, is not merely ethical, but has a rightful place in theology. This doctrine is absolutely necessary to establish that organic union between religion and morality, between theology and ethics, which is one of the characteristics of the Christian religion. When our moral actions are consciously related to the Kingdom of God they gain religious quality.

Without this doctrine we shall have expositions of schemes of redemption and we shall have systems of ethics, but we shall not have a true exposition of Christianity. The first step to the reform of the churches is the restoration of the doctrine of the Kingdom of God.[2]

For Rauschenbusch, the kingdom of God had become spiritualized in orthodox Protestantism, thus losing the first-century social meaning of Jesus's most prominent theme. Rather than understanding the kingdom as heaven, Rauschenbusch followed Ritschl in understanding the kingdom as an earthly fellowship of righteousness ruled by God, namely, humanity organized in this world according to the will of God. By erecting a theological system to guide and theorize the work of his activist colleagues, Rauschenbusch made a powerful claim for legitimacy within the theological mainstream.

SYSTEMATICS OF THE SOCIAL GOSPEL

A Theology for the Social Gospel coherently yet creatively systematized the social gospel under the standard theological categories. At the heart of the social gospel was the kingdom of God. Rauschenbusch insisted that the kingdom of God is at once an earthly and supernatural movement that could never be realized by mere human effort. It can only materialize when humanity collectively works in collaboration with the power of God, seen in the presence of Jesus and the nurturing of the Holy Spirit:

The Kingdom of God is divine in its origin, progress, and consummation. It was initiated by Jesus Christ, in whom the prophetic spirit came to its consummation, it is sustained by the Holy Spirit, and it will be brought to its fulfillment by the power of God in his own time. . . . The Kingdom of God, therefore, is miraculous all the way, and is the continuing revelation of the power, the righteousness, and the love of God. The establishment of a community of righteousness in mankind is just as much a saving act of God as the salvation of an individual from his natural selfishness and moral inability.[3]

Two aspects of the kingdom of God emerged as crucial for Rauschenbusch: the kingdom as the realm of love, and the kingdom as the commonwealth of labor. Regarding love, Rauschenbusch held that it is not enough to conceive of the kingdom as the prevalence of goodwill, for goodwill is consistent with institutions and laws that permit unrestricted exploitation and accumulation.

Rather, the self-giving love that Jesus lavished on us must be the supreme law of human conduct. Regarding labor, Rauschenbusch insisted that we actively love others by serving their needs with our abilities. Accordingly, a divinely ordered community would offer to all the opportunities for intellectual and moral education, meaningful work, bodily protection, and sufficient food, clothing, and shelter. However, sin presently blocks this religious ideal of society.

Rauschenbusch viewed the human condition as sin or a "Kingdom of Evil"[4] marked by "despotic governments,"[5] "war and militarism," "landlordism," and "predatory industry and finance."[6] These manifestations of sin are transmitted down through history by culture's "idealization of evil,"[7] or its predisposition to exalt the bestial and suppress the beautiful. Rauschenbusch argued that the true nature of sin has been hampered by the traditional Augustinian understanding of the fall, which he found nowhere in either the Old Testament or the teachings of Jesus. Viewing the injustices of the entire human race as inescapable consequences of Adam's original sin, the Augustinian understanding gave up hope of remedying these injustices in society at large. Only personal salvation from sin could be found through the church. Rauschenbusch drew together these threads as follows: "The traditional doctrine of the fall has taught us to regard evil as a kind of unvarying racial endowment, which is active in every new life and which can be overcome only by the grace offered in the Gospel and ministered by the Church."[8] While he believed he neither denied nor downplayed the need for personal salvation, Rauschenbusch argued that Jesus called his followers to nothing less than colaboring with God for the transformation of society. Hence the church must assert that, because of the work of Jesus, evil is not a necessary but a variable factor in the life of humanity, which it is our duty to diminish for every new life and every new generation. The replacement of the kingdom of evil with the kingdom of God constitutes the goal toward which the church should be moving.

In Rauschenbusch's program, the kingdom of God is not a mere doctrinal concept, religious ideal, or hope for the hereafter, but a historic force at work in humanity. Human striving for social justice is a necessary but not sufficient condition for the replacement of the kingdom of evil with the kingdom of God. Such a replacement can only be accomplished when God's power supplements human striving: "The passive and active resistance of the Kingdom of Evil at every stage of its advance is so great, and the human resources of the Kingdom of God so slender, that no explanation can satisfy a religious mind which does not see the power of God in its movements."[9] The personal example of fulfilling the ideal of the kingdom of God is Jesus, who revealed the infinite worth of human life and whose salvation seeks the restoration and fulfillment of even the least of persons. From this it follows that the kingdom of God, at every stage of human maturity, inclines toward a social order that best guarantees to all persons their freest and highest development. That order involves the redemption of social life from the hampering influence of religious bigotry, from the upper classes' repression of the lower classes' self-assertion, and from all forms of slavery in which human beings are treated as mere means to serve the ends of others. Since love is the supreme law of Jesus, the kingdom of God demands a progressive reign of love in human affairs. For Rauschenbusch, we can see the kingdom of God advance wherever love supersedes the use of force and legal coercion to regulate the social order. Among the social changes this advancement entails are "the redemption of society from political autocracies and economic oligarchies; the substitution of redemptive for vindictive penology; the abolition of constraint through hunger as part of the industrial system; and the abolition of war."[10]

The kingdom of God, asserted Rauschenbusch, stands as the externalization and goal of Christianity, which once and for all translates Jesus's message from the abstract to the concrete:

> The Kingdom of God contains the teleology of the Christian religion. It translates theology from the static to the dynamic. It sees, not doctrines or rites to be conserved and perpetuated, but resistance to be overcome and great ends to be achieved. Since the Kingdom of God is the supreme purpose of God, we shall understand the Kingdom as far as we understand God, and we shall understand God so far as we understand His Kingdom. As long as organized sin is in the world, the Kingdom of God is characterized by conflict with evil. But if there were no evil, or after evil has been overcome, the Kingdom of God will still be the end to which God is lifting the race. It is realized not only by redemption, but also by the education of mankind and the revelation of his life within it.[11]

Because it is the supreme end of God, Rauschenbusch proclaimed that the kingdom of God must be the purpose for which the church exists. The measure in which it is fulfilling this purpose is directly proportional to the spiritual authority the church possesses at any moment. Moreover, the worship, doctrines, institutions, and activities of the church are only valuable insofar as they help to create the kingdom of God. Every act of worship, doctrine, institution, and activity must in the long run be tested by its effectiveness in bringing about the kingdom of God, and those that are ineffective must be discarded. If any form of church organization that formerly aided the kingdom of God now impedes it, the reason for its existence is likewise gone. For if the church sees itself apart from the kingdom of God and finds its aims in itself, then it commits the same sin of selfish detachment as when an individual selfishly separates himself or herself from the common good. Rauschenbusch observed that the church has the power to save only insofar as the kingdom of God is present in it. If the church is not living for the kingdom of God, its institutions become part of the "world" that Jesus famously condemned, and it devolves into an anti-Christian power.

From the patristic era to his day, Rauschenbusch indicted the church (which Jesus mentioned on only two occasions in the Gospels) of attempting to replace the kingdom of God (which Jesus consistently proclaimed) rather than seeing itself as distinct from yet complementary to the kingdom of God. This replacement has cost theology and Christians at large a tremendous amount. Accordingly, most Christians view Jesus as offering only individual salvation and not social salvation as well. Most Christians also regard the ethical teachings of Jesus in the Synoptic Gospels as unattainable ideals designed to point up human sinfulness rather than a social program to be implemented. Further, most Christians view worship as weekly self-gratifying entertainment in a social setting rather than the glorification of God by working to bring justice to the poor and marginalized. These losses can be summarized under the rubric of the church's individualistic gospel, which is incapable of exposing institutionalized sinfulness or effecting institutionalized redemption: "It has not evoked faith in the will and power of God to redeem the permanent institutions of human society from their inherited guilt of oppression and extortion."[12] To give the true social gospel embodied by Jesus its rightful preeminence, the kingdom of God must be emphasized rather than the church. This correctly placed emphasis carries with it four practical advantages. First, the kingdom of God is not subject to the pitfalls of the church. Second, the kingdom of God has the ability to test and correct the church. Third, the kingdom of God is a prophetic, future-focused ideology and a revolutionary social and political power that regards all creation as sacred. Fourth, the kingdom of God can save the repressive and unjust social order by manifesting love in all its expressions.

Rauschenbusch maintained that the highest expression of love is the free surrender of what is truly our own, such as life, property, and rights. A much lower but perhaps more decisive expression of love is the surrender of any opportunity to exploit other people. Accordingly, no social group or organization can claim allegiance to the kingdom of God, which exploits people for its own ease or resists the effort to abate the fundamental evil of exploitation. Seemingly a century ahead of his time, Rauschenbusch insisted that ending exploitation entails redeeming society from usurpation of the earth's natural resources under the cover of private property and from support of any industrial position that makes monopolies and the resulting exorbitant profits possible. On the political stage, Rauschenbusch declared that the reign of love—the kingdom of God—balances the drive toward the progressive unity of humankind with the safeguarding of individual liberty and of national distinctiveness, as nations work out their own cultural peculiarities and ideals.

ATONEMENT AND THE SACRAMENTS

Among the social gospel's theological manifestations were its distinctive views of the atonement and the sacraments. For Rauschenbusch, humanity, not God, is ultimately responsible for the death of Jesus. Contrary to the substitution-ary theory of the atonement propounded by Princeton theology and Moody, Rauschenbusch articulated an identification theory of the atonement in which Jesus bore the brunt of the social sins in which we all participate and to which our individual sins are causally connected. Rather than a wrathful Father punishing his innocent Son in our place, we are the ones who punished Jesus by engaging, covertly or overtly, in some or all of these six sins that put Jesus on the cross: religious bigotry, the combination of graft and political power, the corruption of justice, the mob spirit and action, militarism, and class contempt. As Rauschenbusch explained, Jesus bore these sins

> not by sympathy, but by direct experience. Insofar as the personal sins of men have contributed to the existence of these public sins, he came into collision with the totality of evil in mankind. It requires no legal fiction of imputation to explain that "he was wounded for our transgressions, he was bruised for our iniquities." Solidarity explains it. . . . Jesus bore these sins in no legal or artificial sense, but in their impact on his own body and soul. He had not contributed to them, as we have, and yet they were laid on him. They were not only the sins of Caiaphas, Pilate, or Judas, but the social sin of all mankind, to which all who ever lived have contributed, and under which all who ever lived have suffered.[13]

Since our sins—the sins of the kingdom of evil in which we all willingly participate—caused the crucifixion, Jesus literally died for (in the sense of "because of") our sins and for us. Moreover, at the cross Jesus saved us from the wrath of God by refusing to invoke God's wrath on us for the atrocity but rather entreating God's forgiveness of us. Had Jesus called down the divine wrath, we would be forever lost to the kingdom of evil and objects of eternal death. But by not calling it down and instead dying as the lamb silent before its slaughterers, Jesus's death ransomed us from the kingdom of evil and afforded us the opportunity to come to God.

But if the Jewish religious aristocracy had embraced Jesus's kingdom inauguration and Israel had adopted Jesus's way of being the light of the world, then humanity would no less have been redeemed from sin. Rauschenbusch therefore charged substitutionary theory with putting the emphasis of Jesus's redemptive work in the wrong place: what God required for humanity's redemption was Jesus's literal embodiment of the kingdom of God, regardless of how we responded to it, and not our negative reaction of brutally executing him. In other words, Jesus's role as Savior was not predicated on inciting others to crucify him. So, for Rauschenbusch, it was not Jesus's crucifixion that invested his embodied kingdom with value, but his embodied kingdom that, consistently with his ability to take the greatest evils and invert them, brought good out of his crucifixion. Although God possessed foreknowledge that if he were to launch his kingdom in the person of Jesus, the Jewish and Roman political leaders would freely crucify him, God still chose to become incarnate in Jesus. Hence God's forgiveness and willingness to overturn the wicked intentions of humanity through forgiveness and resurrection is neither an endorsement of humanity's murderous act nor divine complicity in it. Instead, it exemplifies God's power to redeem.

Regarding the sacrament of baptism, Rauschenbusch pointed out that when baptism was initiated by John the Baptist and continued by Jesus, it was not a ritual act of individual salvation, but an act of dedication to a new religious and social movement. Baptism at the Jordan River was received in view of the impending salvation by the Messiah and as an act of allegiance to a new order of things. The baptism of John and Jesus cannot be separated from their preaching; the former obtained its meaning and content from the latter. Their preaching called people to repent of their old way of living and to begin to live in fraternal love and helpfulness. Consequently, Rauschenbusch held that baptism constituted the dramatic expression of an inward consent and allegiance to the higher standards of life that prevail in the kingdom of God. It is therefore the symbol of initiation into a revolutionary movement. When a believer in Jesus senses the evil of the present world order and wishes to express her solemn dedication to the tasks of the impending Christian world order, that individual should be baptized, accepting her rights as a child of God within his kingdom.

Regarding the sacrament of the Lord's Supper, Rauschenbusch argued that Jesus's purpose was to create an act of loyalty among his followers that would keep memory and faithfulness alive until he returned, eating and drinking with them in the kingdom of God. In the New Testament church, this memorial act comprised part of a fraternal meal in which the Christian group met in privacy to express its distinctive unity and purpose. Because all members contributed a portion of food, the meal produced feelings of solidarity among the community. At the same time, the meal celebrated the imminent parousia, which would usher in Jesus's millennial reign of peace and righteousness on earth. Hence Rauschenbusch observed that the Lord's Supper was inextricably linked to the realization of the church's social ideals and hopes. In partaking of the Lord's Supper, therefore, contemporary believers should reaffirm their supreme allegiance to Jesus, who taught them to know God as their common Father and to recognize that all persons are their sisters and brothers. Amid a world of divisive selfishness, believers accept kinship as the ruling principle of their lives and undertake to implement it in their private and public activities. For Rauschenbusch, eating the bread and drinking the wine meant that believers shun the selfish use of power and wealth for the exploitation of other human beings. It equally meant that believers dedicate themselves to establish the kingdom of God and to win humanity to its principles, accepting the possibility of risk, loss, and death as the obligation of the cross.

CONCLUSION

The social gospel received a great deal of attention from church groups and seminaries, which frequently elicited sociologists to assess the conditions of American life and discern possible means to improve them. Individuals with ministerial training also began entering the field of sociology—including Albion W. Small (1854–1926) and Charles R. Henderson (1848–1915), who emerged as two of its foremost experts. In an attempt to solve the problems of economic injustice, racial inequality, and war, public social thinkers such as Scott Nearing (1883–1983) promoted a visibly religious approach to social concerns. Ties between religion and the American academic establishment were very close in the early decades of the twentieth century, such that the sociologists who shaped the discipline at American universities viewed their mission as the improvement of society rather than simply the analysis of groups. In 1908 American churches adhering to the social gospel formed the Federal Council of the Churches of Christ in America (later absorbed into the National Council of the Churches of Christ in the USA). The council morally and physically supported the labor of social reconstruction, delivering declarations and study documents and sporadically calling for strikes against unjust working conditions.

FOR FURTHER READING

Primary Sources

Rauschenbusch, Walter. *Christianity and the Social Crisis*. New York: Macmillan, 1907.
———. *Christianizing the Social Order*. New York: Macmillan, 1912.
———. *A Theology for the Social Gospel*. New York: Macmillan, 1917.

Secondary Sources

Dorn, Jacob H., ed. *Socialism and Christianity in Early 20th Century America*. Westport, CT: Greenwood, 1998.
Dorrien, Gary J. *Reconstructing the Common Good: Theology and the Social Order*. Maryknoll, NY: Orbis, 1990.
Handy, Robert T., ed. *The Social Gospel in America, 1870–1920*. Oxford: Oxford University Press, 1966.
Minus, Paul M. *Walter Rauschenbusch: American Reformer*. New York: Macmillan, 1988.
White, Ronald C., Jr., and C. Howard Hopkins. *The Social Gospel: Religion and Reform in Changing America*. Philadelphia: Temple University Press, 1976.

CHAPTER 11

CHRISTIAN
FUNDAMENTALISM

T he most visceral response to modern liberalism was found in Christian fundamentalism, a distinctive form of Protestantism that emerged around 1910 with the publication of a series of booklets called *The Fundamentals*. Stimulated by the grand revivals of evangelist D. L. Moody, distraught and outraged by the increasing hold of liberal theology, and empowered by the burgeoning Protestant orthodoxy of B. B. Warfield and others, two affluent Christian businessmen—R. A. Torrey and A. C. Dixon—underwrote the printing and free circulation of twelve volumes of articles by prominent conservative Protestant scholars to thousands of pastors, professors, denominational leaders, and YMCA directors throughout the United States. The first collection included defenses of Jesus's virginal conception by Scottish theologian James Orr (1844–1913) and of Jesus's deity by Warfield, as well as an attack on the higher criticism of the Bible by Canadian Anglican canon Dyson Hague (1857–1935). Fundamentalism tapped into a wellspring of conservative Protestant anxiety and helped galvanize a conservative response to liberal theology and its increasingly popular social gospel. This chapter illustrates how fundamentalists placed at the heart of Christian faith doctrines perceived as threatened by liberalism.

HISTORY OF THE MOVEMENT

Throughout the 1910s, several groups of fundamentalists devised lists of essential Christian doctrines. While some of these lists merely preserved the faith "once for all delivered to the saints," others contained beliefs never previously regarded as essential Christian doctrines by any sizable group of Christians, such as the premillennial return of Christ. The belief that Jesus would return bodily to rule on earth for one thousand years before the final resurrection and judgment was considered "a fundamental of the faith" by the World's Christian Fundamentals Association, founded in 1919 by prominent fundamentalist pastor William Bell Riley (1861–1947). They placed this doctrine alongside the Trinity, humankind's fall into sin, and Jesus's virginal conception, substitutionary atonement, bodily resurrection, and ascension. Several highly conservative Protestants were shocked by this since Protestant orthodoxy in general and Princeton theology in particular never held to premillennialism. Here we see that Riley and certain other fundamentalists elevated to essential status controversial doctrines that no one with even moderately progressive views would endorse. This move launched the trends within fundamentalism of sectarian divisiveness that used theological shibboleths to judge whether Christians were truly sound in doctrine. The first group of any size to explicitly label its members as fundamentalists was the Fundamentalist Fellowship founded in 1920 by Curtis Lee Laws (1868–1946), editor of a leading conservative Baptist magazine called the *Watchman-Examiner*. Laws was initially more moderate than Riley and attempted to maintain fundamentalism as a movement within the larger church for the preservation and defense of true essentials of Christian faith. But during the 1920s and 1930s, moderate and more militant fundamentalists grew closer together as they perceived their common enemy, liberal theology, increasing in strength.

During the height of early fundamentalism in the 1920s, its leading academic theologian was J. Gresham Machen (1881–1937). Machen was an esteemed scholar who studied New Testament and theology at German universities and at Princeton Theological Seminary under Warfield. Even his liberal theological opponents could not fault his scholarship or reject him out of hand as a crazed doctrinaire, as they frequently did with other fundamentalists. Teaching New Testament at Princeton from 1906 to 1929, Machen inherited the mantle of leading the tradition of Princeton theology when Warfield died in 1921. Machen proceeded to engage in theological and ecclesiastical battles against what he viewed as the mounting tide of liberal theology in mainstream American Protestantism generally and his denomination of Presbyterianism particularly. In his provocative 1923 book *Christianity and Liberalism*, Machen argued that liberal Protestant theology constituted a different religion from Christianity and that its adherents ought to be candid enough to admit their departure from Christianity. As Machen boldly declared, "If a condition could be conceived in which all the preaching of the Church should be controlled by the liberalism which in many quarters has already become preponderant, then, we believe, Christianity would at last have perished from the earth and the gospel would have sounded forth for the last time."[1] Machen furnished strong evidence for this thesis based on his thorough knowledge of biblical studies, including higher-critical methods, and the history of Christian thought. As a result, Walter Lippmann (1889–1974), a leading secular commentator, concurred with Machen's thesis and challenged the influential New York liberal pastor Harry Emerson Fosdick (1878–1969) to refute it. This challenge was never met. Hence fundamentalists heralded Machen as a hero and Lippmann's reception of his book as a great victory.

Although Machen permitted Christian fundamentalists to laud him as their academic spokesman, he did not completely fit their mold. While he staunchly defended Protestant orthodoxy and biblical inerrancy, Machen dissented from the antievolutionism and premillennialism of the fundamentalists. He concurred with Hodge and Warfield that evolution amounted to a creative mechanism of God and championed a traditional Reformed amillennial view of the kingdom of God. However, Machen's stature rose among fundamentalists as he gradually distanced himself from mainstream Presbyterianism under enormous pressure from its more liberal hierarchy. In 1929 Machen was expelled from his own denomination for "insubordination" at an infamous church trial where he was not even allowed to defend himself. As a result, he was heralded as a martyr even by fundamentalists who rejected his views on evolution and eschatology.

A turning point for fundamentalism occurred in 1925 with the notorious "Scopes Monkey Trial" in Dayton, Tennessee, the subject of the Broadway play *Inherit the Wind* and a pair of movies based on it. One of the burgeoning leaders of fundamentalism was the Nebraska politician and statesman William Jennings Bryan (1860–1925), a former candidate for president and President Woodrow Wilson's secretary of state. Upon his retirement from politics, Bryan indefatigably campaigned against "godless evolution." In 1925 the newly founded American Civil Liberties Union (ACLU) orchestrated the arrest of a high school biology teacher named John Scopes for teaching evolution in opposition to Tennessee state law; the purpose of the arrest was for the court to strike down the law as unconstitutional. Supporting this and similar state laws, fundamentalists arranged for Bryan to be the visiting celebrity prosecutor of the case. The ACLU hired famed Chicago trial lawyer and agnostic Clarence Darrow to defend Scopes. As the first ever live coast-to-coast broadcast on radio, the trial degenerated into a media circus, accentuated by nationally renowned antifundamentalist journalist H. L. Mencken (1880–1956) in his newspaper columns. While resulting in the conviction of Scopes, the trial's more important consequence was the utter humiliation of fundamentalism. Bryan's replies to Darrow's questions on the witness stand were pathetically naive, and Darrow and Mencken together portrayed Bryan and the forces of fundamentalism mounted against evolution as obscurantist idiots fixed on turning the cultural clock back to premodern and prescientific times. Bryan died in disgrace a mere five days after the trial, and the antievolution laws were quickly struck down by higher courts.

Prior to 1925, Christian fundamentalism constituted a serious cultural and theological force that possessed a strong chance to reverse the tide of liberal theology and bring many mainstream Protestant denominations back to Protestant orthodoxy. But in the judgment of many scholars, Christian fundamentalism consigned itself to cultural and theological obscurity by making antievolutionism its rallying cry and placing relatively minor doctrines such as premillennialism at the top of its theological agenda. The importance fundamentalists placed on the premillennial return of Christ could be seen as an overreaction to the liberal spiritualization of the kingdom of God and the return of Christ. In any case, there is no dispute that fundamentalism entered a lengthy period of retreat after 1925. Fundamentalist leaders fought among themselves about strategy as well as disputed theological issues and fine points of lifestyle, church government, and degrees of separation. Developing as powerful voices within the movement were John R. Rice (1895–1980), Bob Jones (1883–1968), and Carl McIntire (1906–2002), who demanded the practice of "biblical separation," namely, the refusal to fellowship or cooperate with other conservative Christians who fellowshiped or cooperated with nonfundamentalist Christians.

COMMON THEOLOGICAL FEATURES

Four theological features unite the fundamentalist movement. First, Christian fundamentalism held that the evils of modern theology sprang from defections from a robust conviction in the plenary verbal inspiration and inerrancy of the Bible. Following Warfield and Machen, fundamentalism traced the disease of modernism directly back to this single virus and impugned Schleiermacher for injecting it into Protestant theology. Liberals charged that the Protestant Reformers and Pietists, despite their adherence to *sola scriptura*, did not propound anything remotely close to plenary verbal inspiration or inerrancy. But fundamentalists responded that these doctrines were presupposed by and implicit in the writings of the Protestant Reformers and Pietists. There was no need for sixteenth- and seventeenth-century Protestantism to accentuate these crucial doctrines, because they were undisputed by Protestants and Catholics alike. Only when liberal theology challenged the authority of Scripture did it become necessary for plenary verbal inspiration and inerrancy to come to the fore. Most often, fundamentalists construed inerrancy along the lines of a literalistic hermeneutic that stipulated that the Bible contains no errors when taking literally every scriptural pericope, or discrete unit of text, that it is possible to take literally (regardless of its original literary genre). This meant that the opening chapters of Genesis and the book of Revelation must be read literally wherever possible, which gave rise to the movement's young earth creationism and antievolutionism on the one hand and its premillennial dispensationalism on the other hand.

Second, Christian fundamentalism exhibited militant—not "violent" but "stringent, vocal, unrelenting, and uncompromising"—opposition to liberal Protestant theology in all its forms. Machen enunciated this theme clearly in *Christianity and Liberalism*: "If we are to be truly Christians, then, it does make a vast difference what our teachings are, and it is by no means aside from the point to set forth the teachings of Christianity in contrast with the teachings of the chief modern rival of Christianity. The chief modern rival of Christianity is 'liberalism.' An examination of the teachings of liberalism in comparison with those of Christianity will show that at every point the two movements are in direct opposition."[2] As Martin Marty and R. Scott Appleby have pointed out, this militancy branches out from theological opposition to liberalism into nine distinct sociological characteristics.

1. For fundamentalists, their religion forms their identity, both personal and communal.
2. Fundamentalists hold that there is one and only one truth, and it is theirs.
3. Fundamentalists are purposefully shocking. (To this fundamentalists would have responded that they were merely fighting back; it was modern liberalism that had landed the first blows and was attempting to destroy the faith.)
4. Fundamentalists see themselves as a part of a cosmic struggle.
5. Fundamentalists interpret historical events as part of their cosmic struggle.
6. Fundamentalists try to make any opposition to themselves look bad and immoral.
7. Fundamentalists only emphasize some parts of their heritage, ignoring what it is convenient to ignore.
8. Fundamentalist leaders are typically male.
9. Fundamentalists try to rebel against the current distribution of power.[3]

Third, fundamentalism identified authentic Christianity with a coherent system of doctrinal propositions called Protestant orthodoxy. While fundamentalists did not deny that the personal experience of repentance and conversion was necessary for authentic Christianity, they did not find it sufficient for authentic Christianity. Due to the threat they found in liberal theology, they located agreement with unrevisable doctrinal propositions as the essential and timeless core of Christianity. Theologian Roger Olson makes this point well: "Whereas the motto of many pietists had become 'If your heart is warm, give me your hand,' fundamentalists would say, 'If your beliefs are correct, give me your hand.'"[4] Fundamentalism harbored suspicion of religious experience and affections since liberals could purport to have them, and there existed no objective test for right experience of God. Right doctrine, by contrast, could be measured. Because scarcely any liberal theologian would agree to Jesus's literal virginal conception, substitutionary atonement, bodily resurrection, or personal return to earth in glory, fundamentalists zeroed in on these doctrines as tests of authentic Christianity. Those fundamentalists uncertain as to whether these central doctrines were enough to root out liberalism added premillennialism and then a literal week of creation that occurred about six thousand years ago. Other doctrines peripheral to classical Protestant orthodoxy were also added.

Fourth, fundamentalism mandated biblical or first-degree separationism and second-degree separationism. According to first-degree separationism, doctrinally pure Christians must have no association with "false Christians" and their organizations, whether churches, ministries, or societies. Second-degree separationism extends to persons who identify as fundamentalist or evangelical but take part in fellowship, dialogue, or cooperation with doctrinally impure Christians. As Bob Jones University professor George W. Dollar explained, "It is clear that the Bible commands separation from those who aid and encourage any kind of compromise with infidelity."[5] Fundamentalists averred that separationism was implied in the very word "church" (*ekklesia*), which literally means "a called-out assembly." They pointed to Revelation 2:14–15, where Jesus warned the church of Pergamum not to tolerate those who taught false doctrine. Hence fundamentalist groups must take a stance against ecumenical alliances that would unite the church with perceived apostates. Accordingly, a definitive break with other sectors of conservative theology occurred in the early 1940s when Carl McIntire, a self-professed "Bible Presbyterian" who indicted various conservative Protestants for departing from fundamentalism, formed the American Council of Christian Churches (ACCC) as an overarching organization for "pure, separated" fundamentalist churches and denominations.

LEGACY OF FUNDAMENTALISM

Undoubtedly the main legacy of fundamentalism has occurred at the level of grassroots Christianity. Today literally thousands of pastors and congregations and hundreds of national ministries of different kinds are fundamentalist. Virtually every American city of any size includes large, active fundamentalist congregations, prosperous fundamentalist bookstores, and relatively small but established fundamentalist Bible colleges or institutes. Although they exert almost no influence in the hierarchies of mainstream Protestant denominations, they wield enormous influence on American social, political, and religious life through their own institutions, such as Liberty University founded by fundamentalist Baptist preacher Jerry Falwell (1933–2007) and Regent University founded by fundamentalist televangelist Pat Robertson (1930–).

Indeed, the latter half of the twentieth century witnessed an outpouring of interest in organized political activism by American fundamentalists that continues to the present. Fundamentalists of a dispensational bent viewed the 1948 establishment of the State of Israel as an important sign of the fulfillment of biblical prophecy, and support for Israel against the Palestinians emerged as the centerpiece of their approach to American foreign policy. American Supreme Court decisions also sparked fundamentalists' interest in organized politics, particularly the 1962 *Engel v. Vitale* decision that banned state-sanctioned prayer in public schools and the 1963 *Abington School District v. Schempp* decision that banned mandatory Bible reading in public schools. By the time Ronald Reagan ran for president in 1980, fundamentalist preachers were organizing their congregations to vote for receptive candidates. Leaders of the newly political fundamentalism included Jerry Falwell and Robert Grant (1936–). Starting with Grant's American Christian Cause in 1974, Grant's Christian Voice throughout the 1970s, and Falwell's Moral Majority in the 1980s, the Christian Right exercised a major impact on American politics. In the 1980s and 1990s, the Christian Right influenced several elections and policies through such groups as James Dobson's (1936–) Family Research Council and Pat Robertson's Christian Coalition, assisting conservative politicians, especially Republicans, to win state and national elections.

FOR FURTHER READING

Primary Sources

Machen, J. Gresham. *Christianity and Liberalism*. Grand Rapids: Eerdmans, 1985.

Torrey, R. A., and A. C. Dixon, eds. *The Fundamentals: A Testimony to the Truth.* 12 vols. Grand Rapids: Baker, 2003.

Secondary Sources

Dollar, George W. *A History of Fundamentalism in America.* Greenville, SC: Bob Jones University Press, 1973.

Hart, D. G. *Defending the Faith: J. Gresham Machen and the Crisis of Conservative Protestantism in Modern America.* Baltimore: Johns Hopkins University Press, 1994.

Marsden, George. *Fundamentalism and American Culture: The Shaping of Twentieth-Century Evangelicalism, 1870–1925.* Oxford: Oxford University Press, 1980.

———. *Understanding Fundamentalism and Evangelicalism.* Grand Rapids: Eerdmans, 1991.

Marty, Martin E., and R. Scott Appleby, eds. *The Fundamentalism Project.* 5 vols. Chicago: University of Chicago Press, 1991–95.

Olson, Roger E. *The Story of Christian Theology: Twenty Centuries of Tradition and Reform.* Downers Grove, IL: IVP, 1999.

CHAPTER 12

KARL BARTH AND NEO-ORTHODOXY

Two destructive world wars, the Great Depression, and the diabolic nature of right- and left-wing totalitarianism after World War I made the optimistic anthropology of liberalism increasingly irrelevant. In this light, Karl Barth (1886–1968) initiated neo-orthodoxy, to be followed by Emil Brunner (1889–1966) and the Confessing Church in Germany, which opposed the Nazis. This chapter probes the common ideas of neo-orthodoxy as articulated by Barth, comparing and contrasting these ideas with liberal theology and fundamentalist theology. Self-consciously rejecting any endeavor to bridge those approaches, Barth perceived the possibility of transcending both of them and their discord through theoretical analysis of the Word of God.

MAJOR EVENTS IN BARTH'S LIFE

Born in Basel, Switzerland, to a professor of theology who moved to the University of Bern a few years later, Barth grew up in the Swiss capital and determined to become a theologian at the time of his confirmation when he was sixteen years old. He went on to study theology under many of Europe's preeminent liberal Protestant thinkers, including Adolf von Harnack (1851–1930), and became a minister of the Reformed church first in Geneva and then in Safenwil on the Swiss-German border. But Barth learned that the liberal theology of his education failed to connect with the lives of ordinary parishioners. He also grew disillusioned with liberal Protestantism when mentors such as Harnack and other German professors openly supported the war efforts of the Kaiser in 1914. World War I itself caused a crisis in Barth's theology. He realized that he needed to hear a word from God, and his liberal theology only taught him to speak of himself in a loud voice. Turning to the book of Romans for theological renewal, Barth published his landmark commentary *The Epistle to the Romans* (*Der Römerbrief*) in 1919, a work that many historians mark as the birth of distinctively twentieth-century theology. Here Barth delineated the essential principles for the neo-orthodox program of dialectical theology, or the "theology of the Word of God." As Barth would later explain in his 1928 book *The Word of God and the Word of Man*, "It is not the right human thoughts about God which form the content of the Bible, but the right divine thoughts about men."[1]

Following World War I, Barth was invited to teach theology in Germany, taking successive posts at the Universities of Göttingen, Münster, and Bonn. While teaching at Bonn, he started his life's great project of writing a complete system of theology based on the Word of God titled *Church Dogmatics*. At his death, it remained incomplete at thirteen huge volumes. *Church Dogmatics* intended to make the gospel the basis of a Christian theology that transcended the split between liberalism and fundamentalism, which he charged with being equally imprisoned by modernity. Liberal theology stood captive to modernity through its accommodation to modernity, inaugurating modern categories of thought as superior and judging divine revelation by them. Fundamentalism stood captive to modernity by its reactionary obsession to uproot everything "modern" and "liberal." Aiming to relativize modernity, *Church Dogmatics* viewed modernity as a passing cultural trend that would eventually pass away while the Word of God stood forever. Contrary to most other systems of theology, whether liberal or fundamentalist, Protestant or Catholic, *Church Dogmatics* contains no prolegomena, or foundational section on natural theology or rational evidences for belief in God and Scripture. Rather, Barth proceeded directly into an exposition of special revelation, namely, the Word of God in Jesus Christ, the church, and Scripture. His foundational maxim is that "the possibility of knowledge of God lies in God's Word and nowhere else."[2] Because Barth viewed Jesus Christ as identical to the Word of God—God's Word in person—he insisted that "the eternal God is to be known in Jesus Christ and not elsewhere."[3] Barth repudiated any conceivable foundation for Christian knowledge of God apart from the self-authenticating gospel of Jesus Christ himself.

In 1934 Barth was chiefly responsible for the composition of the *Barmen Declaration*, which he personally mailed to Hitler. Among the founding documents of the Confessing Church, the declaration rejected the influence of Nazism on German Christianity by contending that the church's allegiance to Jesus Christ compels it to reject the influence of other lords, such as the German

Führer. Along with Barth, other prominent members of the Confessing Church included the Lutheran theologians Martin Niemöller (1892–1984) and Dietrich Bonhoeffer (1906–45). Bonhoeffer became director of the Confessing Church seminary in Finkenwalde, smuggled several Jews to safety in Switzerland, and was later executed in a Nazi concentration camp. When Barth refused to swear an oath to Hitler in 1935, Barth was removed from his professorship at the University of Bonn and expelled from Germany; returning to his native Switzerland, he received a chair in systematic theology at the University of Basel. Hundreds of students came to Basel to study under Barth, and over the next three decades he became the dominant force in Protestant theology throughout the world.

DOCTRINE OF THE WORD OF GOD

Among the most contested ideas in modern Christian theology is divine revelation. Where and how does God reveal himself? Liberal theologians underlined the general revelation of God in human religious experience or in world history, and they downplayed special revelation as a supplementary depiction of what can already be known about God generally. For Barth, this denigrated the uniqueness of the Christian gospel and essentially relegated it to a philosophy of religion or an ethical agenda. Fundamentalist theologians identified revelation with the propositional content of the Bible. While admitting the reality of God's general revelation in nature, they denied its salvific character; saving knowledge of God only came through special revelation in Scripture. For Barth, this overintellectualized the gospel as a doctrinal system to be learned and embraced. Repudiating both the liberal and fundamentalist approaches, Barth asserted that the content of revelation is God himself—God's self-disclosure—rather than propositions about God. Hence God's Word is God communicating not something, such as information or an experience, but himself to humanity in his speech.

The proposition *Deus dixit* (God speaks), Barth insisted, signifies the spirituality, the personal character, and the purposiveness of the Word of God. The spirituality of the Word of God means that the Word is spiritual as distinguished from naturalness or corporeality. The personal character of the Word of God means that the Word is not a proposition or a thing to be described, but a divine person coming to a human person with the subject as God himself, for what God says is himself. God discloses himself, and his Word is truth because it is his person who speaks. Unlike a concept to be defined, God's Word is fulfilled, concrete (*concretismus*) reality that can never be repeated. God is not bound by his Word, but his Word is bound to him. The purposiveness of the Word of God means that God never says something without a purpose, for God teaches each person something special for her or him. One cannot repeat what God says via nonverbal encounter, or else it will be distorted. Hence no written source such as the Bible can be revelation. God's Word is a genuine ineffaceable encounter not to be dissolved into fellowship, an encounter that tells us something new that we could never have heard from someone else. This is the encounter with Jesus Christ, who is God's Word or revelation to humanity. When Barth equated divine revelation with Jesus Christ, he was not denoting Jesus's teachings or example. To know Jesus Christ (with or without awareness of his human name) is to know God, and one cannot know God without knowing Jesus Christ (with or without awareness of his human name). Purposiveness also ensures that God's Word is necessary for renewal between humanity and God, since God announces himself to human beings in Jesus Christ in the prehistory, history, and posthistory of the incarnation as the contents of our future.

Barth concluded that a major problem with liberalism, fundamentalism, Nazism, and all theological error was natural theology. Moreover, human reason is the cause of all problems. To destroy even the possibility of natural theology, Barth denied the possibility of general revelation. All revelation is special, and must be nothing other than Jesus. Barth engaged in a famous debate on these points with his fellow Swiss neo-orthodox theologian Emil Brunner (1889–1966). In 1934 Brunner published an article titled "Nature and Grace," in which he argued that the gospel provides a "point of contact" (*Anknüpfungspunkt*) for human reason and natural theology. Barth responded with an impassioned and terse essay titled *"Nein!"* ("No!"), in which he rejected all points of contact between the Christian and the non-Christian, classical apologetics, and proofs of God's existence. For Barth, the gospel is its own proof, and the only apologetic is proclamation.

Barth emphasized that God's Word is God's act, by which he meant three things. First, God's Word is contingent contemporaneousness, as God does not have to speak at any set time, but he speaks and acts at various points in history and becomes contemporaneous with us. Further, we do not need to look back to the contingent revelation of the past, like the Bible, for God's act bridges the gap between the contingent facts of history and modern times. There are many different contingent times for God's Word: the time of original, direct utterance by Christ; the apostolic time; the canonical time; and the modern time. Second, God's Word possesses power to rule, as the speech of God is a ruling action on whom he speaks. Third, God's Word is a decision made freely and indeterminately by God, since God has the choice to speak to anyone by his grace, which becomes operative in the decision of the human being to hear the Word and heed it (i.e., belief or unbelief). Barth never adopted the position that it is impossible to know God sans awareness of the facts of Christ's earthly life, for Christ's earthly life does not exhaust his divine-human reality. Barth's perspective on divine revelation is that the person Jesus Christ is, from eternity to eternity, God's perfect and complete self-expression, and not simply a historical figure who served as a model, representative, or prophet. Any other authentic revelations of God revolve around Jesus Christ as promise, hope, and memory.

According to Barth, God's language is God's mystery, which similarly involves three facets. First, God's language is God's mystery in its worldliness. We always possess God's language in a form that is not the Word of God but is an indirect presentation in a this-worldly garb that hides him. For example, Barth claims that the incarnation is neither direct nor indirect. Second, God's language is God's mystery in its one-sidedness. God's Word meets us both as veiled and unveiled, not partly veiled or partly unveiled. Indeed, God's speech and action are different from all other speech and action. It is, paradoxically, God's veiling of himself in which he unveils himself and God's unveiling of himself in which he veils himself. In other words, the invisible God must reveal himself by hiding himself in creaturely forms. The same human nature of Jesus that fully reveals God also fully conceals God, for our own protection. No one can see God and live! Third, God's language is God's mystery in its spirituality. Barth claimed that the Word of God is uttered to humanity so that they must listen to it and be open and ready to hear it. When it is real and believed by the individual, it becomes the ground of apprehending God, to which the correct response is belief. As for the Bible, it is the God-ordained witness to God's Word in the person of Jesus Christ, and it becomes God's Word whenever Jesus Christ chooses to use it to encounter and confront people with his gospel: "The Bible is God's Word to the extent that God causes it to be His Word, to the extent that He speaks through it."[4] The Scriptures are a secondary Word because they witness to past encounters with Jesus.

Three factors led Barth and other neo-orthodox thinkers to their view of revelation. First was the conjunction of (1) Gotthold Ephraim Lessing's (1729–1781) infamous broad, ugly ditch between the necessary claims of religion and the contingent facts of history with (2) utter skepticism toward historical investigation. Thus neo-orthodox thinkers believed we cannot be sure of anything historically stipulated of God, for there is a tremendous—and in principle unbridgeable—ditch of time between our day and events two thousand years earlier. According to Barth, we simply cannot verify whether the things recorded by Scripture are true. Second, the neo-orthodox thinkers adopted wholesale the results of German higher criticism of the Bible, formulated before the leavening advent of biblical archaeology. Taking German scholarship very seriously, they believed many scholars had made findings that demonstrated that the Bible contained errors. Third, neo-orthodoxy was concerned with upholding the truthfulness of God. Because they thought the Bible contained errors, neo-orthodox theologians reasoned that if the Bible was God's Word, then either God lied or God lacked knowledge of the future, where the former option contradicts God's perfection and the latter option contradicts God's omniscience. By asserting that the Bible is not the Word of God but paradoxically becomes the Word of God when it is the vehicle for an existential encounter with Christ, Barth safeguarded the perfection of God at a very high price.

For Barth, the Word of God comes to us in three forms: as preached Word, written Word, and/or revealed Word. The Word of God can come through any of these forms or through the unity of the three. The preached Word means that the Word of God is only truly proclaimed when God himself speaks through the words of the human preacher, and if God does not speak, then the sermon is an invalid presentation of the Word of God. Hence if Jesus does not encounter us in the sermon, then the preacher does not preach the Word of God. Notice that the act of revelation is not in the preacher's control; it is controlled solely by Jesus himself. The written Word means the record that helps us recollect times in which God revealed himself. Thus the Bible is a witness or signpost to revelation, not revelation itself. The Bible becomes the Word of God in the same way the words of the preacher do; God uses human words to speak to humans and encounter them. At this point, the Bible becomes revelation, and the Bible is God's Word for us as God allows it to be and speaks through it. However, Barth insisted that the Bible is a better witness to revelation than any other book. The revealed Word of God means the unveiling of that which is veiled, namely, Jesus Christ. The quintessential, but not the only, expression of the revealed Word of God is the incarnation. When these three forms are unified, the revealed form of the Word, Jesus Christ, is the one who encounters us in preaching and in Scripture.

By calling Scripture a witness to revelation or a signpost to revelation, Barth meant that it points toward the real authority, Jesus Christ, rather than itself being authoritative. Barth held that the Bible was a fallible human book filled with errors and contradictions. He believed that the Bible's capacity for error extends beyond the historical and scientific to the religious and theological. Barth stated that we may therefore take offense at the Bible, and such offense can only be prevented by the miracle of faith. For instance, we may not like what Paul, Moses, or James tell us. God has always used imperfect and even sinful witnesses, and the biblical literature comprises precisely such witnesses. Hence Barth felt that the Bible is a signpost to Christ comprised of the witness of fallible, erring humans like ourselves. Despite his strong repudiation of the doctrine of inerrancy, Barth held the Bible in high esteem. His denials were not meant to degrade the Bible but only to elevate Jesus Christ above it, for Jesus is Lord and the Bible is not. But Barth concurred with the Protestant doctrine of *sola scriptura*, since the Bible is the only source of knowledge of Jesus Christ and the exclusive book God employs to call individuals to decision about Jesus's lordship. Further, it is the one and only record of past revelation and the indispensable tool the preacher uses for proclamation. Hence Barth used Scripture frequently and richly in his *Church Dogmatics*, and his exegesis often ran for multiple pages of fine print. So despite his lower view of Scripture, Barth used the Bible as much as any fundamentalist, and more than many.

So what did Barth make of the doctrine of inspiration? Barth understood inspiration as the use of fallible human words, namely, the Bible, by the Word of God to speak to humanity. What Barth called inspiration is what the Princeton theologians referred to as illumination. Scripture becomes the Word of God and revelation when God freely decides to speak through it. But how can God speak through potentially false statements in Scripture? This was not problematic for Barth because he rejected propositional revelation, or the concept that when God wants to communicate to humans, he communicates information in truth statements. God can use any statement, true or false, to evoke an existential encounter with Jesus Christ. Thus Barth redefined verbal inspiration as God's use of the faulty human word and the human reception of this word in spite of its fallibility. The true authority is not the Bible, but the Word of God who reveals himself. The scriptural witness possesses authority in that it claims no authority for itself and in that its witness amounts to letting the "Something Else" (i.e., Jesus Christ in personal encounter) be the authority himself and by his own agency. We therefore bestow upon the Bible an honor unwelcomed to itself when we directly identify it with the Word of God. Biblical authority, for Barth, is entirely derivative from its function as a vehicle through which God can speak.

Barth maintained that experiencing the Word of God consists in acknowledgment, which involves the following nine aspects. First, acknowledgment consists of gaining knowledge since the Word is God's language, communication, and intellect. Second, acknowledgment involves the fact of being concerned with the relationship between the individual and God. Third, it includes the presence of definite power in regard to acknowledging a Person. Fourth, it involves an awareness of the fact revealed by the Word of God that we are in our own, contemporary, individual existence. Fifth, it consists in the approval of the Word of God by individuals as they make the decision to submit to the one totally above them. Sixth, it involves our decision to respond to God's decision, as God freely comes to us to give grace and to execute judgment. Seventh, it includes a ceasing to question the enigma of Christianity and the willingness not to figure it out. Eighth, it consists of the act of individuals where they recognize God's mystery, realize that it unveils God, and move toward the unveiled God. Finally, it includes giving way before the Person acknowledged, that is, a yielding of authority to God.

DOCTRINE OF GOD

Barth maintained that God is wholly other and totally transcendent; in his transcendence, nothing can be known about God. So God is the *deus absconditus*, the hidden God to whom there is no way to bridge and about whom there is no way to learn or say anything. Nevertheless, God met humanity on his own initiative by becoming *deus revelatus*, or God revealed. This does not mean that the God who is revealed is actually the *deus absconditus* or the transcendent God, but that the transcendent God has taken on a certain form in order to reveal himself to us. This form is God's distinguishing himself from himself, or a new mode of existence that is not subordinate to but simply different from his first mode of existence. But for Barth, the fact that God has taken on this new mode does not mean that the mode fully reveals him. Barth claimed that it is not the form that reveals, but God in the form. Further, this mode is not the subject of revelation, because this would mean that God could be unveiled to humanity in our finitude after all and that there would be no further need of the transcendent God to reveal himself to humanity in the new creation. We should note that Barth adopted a mediating position between two extremes: that we cannot know God in his transcendence, and that the *deus revelatus*, Jesus Christ, is the subjective revelation who reveals God to a sufficient degree that the transcendent God is no longer needed. Hence Barth's position held that Jesus Christ comes to us in a form that is unsuitable for the self-presentation of God, as his form does not correspond to the transcendent God but rather contradicts him. In so doing, it veils what it unveils. Obviously Christ is God and God's revelation, but he is not identical in form with the transcendent God. We cannot know the transcendent God except as we see him in Christ, but that is not to see him as he really is.

Things that are human, like Jesus, can never correspond to the nature of God, or to God in his transcendence. Since we can only know Christ and not the transcendent God, the neo-orthodox focus on Scripture is exclusively christological. The result of these views is that our primary concern has to be with Christ as the Word of God, but we can neither ignore nor discard the *deus absconditus.*

Barth endeavored to balance God's transcendence and immanence by defining God as "He who loves in freedom."[5] The supreme paradox in the Christian doctrine of God stems from the fact that God is both completely loving and completely free both within his own eternal Trinitarian being and in his relationship with creation. In time and eternity, God reveals himself as the one who loves freely. This does not imply that humans can fully comprehend the depths and riches of God's love or freedom, but it does imply that we have been afforded a significant glimpse into these attributes in Jesus Christ. Analysis of God's revelation results in the unfolding of other divine attributes or perfections such as eternity (lordship over time) and immutability (faithfulness to himself). These perfections reveal God to be Lord over all, for nothing outside of God conditions God. God is totally free in all his relationships *ad extra* (toward creation). But equally important in God's revelation is that God's total freedom does not preclude him from binding himself to creatures in love. God's very essence is love within the community of the three Trinitarian persons. This love overflows voluntarily in creation and redemption so that humans are caught up into it through Jesus Christ. Further divine perfections emerging from this scenario are mercy and grace. For Barth, the paradox of God consists in the notion that God actualizes himself in his relation with the world (following Hegel) while being completely free in that self-actualizing relationship. While Barth insisted that "God is not swallowed up in the relation and attitude of Himself to the world and us as actualized in His revelation,"[6] still his relationship with the world is not something simply contingent and external to his own being. God's being is being-in-act, not a static essence detached from God's dynamic relationship with the world. God's love for the world means that he is genuinely involved in it and that the world affects God. Barth departed sharply from classical Christian theism on several counts because he judged them to be poisoned by static Greek categories of being. Nevertheless, based on Scripture, Barth asserted that even in his loving, suffering, fully involved relationship with the world, God remains always the Lord of that relationship.

In the last analysis, Barth deduced that God is fully actualized in his own Trinitarian being from all eternity. The world adds nothing essential to God, for "if we are not careful at this point we inevitably rob God of His deity."[7]

However, God freely chooses from all eternity to possess a relationship with the world in which he actualizes his already fully self-actualized being in and through the covenant he makes with humanity in Jesus Christ. Therefore God's love for the world proves eternal but not necessary.

DOCTRINE OF SALVATION

A third significant contribution of Barth's theology is his doctrine of salvation, which aimed to transcend the polarization between liberalism and fundamentalism. On the one hand, liberal theology repudiated God's wrath as a primitive notion that Jesus dispelled by showing God's universal fatherhood of humankind. Thus hell, damnation, and eternal punishment were consigned to the stockpile of outdated theological relics. On the other hand, fundamentalism portrayed hell in vivid and grotesquely realistic terms, making the eternal suffering of the wicked in literal flames a matter of undebatable dogma for many conservative theologians. Seeking a middle way, Barth drew on Scripture to affirm the reality of God's wrath and judgment and the superior reality of God's mercy and grace. As a Reformed theologian in the Calvinist and Zwinglian tradition, Barth declared the sovereignty of God in election and rejected synergism. Indeed, Barth was a supralapsarian, affirming that God's decree to elect and reject precedes his decree to create the world and his decree to permit humanity's fall into sin. God's ultimate purpose in creation is salvation, and election is an inherent part of salvation by grace alone. But Barth dubbed his doctrine of salvation and election "purified supralapsarianism," by which he indicated that God's total purpose in election is love. While God permits evil from the very beginning, he negates it through Jesus Christ. For Barth, God does not will and reprobate a portion of his creation to be eternally lost for some abstract self-glorification. Instead, God wills, foreordains, and decrees to permit sin and evil and brings about their absolute negation in Jesus Christ via his death and resurrection.

Consequently, God's no is not pronounced against humanity in part or in whole, but only against humanity's ultimate representative, namely, himself in Jesus Christ. For Barth, God truly utters a yes and no in double predestination. But double predestination does not connote a twofold determination of humans—some to salvation and others to damnation—but of Jesus Christ, who is the one elect *and* reprobate man. As Barth explained, "In the election of Jesus Christ which is the eternal will of God, God has ascribed to man . . . election, salvation, and life; and to Himself He has ascribed . . . reprobation, perdition and death. . . . Predestination means that from all eternity God has determined upon man's acquittal at His own cost."[8] That cost is the journey of the Son of God into a far country and his crucifixion at the hands of sinners.

It is a matter of dispute whether Barth's doctrine of salvation implies universalism, a twentieth-century revision of Origen's *apokatastasis panton* (restitution of all things). When queried whether he endorsed universalism, Barth replied equivocally that he neither taught it nor did he not teach it. But the internal logic of his doctrine of election certainly appears to imply universal salvation. Regarding God's decree of salvation, Barth pointed out that "on the basis of this decree of His, the only truly rejected man is His own Son. . . . By permitting the life of a rejected man to be the life of His own Son, God has made such a life objectively impossible for all others."[9] Barth's potential universalism has a different starting point from Origen's. Barth's stemmed from divine sovereignty, while Origen's arose from human freedom (i.e., eventually everyone would return to God). That said, Barth was a dialectical theologian and accordingly cannot be locked into a completely logical position. Hence Barth left open the possibility that the final number of the elect may not correspond exactly with the total of all humans who ever live while simultaneously prohibiting any limitation of salvation to less than that number. God's freedom and love demand that the possibilities be left open.

CONCLUSION

Barth's theology can be summarized along the following lines. God is "wholly other" than humanity, an eternally transcendent holy being. Humanity is helplessly finite and sinful. The Bible is a human book subject to historical criticism like any other book. It is a record of and witness to revelation rather than being an inspired, objective, historical, propositional revelation in itself. The Bible becomes revelation to the individual in the moment of crisis, when the Holy Spirit uses it to effect a personal encounter with God. Thus revelation is understood to be encounter rather than communication of information. Divine history, or salvation history, is separate from the social and intellectual history produced by the historian. People are in Christ, already elected to salvation, and need only to be made aware of this fact.

FOR FURTHER READING

Primary Sources

Barth, Karl. *Church Dogmatics*. 4 vols. Edinburgh: T&T Clark, 1936–62.

———. *The Epistle to the Romans*. 6th ed. Trans. Edwyn C. Hoskyns. Oxford: Oxford University Press, 1968.

———. *The Word of God and the Word of Man*. Trans. Douglas Horton. Gloucester, MA: Peter Smith, 1958.

Secondary Sources

Allen, R. Michael. *Karl Barth's Church Dogmatics: An Introduction and Reader*. Rev. ed. Edinburgh: T&T Clark, 2012.

Berkouwer, Gerrit C. *The Triumph of Grace in the Theology of Karl Barth*. Trans. Harry R. Boer. Grand Rapids: Eerdmans, 1956.

Bromiley, Geoffrey W. *An Introduction to the Theology of Karl Barth*. Grand Rapids: Eerdmans, 1979.

Busch, Eberhard. *The Great Passion: An Introduction to Karl Barth's Theology*. Ed. Darrell L. Guder and Judith J. Guder. Trans. William H. Rader. Grand Rapids: Eerdmans, 2004.

Hunsinger, George. *Reading Barth with Charity: A Hermeneutical Proposal*. Grand Rapids: Baker Academic, 2015.

CHAPTER 13

CHRISTIAN REALISM

E mploying the term *Christian realism* to describe their approach to ethics, brothers Reinhold Niebuhr (1892–1971) and H. Richard Niebuhr (1894–1962) were concerned, in a post–World War II and Stalinist climate, to recover the language of sin and to account seriously for its full impact on the human moral condition. This chapter explains their attempts—sometimes dissenting from one another—to reevaluate realistically Christian ethical standards, rather than evaluating them idealistically as adherents to the social gospel had done.

THE NIEBUHRS' PILGRIMAGE TO REALISM

Theologically, the Niebuhr brothers were refugees from Protestant liberalism. They were sons of German immigrants; their father, Gustav Niebuhr, was a Lutheran pastor in the American branch of the Prussian Church Union (now part of the United Church of Christ). Studying at Yale during the heyday of the social gospel, the brothers absorbed Protestant liberalism there. Reinhold proceeded to assume his first pastorate at a small German-American church named Bethel Evangelical Church in Detroit, Michigan (1915–28), and H. Richard became president of Elmhurst College (1924–27) in the Chicago area and then professor at Eden Theological Seminary (1927–30) near St. Louis, Missouri.

When Reinhold Niebuhr arrived in Detroit, he began preaching the social gospel, which unavoidably brought him into conflict with Ford Motor Company. Distressed by the dehumanizing effects of industrialization on workers, he emerged as an outspoken critic of Henry Ford (1863–1947). His confrontation of the auto industry led him to the position that the social gospel possessed a credulous understanding of sin and an unrealistic optimism toward human nature. He worried particularly what hope remained for American civilization when "naive gentlemen with a genius for mechanics suddenly become the arbiters over the lives and fortunes of hundreds of thousands." As Reinhold recounted: "About midway in my ministry . . . I underwent a fairly complete conversion of thought which involved rejection of almost all the liberal theological ideals and ideas with which I ventured forth in 1915."[1] His attention was captured by Barth's neo-orthodoxy, especially its robust doctrine of sin. While still in Detroit, Niebuhr began to advocate radical solutions to the human crisis as he perceived it—a new "Christian realism" for theology. Taking up the position of professor of practical theology (later ethics and theology) at Union Theological Seminary in New York (1928–60), Reinhold had the opportunity to formulate his ideas about sin and society, which established him as a permanent fixture in the neo-orthodox movement.

Similarly, H. Richard Niebuhr studied the neo-orthodoxy of Barth, as well as the thought of Jonathan Edwards and Søren Kierkegaard, during a sabbatical leave in Germany in 1930. A year later, H. Richard wrote his classic article "Religious Realism in the Twentieth Century." Here he explained that while Christian realism shares the ethical focus of liberal theology, it stresses "the independent reality of the religious object," such that Christian realism "has shifted the center of interest from the subject to the object, from man to God, from that which is purely immanent in religious experience to that which is also transcendent."[2] Thereafter H. Richard accepted a longstanding invitation to teach theology and Christian ethics at Yale Divinity School (1931–62).

REINHOLD NIEBUHR'S BRAND OF CHRISTIAN REALISM

Reinhold Niebuhr delineated the social ramifications of the doctrine of original sin in one of his most influential books, *Moral Man and Immoral Society: A Study in Ethics and Politics* (1932). In the crucible of World War I and industrial strife, Reinhold denounced as vacuous any faith in the essential goodness and wisdom of humanity and in history's movement toward progress. Whether expressed in the social gospel's dependence on moral suasion or the secular commitment to the power of scientific reason, liberalism exemplified "a kind of blindness to which those are particularly subject who imagine that their intelligence has emancipated them from all the stupidities of the past. . . . Liberalism is not only a form of blindness. It is a blindness difficult to cure, because it is a disease among classes who imagine themselves particularly clear-eyed."[3] Reinhold characterized the tenets of liberalism as follows: injustice is a form of ignorance that will retreat through education; that the advance of civilization precludes challenging the philosophy of gradual improvement; that the character of individuals, not societies, ensures justice; that appeals to love and brotherhood will eventually prevail; that goodness yields happiness, and an increased recognition of this fact will conquer human selfishness; and that wars arise from the tragic errors of foolish people. All these tenets fail to recognize the ineradicable element of egoism in all human action, which guarantees the subordination of reason to interest in the social struggle. For Reinhold, each human is an inherently self-regarding creature, and individuals could barely transcend the taint of self-interest to achieve a measure of mutuality in personal relations. Therefore social groups could never achieve such mutuality.

As a result, collective self interest among social groups is intractable, which inescapably results in social struggle.

> What is lacking among all these moralists, whether religious or rational, is an understanding of the brutal character of the behavior of all human collectivities, and the power of self-interest and collective egoism in all inter-group relations. Failure to recognize the stubborn resistance of group egoism to all moral and inclusive social objectives inevitably involves them in unrealistic and confused political thought. They regard social conflict either as an impossible method of achieving morally approved ends or as a momentary expedient which a more perfect education or a purer religion will make unnecessary. They do not see that the limitations of the human imagination, the easy subservience of reason to prejudice and passion, and the consequent persistence of irrational egoism, particularly in group behavior, make social conflict an inevitability in human history, probably to its very end.[4]

Emphasizing the inevitably tragic and sinful situation of human existence before a holy and transcendent God, Reinhold Niebuhr focused on the lesser of evils as the greatest good achievable in human history.

In his *Nature and Destiny of Man* (2 volumes, 1941 and 1943), Reinhold Niebuhr explored the political ramifications of reckoning seriously with the full impact of sin on the human moral condition. Owing to the devastation of Hitler, Stalin, and the Holocaust, Reinhold asserted that "the doctrine of original sin is the only empirically verifiable doctrine of the Christian faith."[5] While acknowledging the selfless agape love of Jesus as the normative moral guide for Christians, Reinhold stressed the need for justice in dealing with the inevitable and competing assertions of self-interest. Thus Christians must settle for justice as the best-case scenario instead of working for a society ordered according to perfect love, as perfect love is an "impossible ideal"[6] within human history. In other words, justice stands as the closest approximation to love under the conditions of sin. Hence the task of the Christian realist is to craft a way of living with the reality of sin and self-interest: "A realist expects no final resolution to these conflicts, but a stable society must establish a working equilibrium between the claims of liberty and equality, freedom and order, or need and merit."[7] A realist reluctantly accepts that the ethical balancing of social and power disparities necessarily involves coercion. The intrinsically coercive nature of politics makes forceful methods morally neutral, such that the ethical and coercive elements of human life interpenetrate and arrange tentative and uneasy compromises. Hence the question of means and ends in politics posed a pragmatic rather than ethical problem, such that no political action could be deemed inherently immoral. No absolute distinctions, then, could be made between nonviolent and violent types of coercion or between coercion used by governments and coercion used by revolutionaries. Reinhold thus advocated a radical utilitarianism, in which any such distinctions must be justified in terms of the consequences that they effectuate.

Since Reinhold Niebuhr viewed justice as the proximate ethical norm of any particular political action, he distinguished between the morality of the end and the nature of the means employed to secure it, thus implying that the successful establishment of justice determined the moral use of force. Discarding the pacifist leanings of his roots, Reinhold became a staunch advocate for American involvement in World War II. This led to a famous debate between Reinhold and pacifist brother H. Richard in the pages of the *Christian Century*. H. Richard argued for a principled inactivity in the war based on radical trust and obedience in God. Radical trust and obedience required Christian nonviolence, and any other response would spell distrust in God and God's promises.

> The inactivity of radical Christianity is not the inactivity of those who call evil good; it is the inaction of those who do not judge their neighbors because they cannot fool themselves into a sense of superior righteousness. . . . It is not the inactivity of the noncombatant, for it knows that there are no noncombatants, that everyone is involved, that China is being crucified . . . by our sins and those of the whole world. It is not the inactivity of the merciless, for works of mercy must be performed though they are only palliates to ease present pain while the process of healing depends on deeper, more actual and urgent forces.[8]

Those forces are the expressions of the promise of agape in the gospel. But Reinhold countered that while indeed the gospel brings hope of agape, it is an eschatological and not a historical hope. Hence Reinhold insisted, "Love may qualify the social struggle of history, but it will never abolish it, and those who make the attempt to bring society under the dominion of perfect love will die on the cross. And those who behold the cross are quite right in seeing it as a revelation of the divine, of what man ought to be and cannot be, at least not so long as he is enmeshed in the processes of history."[9] There are, accordingly, no absolutes in a fallen world. Christians cannot act as if the kingdom of God has already been established and must sometimes use force to protect the innocent. A living Christian faith must constantly engage in commerce with the culture of its day, appropriating and rejecting according to utilitarian principles.

Within this tough minded brand of Christian realism, Reinhold Niebuhr also became a supporter of anticommunism and the development of nuclear weapons as a way to check the use of nuclear power against the United States. Stressing power politics, Reinhold exerted significant impact on Hans Morgenthau (1904–80) at the University of Chicago, who is widely regarded as the father of political realism.

H. RICHARD NIEBUHR'S BRAND OF CHRISTIAN REALISM

Offering a gentler brand of Christian realism than his brother, H. Richard Niebuhr advocated Christian withdrawal from worldly alliances with capitalism, nationalism, and humanism and a return to faithfulness to Jesus's teachings. Throughout the 1930s, H. Richard attempted to expose the actions of Christians that were based on cultural norms rather than authentic religion. As the global situation continued to deteriorate, H. Richard increasingly voiced concern that churchgoing people were too influenced by "the world" and not sufficiently grounded in the Christian faith. In his 1937 book, *The Kingdom of God in America*, H. Richard aimed to delineate the mission of Christianity as a movement of human redemption in history generally and in America particularly. Arguing that the kingdom of God is, in fact, a multifaceted reality that encompasses but is not limited to the sovereignty of God, the reign of Christ, the presence of God, and the kingdom on earth, H. Richard indicted the social gospel as reducing the kingdom to simply the kingdom on earth. By doing so, he felt that the social gospel proclaimed the empty message of how "a God without wrath brought men without sin into a kingdom without judgment through the ministrations of a Christ without a cross."[10] Hence the social gospel needed to be supplemented by a genuinely broad, faithful, and dynamic Christianity that focused neither on the promotion of controversial doctrines (which would divide Christian groups) nor on the rejection of essential Christian theology (which would separate Christianity from God).

More of an abstract theologian than his brother, H. Richard Niebuhr turned to an attempt to synthesize Barth's insistence on the primacy of revelation with the historical relativism of German religious historian and theologian Ernst Troeltsch (1865–1923). The fruits of this labor emerged in his 1941 book, *The Meaning of Revelation*. Here he contended that the positions of Troeltsch and Barth belonged together because when historical relativism ineluctably exposes our views of God as limited and conditioned, we are humbled to become sufficiently self-critical, faithful, and communal to experience revelation in history. For H. Richard, awareness of the limitations of our knowledge of God does not lead to skepticism or subjectivism. Instead, this awareness leads us to find our starting point in the faith of the historical Christian community where revelation occurs but becomes verified communally. This yields a confessional (rather than proclaimed) theology consisting in confession of narrative or recital of story about God in history. Such theology is not dogmatic or confining but "liberating" as a legitimate "approach to universality."[11] Apart from confessional theology, H. Richard feared that idolatry, aggrandizement, self-defense, and self-justification would become the norm.

H. Richard Niebuhr argued that inner history (history as subjectively experienced in the Christian community) and not outer history (history as objective events) is the locus of revelation as the self-disclosure of God. This revelation in inner history illumines and therefore renders intelligible everything else in history. Moreover, revelation in inner history forms the basis of our reasoning about all other entities that we value, including the economy, politics, culture, and the entire human race. Contrary to any sort of tentative hypothesis about history, revelation in inner history enables a radical reinterpretation of history with Jesus Christ—through whose kenosis the power of God was made perfect—as the ultimate center of reference. But the communal setting of revelation did not imply that all Christians perceived the interplay of revelation and historical relativity in the same way. Thus, in his most widely read book, *Christ and Culture* (1951), H. Richard illustrated the historical diversity of conceptions of the Christ-culture relationship via five typologies. First is the Christ of culture, in which culture is uncritically accepted with Christ as the fulfiller of culture. Second is Christ against culture, in which all worldly things are rejected in favor of Christ's sole authority. Third is Christ above culture, where faith in the supernatural Christ is synthesized with the highest impulses of human culture through the mediation of grace. Fourth is Christ and culture in paradox, where we simultaneously live in the kingdom of God and the kingdom of the world with an unresolved tension between the two. Fifth is Christ the transformer of culture, where believers in Christ genuinely change the culture for the better. While H. Richard cataloged these typologies without explicitly prioritizing between them (since different denominations or church leaders would identify with different typologies), the underlying subtext of his work suggests a progressive relationship between them with Christ the transformer of culture as the goal.

Incisively portraying the theological battles underlying the conflicts of Western culture, H. Richard Niebuhr's *Radical Monotheism and Western Culture* (1960) laid out the conception of radical monotheism by comparing it with modern, demythologized forms of polytheism and henotheism. Polytheism offers many objects of devotion (i.e., gods), such that the adherent's loyalties are divided among various causes including family, economic success, scientific knowledge, and artistic creativity. Henotheism insists on loyalty to one god as the priority over many other gods that possess equal status. In the modern world, henotheism manifests itself in the exaltation of one social group to the exclusion of others, and its instances encompass racism, nationalism, fascism, and communism. By contrast, monotheism asserts that there is only one God as the center of value. For H. Richard, it follows that a community of radical monotheism cannot be a closed society. Whoever participates in such a community bears equal value, derived from the only center of value sans the presence of any privileged group. Hence radical monotheism "is the confidence that whatever is good, is good, because it exists as one thing among the many, which all have their origin and their being, in the One—the principle of being which is also the principle of value."[12] Accordingly, the religion of the Hebrew Bible dispensed justice and fairness to the poor as well as foreigners, and the religion of Jesus expressed love of neighbor.

H. Richard Niebuhr maintained that inevitable problems arise if political life is ordered by polytheistic and henotheistic patterns of devotion. Polytheists reject the principle of equal human worth on the grounds that humans do not equally contribute to economic success, knowledge, or artistic creativity. Henotheists also reject the principle of equal human worth in light of their faith in the supremacy of a particular race or nation. Despite being sternly assaulted by polytheistic and henotheistic loyalties, the egalitarianism of radical monotheism must not be defeated in its crucial battle of faith. For radical monotheism,

asserted H. Richard, has the unique power to generate the positive transformation of our ethics that Reinhold deemed impossible within human history.

H. Richard argued for this thesis in *The Responsible Self* (1963), published
shortly after his death. The argument begins by pointing out that humans are
neither simply teleological (goal-seeking) nor deontological (rule-following)
but responsive, so being responsible: "What is implicit in the idea of responsibility is the image of man-the-answerer, man engaged in dialogue, man acting
in response to action upon him."[13] Responsibility queries what is appropriate to
do in view of the current situation. So if a nationalistic commitment prevails,
the concept of responsibility will be locked into the exclusivist framework of
that commitment. But exclusive commitment to one's nation lacks sufficient
universality. Therefore a Christian view of responsibility, grounded in radical monotheism, is needed. Christians are moved to consider all individuals in
the world, whether Christian or non-Christian, as their companions because
they each participate in the entire community of being. Such a universal society
amounts to the spatial horizon in which Christian reflections on responsibility
must occur. Moreover, Christian reflections on responsibility must occur in the
temporal horizon comprised by the universal history of God's all-encompassing
activity involving creation and redemption. Consequently, the Christian ethic is
one of universal responsibility.

CONCLUSION

Through their versions of Christian realism, Reinhold and H. Richard Niebuhr
wished to recover the great Protestant themes of human depravity, grace above
nature, salvation by faith alone, and especially the transcendence and sovereignty
of God. The Niebuhrs can be seen as furnishing an extended and systematic
discussion of anthropology, or how the human being shall think of herself or
himself. In answer to this question, the Niebuhrs proposed a series of dialectical
relationships: humanity is both free and bound, both limited and limitless, both
sinner and saint, both subject to history and social forces but also the artificer
of history and society, both creature of the Creator but potential lord of the
creation, and both egotistical but capable of living for others. The Niebuhrs
employed the Bible to expound these paradoxes, especially what they styled
the biblical "myth" of creation. Accordingly, humanity was made in the *imago
Dei*, for good and for bad. Humans sinned by refusing to believe that God
could conquer their slavery to hubris and to the will to power that forms the
common human fate. In the person of Christ, however, the Niebuhrs located

a distinctive example of power utilized only for good and not, as with every other person, for evil. The cross of Christ proved an especially important theme for the Niebuhrs since it disclosed the paradox par excellence of powerlessness transformed into power, of a love in justice that conquered the sinful world. The Niebuhrs have been criticized for focusing on the Bible because of its relevance to the modern condition rather than because it constituted God's written Word. Notwithstanding this criticism, the Niebuhrs' works remain among the most widely analyzed of all twentieth-century American theological endeavors.

FOR FURTHER READING

Primary Sources

Niebuhr, H. Richard. *Christ and Culture.* New York: Harper & Row, 1951.
———. "The Grace of Doing Nothing." *Christian Century* 49 (March 30, 1932): 378–80.
———. *The Kingdom of God in America.* Chicago: Willett, Clark & Company, 1937.
———. *The Meaning of Revelation.* New York: Macmillan, 1941.
———. *Radical Monotheism and Western Culture.* New York: Harper & Row, 1960.
———. "Religious Realism in the Twentieth Century." In *Religious Realism,* ed. Douglas Clyde Macintosh, 413–28. New York: Macmillan, 1931.
———. *The Responsible Self.* New York: Harper & Row, 1963.
Niebuhr, Reinhold. "The Blindness of Liberalism." *Radical Religion* 1 (Autumn 1936): 1–5.
———. *Man's Nature and His Communities: Essays on the Dynamics and Enigmas of Man's Personal and Social Existence.* New York: Scribner, 1965.
———. *Moral Man and Immoral Society: A Study in Ethics and Politics.* New York: Scribner, 1932.
———. "Must We Do Nothing?" *Christian Century,* March 30, 1932, 415–17.
———. *Nature and Destiny of Man.* 2 vols. New York: Scribner, 1941, 1943.
———. "Ten Years That Shook My World." *Christian Century,* April 26, 1939, 542.

Secondary Sources

Coffey, John W. *Political Realism in American Thought.* Lewisburg, PA: Bucknell University Press, 1977.
Kegley, Charles W., ed. *Reinhold Niebuhr: His Religious, Social, and Political Thought.* Eugene, OR: Wipf and Stock, 2001.
Rice, Daniel F. *Reinhold Niebuhr and John Dewey: An American Odyssey.* Albany, NY: State University of New York Press, 1993.
Werpehowski, William. *American Protestant Ethics and the Legacy of H. Richard Niebuhr.* Washington, DC: Georgetown University Press, 2002.

CHAPTER 14

PENTECOSTALISM AND LATIN AMERICAN PNEUMATOLOGY

The greatest natural disaster in American history, a massive earthquake destroyed much of San Francisco and claimed thousands of casualties on April 18, 1906. On April 19, a group of underprivileged, racially mixed Christians gathered in a shabby warehouse building on 312 Azusa Street in Los Angeles for prayer and to inquire of God as to the significance of the earthquake. Leading the gathering was William J. Seymour (1870–1922), a one-eyed African American preacher from Louisiana who proclaimed that the earthquake marked the start of the great tribulation. However, Seymour maintained that God was pouring out his Spirit in these end times to furnish a window of opportunity for repentance before Jesus's return. God was restoring the apostolic church of the first century, including a recapitulation of Pentecost through which Christians could be baptized in the Holy Spirit, speak in unknown languages, be enabled for witness, and pursue holy lives. A revival quickly broke out, lasting from 1906 to the beginning of 1909 and drawing tens of thousands of people worldwide, who came to encounter the outpouring of the Holy Spirit during one of the three daily services. Evangelistic and missionary zeal exploded from this revival, which kindled new fires of Pentecostalism throughout the world. The Canadian-American evangelist Aimee Semple McPherson (1890–1944) pioneered the use of modern media in spreading Pentecostalism. Pentecostal movements emerged in Wales, India, China, and Africa, with none more prominent than in Latin America.

CENTRAL TENETS OF GLOBAL PENTECOSTALISM

While a phenomenon encompassing more than 600 million Christians around the world, Pentecostalism is united by four central tenets. First, Pentecostals believe in a postconversion (or postregeneration) experience styled "baptism in (or with) the Holy Spirit" (cf. Acts 2:2–4). Pentecostals maintain that the empowerment of the Holy Spirit must be infused into the life of each Christian. Although this experience could happen on the same day as a person's conversion, it should not be regarded as happening automatically along with the person's faith in Jesus and justification. Nevertheless, differences exist among Pentecostals concerning the exact nature of this baptism, the methods of infusion, and the evidences underscored to prove that a person has been baptized in the Spirit. Second, Pentecostals believe that the complete range of gifts and miraculous manifestations of the Spirit present in the New Testament are available for Christians today. Summed up in the rhetorical question, "Is Jesus Christ the great I Am or is he the great I Was?"[1] Pentecostals repudiate any notion that the spiritual and sign gifts were either limited to the first century or ceased with the apostles. Hence Pentecostals hold that the miraculous powers of Jesus's ministry and the apostolic "signs and wonders" are accessible to Christians today through the Spirit's power. Third, Pentecostals display less formalized and expressive forms of worship, such as raising up of hands, dancing, shouting, and clapping. Fourth, Pentecostals exhibit a special urgency to evangelize the world since they believe we are living in the last days before Christ's return.

THE LATIN AMERICAN FOCUS: PNEUMATOLOGICAL THEORY

Both exemplifying and producing innovations within the Pentecostal tradition is Latin American Pentecostalism, which has affected theological formulation and practice throughout the world. There are three reasons for our focus on Latin America. First, Latin American Pentecostalism is the fastest-growing religious movement in the Western Hemisphere, with eight thousand persons baptized daily and more than 100 million Pentecostals on the continent. As historian of global Christianity Timothy C. Tennent points out, "The vibrant life of this new branch of Christianity in Latin America is almost without parallel and exceeds the growth rate of Protestantism in Central Europe during the time of the Reformation. This transformation deserves our attention."[2]

Second, Latin American Pentecostalism evinces the disintegration of the

Christendom church-state amalgam that has dominated the continent's religious and political landscape since the sixteenth century. Contrary to the longstanding process of acculturation in which people were civilized and so "Christianized," Latin American Pentecostalism has brought robust evangelism to the continent. Such evangelism proclaims the gospel to facilitate a personal encounter with the living Jesus, leading to conversion and discipleship. Among the greatest historical ironies is that only with the collapse of Christendom can there be the birth of legitimate evangelism. While Christendom is quite effective in generating large numbers of nominal Christians, it is useless in biblical evangelism. Latin American Pentecostals are arguably the most effective evangelists in Christian history. Central among the reasons for this is that Pentecostalism constitutes the antithesis of Christendom. Far from being hierarchical, it possesses a popular, grassroots organization. Far from standing at the center of a political and business elite frequently mired in corruption, it exists on the periphery.

Third, the theological discourse of Latin American Pentecostals presents many important challenges to traditional European and North American discourse about the work of the Holy Spirit in the world. In particular, Latin American Pentecostals charge traditional doctrines of the Spirit with being too static and disconnected from the suffering and economic hardships of the peoples of Latin America. Accordingly, we should humbly concede that we have much to learn from this amazing work of God in our time.

The most important contribution of Latin American pneumatology is its shattering of the two-tiered Western Enlightenment universe that separates the natural realm from the spiritual realm. The Enlightenment worldview erects a high wall separating the experiential world of the senses, governed by reason and open to scientific investigation, from the unseen world beyond the wall. Such a world either does not exist, per naturalism, or is essentially unknowable, per deism. Even in conservative Western theology, the basic two-tiered universe remains intact, having merely been altered by punching various "holes in the wall" for God to come into the natural world through the incarnation, revelation, and occasional miracles and for us to access the spiritual world through prayer. But for Latin American pneumatology, there is no real wall of separation, and the space separating the natural realm from the spiritual realm constitutes an open frontier. Hence the entire creation is animated by spirits and various dynamic invisible forces, including angels and demons. As a rule, spiritual explanations are more frequent than naturalistic ones because the worldview of Latin American Pentecostalism is more spiritualistic and relational than naturalistic and mechanical.

Generally, whenever Western missionaries arrived in Latin America with their modified Enlightenment worldview and their hampered, reduced pneumatology, they found themselves at a loss when someone asserted that a drought was caused by God's judgment, when worried parents begged them to exorcise the demon tormenting their daughter, or when someone proclaimed they had received a vision to preach the gospel in a specific new region. Western missionaries had no training or conceptual framework for responding to such a worldview. The only category the missionaries possessed was "superstition," of which they typically availed themselves to account for these "spiritualized" accounts of what must have their grounds, they believed, in naturalistic explanations. Though these missionaries were evangelical in their theology, they were functional deists when applying pneumatology in real-life contexts. As Lesslie Newbigin observed, Western missionaries proved one of the greatest forces of secularization in history.[3]

In contrast, Latin American Pentecostalism arose among uneducated peoples whose worldview was by no means influenced by the truncated Enlightenment worldview. Their personal encounters with the Holy Spirit afforded them reason to believe that the very Spirit who acted supernaturally in the ministries of the apostles is active today in like manner. For Latin American Pentecostal pneumatology, an expectation exists for the Holy Spirit to personally and continually intervene in the world through miraculous healings, prophetic guidance to the church, deliverance from evil, and empowered witness to the world. The Holy Spirit thus consistently brings the "not yet" of the kingdom of God into the "already" of our fallen world. All the future realities of the kingdom are now fully available to all Christians through the Holy Spirit's person and work.

THE LATIN AMERICAN FOCUS: PNEUMATOLOGICAL PRAXIS

The successful evangelism displayed by Latin American Pentecostals is a direct result of their distinctive pneumatology. The Spirit is not only a person of the Trinity—equal to the Father and the Son—who inspired the Bible and regenerates believers; he equally empowers us for effective evangelism. Latin American Pentecostals are fully persuaded that today the Holy Spirit confirms the preaching of the gospel and the truth of Jesus's resurrection through signs and wonders, just as he did to those uneducated fishermen and tax collectors who comprised his initial apostles. Latin American Pentecostals observe that if someone is demon possessed, then casting out the demon in the name of Jesus is still part of the gospel and the practical extension of Jesus's triumph over the principalities and powers (Eph. 6:12; Col. 2:14–15). Tennent expresses this consideration well: "In other words, if the Holy Spirit is alive and real, then he must have the power and means to extend his dynamic life in real and concrete ways into the lives of those who are suffering. If God raised the dead in the first century, why can't he do it in the twenty-first century?"[4] This vigorous pneumatology supplied the theological foundation for an effective Latin American Pentecostal missiology. A standard Pentecostal conviction is that a Christian never witnesses or evangelizes alone since they are always accompanied by God the Evangelist—the Holy Spirit—who speaks and works through them. Such a conception of the Holy Spirit as being really present and ready to display his power in practical ways gives Pentecostals the doctrinal basis for mobilizing the entire laity for evangelism, including the very newest believers. To illustrate, several Pentecostal networks will not permit people to be baptized until they have led at least one person to Christ. Thus the praxis of evangelism constitutes part of the initial catechesis to the Christian faith.

With God the Evangelist present, the success of Latin American Pentecostal efforts did not depend on foreign financial support, attractive buildings, elaborate planning, or professionals with seminary degrees. Theologian Orlando Costas observes that while mission practice from North America emerges from "carefully thought out, written reflection," in South America it emerges as an "oral, popular reflection which is done 'on the road,' prompted by a significant event or a specific issue."[5] Laypeople grasp the struggles and issues at the core of the Latin American experience, and they relate the gospel to these matters. Neither passive nor otherworldly, Pentecostals are in the movement because they have found solutions to practical problems. Their most vigorous growth has occurred in the poorest areas of Latin America, lacking access to modern health care. This has generated a widespread ministry of praying for the sick. Indeed, while speaking in tongues is the primary focus of North American Pentecostalism, divine healing is the primary focus of Latin American Pentecostalism. Like the Gerasene demoniac whom Jesus healed (Mark 5:1–20), those who receive healing and place their faith in Jesus are immediately asked to publicly testify to their faith. Latin American Pentecostals hold that anyone who knows enough to receive Jesus knows enough to lead other people to Jesus. Hence the laity was given free rein for evangelism and witness, and Pentecostalism became known to the Latin American masses as a Protestantism of the people.

As missiologist Gamaliel Lugo Morales notes, the significance of this move cannot be overemphasized: it is a Copernican revolution in which the church went from resting on the point of a pyramid (in the person of a bishop, priest, pastor, or missionary) to resting on its base.[6] The releasing of the laity also meant that churches could be rapidly founded, as they were independent of the construction of church buildings or the hiring of professional clergy. Latin American Pentecostals found that God the Evangelist seemed to be just as pleased to be present in a small house church or a storefront church as in large cathedrals. In fact, Tennent discloses that some of the most powerful moments of worship and sensing the presence of God have occurred in small house churches or thatched roof "prayer sheds" filled with new believers passionately praising God for who he is and thanking him for his mercy in saving them.[7]

The multiplication of churches rather than of individual Christians is one of the primary reasons Latin American Pentecostalism advances so quickly and effectively. Latin American Pentecostals do not simply preach individual salvation but rather plant communities of redeemed people who can implement the kingdom of God in the context of their larger communities with whom they are functionally connected. Moreover, pneumatology affected Latin American Pentecostals' understanding of the Great Commission. They stress that while the Great Commission is never less than a biblical command, it is definitely more than a biblical command. To illustrate, the book of Acts never once cites the Great Commission as the motivation for the early believers' evangelism. For the Great Commission was not so much a command to be obeyed as it was the manifestation of the resurrected Jesus who prepared the way before the early believers and the Holy Spirit who testified to Jesus through them. Thus the Holy Spirit was increasing the presence and power of the living Jesus through the church's witness. This Pentecostal link between Christology and pneumatology has rendered them a powerful force in global missions. In the words of missiologist Paul A. Pommerville, for Latin American Pentecostals "the commission is no longer merely an outward command, an ethical demand. It is now personified by the missionary Spirit's indwelling presence."[8] It is not simply that God gave us a missionary command; by nature, God is a missionary God. In the final analysis, Jesus embodies the Great Commission so that we are not encountered by a command but by Jesus himself.

THE CONTRIBUTION OF LATIN AMERICAN PENTECOSTALISM TO ECUMENISM

Latin American Pentecostals were among the first to appreciate the global implications of transcending the denominational divisions that have marked Protestant identity for centuries. Since Latin American Pentecostalism did not originate in a single church tradition, it was born out of diversity, sweeping through Roman Catholic and mainline Protestant churches. Such a diverse background prompted Pentecostals to adopt unity in spiritual terms rather than in doctrinal or ecclesiastical terms. This is why, in Latin America, *Pentecostal* is often used both as an adjective and a noun in a way not typically found with terms such as Roman Catholic or Methodist. One can regard oneself as a Pentecostal Roman Catholic or a Pentecostal Methodist without fear of contradiction. As a matter of fact, one of the most vibrant Pentecostal movements in Chile came out of the Methodist Church. Because Pentecostals viewed themselves as reviving the apostolic faith rather than splitting off of or springing forth from any existing movements, it enabled them to give a basis for ecumenism around their shared commitment to the biblical witness and their common experience of the Holy Spirit. Accordingly, they could focus outward on evangelism and missions rather than inward on either defining their own identity or defending themselves against their critics.

Further, Latin American Pentecostals have furnished a significant counterbalance to the strong emphasis on evangelizing unreached people groups on the basis of the homogeneous unit principle, which dominates the church-growth movement. Arguing that people prefer not to cross cultural barriers when becoming Christians and prefer to worship with others like themselves, the homogeneous unit principle prescribes focusing on a sector of society in which all the members have some characteristic in common (e.g., social identity, ethnicity, language, and so forth) and generating a people movement within this sector.

But Latin American Pentecostals have refused to embrace this principle in their evangelism and mission work. Just as the original Pentecost was a multicultural event that transcended normal social and ethnic barriers, so the recapitulation of Pentecost furnishes a new ground of unity not rooted in sociocultural factors but on the power of the Holy Spirit, who yokes diverse individuals to Jesus and to each other. Latin American Pentecostals point to the account of Peter and Cornelius in Acts 10. Far from being part of the same homogeneous unit, the two men were utterly separated, both theologically and culturally. One was a Torah-observant Jew and the other was an uncircumcised Gentile and Roman soldier; according to longstanding custom, the two could not even share table fellowship, much less stand together in the presence of God. But once the Holy Spirit descended on the whole household, everything changed, and both Peter and Cornelius found transformation. Peter experienced the enlargement of his truncated view of God, and Cornelius became a full-fledged member of the body of Christ.

CONCLUSION

Latin American pneumatology should serve as a reminder to Western churches that the Holy Spirit breaks down racial, ethnic, sociocultural, and denominational barriers by unifying persons from radically different backgrounds through a new identity in Christ. It should also expand Western perspectives on missions beyond obedience to a divine command, thus liberating Western Christians from the church-centered, anthropocentric view that permeates much of contemporary missionary work. Perceiving God as the embodiment of missions acknowledges the role of the Father in preparing individuals to respond to the gospel before missionaries arrive, the role of Jesus as the risen Lord standing alongside missionaries as they proclaim the gospel in particular cultural contexts, and the role of the Holy Spirit in supernaturally confirming the gospel and empowering new believers to integrate the faith into their real-world circumstances. This framework provides a Trinitarian, God-centered agenda that presents God as the subject of missions instead of the church as the subject focused on the expansion of its institutional life.

FOR FURTHER READING

Primary Sources

Atwood, Leroy, and Elaine Atwood, eds. *El Evangelio Pentecostal*. New Braunfels, TX: Assemblies of God, 1972–92.

Azusa Street Mission. *The Apostolic Faith*. Los Angeles: Apostolic Faith Mission, 1906–8.

Ball, H. C., ed. *La Luz Apostolica*. Kingsville, TX: Latin American District Council of the Assemblies of God, 1916–73.

Secondary Sources

Cleary, Edward L., and Hannah W. Stewart-Gambino. *Power, Politics, and Pentecostals in Latin America*. Boulder, CO: Westview, 1987.

Costas, Orlando. *Theology of the Crossroads*. Amsterdam: Editions Rodopi, 1976.

Morales, Gamaliel Lugo. "Moving Forward with the Latin American Pentecostal Movement." *International Review of Mission* 87 (1998): 504–12.

Newbigin, Lesslie. *Honest Religion for Secular Man*. Philadelphia: Westminster, 1966.

Padilla, C. René. "The Future of Christianity in Latin America: Missiological Perspectives and Challenges." *International Bulletin of Missionary Research* 23, no. 3 (1999): 105–12.

Pommerville, Paul A. *The Third Force in Missions*. Peabody, MA: Hendrickson, 1985.

Robeck, Cecil M., Jr. "Pentecostals and the Apostolic Faith: Implications for Ecumenism." *Pneuma: The Journal of the Society for Pentecostal Studies* 9 (1987): 61–84.

Stoll, David. *Is Latin America Turning Protestant?* Los Angeles: University of California Press, 1990.

Tennent, Timothy C. *Theology in the Context of World Christianity: How the Global Church Is Influencing the Way We Think about and Discuss Theology*. Grand Rapids: Zondervan, 2007.

CHAPTER 15

LUDWIG WITTGENSTEIN, PICTURE THEORY, AND LANGUAGE GAMES

orn in Vienna and teaching for a number of years at Cambridge University, the analytic philosopher Ludwig Wittgenstein (1889–1951) developed two philosophical systems that would prove highly relevant to twentieth-century religious and theological discourse. Departing from the emphasis on philosophical categories in Hegelian and existentialist systems, Wittgenstein's systems emphasize the use of language. The first of these systems was delineated in his *Tractatus Logico-Philosophicus* (1921), which strongly influenced a group of Continental philosophers known as the Vienna Circle who developed logical positivism. The second of these systems was published posthumously as *Philosophical Investigations* (1953). This chapter unpacks the major teachings of the *Tractatus* and *Philosophical Investigations*, including the picture theory of meaning and the theory of language games. In the process, the chapter assesses the implications of these theories for theology in general and for the doctrine of biblical inerrancy in particular.

ONTOLOGY OF THE *TRACTATUS*

Throughout his philosophy, Wittgenstein was always concerned with two key issues: an understanding of the nature of reality and the problem of the meaning of language. We therefore begin by taking up the question of how Wittgenstein conceived reality. Wittgenstein argued that the world is comprised of facts—states of affairs that are elementary in nature—rather than objects—the substance of the world or the stuff out of which the world is made. While Wittgenstein believed in the reality of objects, the world is not the totality of objects but the totality of facts. This is because Wittgenstein held that whatever the world is the totality of, a complete list of these entities ought to tell us what the world is like and provide a complete description of the world. However, this condition is not met if the world is the totality of objects, for a grocery list of objects found in the world fails to tell us what the world is like since we do not know how the objects are arranged in relationship to each other. But if the world is the totality of facts or states of affairs, then a complete description of the world can be given through these facts, because such facts will include descriptions of objects and how they are arranged.

According to Wittgenstein, there are four basic characteristics of facts or states of affairs. First, facts are combinations of objects or things, like the set {2.01, 2.0272, 2.03}. In a fact, objects hang with one another like links of a chain, since objects per se are fixed constant elements of the world. The substance (the fixed constant elements) of the world is independent of facts (states of affairs) but can be combined to form states of affairs, where various configurations of states of affairs are variables. Second, facts are either complex (i.e., molecular) or simple (i.e., atomic), where complex facts are reducible to atomic facts while atomic facts are irreducible. For example, the statement "The dog on the mat is drinking water from a bowl" is a complex fact that can be broken down into four atomic facts: there's a dog on a mat; there's a bowl on or next to that mat; there's water in the bowl; and the dog is drinking the water. All atomic facts are independent of one another: the existence of one simple state of affairs neither entails nor excludes any other simple state of affairs. Thus the dog's being on the mat entails neither that there must be nor that there cannot be a bowl of water which is also on or next to that mat. Nor does the dog's presence on the mat and even the water's presence on or near the mat necessitate that the dog must drink it. Third, facts are either logically possible or logically impossible. Some states of affairs are logically impossible, like the idea that a musical note is red, while it is logically possible for a note to be loud. Fourth, any possible fact or state of affairs may be true or false of any possible world, including the world that is actual. As for the actual world, Wittgenstein distinguished between positive and negative facts. Positive facts describe what something is, and negative facts describe what something is not. The totality of positive and negative facts determines all that is the case and is not the case. If one knows the totality of these facts, one knows everything there is to know about the actual world. The consequence of Wittgenstein's belief that reality is only composed of facts is manifest in his picture theory of meaning.

THE PICTURE THEORY OF MEANING

We now take up the early Wittgenstein's theory of language from the *Tractatus*, known as his picture theory of meaning. The basic idea of the picture theory of meaning is that a proposition is a literal picture of reality, a model of reality as we think it is. When we articulate a proposition, we construct a model of reality. The constituents of language correspond to constituents of reality. The basic constituents of language are simple signs or names, and they correspond to objects, which are the basic constituents of the world. Hence there is a one-to-one correspondence between names (the "simples" of propositions) and objects in the real world (the "simples" of reality). To illustrate, a name means an object, and objects and names cannot be analyzed any further. Similarly, elementary propositions correspond to elementary states of affairs. Just as elementary states of affairs come from basic configurations of objects, so elementary propositions are configuration connections of elementary signs. Finally, complex propositions correspond to complex states of affairs. Complex states of affairs (e.g., the weather) are configurations of elementary states of affairs (e.g., the movement of particular clouds, the strength of the wind, and so forth), and complex propositions (e.g., if *A*, then *B* and not *C*) are configurations of elementary propositions (e.g., *A*, *B*, and *C*).

Wittgenstein described the picturing relation between language and the world in the following way. We think of a literal, real picture; one sees various objects that stand for or correspond to objects in the real world, and the objects in the picture stand together in different relationships (i.e., one object is above, one object is below). The relationships that the objects have in the picture represent the way objects in the world relate to one another. The connection of various elements in a literal picture is the picture structure, and the possibility that the elements can be structured together is called the form of representation of a picture. Because a proposition communicates a state of affairs, it must be essentially connected to the state of affairs. The connection between the proposition and state of affairs is not a spatial picture (like a literal picture), but a logical picture of the state of affairs it describes. In order for one thing *A* to be a logical picture of another *B*, three conditions must be met. First, there must be a one-to-one correspondence between the components of *A* and *B*. Second, to every feature of the structure or form of *A*, there must correspond a feature of the structure or form of *B*. Third, there must be rules of projection connecting the components of *A* and *B*, where rules of projection are rules in which given either *A* or *B*, *B* or *A* can be reconstructed from it. For example, a performance can be reconstructed from a musical score, and a musical score can be reconstructed by listening to the performance.

According to the picture theory of meaning, what a picture represents is its sense. Thus, if a sentence does not picture ordinary states of affairs in the world, it is without sense or nonsense, and it has no meaning. The world is the totality of facts, and propositions are pictures of facts. For Wittgenstein, propositions that have meaning can only be about states of affairs in the world. Thus states of affairs outside of this world are not things that language can picture or that it could be about. Any sentence discussing states of affairs outside of this world does not have a sense or is nonsense, because having a sense means picturing facts or states of affairs in this world. If a proposition is nonsense, then it does not picture ordinary states of affairs in the world, and the thing it purports to speak about does not exist in the world.

Given the picture theory of meaning, four classes of propositions are nonsense to Wittgenstein: propositions of metaphysics, propositions of ethics, propositions of religion and theology, and propositions of philosophy. Propositions of metaphysics are nonsense because they are propositions about realities outside the world and how those realities bring about effects in the world rather than about realities fully located within the world. Thus metaphysical propositions about God and his relation to the world are nonsense. Further, Wittgenstein argued that if one wrote a book and called it *The World as I Found It*, the metaphysical subject "I" would not be in the world because, by evaluating the world, the "I" puts itself into a subject-object relationship with the world, and subjects are categorically distinct from objects. As a result, talk of that metaphysical item would be nonsense. Propositions of ethics are nonsense because they propose that the sense of the world lies outside the world, while no value is attached as an object to any state of affairs in the world.

If I see someone pull out a gun and shoot another person, I will have a negative evaluation of his action, but I do not see a negative evaluation as an object in the world alongside of the gun, the person holding it, and the person hit by the bullet. According to Wittgenstein, propositions of religion and theology are nonsense because he believed that God does not reveal himself in the world, and thus any proposition about God has no sense or is nonsense. Propositions of philosophy are nonsense because they picture nothing about the world, i.e., no states of affairs in the world. Wittgenstein even stated about his own philosophizing: "My propositions are elucidatory in this way: he who understands me finally recognizes them as senseless when he has climbed out through them, on them, over them. He must, so to speak, throw away the ladder after he has climbed up on it. He must surmount these propositions; then he sees the world rightly."[1]

Wittgenstein claimed regarding his picture theory of meaning that every proposition is a truth function on elementary propositions. A truth function of a single proposition P is a proposition whose truth or falsity is uniquely determined by the truth or falsity of P. For example, not-P (i.e., P is false) is a truth function of P. A truth function of two propositions P and Q is a proposition whose truth is uniquely determined by the truth or falsity of P and Q. For instance, the proposition "P and Q are both true" is a truth function of P and Q. In this case, the relevant proposition would be a conjunction, and whether the conjunction is true or false depends on the truth or falsity of each conjunct plus the fact that in the proposition both conjuncts are asserted to be true. Since most propositions that a person would utter are complex propositions, it is clear that those propositions are analyzable into elementary propositions and therefore a truth function on them.

For Wittgenstein, there are three basic kinds of sentences: tautologies (sentences that are true for all possibilities of an elementary proposition), contradictions (sentences that are false for all possibilities), and propositions that are neither always true nor always false. The propositions of logic are all tautologies. This means that they express no thoughts but are not nonsense, because the fact that a certain combination of propositions yields a tautology reveals something about the structure of the constituent propositions. For any other proposition, we discover if it is true or false by looking and seeing whether the picture in the proposition agrees with reality or not. It should be noted that propositions picture discrete states of affairs, which are conceptually independent of one another and do not infer one another.

So, we may ask, what class or classes of propositions are sensical for Wittgenstein? Wittgenstein maintained that those propositions that have sense are the propositions of natural science and history, a commitment evincing the rigorous commitment to empiricism characterizing Wittgenstein's philosophy. Though tempered somewhat by other statements affirming the reality yet ineffability of various transcendental or mystical entities, Wittgenstein infamously asserted that nonsensical propositions should not be uttered: "Whereof one cannot speak, thereof one must be silent."[2] This view was, *mutatis mutandis*, taken up by the logical positivists in their verificationist theory of meaning, according to which a statement is meaningful if and only if it is empirically verifiable. While Wittgenstein never declared that *empirical* verifiability was a necessary criterion for meaning, leaving open other avenues for "looking and seeing" whether the picture in a proposition agrees with reality or not (e.g., intuition, logical coherence), it is easy to see how the logical positivists could get from the picture theory to verificationism.

It follows from the foregoing discussion that Wittgenstein denied that one can have any knowledge of the future. The idea that one proposition can be inferred from another depends on the presupposition that there is an internal structural connection, cause-and-effect relationship, or dependence between the two propositions. However, if all propositions picture states of affairs that are independent of one another and do not infer one another, the existence of one state of affairs cannot be inferred from the existence of a distinct, different state of affairs. Hence the picture theory of meaning eliminates causality. Since causality is required for predicting the future, we cannot infer from one proposition what a future state of affairs would be. Moreover, we do not even know what propositions will be used to picture future states of affairs.

THEOLOGICAL IMPLICATIONS OF THE PICTURE THEORY OF MEANING

On the picture theory of meaning, propositions of theology and ethics are nonsense, and as such, they have no reference to states of affairs in the world. Hence there will be no empirical way to verify our theology or our ethics. The implications for the meaningfulness and defensibility of theology and ethics are dire if one adopts Wittgenstein's views in the *Tractatus*. Theology and ethics should never be spoken, nor can they be defended. Obviously, this rules out most, if not all, of what we know as apologetics. Moreover, because atomic facts are independent and there are thus no causal relationships, it is extremely hard to see how God is part of the world or how he could act in the world, let alone to see how the will of God could affect the world. Therefore the independence of atomic facts precludes God's ability to act in the world or his will to affect the world. The independence of atomic facts also means that one cannot argue from the inspiration of the Bible to its inerrancy. Hence nothing at all follows from an inspired Bible! On the picture theory of meaning, the only way to demonstrate biblical inerrancy is to show that each statement of Scripture possesses sense (on Wittgenstein's understanding) and that it is true, making any attempt to prove inerrancy an almost impossible task.

Even worse, it is a hopeless task to speak of Scripture's inerrancy on the picture theory of meaning because the term *inerrancy* is meaningless. Rather than being a genuine proposition that pictures a state of affairs in the world, the statement "the Bible is inerrant" is nonsense. For if statements of theology, ethics, and religion are nonsense, then they are neither true nor false. Hence any definition of *inerrancy* based on truth is destroyed. So we have no knowledge of what *inerrancy* means—for the term lacks a determinate sense—thereby rendering any statement concerning inerrancy a disingenuous proposition and nonsense. Since nonsensical propositions should not be uttered, one must be silent on the topic of inerrancy.

THE THEORY OF LANGUAGE GAMES

In the 1930s and 1940s, the verificationist theory of meaning propounded by the logical positivists met with severe philosophical criticism on the grounds that it was self-refuting. For if it is the case that a statement is meaningful if and only if it is empirically verifiable, then what about that very proposition? Is it empirically verifiable? Well, clearly not; it is just an arbitrary definition. Hence the verificationist theory of meaning fails to satisfy its own criteria. It is, on its own, meaningless and so cannot be true. Although the picture theory of meaning could evade this criticism because it did not insist on empirical verifiability, Wittgenstein perceived that the picture theory needed to be supplemented by some way to "look and see" that also applied to itself. Further, he came to find the picture theory too restrictive in its claim that metaphysical, ethical, religious, theological, and philosophical propositions were all nonsense. Practically speaking, it seemed that language must make and be prepared to deal with such propositions, as they appear indispensable to human thought. So in his *Philosophical Investigations* (a posthumous collection of material unpublished during his lifetime), Wittgenstein expanded the picture theory of meaning with his theory of language games. He defined a language game as a complete way of doing some activity, including verbal and nonverbal behavior. Thus a language game is more than mere words but a context that involves behavior or a form of life, such as religion, a teaching skill, science, history, and so forth. Every language game is independent of every other language game.

At this point, one wonders how a verbal claim pictures something in a language game and therefore acquires meaning. To answer this query Wittgenstein proposed the use theory of meaning, which claims that words and sentences gain meaning due to their use in a language game. Since there are countless kinds of language games, words and sentences are tools that can be used to make moves in a language game. Because various words or sentences appear in different language games, their meaning in each language game is independent. We may illustrate this point by considering the rules of European and American football. Running with the ball and using one's hands are violations in soccer but not in American football. One scores touchdowns in American football and not soccer. One has to know which game one is playing to make sense of the rules and the instructions for playing.

Wittgenstein clearly grasped the significance of language games for the field of religion. He began by pointing out that the language games of religion, science, and history are independent. Thus how one uses a sentence in the language game of science or history is totally different than how one uses the same sentence in the language game of religion. What is true in one language game may well be false in another, based on the different rules in said games. The language games of science and history are different from the language game of religion because the games of science and history are evidential and based on empirical facts, while the game of religion does not make assertions about the world. Consequently, to speak of propositions of religious belief as though they were scientific or histori- cal propositions to be verified or falsified by appeal to empirical evidence or any other kind of evidence is to make a major blunder. This is not the type of blunder one makes when presenting poor evidence for a scientific hypothesis, but a much more serious blunder indeed. By presenting evidence for the truth of a religious belief, Wittgenstein charged that one manifestly fails to understand the nature of the religious language game. In particular, a proposition in the language game of religion is not the sort of thing for which one presents evidence as though this proposition were a proposition of science or history.

Wittgenstein illustrated his point with the following thought experiment. Suppose someone were to appeal to a dream as evidence that he knows what the last judgment will be like. Suppose another person responds to him that the dream is poor evidence. Now both persons are making a bad mistake. The first person is wrong that the dream is valid evidence for the last judgment, and the second person is wrong that the dream is poor evidence for the last judgment. The dream is not evidence at all, as there cannot by the nature of the case be any evidence for the last judgment. To treat the dream as evidence of any kind is to confuse the language game of religion with the language games of science and history. One does not use beliefs in the language game of religion in the same way as beliefs in the language games of science and history. To say, "The last judgment will occur when Christ returns," is thus a profoundly different kind of statement than to say, "It will rain tomorrow." The former is not factual, as it does not spring from a language game of factuality, while the latter is factual, as it does spring from a language game of factuality. But paradoxically we can be equally certain of both claims. Wittgenstein proposed that there are certain fundamental forms of life basic to human existence, including the language game of religion, that can neither be justified nor doubted but must simply be accepted as given. The fundamental forms of life, or fundamental language games, do not rest on any ground or evidence but are rather simply there. Since claims made in these games are not facts, one cannot doubt them or even know how to doubt them. Hence these claims possess a certainty deriving from the essential nature of their corresponding games.

To make sense of the foregoing analysis, it is very important to observe here that Wittgenstein's theory of language games draws a distinction between truth and fact. According to the rules of some language games like science and history, truth is defined as fact. Thus the scientific proposition "The temperature is 0° C" is true if and only if it is a fact that the temperature is 0° C, and it is false if the temperature is anything other than 0° C. Likewise, the historical proposition "Immanuel Kant wrote the *Critique of Pure Reason*" is true if and only if it is a fact that Kant wrote the *Critique of Pure Reason*, and it is false if Kant did not write the *Critique of Pure Reason*.

But according to the rules of the language game of religion, truth is not the same as fact. Actually, fact is irrelevant to truth. Rather, the rules of the language game of religion stipulate that a proposition R is true to the degree that it enables an individual to tap into the depth dimension of human experience— the dimension of meaning, value, and being that is inaccessible to the five senses but that we all directly know exists via spiritual reflection. R is false to the degree that it does not enable an individual to tap into the depth dimension of human experience. Any individual can use his powers of spiritual reflection to "look and see" whether R does or does not enable him to access the depth dimension. This is a pragmatic view of truth.

Contrary to the picture theory of meaning *simpliciter*, enhancing the picture theory with the theory of language games renders religious propositions meaningful. So the religious proposition "The last judgment will occur when Christ returns" is, for Christians, true because it enables them access to the depth dimension of human experience, even though it would be false for Buddhists because it gives them no access to the depth dimension. In any case, Wittgenstein held it to be factually inaccurate that "the last judgment will occur when Christ returns," believing neither in a factual last judgment nor a factual return of Christ. But for Wittgenstein, this does nothing to undermine the proposition's truth. For Christians, the proposition meets the religious test of truth and is therefore certain for them.

THEOLOGICAL IMPLICATIONS OF THE THEORY OF LANGUAGE GAMES

Unlike the picture theory of meaning, one might use Wittgenstein's theory of language games to defend the inerrancy of Scripture, but at a very steep price. When a critic alleges that an error is found in Scripture, one may reply that it would indeed be an error if the rules of the language game of religion were the same as the rules of the language game of science or history. Many would find this admission of factual error highly objectionable. But the respondent may continue to say that the alleged error is actually true in the religious language game because of its power to facilitate one's access to the depth dimension of human experience and is hence no error at all. Here we see that, on Wittgenstein's analysis, the doctrine of biblical inerrancy and all other religious statements become highly subjective. For the critic playing the religious language game could respond that the alleged error is indeed false because it prevents the critic from accessing the depth dimension of human experience. So the Bible is inerrant for those individuals who find each of its propositions spiritually life affirming, and the Bible is not inerrant for those individuals who find some of its propositions spiritually life denying. The same goes for any particular theological assertion inside or outside Scripture: it is true for persons who find it spiritually life affirming and false for persons who find it spiritually life denying. Wittgenstein's theory of language games therefore introduces into religion a dangerous relativism, which has come to permeate much of Western culture. For whenever someone replies to a religious proposition, "That's true for you, but not for me," they are—whether they realize it or not—arguing on the basis of the theory of language games.

FOR FURTHER READING

Primary Sources

Wittgenstein, Ludwig. *Philosophical Investigations*. 3rd ed. Paramus, NJ: Prentice Hall, 1973.
———. *Tractatus Logico-Philosophicus*. New York: Harcourt, Brace & Company, 1922.

Secondary Sources

Cooper, Neil. "The Religious Language Game." *Scottish Journal of Religious Studies* 9 (1988): 29–39.
Feinberg, John S. "Noncognitivism: Wittgenstein." In *Biblical Errancy: An Analysis of Its Philosophical Roots*, ed. Norman Geisler. Grand Rapids: Zondervan, 1981, 163–201.
Grayling, A. C. *Wittgenstein*. Oxford: Oxford University Press, 1988.
Harvey, Michael G. "Wittgenstein's Notion of 'Theology as Grammar.'" *Religious Studies* 26 (1989): 89–103.
Hudson, W. Donald. *Wittgenstein and Religious Belief*. New York: St. Martin's, 1975.
Martin, Michael. "Wittgenstein's Lectures on Religious Belief." *Heythrop Journal* 32 (1991): 369–82.

CHAPTER 16

THE BIRTH OF CONTEMPORARY EVANGELICALISM

After World War II, a new spirit of intellectual inquiry and scholarship emerged among historic orthodox Christians that gave rise to a contemporary evangelicalism distinct from fundamentalism. Self-designated as "new evangelicals," younger thinkers subscribing to traditional Christianity aimed to carve out new space in the American religious landscape between fundamentalism and liberalism. Holding to a more historically nuanced and less literalistic doctrine of biblical inerrancy than the fundamentalists, evangelicals proved willing to engage culture rather than separate from it as the fundamentalists had done. This new approach appealed to a broad constituency of groups crossing denominational lines, such as conservative Baptists, conservative Presbyterians, Holiness Wesleyans, Scandinavian Lutherans, Dutch Calvinists, Mennonites, and several others. While many thinkers played important roles, three leaders figured quite prominently in the new evangelical movement: the pastor Harold John Ockenga (1905–85), the theologian Carl F. H. Henry (1913–2003), and the evangelist Billy Graham (1918–2018).

HAROLD JOHN OCKENGA AND HIS INFLUENCE

The principal catalyst of the new evangelicalism, Ockenga grew up as a Methodist but became a star pupil of J. Gresham Machen at Princeton Theological Seminary. When Machen departed from Princeton to found Westminster Theological Seminary in 1929, Ockenga accompanied his teacher and stood among the seminary's first graduating class, later earning his doctorate in philosophy at the University of Pittsburgh. However, Ockenga's respect for Machen waned after Machen defied the Northern Presbyterian Church and established a competing mission board, the Independent Board for Presbyterian Foreign Missions (1933). Ockenga grew to resent the increasingly separatist disposition of Machen's fundamentalist movement and instead desired to generate a more irenic, socially engaged movement that avoided the divisiveness and vitriolic rhetoric characterizing the fundamentalist-modernist controversy. In 1937 Ockenga was installed as pastor of the historic Park Street Church in Boston and quickly spearheaded neo-evangelicalism (later shortened to *evangelicalism*), using his platform to proclaim its agenda. By deliberately appropriating the evangelical moniker, the new evangelicals were claiming a long historical heritage, insisting that they—not the fundamentalists—represented the legitimate offspring of centuries of evangelical movements stretching back to the Reformation era.

Ockenga and his colaborers denounced the anti-intellectualism, internal backbiting, and disdain for the social implications of Christianity that attended fundamentalism. Rather, they strove, in Ockenga's words, to display "a spirit of cooperation, of mutual faith, of progressive action and of ethical responsibility."[1] The new evangelicals directed attention toward a new social responsibility, formulating intellectually credible apologetics, manifesting bold public evangelism, founding educational institutions committed to scholarship, and exhibiting transdenominational cooperation with other like-minded progressives. To these ends, Ockenga and other new evangelicals launched the National Association of Evangelicals (NAE) on April 7, 1942. The NAE sought to both reinvigorate traditional Christianity and furnish a credible alternative to the more liberal National Council of Churches and the fundamentalist American Council of Christian Churches. In the opening NAE address to 150 delegates assembled in St. Louis, Ockenga declared, "I believe we must first of all seek unity. . . . A terrible indictment may be laid against fundamentalism because of its failures, division and controversies. This must be admitted by those of us who believe in the fundamentals and who also seek a new outlook."[2] The NAE united into its membership a broad spectrum of evangelicals, including Baptists, Methodists, Lutherans, Christian Reformed, the Salvation Army, and Pentecostals.

Ockenga participated in virtually all the early neo-evangelical initiatives. In addition to founding the NAE, he served as the first president of Fuller Theological Seminary in Pasadena, California (though staying in Boston as pastor of Park Street Church). The concept of a new seminary first occurred in 1939 to Charles Fuller, a famous radio evangelist who hosted the *Old Fashioned*

Revival Hour, but it only came to fruition when Fuller and Ockenga collaborated in 1947. Within a few years of Fuller's founding, Billy Graham came to serve as a member of its board. Church historians John D. Woodbridge and Frank A. James III point out the monumental nature of these alliances: "Since Graham and Fuller were the two leading evangelists of the day, their joint association with Fuller Seminary gave powerful credibility and stature to the new evangelicalism."[3] Among the most significant achievements of neo-evangelicalism was the 1955 institution of the national magazine *Christianity Today* by Billy Graham, Graham's father-in-law Nelson Bell, and Sun Oil tycoon J. Howard Pew, with Ockenga as chairman of the board and Carl Henry its first editor. Envisioned to function as the flagship publication of evangelicalism, *Christianity Today* aimed to reach a wide audience and supply an evangelical alternative to the more liberal magazine *The Christian Century*. At present, *Christianity Today* exerts tremendous influence over the evangelical world.

CARL F. H. HENRY AND HIS INFLUENCE

Just as Ockenga was the principal organizer of the new evangelicalism, so Carl Henry was the chief theologian of the new evangelicalism. Henry's magnum opus is his six-volume *God, Revelation and Authority*, which covers the broad theological spectrum. It rejects Hegelian and existentialist theologies while defending propositional revelation, the infallibility of Scripture, and traditional Christian doctrines from the Trinity to the last judgment. When Ockenga, as president of Fuller Seminary, recruited the institution's first faculty, he hired Henry as dean and professor of theology and philosophy, Everett Harrison (1902–99) as professor of New Testament, Wilbur Smith (1894–1977) as professor of apologetics, and Harold Lindsell (1913–98) as professor of missions. Undoubtedly Ockenga placed his hopes for a new evangelicalism on the shoulders of Henry, previously professor at Northern Baptist Theological Seminary. Soon after the opening of Fuller, Henry published his platform for neo-evangelicalism titled *The Uneasy Conscience of Modern Fundamentalism* (1947). It charged fundamentalists with withdrawing from the full-gospel mission and failing to preach against "such social evils as aggressive warfare, racial hatred, intolerance."[4] Putting a high value on rationality, Henry proclaimed against fundamentalism that "faith without reason is not worth much, and that reason is not an enemy but an ally of genuine faith."[5] Indeed, Henry indicated that human rational faculties were not incapacitated by the fall, such that the truths of Christianity were as open to non-Christians as the truths of natural science. Warning that American evangelicalism was on the verge of becoming a "wilderness cult in a secular society,"[6] Henry contended that evangelicalism must dissociate itself from fundamentalism to survive into the future. On the heels of the fundamentalist-modernist controversy, the scholarly Christian traditionalists—who lacked the fundamentalists' moral reservations about smoking, alcohol, movies, and dancing and who regarded dispensationalism as one of many valid eschatological views—rejected the more stringent fundamentalism and increasingly emerged from their cultural isolation.

Under Henry's direction, the new evangelicals ardently supported biblical inerrancy but refused to take part in cultural separatism. They were directed by a different principle. Instead of pitting Christ against culture, they adopted the notion that Christ transforms culture, entailing their participation in the secular realm. Hence the new evangelicals aimed for intellectual credibility. This led to the birth of the Evangelical Theological Society (ETS) in 1949 as a transdenominational forum for evangelical scholarship. It possesses two theological requirements for membership, namely, subscriptions to inerrancy and to the doctrine of the Trinity. In the words of the ETS Doctrinal Basis, "The Bible alone, and the Bible in its entirety, is the Word of God written and is therefore inerrant in the autographs. God is a Trinity, Father, Son, and Holy Spirit, each an uncreated person, one in essence, equal in power and glory."[7] Guided by Henry's leadership, Fuller Seminary acquired a strong intellectual direction, which quickly laid the foundations for the reassessment of some of evangelicalism's most esteemed theological commitments. Finally deciding that he could not leave Park Street Church, Ockenga turned over the presidency of Fuller to the distinguished evangelical theologian Edward J. Carnell (1919–67). Carnell was open to reexamining the doctrine of biblical inerrancy, foundational to both fundamentalism and neo-evangelicalism. He investigated the earlier views of Scottish evangelicals James Orr (1844–1913) and James Denney (1856–1917), who argued that the Princeton conception of inerrancy could not be intellectually defended. It is important to note that Carnell never departed from the doctrine of inerrancy; rather, he endeavored to expand its domain of meaning beyond any narrow construal. But this laid the groundwork for other Fuller faculty to more aggressively press the issue in later years.

Henry firmly supported the inerrancy requirement for ETS membership but just as firmly resisted the more combative position that inerrancy constitutes the litmus test for qualification as an evangelical. Thus he castigated what he described as the "somewhat reactionary elevation of inerrancy as the super-badge of evangelical orthodoxy."[8] Regarding evangelicals who dissented from the doctrine of inerrancy, such as renowned British biblical scholar F. F. Bruce (1910–90) and renowned Dutch theologian G. C. Berkouwer (1903–96), Henry remarked: "I think it highly unfortunate that the primary thing that should be said about men like F. F. Bruce and G. C. Berkouwer, men who have made significant contributions to the conservative position . . . is that they are not evangelicals because of their positions at this one point."[9] Here Henry echoed the position of Machen, who had stated in *Christianity and Liberalism*: "There are many who believe that the Bible is right at the central point, in its account of the redeeming work of Christ, and yet believe that it contains errors. Such men are not really liberals, but Christians."[10] Henry readily admitted that inerrancy is not explicitly taught in Scripture but is logically deduced from the doctrine of biblical inspiration, which is explicitly taught in Scripture (2 Tim. 3:16; 2 Peter 1:21).

During the 1960s and 1970s, several faculty and trustees at Fuller Seminary became unconvinced that inerrancy is a necessary inference from inspiration. These faculty and trustees drew a distinction between the inerrancy of Scripture and the infallibility of Scripture. While inerrancy meant that the Bible contained no false or misleading statements of any kind, infallibility meant that the Bible contained no false or misleading statements on matters of faith and practice. But infallibility leaves open the possibility that the Bible contains false or misleading statements on matters of history, science, and the like. In 1971 the board of Fuller Seminary voted unanimously to adopt a new doctrinal statement in which the original phrase describing Scripture as "plenarily inspired and free from all error in the whole and the part" was dropped: "Scripture is an essential part and trustworthy record of this divine self-disclosure. All the books of the Old and New Testaments, given by divine inspiration, are the written Word of God, the only infallible rule of faith and practice."[11] This decision was taken to task by former Fuller professor Harold Lindsell, whose 1976 book, *The Battle for the Bible*, overtly denied that anyone could legitimately "claim the evangelical badge once he has abandoned inerrancy."[12] At the same time, European evangelicals generally rejected the term *inerrancy* as an inadequate expression of biblical inspiration while embracing the trustworthiness and supreme authority of Scripture.

Concerned with the defection among Christians in general and a significant number of evangelicals in particular from adherence to the complete truthfulness of the Bible, the International Council on Biblical Inerrancy (ICBI) was founded in 1977 to clarify and defend the doctrine of biblical inerrancy. At its first summit in Chicago (1978), nearly three hundred noted evangelical scholars, including Henry and Ockenga, produced the Chicago Statement on

Biblical Inerrancy, which delineated a sophisticated and intellectually defensible doctrine of inerrancy that avoided many of the criticisms previously launched against the idea. The Chicago Statement insisted on both the infallibility and inerrancy of Scripture, claiming that these two symbiotically related doctrines could not validly be separated. Hence the Chicago Statement commented concerning infallibility and inerrancy:

> We affirm that Scripture, having been given by divine inspiration, is infallible, so that, far from misleading us, it is true and reliable in all matters it addresses. We deny that it is possible for the Bible to be at the same time infallible and errant in its assertions. Infallibility and inerrancy may be distinguished, but not separated. . . . We affirm that Scripture in its entirety is inerrant, being free from all falsehood, fraud, and deceit. We deny that Biblical infallibility and inerrancy are limited to spiritual, religious or redemptive themes, exclusive of assertions in the fields of history and science.[13]

Explicitly linking the inspiration of Scripture to its inerrancy, the Chicago Statement went on to declare: "We affirm that inspiration, though not conferring omniscience, guaranteed true and trustworthy utterance on all matters of which the Bible authors were moved to speak and write. We deny that the finitude or fallenness of these writers, by necessity or otherwise, introduced distortion or falsehood into God's Word."[14]

The Chicago Statement was careful to refrain from the fundamentalist construal of inerrancy as the belief that when taking literally every scriptural pericope (discrete unit of text) that it is possible to take literally, the Bible contains no errors. For this construal shows no regard for the original literary genre of any given pericope or the conventions in that genre. Rather, the Chicago Statement affirmed that for each pericope within every document of the scriptural canon, when one first takes into consideration that pericope's original literary genre and the rules in that genre for what does and does not constitute an error, the pericope contains no errors. Hence the Bible contains no errors in what it asserts or teaches, and discerning exactly what it asserts is the task of grammatico-historical exegesis: "In determining what the God-taught writer is asserting in each passage, we must pay the most careful attention to its claims and character as a human production. In inspiration, God utilized the culture and conventions of His penman's milieu. . . . It is misinterpretation to imagine otherwise. So history must be treated as history, poetry as poetry, hyperbole and metaphor as hyperbole and metaphor, generalization and approximation as what they are, and so forth."[15]

Moreover, the Chicago Statement emphasized that one cannot anachronistically superimpose modern standards of accuracy on ancient biblical texts that worked with different standards. This qualification is highly significant, as most if not all cases of alleged biblical "errors" arise from such a superimposition.

Differences between literary conventions in Bible times and in ours must also be observed: since, for instance, non-chronological narration and imprecise citation were conventional and acceptable and violated no expectations in those days, we must not regard these things as faults when we find them in Bible writers. When total precision of a particular kind was not expected nor aimed at, it is no error not to have achieved it. Scripture is inerrant, not in the sense of being absolutely precise by modern standards, but in the sense of making good its claims and achieving that measure of focused truth at which its authors aimed. The truthfulness of Scripture is not negated by the appearance in it of irregularities of grammar or spelling, phenomenal descriptions of nature, reports of false statements (e.g., the lies of Satan), or seeming discrepancies between one passage and another.[16]

Finally, the Chicago Statement stressed that while biblical principles are objectively true for every time and place, the application of those principles may vary considerably from biblical times to our own time: "Although Holy Scripture is nowhere culture-bound in the sense that its teaching lacks universal validity, it is sometimes culturally conditioned by the customs and conventional views of a particular period, so that the application of its principles today calls for a different sort of action."[17] The Chicago Statement's balanced view of inerrancy has since become standard across contemporary evangelicalism, though it has not gone unchallenged.

BILLY GRAHAM AND HIS INFLUENCE

The most recognizable face of the new evangelicalism was the Southern evangelist William Franklin "Billy" Graham Jr. Raised on a dairy farm near Charlotte, North Carolina, Graham grew up in the Associate Reformed Presbyterian Church. Following his 1934 conversion experience, however, he was ordained a Southern Baptist in 1939. Graham graduated from Wheaton College in 1943 and was profoundly influenced by Torrey Johnson (1909–2002), founder of the worldwide ministry Youth for Christ, and Henrietta Mears (1890–1963), director of Christian education at the First Presbyterian Church of Hollywood. With the passion of a new convert, Graham and Charles Templeton (1915–2001) traveled the United States and Europe as evangelists for Youth for Christ.

But Graham and Templeton parted company when Templeton, starting on his eventual road to agnosticism, expressed doubts about the authority of the Bible. As an evangelist, Graham famously summarized the gospel message in four simple steps, which he would employ throughout his meteoric career: God is love and so loves every person; humans are sinful and separated from God; Jesus died to save us from our sins; and anyone can find salvation by repenting of their sins and embracing Jesus as Lord and Savior. At age thirty, Graham was the youngest person ever to become a college president when in 1948 he was appointed to the presidency of Northwestern College in Minnesota (now the University of Northwestern–St. Paul). He served in that position until 1952.

Graham was launched into worldwide stardom by journalism moguls William Randolph Hearst (1863–1951) and Henry Luce (1898–1967), who mistakenly thought Graham would prove an ally in advancing their conservative anticommunist position. Amid a 1949 series of Graham's evangelistic meetings in Los Angeles, Hearst sent a telegram to his newspaper editors ordering them to "puff Graham."[18] Due to the increased media exposure, the crusade event ran for four weeks longer than planned. Luce then proceeded to put Graham on the cover of *Time* magazine. Given this newfound popularity, the Billy Graham Evangelistic Association was founded in 1950, and Graham proceeded to hold evangelistic crusades worldwide. From the start of his career, Graham associated with the new evangelicals. Quickly following the institution of the NAE, Graham joined with Ockenga and Henry as a leader in the NAE specifically and in neo-evangelicalism generally. Graham self-consciously repudiated fundamentalist anti-intellectualism and divisiveness and, though not a scholar himself, played an important role in promoting the intellectual enlightenment of evangelicalism. As church historian Mark Noll observes, "Graham provided the evangelical equivalent of an imprimatur for serious intellectual labor. More than any other public figure, Graham protected evangelical scholars from the anti-intellectualism endemic to the movement."[19] Lending his name and influence to many colleges and seminaries that strove to reestablish evangelical academic respectability, Graham was also chiefly responsible for the birth of *Christianity Today* out of a longing to form a serious evangelical counterpart to mainline Protestant and Catholic popular publications.

Nevertheless, Graham showed a remarkable ecumenism in working together with a wide variety of Christian nonevangelicals. But to quote the verdict of Woodbridge and James, "his willingness to associate with mainline Christians and his avoidance of invective toward liberals predictably earned him the anathemas of many fundamentalists."[20] These tensions came to a head during the New

York City Crusade of 1957, in which Graham allowed nonevangelicals to take part. The fundamentalists John R. Rice (1895–1980), Jack Wyrtzen (1913–96), and Bob Jones Jr. (1911–97) immediately sounded alarm bells, requiring their adherents to practice "second-degree separation." Accordingly, a Christian must separate from any Christian who is not practicing "first-degree" or "biblical" separation from liberals and persons sliding down the slippery slope toward liberalism. As a result, many fundamentalists separated both from Graham and from anyone who did not separate from Graham. Jones went so far as to call Graham "the most dangerous man in America." In many fundamentalist circles, the principle of separation emerged as a new doctrinal litmus test.

In the same fashion as his fellow new evangelicals Ockenga and Henry, Graham publicly confronted many of the central social issues of his day, especially racial injustice. Opposing segregation in the southern United States during the 1960s, Graham argued, "The ground at the foot of the cross is level, and it touches my heart when I see whites standing shoulder to shoulder with blacks at the cross."[21] Graham posted bail for Dr. Martin Luther King Jr. (1929–68)—one of the nonevangelicals who had preached with him at the New York City Crusade—to be released from jail during the height of the civil rights protests in Birmingham. During the apartheid era in South Africa, Graham steadfastly refused to visit the nation until the government allowed his audiences to be desegregated. When the South African government relented in 1973, Graham openly denounced apartheid at his first crusade in the country.

Graham became history's most visible evangelical, primarily because of his more than forty crusades since 1948. Throughout the course of his ministry, Graham preached to live audiences of nearly 215 million people in more than 185 countries and reached hundreds of millions more through media outlets. Among Graham's most significant accomplishments was the organization of the 1974 International Congress on World Evangelization in Lausanne, Switzerland (otherwise known as the Lausanne Congress), where 2,700 participants from 150 nations gathered to strengthen the global church for evangelization, to engage sociological and ideological trends that bore on the evangelistic task, and to produce the Lausanne Covenant, an ecumenical doctrinal statement considered one of modern Christianity's most influential documents.

CONCLUSION

In the second half of the twentieth century, evangelicalism reascended to the heights from which it had fallen before its early twentieth-century co-option by fundamentalism and its embarrassment during the fundamentalist-modernist controversy. The American Association of Bible Colleges, the transformation of many Bible schools into four-year institutions of liberal arts and sciences, the Evangelical Theological Society, the National Association of Evangelicals, Christian academic publishers, evangelical scholarly journals, and parachurch agencies raised the level of evangelical culture. Contemporary evangelicals hold certain ideas in common. They believe the Scriptures are the inspired, infallible rule of faith and practice, with most evangelicals also professing the Scriptures as the inerrant expression of all they assert or teach. They believe in human depravity and vigorously stress Jesus's deity, virginal conception, atonement, bodily resurrection, and glorious return. Through faith in Jesus, spiritual rebirth and a life of righteousness become realities. While demanding priority on gospel proclamation, evangelicals have frequently stood in the vanguard of social action in America. Standing in basic agreement on essential biblical truths, evangelicalism is a rich montage of groups exhibiting diversity on such matters as glossolalia, a second work of sanctification resulting in perfection, the mode of baptism, and dispensationalism.

FOR FURTHER READING

Primary Sources

Adler, Mortimer J., and Charles Van Doren, eds. *The Annals of America, Vol. 16: 1940–1949.* New York: Encyclopædia Britannica, 1968.

The Chicago Statement on Biblical Inerrancy. In *Inerrancy*, ed. Norman L. Geisler, 493–502. Grand Rapids: Zondervan, 1990.

Henry, Carl F. H. *Confessions of a Theologian: An Autobiography.* Waco: Word, 1986.

———. *Evangelicals at the Brink of Crisis.* Waco: Word, 1967.

———. *God, Revelation, and Authority.* 6 vols. 2nd ed. Wheaton, IL: Crossway, 1999.

———. "Reaction and Realignment." *Christianity Today* 20 (July 2, 1976): 30.

———. *The Uneasy Conscience of Modern Fundamentalism.* Grand Rapids: Eerdmans, 1947.

Lindsell, Harold. *The Battle for the Bible.* Grand Rapids: Zondervan, 1976.

———. *Park Street Prophet: A Life of Harold John Ockenga.* Wheaton, IL: Van Kampen, 1951.

Ockenga, Harold John. "Can Fundamentalism Win America?" *Christian Life and Times* 2 (June 1947): 13–15.

Secondary Sources

Dorrien, Gary J. *The Remaking of Evangelical Theology.* Louisville: Westminster John Knox, 1998.

Marsden, George M. *Understanding Fundamentalism and Evangelicalism.* Grand Rapids: Eerdmans, 1990.

Noll, Mark A. *American Evangelical Christianity: An Introduction*. Hoboken, NJ: Wiley-Blackwell, 2000.

Rosell, Garth M. *The Surprising Work of God: Harold John Ockenga, Billy Graham, and the Rebirth of Evangelicalism*. Grand Rapids: Baker Academic, 2008.

Tchividdjian, Basyle, and Aram Tchividdjian. *Invitation: Billy Graham and the Lives God Touched*. Colorado Springs: Multnomah, 2008.

Woodbridge, John D., and Frank A. James III. *Church History*. Vol. 2, *From Pre-Reformation to the Present Day*. Grand Rapids: Zondervan, 2013.

CHAPTER 17

RUDOLF BULTMANN

Demythologization

While conservatives in America were making a comeback in the mid-twentieth century, other, more liberal movements were happening in Europe. One significant leader was the epochal German New Testament scholar and existentialist theologian Rudolf Bultmann (1884–1976). Bultmann delineated a unified and provocative theological vision that called on modern interpreters to demythologize the New Testament so that the Christian gospel might be separated from its mythological trappings. Bultmann's system is best viewed as a philosophically driven synthesis of nineteenth-century German theological liberalism and Barth's ensuing critique of that movement. *Pro* Barth, Bultmann desired to proclaim the saving act of God in Christ; *pro* liberal theology, Bultmann desired to remove from this proclamation what he considered unnecessary stumbling blocks to modern listeners. This chapter analyzes Bultmann's system through an exploration of its philosophical presuppositions, its hermeneutics, and its eschatology.

PHILOSOPHICAL PRESUPPOSITIONS OF BULTMANN'S SYSTEM

Bultmann suggested that every interpreter comes to Scripture with some set of presuppositions; this is unavoidable. It is impossible to interpret anything without some sort of presuppositions. Acknowledging that presuppositions with respect to results are inappropriate, Bultmann held that presuppositions with respect to methods are appropriate. In other words, it is problematic to presuppose the content of what one will believe without ever having furnished any evidence for it, but it is not problematic to hold certain assumptions about the best way to discover truth and investigating topics. The key question then becomes, what are the right presuppositions of method to employ for the tasks of interpreting Scripture and shaping theological ideas? Bultmann insisted that the basic presupposition for every form of exegesis of any piece of literature (not simply the Bible) is that one's own life relationship to the subject matter prompts the questions one brings to the text and elicits the answers one derives from the text. When we read the Bible, then, our interest is not merely to acquire a historical awareness of the situations discussed. Rather, our interest is really to hear what the Bible has to say for our actual present, namely, the truth about our life and our soul right now. Moreover, Bultmann proposed, if it is true that the right questions to bring to any text are concerned with the possibilities of understanding human existence, then it is necessary to discover the adequate conceptions whereby such understanding may be expressed. To discover these conceptions is the task of philosophy. This situation entails that our exegesis must, in a certain respect, be controlled by our philosophy, a fact that necessarily holds for every person in every age.

So, for Bultmann, the issue is not whether we should allow philosophy to control our exegesis, as this will happen in any case. Instead, the issue is determining which philosophy will be the right one for today in our life situation. To this issue Bultmann has a very specific answer: the best philosophy for our day is existentialism, since it makes human existence the direct object of attention. Due to the influence of French philosophers Jean-Paul Sartre (1905–80) and Albert Camus (1913–60), existentialism became very popular in the middle of the twentieth century. Indeed, two world wars, modernity, and increasingly technology contributed to a crisis of human meaninglessness that existentialism attempted to solve. Bultmann felt that the existentialist school of thought had reached its zenith in the work of Martin Heidegger (1889–1976), as Heidegger showed what it means to exist but without dictating the way we must exist. Regarding Heideggerian existentialism, Bultmann declared, "Existential philosophy, while it gives no answer to the question of my own personal existence, makes personal existence my own personal responsibility, and by doing so it helps me be open to the word of the Bible. Existential philosophy, then, can offer adequate conceptions as presuppositions for the interpretation of the Bible, since the interpretation of the Bible is concerned with the understanding of existence just as existentialism is."[1]

In existentialist fashion, Bultmann maintained that unless a person in responsibility takes it upon himself to be, so displaying readiness to be a human being, that person cannot understand a single word of the Bible. Further, hearing the word of the Bible can only occur in personal decision. Accordingly, Bultmann pronounced that "scientific interpretation of the Bible does require the existentialist conceptions in order to explain the biblical understanding of human existence."[2] In the end, both the Bible and existentialism are after the same thing: to help us understand the meaning of existence. Hence interpreting the Bible through the existentialist lens is entirely justified because that lens provides us with the right questions to use in approaching the Bible.

BULTMANNIAN HERMENEUTICS

Bultmann affirmed German liberalism's dichotomy between the Jesus of history and the Christ of faith, such that the message of the historical Jesus (much like the message of the Old Testament prophets) is a presupposition for New Testament theology rather than a part of New Testament theology. The New Testament has so covered the historical Jesus with layers of myth and dogma that we can know virtually nothing about him, save the bare fact of his existence. In Bultmann's words, "I do indeed think that we can now know almost nothing concerning the life and personality of Jesus, because the early Christian sources show no interest in either and also are fragmentary and often legendary."[3] But this, for Bultmann, is of no concern, since the only thing important about the historical Jesus is the simple "dass *seines Gekommenseins*," namely, the *that* of his coming. Beyond this, the "kerygmatic" Christ of faith was what really mattered to the early church. At this juncture, Bultmann's understanding of myth comes to the fore. Bultmann construed myth as a form of imagery where that which transcends the world is represented as though it were of this world and, indeed, in human terms. Every myth contains an underlying core of truth, presented in legendary terms; there is a kernel of truth in the husk of myth. This conviction led Bultmann to formulate his method of biblical interpretation, known as demythologization: "We must ask whether the eschatological preaching and the mythological sayings as a whole contain a still deeper meaning that is concealed under the cover of mythology. If that is so, let us abandon the mythological conceptions precisely because we want to retain their deeper meaning. This method of interpretation of the New Testament, which tries to recover the deeper meaning behind the mythological conceptions, I call *de-mythologizing*."[4]

According to Bultmann, demythologizing the New Testament *in toto* (rather than simply the words and deeds of Jesus) is necessary because the Christian Scriptures presuppose a mythological worldview from top to bottom.

Bultmann maintained that we recognize the mythic nature of this worldview by virtue of its difference from the worldview established by modern science and accepted by all modern humans. Modern science does not believe that the nexus between cause and effect can be interrupted or perforated by supernatural powers. Examples of the mythological worldview of the Bible that Bultmann cited include a three-story conception of the universe (heaven, earth, and hell), miracles, the intervention of supernatural forces in the life of the soul, Satan, and evil spirits. In addition, Bultmann deemed as mythical New Testament views about eschatology, a redeemer, and redemption. Since they are inherently unscientific, Bultmann claimed that it is absurd to try to present evidence for modern humans to believe these myths. Given this approach, Bultmann could not accept the historicity of Jesus's resurrection but ruled it out in advance of any evidential considerations: "The resurrection, of course, simply cannot be a visible fact in the realm of human history."[5] Rather, the resurrection was simply the product of the disciples' reflection on Jesus and his message.

Consequently, Bultmann declared that we need to strip away the mythical elements of the New Testament to arrive at the kerygma, the timeless central message of the text. Ironically, for Bultmann, demythologizing serves an apologetic function and has an apologetic purpose. Since it is impossible for modern humans to believe the myths of Christian Scripture, they are stumbling blocks that prevent modern humans from coming to Christ. Bultmann felt that this was unfortunate, as they substitute false stumbling blocks for the true stumbling block that any person must face to become a Christian. Christianity indeed contains a legitimate stumbling block, and that is the kerygma. Bultmann identified the kerygma as the word of the cross that calls men and women out of their human-made security and inauthentic existence. In line with existentialism, authentic existence entails taking complete responsibility for one's identity and making decisions out of that identity. However, this kerygma is so covered over by myth that most people are offended at the myth and never even encounter the true stumbling block. Hence demythologizing is a hermeneutical program that begins with the insight that Christian preaching is kerygma, a proclamation addressed not to the theoretical reason but to the hearer as a self. In Bultmann's estimation, Paul's exclusive commitment to the word of the cross—to know nothing but Christ crucified (1 Cor. 2:2)—is the reason he commended himself to every person's conscience in the sight of God (2 Cor. 4:2). It is the task of the theologian, then, to bring people to the real stumbling block so that they can become Christians by totally stripping away (this must be complete—all or nothing) the shell of an antiquated worldview to expose the true kernel of kerygma.

In view of the hermeneutic of demythologization, Bultmann turned to the interpreter's interaction with the scriptural text. Bultmann remarked that every person comes to the text with certain questions that arise from the conceptions by which he understands life and from his own life experiences. The corresponding presupposition of exegesis is that each of us has a relationship to the subject matter we are reading about, which Bultmann called the life-relation. When an interpreter comes to Scripture, he does not come to it in a disinterested way but has something at stake; namely, he has a life-relation with it. The interpreter has a certain view of the world that comes from his life and experiences and certain questions he wants to ask of the text and hopes that the text can answer. In the process of exegeting a text on a particular matter, Bultmann held that the interpreter must put his understanding of the matter into the interpretation. Thus exegesis is not merely a matter of the text operating on the interpreter, so that the interpreter then tells us what the biblical writer said and meant. Instead, there is a need for the interpreter to interact with the writer and to impose the interpreter's understanding of the issue in the interpretive process. The result may well be that the interpreter does not arrive at what the text actually says or the writer truly means, but instead arrives at what the text says insofar as the interpreter molds it to fit the interpreter's understanding of the subject. This exegetical procedure is known as the hermeneutical circle. Placing myself in a circle with the text, Bultmann alleged that the "two of us together" derive the text's meaning. Both the interpreter and the text come up with the meaning as the interpreter encounters, interacts with, and adds to the text while the text encounters, interacts with, and adds to the interpreter. Here it is instructive to note that the hermeneutical circle bears significant resemblance to the Hegelian dialectical method: there are two sides of an issue, and in the synthesis of the two sides into a greater whole, one finds the true meaning. While it is quite doubtful that Bultmann deliberately borrowed from Hegel on this score, the unintended closeness of the two thinkers serves to indicate just how important Hegelian dialectic is to contemporary theology.

BULTMANNIAN ESCHATOLOGY

Contrary to orthodox theologians, Bultmann insisted that there will be no future coming of Christ to set up a kingdom, for this is part of Scripture's myth. For Bultmann, the proof that the coming kingdom is mythological lies in the mistaken kingdom expectation of Jesus. Since Jesus allegedly expected the kingdom to come during the first generation after his death and it never came,

Jesus was mistaken, and anyone who expects as he did for a future kingdom to be established is equally mistaken. But if eschatology does not deal with a future kingdom, then, one may ask, what does it deal with? Bultmann replied that eschatology is to be thought of in two complementary senses, neither of which is Jesus's notion of a coming kingdom. First, we understand eschatology to be wrapped up with the imminent end of the world, with imminent judgment, and with a new time of salvation and of eternal bliss. At this point, Bultmann left it ambiguous as to whether this "end of the world" is to be taken as a literal termination of the universe or in some other way. But he did clarify that eschatology in the first sense speaks of human finitude, of the human ability to self-destruct and of that self-destruction as God's judgment. Eschatology then means to be open to God's future, which is imminent for all of us. We must be ready for God's future, which will come like a thief in the night and will judge those who are bound to this world. Those who are not judged will be put into a state of bliss where they live as authentic selves. Although Bultmann did not expound on the nature of this state of bliss, he did reformulate the Pauline doctrine of justification in relation to it. For Bultmann, justification meant turning from one's inauthentic existence to authentic existence through faith in Christ. Moreover, Bultmann saw the gospel as offering people the possibility of such justification.

The second way Bultmann understood eschatology was as realized eschatology. Realized eschatology begins by asserting that the only physical, eschatological coming of Christ was his first coming. The event of Christ—namely, everything that he did—was the eschatological event, and we must look for no other. This is paradoxical because mere history does not see Jesus as the eschatological event. The historian can see nothing more than that Jesus of Nazareth is simply a human being, a historical person. The historian cannot become aware of what God has done in Christ as the eschatological event. On the other hand, for believers the eschatological event of Jesus Christ has already been realized in two respects. It has been realized, first of all, in history, as Jesus indisputably came once. Second, it is realized in the present when Christ comes individually to each person who encounters him and makes that person a new creature. This leads to a further paradox of realized eschatology: while Christ's coming occurred back in history, it also occurs here and now when the Word of God is being preached and men and women encounter God. Christ is the once-for-all Word of God that is continually happening in our lives and preaching. According to Bultmann, we must be open for God's future to encounter us in this way rather than in terms of any traditional notion of the Second Coming. Bultmann explained his notion of

God's future—including both judgment and salvation—as occurring in the here and now and in every "there and then" since Jesus's ministry:

> In the Fourth Gospel, as we have seen, the cosmological eschatology is understood from our point of view as an historical eschatology. We have also seen that, for Paul, the believer is already a new creation. The old has passed away; behold, the new has come (2 Cor. 5:17). We must therefore say that to live in faith is to live an eschatological existence, to live beyond the world, to have passed from death to life (cp. John 5:24; 1 John 3:14). Certainly the eschatological existence is already realized in anticipation, for "we walk by faith, not by sight" (2 Cor. 5:7). This means that the eschatological existence of the believer is not a worldly phenomenon, but is realized in the new self-understanding. This self-understanding, as we have seen before, grows out of the Word. The eschatological event which is Jesus Christ happens here and now as the Word is being preached (2 Cor. 6:2; John 5:24), regardless of whether this word is accepted or rejected. The believer has passed from death to life, and the unbeliever is judged. The wrath of God rests upon him, says John (John 3:18, 36; 9:39). The word of the preaching spreads death and life, says Paul (2 Cor. 2:15ff.). Thus the once-for-all is now understood in its genuine sense, namely, as the once-for-all of the eschatological event. For this once-for-all is not the uniqueness of an historical event, but means that a particular historical event—that is, Jesus Christ—is to be understood as the eschatological once-for-all. As an eschatological event, this once-for-all is always present in the proclaimed Word, not as a timeless truth, but as happening here and now.[6]

Here the notion of Jesus as the eschatological once-for-all emerges as central. For Bultmann, it entails the omnipresent nature of divine judgment and salvation from the time of Jesus into the future. The ubiquity of the salvific possibility since Jesus's kingdom proclamation implies that the mechanism of salvation—namely, the prevenient grace of God that draws inauthentic men and women into freely finding existential authenticity through Christ—is always available. It becomes especially effective in the preaching of the Word of God. Bultmann drew together these threads:

> Certainly the Word says to me that God's grace is a prevenient grace which has already acted for me, but not in such a way that I can look back on it as an historical event of the past. The acting grace is present now as the

eschatological event. The Word of God is Word of God only as it happens here and now. The paradox is that the Word which is always happening here and now is one and the same with the first Word of the apostolic preaching crystallized in the scriptures of the New Testament and delivered by men again and again, the Word whose content may be formulated in general statements. It cannot be the one without the other. This is the sense of the once-for-all. It is the eschatological once-for-all because the Word becomes event here and now in the living voice of the preaching.[7]

CONCLUSION

To close our discussion, it is instructive to see how Bultmann integrates his philosophical presuppositions, hermeneutics, and eschatology in arriving at his full doctrines of anthropology and soteriology. For Bultmann, persons in their truest nature, or essence, are makers of decisions. If decision making constitutes a person's essence, then the future instead of the past represents that person's spiritual element. For only the future contains options, and only where there are options can there be decisions. Bultmann held that persons do many things to evade facing the fact that they are decision makers. For instance, persons often live by dead traditions; persons allow legalistic ethical systems to make decisions for them; persons conceive of themselves as having fixed character traits from which their actions necessarily issue; and persons define themselves by reference to their social roles and relationships to other people, so refusing complete responsibility for their identity. In these and similar ways, a person is inauthentic, that is, not one's self. Bultmann maintained that inauthenticity is precisely what the New Testament means by "sin" and by speaking of persons as "sinners" and under the sway of "death." It follows from this that salvation is radical openness to the future, namely, a person's complete recognition that they are a decision maker. Salvation can only be found by grace when a person receives it as a gift. Hence Bultmann contended that humans are in need of a savior and that authenticity can be realized only through the once-for-all fact of Jesus Christ.

FOR FURTHER READING

Primary Sources

Bultmann, Rudolf. *Jesus and the Word*. New York: Scribner, 1958.

———. *Jesus Christ and Mythology*. New York: Scribner, 1958.

———. *Theology of the New Testament*. 2 vols. Trans. Kendrick Grobel. New York: Scribner, 1951–55.

Secondary Sources

Cahill, P. Joseph. "Theological Significance of Rudolf Bultmann." *Theological Studies* 38 (1977): 231–74.

Jones, Hans. "Is Faith Still Possible: Memories of Rudolf Bultmann and Reflections on the Philosophical Aspects of His Work." *Harvard Theological Review* 75 (1982): 1–23.

Macquarrie, John. *The Scope of Demythologizing*. London: SCM, 1960.

Ogden, Schubert M. *Christ without Myth*. New York: Harper, 1961.

———. "The Significance of Rudolf Bultmann." *Perkins Journal* 15 (1962): 5–17.

Perrin, Norman. *The Promise of Bultmann*. Philadelphia: Lippincott, 1969.

CHAPTER 18

PAUL TILLICH

Theology of Culture

L ike Bultmann, German émigré theologian Paul Tillich (1886–1965) oper-
ated from an existentialist foundation, though he developed it in a markedly different way. Dismissed from his professorship at the University of
Frankfurt in 1933 after publicly opposing the Nazis, Tillich articulated a theology of culture throughout his subsequent career at Union Theological Seminary,
Harvard University, and the University of Chicago. Tillich argued that a theological system must state the truth of the Christian message and interpret that
truth for every new culture. This chapter unpacks the central ideas of Tillich's
three-volume magnum opus, *Systematic Theology*, which feature prominently
throughout his literary corpus. In the process, Tillich's concept of God as being-
itself, or the suprapersonal ground, power, and structure of being, is explained.
Given Tillich's concept of the fall as the state of human existential estrangement
from essential humanity, the quest for the new being becomes the implicit or
explicit quest of all religions. Tillich maintained that the new being—essential
being under the conditions of existence without being conquered by them—has
appeared in the personal life of Jesus of Nazareth. As a result, the new being in
Jesus as the Christ overcomes the estrangement between existential and essential
being for all who follow him, enabling them to obtain qualitatively eternal life.

TILLICH ON THE NATURE AND METHOD
OF SYSTEMATIC THEOLOGY

For Tillich, a theology of culture or "kerygmatic theology" should satisfy two
basic needs: it must state the truth of the Christian message and interpret that
truth for every new generation.[1] Thus a kerygmatic theology should move

between the two poles of eternal truth and temporal needs, while fundamentalism has erred by only recognizing eternal truth and failing to realize temporality. The kerygmatic theology must apply the kerygma, interpret it to the systems of our day, and serve as apologetic theology by answering questions put before it. Tillich explained the nature of systematic theology as a theological circle. One cannot simply attempt to inductively or deductively answer theological questions as a disinterested observer. Hence a kind of mystical experience is a priori for the theologian to enter the "circle" or sphere where theological concepts reside.[2] The theologian enters this circle by a voluntary act of commitment. If one attempts to enter by induction or deduction, then one is really in the religious-philosophical circle instead of the theological circle. But if one enters by making a commitment of will, then one is truly a theologian. Moreover, the theologian must be in a situation of faith, but she is paradoxically alienated as she is both in faith and doubt (the doubt is Kierkegaardian, the paradox Hegelian). As a result, the theologian is simultaneously inside and outside the theological circle, and she is never certain which side ultimately prevails. Tillich insists that being a theologian does not depend on regeneration, sanctification, or on whether one wants to accept or attack the theological circle.

Tillich posited that the two formal criteria for every theology are as follows. First, the object of theology is what concerns us ultimately. Only those propositions are theological that deal with their object insofar as it can become a matter of ultimate concern for us. The religious concern is ultimate and excludes all other concerns from being ultimate by making them preliminary. In Tillich's words, "Ultimate concern is the abstract translation of the great commandment: 'The Lord, our God, the Lord is one; and you shall love the Lord your God with all your heart, and with all your soul and with all your mind, and with all your strength.'"[3] The object of theology is called a "concern" to indicate the existential character of religious experience.[4]

Second, our ultimate concern is that which determines our being or not-being. Only those statements are theological that deal with their object insofar as it becomes a matter of being or not-being for us. Tillich defined being as "the whole of human reality, the structure, the meaning, and the aim of existence."[5] Tillich held that every theology discusses God, whether Christian or not, but Christian theology has its foundation in the Logos becoming flesh, thus implying its uniqueness and superiority: "If this message is true, Christian theology has received a foundation which transcends the foundation of any other theology and which itself cannot be transcended."[6] Christian theology focuses on the union between the infinite and the finite—the ultimate problem of existence—and provides a solution through the incarnation. Tillich proceeded to stipulate that the norm of Christian systematic theology is "the New Being in Jesus as the Christ as our ultimate concern."[7] In other words, the new being in Jesus as the Christ is the essential axiom through which one can address the fundamental existential questions about being and non-being. The new being in Jesus as the Christ, rather than the Bible, constitutes the theological norm, though it is derived from the Bible through an encounter with the church. As the norm for systematic theology, the new being in Jesus as the Christ determines how we use the sources for theology and mediates the criteria to which all the sources must be subjected.

On Tillich's reckoning, there are three sources of systematic theology: the Bible, church history, and material from the history of religion and culture. The Bible is the basic source because it is the original event and document on which the Christian church is founded, but it is only a witness to revelation rather than being itself revelation. Tillich understood the inspiration of the biblical authors as consisting of their participation and creativity, namely, their receptive and creative response to potentially revelatory facts. The Bible relates to church history in that the genesis of the Bible is an event in church history. So, in using the Bible, one is implicitly and explicitly using church history. Further, every person who encounters a biblical text is guided in her understanding of it by the understanding of all previous generations in church history. Material from the history of religion and culture forms the broadest source of systematic theology, as a person's spiritual life is influenced by the language she speaks and the cultural situation in which she has grown up. Every person formulates the existential question implied in her religion and culture, for which she intends systematic theology to answer. All three of Tillich's sources relate to the new being in Jesus as the Christ in the following way. The theologian has a vast amount of material on which to draw, but she cannot incorporate everything. Consequently, those items that most highly relate to the appearance of the new being in Jesus as the Christ must receive the most emphasis, while those items with a less direct or indirect emphasis on the appearance of the new being in Jesus as the Christ should receive less emphasis.

According to Tillich, experience is the medium of reception for the materials of systematic theology. He explained that experience may be thought of in three senses: an ontological sense, a scientific sense, and a mystical sense. The ontological sense is a consequence or result of philosophical positivism. Thus the only reality about which we can meaningfully speak is what is positively given through experience. If we incorporate the ontological sense for systematic theology, then systematic theology can incorporate nothing outside our five senses, thereby excluding a transcendent God. The scientific sense is an experimentally driven discipline of science that combines rational and perceptual elements in a never-ending process of experimenting and testing. Tillich declared that the scientific sense can never be part of systematic theology for two reasons: the object of theology is not an object within the whole of scientific experience but can only be found in an act of surrender and participation; and the object of theology cannot be tested by scientific methods of verification. The mystical sense is the key to experiential theology and is defined as experience by participation. Such experience by participation is secretly presupposed by the ontological and scientific senses. Hence the experience of the individual who has the Holy Spirit is greater than the law and is the source of both religious truth and systematic theology. Tillich alleged that the letter of the Bible and the doctrines of the church remain useless unless the Spirit interprets them in the life of each individual Christian. Therefore experience through the interpretive power of the Spirit is the ultimate source of theology.

Systematic theology's method, for Tillich, is the method of correlation. Tillich's method of correlation begins with an analysis of the human situation, for it is out of this analysis that existential questions arise (i.e., questions concerning the nature of existence). Next, the method demonstrates that the symbols used in systematic theology constitute answers to these questions, thereby correlating the symbols with the questions. The method of correlation is done in existential terms, or by determining the very meaning of existence, and implies the materials made available in humankind's creative self-interpretation in all realms of culture, like philosophy and sociology, to answer the question of human existence. The theologian organizes these materials and analyzes the human situation in terms of them in relation to the answer given by the Christian message.

Tillich provided three examples of how his method works. First, the problem of finitude is analyzed, which raises the dilemma that humankind is faced with the threat of non-being. The answer is God in correlation with the problem, namely, that God must be identified as the infinite power of being that resists the threat of non-being. Second, the problem of anxiety is analyzed, which yields an awareness of being finite. The answer is that God must be identified as the infinite ground of courage, a notion encapsulated in classical theology by God's universal providence, or the notion that God is in control of all things. Third, the problem of historical existence is analyzed, which raises the question of whether this riddle appears in the concept of the kingdom of God. The answer is that if the riddle does appear in God's kingdom, then the kingdom must be identified as the meaning, fulfillment, and unity of history to indicate that history is going somewhere and has a purpose.

According to Tillich, the three inadequate methods that the method of correlation replaces are the supranaturalistic method, the naturalistic or humanistic method, and the dualistic method. The supranaturalistic method takes the Christian message to be the sum of revealed truths that have fallen into the human situation like strange bodies falling from a strange world. Tillich claimed that this method must first create a new, foreign situation before these revealed truths can be received at all. Moreover, this method forces humans to receive answers to questions they have never asked, such that the answers are meaningless for our situation. The naturalistic or humanistic method derives the Christian message from humankind's natural state or existence, blissfully ignorant that human existence is the question desperately needing to be answered. The dualistic method builds a supranatural structure on a natural substructure and tries to explain the divine-human relationship as a body of theological truth that humans can reach through their own efforts, that is, through the use of natural revelation. Tillich claimed that the arguments produced by this method are true insofar as they analyze human finitude, but they are false insofar as they derive answers to the problem of finitude from finitude itself.

TILLICH'S CONCEPT OF GOD

Tillich's exploration of the concept of God begins with the question of being. The question of being asks the ontological question of what being-itself is. In other words, what is it that is not a particular being or group of beings, not something concrete or abstract, but the very nature and basis of being-itself which is always thought implicitly and sometimes explicitly if something is said to be? For Tillich, the answer to the question of being is God. Hence God is being-itself, the ultimate ground, basis, power, and structure of being and existence, who remains the subject in ontological discussions even when he is the logical object. Humanity's finitude causes us to ask the question of being, as there are four aspects of finitude that demand the question. First, finitude is the union of being and meontic non-being. To understand what Tillich meant by meontic non-being (from the Greek *mē*, indicating negation), we must contrast it with another sort of non-being, namely, oukontic non-being (from the Greek *ouk*, indicating strong negation). Oukontic non-being is the nothing that has no relation at all to being; it is the absolute opposite of being, or the total absence of any kind of being. It is absolute nothingness—the most radical form of non-being with no potentiality for existence whatsoever. However, meontic non-being is the nothing that has a dialectical relationship to being. It does not exist but has the potential to exist. Hence contingent being comes out of meontic non-being and still faces the danger of future nonexistence even when it exists. Second, humanity is estranged from the infinite. Third, humanity—as a form of finite or contingent being—is threatened by non-being. Fourth, the question remains whether contingent being can overcome and conquer non-being. Tillich argued that God, properly understood, is the infinite to whom humans can be reconciled and through whom humans can conquer non-being.

By saying that God is being-itself or the ground of being, Tillich meant that God is not a being alongside or above other beings or even the highest of all beings, in which case he would only be a specific being subjected to the categories of finitude. Rather, God is the power and subject-object structure of being who is not himself subject to the structure of being. For Tillich, only statements predicated on the notion that God is being-itself—being *qua* being—can be uttered about God in a nonsymbolic way. If one says that God is just, loving, or the Creator, one is using anthropomorphisms that cannot be understood literally. However, it is literally true that God has the power of determining the structure of everything that has being. While life is a process where potential being becomes actual being, in God there is no distinction between potentiality and actuality. More precisely, God transcends this distinction. So it is improper to speak of God as living or existing, as God is beyond such allegedly finite categories. While Tillich certainly asserted "the reality of God,"[8] "the actuality of God,"[9] and that "God is,"[10] his metaphysics caused him to regard the phrase "God exists" as a contradiction in terms, for "as being-itself God is beyond the contrast of essential and existential being . . . beyond essence and existence."[11] Tillich pointed out that "existence" comes from the Latin *existere*, which means "standing out of non-being."[12] But being-itself has no relation to non-being; it infinitely transcends and stands diametrically opposed to non-being. Since he believed the affirmation "God exists" implies God's emergence from non-being and possible future defeat by non-being, Tillich held that it is just as atheistic to say "God exists" as it is to say "God does not exist." In an attempt to prevent misunderstanding on this score, Tillich went on to assert that God lives insofar as he is the ground of life, but there could not be any process through which God is either potentialized or actualized. Thus God himself did not come into existence, but he is that which makes it possible for any specific being to move from potentiality to actuality.

As the ground and structure of being, God is the foundation of the three pairs of ontological elements. Tillich identified these pairs as individuality and participation, form and dynamics, and freedom and destiny. Individuality and participation relate to God because he is the ground of everything personal and carries within himself the ontological power of personality. On Tillich's view, God is not *a* person, but he is personal; historically, the Latin term *persona* was used to distinguish each of the three Trinitarian hypostases instead of the one God. Concerning form and dynamics, Tillich understood dynamics symbolically as divine creativity. God's participation in history includes an outgoing character where a "not yet" is always balanced by an "already" in the divine life. Form expresses the actualization of divine potentiality, which inescapably unites possibility with fulfillment. Tillich proposed that freedom and destiny are one in God. God's freedom is freedom from anything prior to God or alongside God, or his aseity or self-derived nature. The ultimate concern of humanity, namely, God, is independent of humanity or any finite being or concern. The relationship between destiny and history can be expressed in the statement "God is his own destiny,"[13] which avoids the connotation of a destiny-determining power above God. This statement demands that God is his own law and points both to the infinite mystery of being and God's becoming in history.

In the history of religious thought, Tillich differentiated between three kinds of monotheism, of which he advocated the third: monarchic, mystical, and exclusive. *Monarchic monotheism* is the boundary line between monotheism and polytheism, since it affirms God as the monarch over a hierarchy of inferior gods or lower godlike beings. In monarchic monotheism, the divine powers of polytheism are subject to the ultimate monotheistic divine power. An example of monarchic monotheism is the Greco-Roman pantheon, which featured a number of gods with one supreme over all. For Tillich, monarchic monotheism is unacceptable because it affirms the reality of the polytheistic gods and renders the supreme god as merely one being among many.

In polar contradistinction to monarchic monotheism, *mystical monotheism* claims that God transcends all realms of being, value, and their divine representatives in favor of the divine ground and abyss from which they came and in which they disappear. Thus God is the One or the Ultimate; there is only one God, but he totally transcends all concrete reality. Tillich charged mystical monotheism with wrongfully surrendering God's concreteness, which is part of . humanity's ultimate concern.

Exclusive monotheism—which Tillich viewed as the monotheism of Christianity—is created by the elevation of a concrete God to ultimacy and universality without the loss of his concreteness and without asserting some sort of demonic power about this God. This dilemma raises the Trinitarian problem, which for Tillich is not a matter of the number three, how three can be one, or how one can be three. Rather, it is a qualitative, not quantitative, attempt to speak of a living God in whom concreteness and ultimacy are united. Hence the Trinitarian problem is founded on the paradox that God became incarnate in a human life, Jesus of Nazareth, who made an unapproachable God concrete in time and space and served as the basis of religious experience.

TILLICH'S CHRISTOLOGY

Tillich insisted that the issue of Christology is made urgent by the existentialist problem. This problem is that we as individuals, while something not currently lacking being and standing out of absolute (oukontic) non-being, are relatively non-being (meontic), in that we will (apart from divine intervention) die, cease to exist, and thereby come to nothing. Accordingly, there will be a moment when "I" will no longer exist, which creates ultimate existential despair, hopelessness, and meaninglessness. But this problem demands that we also analyze how we came into being. Prior to our coming into being, we participated in potential being even though we were not yet actualized, and thus we were not a total nothing or blank in potentiality despite our participation in meontic non-being. Paradoxically, we were both relative non-being and already at least a something. Such a split in reality between potentiality and actuality is deemed by Tillich as the first step toward the solution of the existentialist problem. In philosophical discussion, the potential realm is equated with the essential realm (the essence of things or the ideal form of description), and the actual realm (what really exists) is equated with the existential realm. For humans to exist, therefore, means to stand out of our essence as one would in a fall. Tillich's concept of the fall is therefore the state of human existential estrangement from essential humanity, or the seemingly unbridgeable gap separating what we actually are from what we could potentially be. Thus Genesis 1–3 "can guide our description of the transition from essential to existential being. It is the profoundest and richest expression of man's awareness of his existential estrangement and provides the scheme in which the transition from essence to existence can be treated."[14] This concept amounts to a tremendous protest against Hegel's essentialism, as it yields the conclusion that humanity's existential situation is its state of estrangement from its essential nature. Contrary to Hegel's claim that everything humanity could potentially be has been actualized, the existentialist affirms that there is a gap between potentiality and actuality, for the estrangement has not been overcome. Existence, Tillich contended, is estrangement and not reconciliation; it is dehumanization, not the expression of essential humanity. Existence is a process in which someone becomes a thing and ceases to be a person. Moreover, history is not, *pace* Hegel, the divine self-manifestation, but a series of unreconciled conflicts threatening humanity with self-destruction. Tillich judged that existence is filled with anxiety and terrorized by meaninglessness, while Hegel's essentialism comprises an attempt to hide the truth about humanity's actual state.

The existentialist problem leads humanity on a quest for the new being. Tillich conceived of the new being as the transformed reality and transformed history that occurs in and through a historical process that is unique, unrepeatable, and irreversible. This new being solves the existentialist problem by bridging the gap of existence and essence in the person of Jesus Christ, as the Messiah or Christ conquered humanity's estrangement from God through a new reality that defeats the old reality. According to Tillich, existentialism has analyzed the old eon, namely, the predicament of humanity and its world in the state of estrangement. In doing so, it has become the natural ally of Christianity—or "the good luck of Christian theology"[15]—because it points to the great need of humanity and prepares individuals for what Christianity says about Christ. Therefore Christianity is especially important in the quest for the new being because its decisive event gives history its center. It balances the "not yet" of Judaism with the "already" of the kingdom of God through the revelatory possibility of any moment in history. All of this is embodied in the title "the Christ," the name Christianity applies to the bearer of the new being in its final manifestation. Hence Christianity contains within it what all other religions are searching for: the bearer of the new reality that conquers human estrangement from God and bridges the gap of existence and essence, namely, Jesus Christ.

For Tillich, the historical person Jesus of Nazareth constitutes essential being under the conditions of existence without being conquered by them, which makes him the Christ. The fate of each individual as well as the entire universe is bound up in him: "The function of the bearer of the New Being is not only to save individuals and to transform man's historical existence but to renew the universe. And the assumption is that mankind and individual men are so dependent on the powers of the universe that salvation of the one without the other is unthinkable."[16] The birth of Christianity, Tillich alleged, occurred not at Pentecost but at Caesarea Philippi when Simon Peter recognized Jesus as the bearer of the new being, the conqueror of the existential predicament. Anxious to preclude any mythological understanding of a deity siring a son, Tillich insisted that referring to Jesus as the "Son of God" must be understood in a symbolic sense rather than any family relationship in the life of the divine. Being the "Son of God" meant for Tillich that Jesus represented the essential unity between God and humanity under the conditions of existence and reestablished the unity between God and humanity for all those who participate in his being.

Tillich maintained that individual salvation bears a threefold character. First, salvation is participation in the new being, or regeneration. Tillich defined regeneration (i.e., new birth, being a new creature) as the new state of things universally, the new eon, which the Christ brought. The individual enters it, and in so doing the individual participates in it and is reborn through participation. Hence the objective reality of the new being precedes individual participation in it. Tillich therefore cast conversion in existential terms: "The message of conversion is, first, the message of a new reality to which one is asked to turn; in the light of it, one is to move away from the old reality, the state of existential estrangement in which one has lived."[17]

Second, salvation is acceptance of the new being, or justification. Tillich identified justification as the immediate consequence of the doctrine of atonement and the heart and center of salvation. Like regeneration, justification is first an objective event and then a subjective reception. In the objective sense, justification is "the eternal act of God by which he accepts as not estranged those who are indeed estranged from him by guilt and the act by which he takes them into the unity with him which is manifest in the New Being in Christ."[18] For Tillich, there is nothing in humanity that enables God to accept humanity. But the individual must accept in faith—justifying faith—that she is accepted by God because of Christ.

Third, salvation is transformation by the new being, or sanctification. Tillich described sanctification as the process in which the power of the new being transforms personality and community inside and outside the church. Persons who possess salvation are centered, self-conscious selves who cannot be excluded from eternal life: "The dimension of the spirit which in all its functions presupposes self-consciousness cannot be denied eternal fulfilment, just as eternal fulfilment cannot be denied to the biological dimension and therefore to the body."[19] Eschatologically, Tillich felt that more than this cannot be said.

CONCLUSION

Tillich is a controversial and provocative theologian. Whether Tillich has successfully transposed the Christian message into the language of existentialism or has significantly altered the Christian message under the guise of such transposition is a matter of continuing debate. In either case, Tillich is responsible for advancing the conversation between the realms of Christian theology and existentialist philosophy in a way somewhat similar to but far exceeding in breadth and depth the way charted by Bultmann.

FOR FURTHER READING

Primary Sources

Tillich, Paul. *Biblical Religion and the Search for Ultimate Reality*. Chicago: University of Chicago Press, 1955.

———. *The Courage to Be*. New Haven, CT: Yale University Press, 1952.

———. *Love, Power, and Justice*. Oxford: Oxford University Press, 1960.

———. *Systematic Theology*. 3 vols. in 1. Chicago: University of Chicago Press, 1967.

Secondary Sources

Clayton, John. "Tillich, Troeltsch and the Dialectical Theology." *Modern Theology* 4 (1988): 323–44.

Hummel, Gert, ed. *God and Being: The Problem of Ontology in the Philosophical Theology of Paul Tillich*. Berlin: de Gruyter, 1988.

Manning, Russell R., ed. *The Cambridge Companion to Paul Tillich*. Cambridge: Cambridge University Press, 2009.

McDonald, H. D. "The Symbolistic Christology of Paul Tillich." *Vox Evangelica* 18 (1988): 75–88.

Otto, Randall E. "The Doctrine of God in the Theology of Paul Tillich." *Westminster Theological Journal* 52 (1990): 303–23.

CHAPTER 19

DEATH OF GOD
THEOLOGIES

O n April 8, 1966, *Time* magazine featured a cover that was completely black except for three words emblazoned in bright, red letters against the dark background: "Is God Dead?" In the counterculture movement, many "baby boomers" rejected the ambitions, morals, politics, and social values of their parents in favor of something that was uniquely their own. These baby boomers resonated with the open hostility to Christianity shown by German philosopher Friedrich Nietzsche (1844–1900). Nietzsche had asserted that "God is dead" and that humankind must learn to live without him. Reaching the height of their popularity in the 1960s, death of God theologies asserted either the meaning-lessness of the concept of God in a secular world or God's ceasing to exist. The former was most famously asserted by Paul Van Buren (1924–88), and the latter was most famously asserted by Thomas J. J. Altizer (1927–). This chapter traces the thought of Van Buren and Altizer, exploring why each figure proclaimed, "God is dead," and preferred Jesus over God in his radical recasting of the gospel.

VAN BUREN'S SECULAR MEANING OF THE GOSPEL

Representative of Van Buren's thought is his 1963 book *The Secular Meaning of the Gospel*. Van Buren began by employing three recent figures to illustrate what he saw as the problem of the Christian living in a modern, secular world.

First is German theologian and anti-Nazi dissident Dietrich Bonhoeffer (1906–45), who spoke of Christians living in a world "come of age." Van Buren gave his own spin to Bonhoeffer's thought, one that Bonhoeffer himself, who remained an orthodox Christian, would have rejected. For Van Buren, in a world "come of age," men and women no longer believe in a transcendent realm where their longings will be fulfilled by and by. Thus one must live as if there is no God. Not wanting to throw out Christianity altogether, Van Buren picked up on Bonhoeffer's non-religious interpretation of biblical concepts and advocacy of a "religionless Christianity." While Bonhoeffer meant by this phrase that the boundaries between organized religion and everyday life should be removed, Van Buren took it to mean a godless Christianity. For Van Buren, Bonhoeffer's work ultimately leaves us with this question: How can Christians who are themselves secular persons understand the gospel in a secular way?

The second figure Van Buren cited is English philosopher Antony Flew (1923–2010), who told the parable of the invisible gardener. In this parable, two explorers in a jungle come upon a clearing with many flowers and many weeds. One explorer says, "Some gardener must tend this plot." The other disagrees: "There is no gardener." So they pitch their tents and set a watch, and no gardener is ever seen. The first explorer responds, "But he is an invisible gardener." So they set up an electrified barbed-wire fence and patrol it with bloodhounds, but no shriek ever suggests that some intruder has received a shock, no movement of the wire ever betrays an invisible climber, and the bloodhounds never give cry. Yet still the first explorer is unconvinced, protesting: "But there is a gardener, invisible, intangible, insensible to electric shocks, who has no scent and makes no sound, who comes secretly to look after the garden he loves." At last the second explorer retorts, "But what is left of your original assertion? How does what you call an invisible, intangible, eternally elusive gardener differ from no gardener at all?" By postulating that the gardener has one more mysterious attribute after another, the hypothesis of the gardener finally dies what Flew called the death of a thousand qualifications. Interestingly, while Flew spent most of his career as an atheist, he became a theist toward the close of his career, arguing on the basis of cosmological and teleological arguments that verifiable affirmations can be made of God, who does not therefore suffer the fate of the gardener. But Van Buren argued that religious assertions about belief in God are of the same nature as assertions about the invisible gardener. Ultimately, they amount to nothing, dying the death of a thousand qualifications, and bear the same meaning as the statement, "There is no God."

Third, Van Buren turned to Rudolf Bultmann, specifically his belief that the Bible presents a mythological worldview. In light of the scientific revolution, Van Buren maintained that we have a different way of seeing and thinking about the world than the ancients, necessitating that we employ various tools to uncover the demythologized meaning of the gospel.

These tools, Van Buren insisted, come from the field of linguistic analysis, especially as influenced by logical positivism and Ludwig Wittgenstein. Van Buren appealed to the positivists' verificationist principle of meaning, observing that on that principle language about God as invisible and transcendent is absolutely meaningless. Despite its criticism as self-referentially incoherent, Van Buren believed that the verificationist principle continues to be important in a modified form, which asks what sort of things would count for an assertion and what sort of things would count against it. For if we know that, then we can say in which language game the assertion is at home. This assumes Wittgenstein's claim that the meaning of a sentence is its use in its language game. Consequently, Van Buren's answer to the problem of the meaning of the gospel is to submit its language to linguistic analysis to see how that language is used or functions. In doing so, we must take seriously three factors: the concern for Christology, the need for a contemporary way of thinking, and the logical analysis of theological statements.

Van Buren then turned to the analysis of religious language. Defining religion as "the attempted enlargement of reality by means of God,"[1] Van Buren commented that religion invokes God to explain, justify, or fill in our picture of the world or our understanding of human affairs. By contrast, a religionless posture involves "coming to terms with reality apart from God,"[2] or at least without use of the God hypothesis. For Van Buren, the problem with the views of his theological contemporaries—from Barth on the right to Bultmann on the left—is that they continue to speak about God despite that a considerable proportion of people do not even understand what "God" means. Van Buren noted that the solution proposed by some existentialists consists of continuing to use the term *God* while eliminating all objectification of God in thought and word, that is, all thinking of God as a distinct being with objective reality outside the human mind. But this solution must be rejected because it meaninglessly uses *God* as a symbol for some facet of human experience that cannot be verified, such as a numinous encounter or viewpoint. Van Buren summed up the problem empirical, modern humanity has with objective and nonobjective God-language alike:

> The empiricist in us finds the heart of the difficulty not in what is said about God, but in the very talking about God at all. We do not know what God is, and we cannot understand how the word "God" is being used. It seems to function as a name, yet theologians tell us that we cannot use it as we do other names to refer to something quite specific. If it is meant to refer to an existentialist encounter, a point of view, or the speaker's self-understanding, surely a more appropriate expression could be found. The problem is not

solved, moreover, by substituting other words for the word "God." One could supply the letter X—Flew used the word "gardener" in his parable—and the problem would remain. For the difficulty has to do with how X functions. The problem of the gospel in a secular age is a problem of the logic of its apparently meaningless language, and linguistic analysts will give us help in clarifying it.[3]

From this Van Buren proceeded to the analysis of religious assertions, as opposed to terms alone, and queried how they are used.

Synthesizing the work of English philosophers R. M. Hare (1919–2002) and R. B. Braithwaite (1900–1990), Van Buren formulated a noncognitive understanding of theological language. In conversation with Flew's parable of the invisible gardener, Hare offered his own parable about a student with an insane fear that there are people trying to kill him. No matter how much his friends present evidence to the contrary, this student is convinced beyond a shadow of a doubt that people are out to kill him. The student with this insane view has what Hare dubbed a different "blik" than everyone else has. By "blik" Hare meant a fundamental attitude, a particular way of seeing the world, or a mind-set. A blik is not something that one achieves by empirical investigation, nor does one discard it by rational or empirical argumentation. Rather, a blik captures our basic conceptual grid of the world. For Hare, the person who uses religious language uses it as an expression of a blik, namely, his or her orientation or commitment to see the world in a particular fashion and to live accordingly. Thus Van Buren maintained that religious language is meaningful, but that meaning does not lie in any attempt to literally make assertions about God and his relationship to the world. Its meaningfulness lies in the fact that it expresses a commitment to view life and the world in a specific way. Similar to Hare, Braithwaite argued that religious language is not like the language of empirical observation, the language of a general theory, or the language of mathematics and logic, the three types of language meaningful in light of the verification criterion. However, religious language is meaningful because it is used conatively, or as an expression of the user's intention to act in a certain way. Hence Christians have historically used religious language to express their intention to live an agape-istic way of life, an assessment with which Van Buren concurred. Religious language also expresses an association of certain stories—whether Bible stories for Christians or other scriptural stories for adherents to non-Christian religions—with the user's intention to act. While these stories are not assertions of fact but are rather mythological, they possess a psychological and causal relation to the user's intention to act, as perceiving a course of behavior as God's will increases the likelihood that the user will carry it out. Consequently, Van Buren's conception of the meaningfulness of religious language binds together worldview, sacred stories, and action as respectively supplying the framework to make sense of a behavior, the motivation to perform that behavior, and the execution of that behavior.

But for modern Christians who do not wish to play the language game of conative bliks but only wish to utter the empirically meaningful language of secularism, Van Buren submitted that linguistic analysis raises the question, What is the real issue of Christian faith: Jesus or God, Christology or theology? Van Buren chooses the former term in each related pair, for now the traditional concept of God revealed in and through the language of Scripture is dead. Accordingly, the secular meaning of the gospel focuses on Jesus Christ, a first-century Jew whose existence can be historically verified. But linguistic analysis still bears the further task of demythologizing those statements about Jesus that cannot be taken as straightforward literal empirical assertions, such as the New Testament accounts of Easter. For the secular meaning of the gospel hinges not only on the historical fact of Jesus's life but also on the historical reality behind the Easter narratives. This historical reality, judged Van Buren, is that certain people, including the disciples, sincerely believed they saw Jesus alive after his death (even though their belief was mistaken but arose purely from psychological processes) and therefore viewed Jesus in a new way. This view awakened in them the same kind of freedom that Jesus had, namely, the freedom from self and the freedom to be for others. Hence the secular meaning of the gospel is that Jesus, though a figure of the past, offers modern humans the selfless, agape-istic freedom that he embodied.

ALTIZER'S GOSPEL OF CHRISTIAN ATHEISM

Even more radical than Van Buren was Altizer. Holding to the literal meaning of the term *God*, Altizer claimed that the Christian alone can speak of God in our time. But the message the Christian proclaims is the gospel, the good news or glad tidings, of the death of God—namely, that the transcendent, personal creator of the universe who once existed has ceased to exist, and has ceased to exist for the sake of humanity. Such a message, alleged Altizer, serves as a breath of fresh air in a modern culture that finds the traditional concept of God irrelevant. Altizer declared that for many years science has removed God from contemporary thought, thus isolating faith from concrete human experience. In reaction, theology ceased to speak about the Word of faith and dared to attack the outside world of anti-faith. But the Christian can now herald the rejection of the transcendent God and the affirmation of a totally incarnate Word. This offers a form of faith totally engaged with the world and rejects all forms of faith that disengage from the world and flee from it as though the world were unimportant.

Central to Altizer's death of God theology is his Christology. Altizer remarked that the nature of oriental mysticism, out of which most world religions spring, is a radical world negation. Such a world negation was roundly criticized by such prominent nineteenth-century thinkers as Friedrich Nietzsche (1844–1900), William Blake (1757–1827), and G. W. F. Hegel (1770–1831), as any healthy and morally responsible system of thought must embrace the value of the world and focus on solving its problems. Thus it is vitally significant that, regarding world negation, Christianity stands in sharp contrast to other religions. For Altizer, the uniqueness of Christianity is that the Christian Word comes neither in a primordial nor eternal form, but as an incarnate Word, a Word that is real only to the extent that it becomes one with human flesh. Altizer argued that from eternity past, the transcendent God existed. This God was a unitarian, not a Trinitarian, being and thus comprised one person; moreover, God was endowed with the great-making character attributes of classical theism, including being all-loving and all-just. God proceeded to create humankind, depending on the hope that they would always do right and hence receive his rewards. But humanity fell into sin, and God foreknew that every future human would also commit sin, such that the following scenario would forever be true of the human race: "'There is no one righteous; not even one.... All have turned away, they have together become worthless; there is no one who does good, not even one.'... For all have sinned and fall short of the glory of God" (Rom. 3:10, 12, 23). Hence God realized that his justice would compel him to eternally condemn every human being to hell—that is, if he continued to exist.

To save humanity from damnation, God committed deicide or self-annihilation by the *kenosis* of becoming totally incarnate in Jesus Christ. On Altizer's account, kenosis, or the emptying of Christ, becomes very important, but not in the orthodox sense. In the orthodox sense, Christ emptied himself by taking on full humanity, thereby laying aside for a time the exercising of the power and privileges unique to his deity in order to save us. But Christ never abandoned his deity. In contrast to the orthodox conception, kenosis for Altizer means a radical transformation and metamorphosis of the primordial God into flesh. God in becoming incarnate literally died in his transcendent, primordial form, which is forever abandoned or negated. At the moment of Jesus's conception in the womb of Mary, therefore, atheism became true. Here we see that Altizer reversed the orthodox confession that Jesus is God. Instead of saying

Jesus is God, Altizer said God—or rather the person formerly known as God—is Jesus. Altizer insisted that in committing deicide to redeem humanity, God was finally able to manifest his all-loving nature by becoming love:

> Already in the Gospel of John we find the revolutionary Christian proclamation that God is love. But despite the fact that Christian faith has invariably given witness to the reality of the compassion of God, Christian theology has been unable to incorporate this primary core of faith, if only because it has ever remained bound to an idea of God as a wholly self-sufficient, self-enclosed, and absolutely autonomous being. Even when theologians have rediscovered the *agape*, or total self-giving of God, they have confined it to the movement of the Incarnation, and thus have dualistically isolated God's love from the primordial nature and existence of God himself. So long as God is known in his primordial form as an eternal and unchanging being, he can never be known in his incarnate form as self-giving or self-negating being. The radical Christian refuses to speak of God's existence . . . because he knows that God has negated and transcended himself in the Incarnation, and thereby he has fully and finally ceased to exist in his original and primordial form. To know that God is Jesus is to know that God himself has become flesh. No longer does God exist as transcendent Spirit or sovereign Lord; now God is love.[4]

But this, for Altizer, is not enough, because it only serves to rescue us from hell and assuage our fear of damnation. The kenotic self-emptying of the Word must continue until it reaches and morally changes every human being for the better.

The consummation of the Word's kenotic self-emptying occurs when Jesus dies on the cross. At this point, the person who had once been God finally ceases to exist. Jesus pours out himself at Calvary, thus uniformly diffusing his very being—the Word, the essence of love—throughout the universe. Hence the incarnate Word experiences a forward movement from Jesus to all humanity, such that the love of God is now seen in every human visage: "The Word continues its kenotic movement and direction by moving from the historical Jesus to the universal body of humanity, thereby undergoing an epiphany in every human hand and face."[5] Echoing Bultmann, Altizer maintained that this totally immanent Word offers each person the power of existential transformation, so that each person may freely tap into the Word at the core of his being and find authentic, qualitatively eternal life. "A fundamental problem posed by the radical Christian vision of Christ is the concrete identity of the incarnate Word. Here, as we have seen, the Word is not confined to the particular man Jesus of Nazareth. . . . No, the totally incarnate Word can only be the Jesus who is present in what Blake called experience, the Jesus who is actually and fully incarnate in every human. . . . The radical Christian knows that God has truly died in Jesus, and that his death has liberated humanity."[6] In the end, Altizer's gospel proclaims the "good news" that, in an outpouring of his love, God ceased to exist both as deity and as a person in order that humans may fearlessly and authentically live. Moreover, the Word perseveres in this world in the quest for justice and liberation.

CONCLUSION

Death of God theologies took to its logical extreme an underlying subtext of much of Western philosophy and theology since Kant—the postulate that a transcendent God at best could not be known and at worst did not exist at all. Indeed, the phrase "God is dead" was first coined by Nietzsche. Since God is not empirically verifiable, death of God theologies propose that nontheistic explanations must now be substituted for theistic ones in all realms of life, including modern Christianity. Humanity may only speak of Christ, not God. Moreover, the death of God actually beckons humanity to look upon Jesus as a moral exemplar of how to live in the secular world. While death of God theologies quickly became regarded as too radical and faded from prominence in the 1970s, they bequeathed to many later systems of thought a commitment to secularism as intellectually normative and ethically good.

FOR FURTHER READING

Primary Sources

Altizer, Thomas J. J. *The Gospel of Christian Atheism*. Philadelphia: Westminster, 1966.

Van Buren, Paul M. *The Secular Meaning of the Gospel: Based on Analysis of Its Language*. New York: Macmillan, 1963.

Secondary Sources

Butler, Clark. "Hegel, Altizer and Christian Atheism." *Encounter* 41 (1980): 103–28.

Caputo, John D., and Gianni Vattimo. *After the Death of God*. Ed. Jeffrey W. Robbins. Columbia, NY: Columbia University Press, 2007.

Cobb, John B., ed. *The Theology of Altizer: Critique and Response*. Philadelphia: Westminster, 1970.

Murchland, Bernard, ed. *The Meaning of the Death of God*. New York: Random House, 1967.

Sabatino, Charles J. "The Death of God: A Symbol for Religious Humanism." *Horizons* 10 (1983): 288–303.

Taylor, Mark C. "The Anachronism of A/theology." *Religion and Intellectual Life* 5 (1988): 22–36.

CHAPTER 20

ROMAN CATHOLIC THEOLOGY FROM VATICAN II TO THE PRESENT

Vatican I's rejection of modernity made the Roman Catholic Church seem reactionary and out-of-date to many Catholics and non-Catholics. Hence a large number of Catholics tried to move the church to catch up with the times. For instance, the activist Dorothy Day (1897–1980) worked for such social causes as pacifism and women's suffrage through the prism of the Catholic Church. Another figure longing for change was the Venetian cardinal Angelo Giuseppe Roncalli (1881–1963), who in 1958 ascended to the papacy and took the name John XXIII (r. 1958–63). Despite his peasant background, Roncalli established himself as a scholar early in life, earning a doctorate in theology in 1904 while still in his twenties. Throughout his career as a priest and patriarch (cardinal-archbishop) of Venice, he distinguished himself as a skillful diplomat and spearheaded humanitarian work. On his becoming pope at the age of seventy-six, Roncalli was presumed to be little more than a temporary sustainer of the status quo, as the College of Cardinals frequently conveys its expectations by the age of the man they elect to the papacy. No one could have predicted that this scholarly and elderly pontiff who desired only to be a "good shepherd" would usher in a new era for the Roman Catholic Church. Yet a new era is precisely what John XXIII intended from the very start of his pontificate. Less than three months after his election, he convened the twenty-first ecumenical council to meet at the Vatican in Rome. The council, known as Vatican II (1962–65), ranks with the Council of Trent (1545–63) and the Fourth Lateran Council (1215) in importance. This chapter will describe the significant changes to Roman Catholicism made by Vatican II and its proceeding developments.

THE SECOND VATICAN COUNCIL AND THE LAITY

As the Second Vatican Council opened on October 11, 1962, questions abounded in the participants' minds as to whether the Catholic Church could modernize and present itself as relevant in the post–World War II secular society. In response, Pope John XXIII proclaimed the goal of Vatican II as *aggiornamento* (updating) of the Catholic Church to the contemporary world, which included a spirit of change and open-mindedness. *Aggiornamento* indicated that the Catholic Church had emerged from the reactionary antimodernist isolation epitomizing Vatican I. Vatican II carried out *aggiornamento* through the influence of the church's leading thinkers. At least four future pontiffs took part in Vatican II: Cardinal Giovanni Battista Montini (1897–1978; r. 1963–78), later Paul VI; Bishop Albino Luciani (1912–78; r. 1978), later John Paul I; Bishop Karol Wojtyla (1920–2005; r. 1978–2005), later John Paul II; and Father Joseph Ratzinger (1927–; r. 2005–13), later Benedict XVI. Moreover, several Catholic luminaries served as *periti*, or theological advisers to the bishops, including Hans Küng (1928–), Henri de Lubac (1896–1991), Yves Congar (1904–95), Marie-Dominique Chenu (1895–1990), Jean Daniélou (1905–74), and Karl Rahner (1904–84). Vatican II applied *aggiornamento* to both praxis and theology, thereby throwing "open the windows of the church to let the fresh breezes blow through it."[1]

When Pope John XXIII died in 1963, Vatican II was automatically suspended according to the dictates of canon law. But his successor, Pope Paul VI, immediately reconvened Vatican II and saw it to completion. Paul VI overtly embraced John XXIII's ideology for himself: "We cannot forget Pope John XXIII's word *aggiornamento* which we have adopted as expressing the aim and object of our own pontificate. Besides ratifying it and confirming it as the guiding principle of the Ecumenical Council, we want to bring it to the notice of the whole Church. It should prove a stimulus to the Church to increase its ever growing vitality and its ability to take stock of itself and give careful consideration to the signs of the times."[2]

Vatican II went on to make practical changes specifically geared to make the church more receptive to the laity. The vernacular was substituted for Latin in the Mass—a step many Catholics deemed to be long overdue—such that the laity could now understand what was being said. Eradicating the Index of Prohibited Books, a creation of Trent, proved to be another step toward modernization and gave the laity greater intellectual freedom. New translations and editions of the Bible were made to render the Scriptures more accessible to lay Catholics, who had tended to regard the Bible as the province of the clerical specialists and thus as off-limits to them. The laity were assigned a more active role in church affairs, as teachers, as eucharistic ministers who distribute the Communion elements, and as partners in ongoing consultations with the clergy. Vatican II, therefore, attempted to bridge the ancient chasm separating laity and priesthood in as many ways as possible without eliminating the essential difference between the two.

Time-honored symbols of the clergy-laity separation fell to the wayside in favor of new symbols affirming the unity of the two groups. Abolished was the custom of the priest's reciting Mass at the altar, placed at the east end of the church, while facing away from the people. Now the priest of the post-Vatican II church stands facing the people to celebrate Mass at a special Communion table placed much closer to the congregation. Vatican II incorporated new musical forms, stretching from the popular to the esoteric, into the liturgy. It also allowed the laity to receive both the host (consecrated bread) and the cup (consecrated wine)—both kinds—in the Eucharist, a privilege formerly reserved for the clergy. Since the Fourth Vatican Council, laity had only been permitted to receive the host. Moreover, females were empowered to serve as altar girls, and they presently outnumber their male counterparts in many parts of the world. Vatican II authorized laypeople to deliver the Eucharist to the sick in hospitals and to furnish other forms of pastoral care.

Aside from liturgy, Vatican II introduced many other new forms of lay involvement in the life of the church. Laity are now consulted in matters of faith, where several committees and advisory boards within parishes and dioceses consult with their priests and bishops as to their own needs and desires. One of the most significant areas of lay involvement in the work of the church is the endeavor to bring new members into the Catholic fold. The Rite of Christian Initiation for Adults (RCIA) is a parish-level movement that pairs lay Catholics with prospective members from other Christian churches, other religions, or no religious background at all, so as to help them learn about Catholicism. Throughout the process, sponsors (the members) and catechumens (the inquirers) meet weekly to discuss the week's Scripture passages and facets of Roman Catholic doctrine. Instead of being authoritatively instructed by clergy as previous generations were, today's initiates share in a partnership and so feel part of the community before they have officially joined it.

THE SECOND VATICAN COUNCIL AND ECUMENISM

One of the most distinguishing features of Vatican II was its new ecumenical outlook. Before Vatican II, Catholics' relationships with other Christians were defined by the former attempting to persuade the latter to repent of their heresy by returning to the mother church. By contrast, the ecumenism of Vatican II emphasized first the need for reform from within the Roman Church itself. This reform would, in turn, constitute a basis for genuine dialogue that attempted to both understand other viewpoints and explain Roman Catholic teaching. As Vatican II explained in its decree *Unitatis Redintegratio* (Restoration of Unity) of November 21, 1964:

> There can be no ecumenism worthy of the name without a change of heart. It is from renewal of the inner life of our minds, from self-denial, and from an unstinted love that desires of unity take their rise and develop in a mature way. We should therefore pray to the Holy Spirit for the grace to be genuinely self-denying, humble, and gentle in the service of others and have an attitude of brotherly generosity towards them. . . . The words of St. John hold good about sins against unity: "If we say we have not sinned, we make him a liar, and his word is not in us." So we humbly beg pardon of God and of our separated brethren, just as we forgive them that trespass against us.[3]

Vatican II quickly made good on its word. It declared that Protestants were no longer to be dismissed as heretics but regarded as "separated brethren" (*fratres seiuncti*) who possessed "many elements of sanctification and of truth."[4] On December 7, 1965, Pope Paul VI and the Orthodox patriarch of Constantinople, Athenagoras, issued simultaneously in Rome and Istanbul a joint declaration of remorse for past actions that issued in the Great Schism of 1054 between the Western and Eastern churches. Paul VI officially revoked the 1054 Roman Catholic excommunication of the Orthodox Church that finalized the split. Vatican II invited to its proceedings a large number of non-Catholic theologians and religious leaders, and their attendance amounted to more than a gesture of goodwill: it was intended to be the beginning of lasting dialogue.

Among the various bodies established by the council to implement its decisions was the Secretariat for the Promotion of the Unity of Christians. The secretariat's *Decree on Ecumenism* called for a more complete communion among Christian communities. Astonishingly, it recognized that certain articles of Catholic belief were "negotiable"[5]—subject to respectful disagreement by other Christians—while others were held in common with other Christians and hence outside of debates about potential alteration. For a church that since the Middle Ages had seen itself as the only true and valid one, this constituted an extraordinary move toward appeasement. This move has brought Roman Catholicism into conversation with the writings of contemporary Eastern Orthodox theologians John Meyendorff (1926–1992) and John Zizioulas (1931–).

Moreover, Vatican II acknowledged, not uncontroversially, the possibility of salvation in various non-Christian religions, such as Judaism and Islam, in which the creator God is worshiped. In *Nostra Aetate*, the council declared that those who have not yet embraced the Christian gospel are related in various ways to the people of God. Jews, in particular, remain dear to God. With the Holocaust still a clear memory, the council proclaimed that the Jewish people as a whole were not responsible for the death of Jesus, such that Jews cannot be considered accursed by God. The council therefore declared that Catholics now pray *for* Jews, not for the *conversion* of Jews. The plan of salvation also includes all who acknowledge the Creator, including Muslims, on whom the church looks with esteem. According to Vatican II, persons who through no fault of their own do not know the Christian gospel but who strive to do God's will by conscience can be saved. Vatican II insists that salvation still comes through the church, whether or not such recipients realize it.[6] Although couched in ambiguous language, these statements could easily be taken as a radical reinterpretation of the nature of the Catholic Church, according to which great numbers of non-Christians are specifically related to the church.

Following the council, ecumenical efforts between prominent Catholic, Protestant, and Orthodox theologians led to the weakening of theological barriers between their confessions. In 1972 the Secretariat for the Promotion of the Unity of Christians spelled out conditions under which members of other Christian denominations could participate in Catholic Communion. Since the Eucharist has been the central experience in Catholic life, defining who can and cannot come together at the altar is virtually synonymous in Catholic thought to determining who is and is not a Christian. While non-Catholics have always been welcome to attend and observe the Mass, receiving the Eucharist is a form of being present at the Last Supper and sharing in that mysterious oneness with Jesus. The secretariat permitted any Christian who has a "serious spiritual need for the Eucharistic sustenance" and who believes in a sacramentally ordained clergy to partake of the "ecclesial communion" of the eucharistic sacrament. But only in the case of "urgent necessity" (left undefined by the secretariat) can someone who fails to meet these conditions join in eucharistic Communion.[7] Through discussions over the ensuing decades, several churches that originated in Reformation-era divisions from the Roman Church have found themselves in "full communion" with it, in a coexistence that many theologians on all sides consider the best of both worlds. Many Lutherans and Anglicans (Episcopalians), for example, now enjoy full communion with the Roman Church. The "separated" churches are free to retain their distinct identity, polity, and history without being condemned as heretical, while sharing the sacraments with the church from which they broke away centuries earlier.

In a dialogue lasting more than thirty years, Roman Catholics and Lutherans formulated a joint declaration on the theological issue at the heart of the Protestant Reformation. The *Joint Declaration on the Doctrine of Justification* was issued in 1999 by the Secretariat for the Promotion of the Unity of Christians and the Lutheran World Federation (which does not include conservative Lutherans such as the Missouri and Wisconsin Synods). Both sides concurred with the essential notion that since justification is "by grace alone, in faith in Christ's saving work and not because of any merit on our part, we are accepted by God and receive the Holy Spirit, who renews our hearts while equipping and calling us to good works."[8] Although the declaration neither solves nor even treats all Catholic and Lutheran disagreements, it maintains that "the remaining differences in language, theological elaboration and emphasis in the understanding of justification . . . are acceptable."[9] Accordingly, the outstanding differences are no longer the object of mutual condemnation: the *Declaration* took the extraordinary step of revoking prior excommunications concerning the doctrine of justification pronounced by the Council of Trent and by the Lutheran Confessions. In 2006 the World Methodist Council voted unanimously to adopt the *Declaration* as well.

LIBERAL AND CONSERVATIVE THEOLOGICAL FORCES

The theological style of the Roman Catholic Church was beginning to change on both the left and right. Progressive thinkers such as Hans Küng and Karl Rahner were theologians present at Vatican II, reconceptualizing Catholic and Christian identity in strikingly new ways. Regarding the doctrine of papal infallibility, Küng went further to the left than the Roman hierarchy wished, and in 1979 he was censured by the church and banned from teaching as a Catholic theologian (a ban later moderated). Ironically, this action only served to heighten his popularity among both Catholic and Protestant audiences.

Less well known on the popular level but far more influential on the scholarly level, Rahner ranks as one of the most prolific theologians in the history of Christianity, whose works exerted as much impact on Catholic thought as Vatican II had on church life. Rahner's thought is best seen in his twenty-three volume *Theological Investigations* (1954–84) and his *Foundations of Christian*

Faith (1982). Central to Rahner's theology is the affirmation that Christianity constitutes the essential structure of human experience. Rahner deemed dependence on a creator-deity and freedom made possible by a redeemer-deity as universal givens of human experience and organizing principles of all the world's great religions. While recognizing their universality, Rahner maintained that these principles reach their most perfect expression in Christianity. Proceeding along the trajectory of Vatican II, Rahner identified all adherents to creative-redemptive religions as "anonymous Christians,"[10] arguing that they really believed in redemption through Christ but were not yet aware of their redeemer's name. Hence Rahner's theological program attempted to balance the distinctiveness of Christianity against the shared experience of all religions. In some ways, Rahner's program is an updated Catholic version of Schleiermacher's theological system, as both are constructed on appeals to common human experience rather than notions of revelation, which will always be exclusive to their recipients.

Ecumenical and theological developments since Vatican II have been viewed by some Catholics as an overliberal tendency within Catholicism and a compromise of its distinctive characteristics. Hence a conservative reaction acquired considerable momentum, especially in the United States and Germany. Conservatives alleged that the Latin liturgy was intrinsically holier than the vernacular Mass ordered by Vatican II. Among the primary vehicles for conservative interests was the organization Opus Dei (the work of God), founded by Josemariá Escrivá de Balaguer (1902–75). Opus Dei became an image of the pre-Vatican II church: hierarchical, aloof, and authoritative. In rhetoric evocative of the Council of Trent, Opus Dei protested the popularization of liturgy as a concession to an increasingly worldly laity, rejected consultations between clergy and laity as acceding to lay pressure for control, and denounced pluralism as an admission that Catholicism was not the one true faith. Via its publishing arm, Ignatius Press, Opus Dei has introduced a number of influential European authors to an American audience: Hans Urs von Balthasar (1905–88), Henri de Lubac (1896–1991), and the Holocaust martyr Edith Stein (1891–1942), all right-of-center Catholics. In so doing, Opus Dei has widened the spectrum of viewpoints within American Catholicism.

CONCLUSION

Notwithstanding conservative reactions, Vatican II caused the boundaries between Catholic theology, Protestant theology, and modern philosophy to grow increasingly more fluid. Priests and theologians educated in Catholic universities and seminaries since the 1960s occupy a different thought world than those educated before the council and without the influence of Rahner. Today priests and theologians are more open to modern thought in general and to the critical revision of Catholic theology in particular. Affirming the entire church as the people of God, they include Protestant and Orthodox Christians within the true church of Christ. With Rahner, modern Catholic thinkers affirm that all persons are gifted by God with a capacity to receive grace and possess an element of grace within, or a "supernatural existential," which affords an opportunity for salvation. Many modern Catholics proceed to advocate a religious inclusivism that holds that anyone who adheres to and develops the supernatural existential will find complete salvation, even if they never hear the explicit message of Jesus. The current *Catechism of the Catholic Church* exemplifies these trajectories.

FOR FURTHER READING

Primary Sources

Catechism of the Catholic Church. 2nd ed. New York: Doubleday, 1994.

The Lutheran World Federation and the Roman Catholic Church. *Joint Declaration on the Doctrine of Justification*. Grand Rapids: Eerdmans, 2000.

Paul VI. *Ecclesiam suam*. Papal Encyclicals Online. http://www.papalencyclicals.net/Paul06/p6eccles.htm.

Rahner, Karl. *Foundations of Christian Faith*. Trans. William V. Dych. New York: Herder, 1982.

———. *Theological Investigations*. 23 vols. New York: Herder, 1965–92.

Vatican Council II. *The Basic Sixteen Documents: Constitutions, Decrees, Declarations*. Ed. Austin Flannery. Northport, NY: Costello, 1996.

Secondary Sources

Congar, Yves. *Diversity and Communion*. London: SCM, 1984.

Faggioli, Massimo. *Vatican II: The Battle for Meaning*. New York: Paulist, 2012.

———. *Vatican II: The Complete History*. New York: Paulist, 2015.

Kerr, Fargus. *Twentieth-Century Catholic Theologians*. Hoboken, NJ: Wiley-Blackwell, 2006.

McBrien, Richard P. *Catholicism*. Rev. ed. New York: HarperOne, 1994.

O'Malley, John W. *What Happened at Vatican II*. Cambridge, MA: Harvard University Press, 2008.

CHAPTER 21

PROCESS THEOLOGY

nfluenced by modern science's discovery that reality is in motion (e.g., whir-ring electrons in mostly empty space) and the twentieth century's height-ened awareness of the problem of evil, process theology reflects a nonstatic, evolving, creative, and subjective reality. Advanced by Alfred North Whitehead (1861–1947), Charles Hartshorne (1897–2000), and John Cobb (1925–), pro-cess theology utilizes a form of empiricism (in which experience gives verifica-tion and meaning to this world) for the purpose of developing a theodicy that explains evil in the world. This chapter explains how, for process theologians, the nature of reality is becoming rather than being. Since the world's creation, God is no longer sovereign or transcendent, and both God and his universe are becoming rather than being. All living existing things react to their environment and to one another in free creative choice, which may cause suffering. But the primordial God, who is also creative, is in love guiding creation to a higher level so that he and his creation may overcome evil and avert chaos in a new order.

PHILOSOPHICAL PRESUPPOSITIONS OF PROCESS THOUGHT

Throughout the history of contemporary theology, we have observed that philos-ophy and theology are virtually inextricable from each other. Unlike Aquinas's conception of philosophy as the handmaiden of theology, liberal theologians frequently regard philosophy at least an equal partner to theology in the enter-prise of shaping doctrine. One branch of recent theology that is both liberal and assigns philosophy the dominant role is process theology.

Process theology comprises an effort by some contemporary Christian thinkers to reconstruct the doctrine of God and indeed all of Christian theology to better harmonize with modern assumptions concerning the nature of the world. Process thinkers start with the working principle that Christian theology must be revised and updated in each new culture in view of its particular concerns, issues, and questions. Further, they insist that a feasible Christian theology cannot stand firm in the teeth of the culture's fundamental convictions about reality. The Greek philosophy that shaped early Christian theology held that perfect being is static, for change represents imperfection. Ultimate reality—God—must be totally simple (noncomposite) and immutable (changeless); elsewise it would be imperfect. Process theologians assert that modern philosophy cannot concur with such a conception of being and perfection; intelligent, thinking modern persons recognize this as flawed metaphysics. Change is not evidence of imperfection; rather, modern philosophy shows that to be is to change. As modern science has shown, reality is in motion. Everything is related to everything else, a doctrine known as mutual interdependence. Being itself is relational, and relationship demands openness to being affected by others within the network of significant relationships. We find that the natural order and the social order operate this way. Being is social, which entails dynamism. Being itself is the process of becoming.

THE SEMINAL CONTRIBUTIONS OF WHITEHEAD

Process theologians are persuaded that a new philosophy is needed to assist Christian thought in casting off its defunct metaphysic of timeless and changeless perfection and reconceive theology to make it tenable in a modern world that privileges becoming over static being. They found that new philosophy in the thought of English mathematician Alfred North Whitehead, who turned from mathematics to speculative philosophy when he left Britain to teach at Harvard University in 1924. According to some commentators, he formulated the most robust metaphysical system of the twentieth century by reconceiving reality itself as a network of interrelated moments of energy called "actual occasions." Rather than construing reality in terms of objects, either physical or spiritual, Whitehead reconceptualized all of reality as occasions, or drops of experience. Reality is thus a sequence of happenings instead of a great chain of being. To be real is to "happen" vis-à-vis other happenings and to "experience" within a network of experiencing objects.

Whitehead considered God as a great cosmic organizing principle who creates the world by unifying it insofar as possible. While God can be spoken of in personal pronouns, Whitehead believed that God is suprapersonal, or transcending the distinction between personality and impersonality. In Whitehead's philosophy, God is neither omnipotent nor timeless. God contains the world and is contained in it; accordingly, "It is as true to say that the World creates God as that God creates the World."[1] God is superior to the world at any given moment but is always able to become superior to himself as well. Indeed, at any particular moment God is becoming superior to himself. God evolves with the world and under its direction.

A central idea of Whitehead's philosophy is the "dipolarity" or "bipolarity" of each actual entity. "Actual entity" or "actual occasion" refers to one of the basic building blocks of reality. Nothing but actual entities are real, and each one possesses two aspects or poles: mental and physical. The mental pole is the aspect of the entity that feels the past as object or given. The physical pole harmonizes the past in conjunction with an understanding of possibility in the future. God's two poles, mental and physical, may be respectively characterized as "primordial" and "consequent." God's primordial pole is God's essential, unchanging nature containing ideals yet to be achieved; this pole is potential and abstract rather than actual and concrete. Hence God, in his primordial pole, is the soul or immaterial mind of the world. God's consequent pole is his lived reality or actual experience, which constantly changes as God "feels" the world. Hence God's consequent pole designates the world as the body of God. Just as the condition of the world affects God and even comprises God's concrete existence (his body), so God (as soul) affects the world. God imports into the world the ideals of his primordial nature and tries to woo or persuade the world's actual occasions to realize these ideals in order to optimize harmony, beauty, and enjoyment. But God cannot compel any actual entity to realize its "ideal subjective aim"[2]; he can only attempt to persuade it. Every actual entity possesses some degree of free will and self-determination and may act in line with God's ideal or reject it. Evil is the result of the rejection of God's ideals by actual entities, and it causes God to suffer. God is both augmented and diminished by the world's responses to his persuasive influence.

Personal immortality did not comprise an essential part of Whitehead's philosophy. Though seeing no scientific evidence for it, he did not oppose personal immortality. He did, however, observe that a purely spiritual being would necessarily be immortal, since an immaterial being is indestructible. Making no reference to Jesus Christ, Whitehead was not a Christian in any sense of the term. His own faith constituted a natural religion stemming from his philosophy.

Nevertheless, several liberal Christian thinkers discovered something valuable in his philosophy for reconceiving Christian doctrine in line with modern knowledge.

LIBERAL CHRISTIAN MANIFESTATIONS OF PROCESS THEOLOGY

Those who attempted to synthesize Christian theology with Whitehead's philosophy became known as process theologians, and by the 1970s their numbers were growing. Entire mainstream Protestant seminaries and university divinity schools in the United States and Canada embraced process theology as their primary emphasis and approach. The United Methodist–affiliated Claremont School of Theology (California) became a hub of process theology. Located there are the Center for Process Studies and the editorial offices of the journal *Process Studies*. Charles Hartshorne worked to transform Whiteheadian process philosophy into process theology. Hartshorne maintained that process theology is panentheistic (God is in all), as opposed to both pantheism (God is all) and classical theism. Contra classical theism, process theology asserts that God is not in all senses independent of the cosmos. Rather, all finite things are related to him insofar as they are included in him, specifically his body. Thus everything is in God. However, God is more than the sum total of all finite things. His relation to the universe constitutes only one aspect of God. Since there is another aspect of God—his soul—which transcends the cosmos, panentheism is not identical with pantheism. Hartshorne described the metaphysic of process theology as "neo-classical metaphysics."[3] Far from the classical metaphysics of "being" or "substance," neo-classical metaphysics consider events as primary. Relativity is not deemed inferior to absoluteness, nor is possibility inferior to necessity. Ultimate reality is in a state of dynamic process, taking evolution into account as well as the dynamics of both the physical world and human personality.

The most prominent Protestant advocate of process theology from the 1960s to the 1990s was John Cobb, a United Methodist minister and Claremont theology professor. Cobb wrote many books applying Whitehead's philosophy to Christian theology, including *A Christian Natural Theology* (1965), *God and the World* (1965), and *Christ in a Pluralistic Age* (1975). A common thread running throughout each book is the mutual relationship of interdependence between God and the world. Also emphasized is the principle of creativity, which is seen as necessary and eternal because there is nothing more general or ultimate above it. The principle of creativity expands beyond human beings to literally everything in the nonhuman as well as in the human world. This feature of process theology has evinced great interest from theologians concerned with ecological issues.

Cobb and his fellow process theologians desire to redistrict Christian theology away from the classical theism of the patristic and medieval church. Process theologians stress God's immanence rather than God's transcendence. They emphasize God's personal nature over against God's absoluteness. Divine love, including vulnerability and suffering, trumps power and sovereignty. Moreover, Cobb and other process theologians denounce monergism and any account of God's work in the world as compulsive. God never forces any actual entity, including humans, to do anything. God never works except through persuasion. God summons the world to its own fulfillment in the complete wholeness and harmony of his kingdom, but free creatures choose whether and how to respond. While traditional theology maintained that humanity proposes but God disposes, process theology maintains that God proposes but humanity disposes. It should be emphasized that process theology is naturalistic, as it utterly discards the notion of supernatural interventions by God in the natural world. Although not precluding special persuasive acts of God, process theology does preclude bona fide miracles and naturally inexplicable signs and wonders. God works directly on each actual entity by furnishing it with its initial goal and drawing it toward his vision for what it should become, but God neither interrupts the natural order of events nor forces anything to happen against nature or free will. Indeed, God cannot even know the future in full detail with complete certainty since it will only be filled in by free choices of actual entities that do not yet exist. The future is thus as open to God as it is to us.

Process theology is a distinctly twentieth-century manifestation of liberal Protestant theology. Some Roman Catholic theologians have also embraced facets of it. Its appeal primarily resides in the solution it provides to the problem of evil and innocent suffering. World War II and the Holocaust dramatically rocked many theologians' ideas about God and suffering. Where was God when the Nazis gassed and burned to death six to nine million Jews? The horrors of twentieth-century war and genocide appeared to many contemporary theologians to demand wholesale revision of traditional Augustinian notions of God's power and sovereignty. If God could have stopped the mass extermination of innocent men, women, and children, they argue, he should have. But God always does what God should do. Hence it must be the case that God could not stop the Holocaust. Process theologians found comfort and security in Whitehead's depiction of God as "the fellow-sufferer who understands"[4] and who cannot compel actual entities or societies to do good instead of evil.

But Cobb insists that the process is not in a final state of chaos since it depends on a unifier who envisions possibilities, experiences all that happens, synthesizes, and gives directions. This unifier is God, a reality who surpasses all and is capable of bringing harmony out of growing complexity. Modifying Whitehead, Cobb claims that without God there could be no process. Therefore God can indeed be described as creator. While not the creator of the world *ex nihilo* (out of nothing), God is the creator *ex materia* (out of preexistent material), where the material is actually God's physical dimension or pole, rendering creation ultimately *ex deo* (out of God). Furthermore, God is the prime transformer and shaper of the world and each state thereof.

Cobb and his fellow theologians are quite concerned with Christology and hence the Christianizing of Whiteheadian philosophy. Adopting a "process conceptuality," process theologians recognize that Jesus Christ made a decisive difference to the world. They proclaim the complete, unqualified humanity of Jesus. But they are suspicious of traditional two-nature Christologies as diminishing the full humanity of Jesus and presupposing a metaphysic in conflict with contemporary ways of understanding the world. Process theologians disclaim any idea of God's "intrusion" into the world in Jesus that is at all an exception to "the creative process." Instead, God's incarnating activity is conceived as not being "confined" to Jesus, as God incarnates himself to the extent that his "initial aim" is accepted and his purpose actualized. But God's incarnating activity is "defined" by Jesus. In Jesus, divine action and human response are so integrated that Jesus can be identified as "the classic instance of divine activity in manhood, love 'enmanned.'"[5] Jesus is God's decisive act because he is the decisive revelation or representation of a certain possibility for human existence on the one hand, and of God's being and action on the other hand. The vision of reality delineated through Jesus's words and actions constitutes the supreme manifestation of God's character, purpose, and mode of agency—the self-expression of God. Cobb focuses on Jesus in terms of his authority as revelation, as example, and as Lord and Savior, introducing a new structure of existence in which Christians participate. Without forsaking process conceptuality, Cobb constructs a full *Logos* Christology that aims to be consistent with the pluralism of our age. Accordingly, Christ is present wherever and whenever "creative transformation" occurs.

Regarding the "end" of creation, marked divergence exists between process theology and traditional Christian doctrine, whether "end" is viewed as temporal (*finis*) or as final purpose (*telos*). Process theologians contend that there can be no temporal end, for if the time-space universe ends, God ceases to be God.

It is rather the *telos* that is significant, defined as "the attainment of value in the temporal world," or the achievement of "a creative harmony present in all things from atoms to deity."[6] The *telos* is described either as the continual consummation of everything in the life of God or as the kingdom of God, understood not as a physical reign but as the fulfillment of God's being in relation to every creature, an infinite realm of creative life. In either case, "Christ enables those who follow him to live authentic life in love—and to the extent that life is so lived, a constant consummation occurs."[7] Some process theologians espouse a doctrine of objective immortality, in which everything is preserved eternally in the memory and life of God due to God's omniscience. In the memory and life of God, everything is being transformed for use in the ongoing process of creation. Cobb develops the concept of the kingdom of God as an image of hope, positioning it alongside other images of hope such as the resurrection of the dead and the city of God. For Cobb, persons inhabit the kingdom in both objectivity and subjectivity. As a result, in God each person experiences an enlarged and enlarging world that contains new occasions as they come into being. In the kingdom, persons and events are open to each other and to God. The kerygma of Jesus realizes the kingdom in anticipation, and the structure of Jesus's existence prefigures what existence in the kingdom is to be.

CONCLUSION

Process theologians seek a comprehensive view of reality, realizing the inadequacy of a fragmentary understanding of various parts of the world. Process theology stipulates an intimate relation between God and the world without eviscerating that relation, as does pantheism. God is in the world but not identical to it. The presence of God in the universe does not extinguish the diversity that humans experience but instead preserves it and bequeaths it with purpose and meaning. Affirming the existence of a supreme being, process theologians illustrate that the world depends on God for its origin and preservation; without God the world would not continue to exist. In addition, process theologians genuinely relate their worldview to contemporary scientific theories.

However, many critics of process theology contend that it strayed too far in the opposite direction from Augustinian monergism. The God of Whitehead and Cobb is impotent to do most of the things Christian theology traditionally places under the rubrics of God's creation and redemption. The God of process theology did not create the world *ex nihilo*. The world is literally the body of God and God is literally the soul or mind of the world, such that God and the world are always inseparable and interdependent. Even more radically, for process theologians there is no guarantee or even reason to think God will ultimately defeat the stubborn resistance to his vision of good. Even given the process kingdom vision, the future may well be simply more of the same. Consequently, debate raged in theological circles during the 1970s and 1980s over whether process theology can even be considered "Christian." Today it continues to be taught as a legitimate version of Christian theology in several liberal, mainstream Protestant seminaries while simultaneously being condemned as heresy by most conservative theologians.

FOR FURTHER READING

Primary Sources

Cobb, John B., Jr. *A Christian Natural Theology: Based on the Thought of Alfred North Whitehead.* 2nd ed. Louisville: Westminster John Knox, 2007.

———. *Christ in a Pluralistic Age.* Philadelphia: Westminster, 1975.

———. *God and the World.* Philadelphia: Westminster, 1965.

Hartshorne, Charles. *The Divine Relativity: A Social Conception of God.* New Haven, CT: Yale University Press, 1948.

———. *A Natural Theology for Our Time.* La Salle, IL: Open Court, 1967.

Whitehead, Alfred North. *Process and Reality: An Essay in Cosmology.* New York: Harper Torchbooks, 1929.

Secondary Sources

Geisler, Norman L. "Process Theology." In *Tensions in Contemporary Theology*, ed. Stanley N. Gundry and Alan F. Johnson, 237–86. Chicago: Moody, 1976.

Griffin, David R. *A Process Christology.* Philadelphia: Westminster, 1973.

Gruenler, Royce Gordon. *The Inexhaustible God: Biblical Faith and the Challenge of Process Theism.* Grand Rapids: Baker, 1983.

Ogden, Schubert M. *The Understanding of Christian Faith.* Eugene, OR: Cascade, 2010.

Pittenger, Norman. *The Lure of Divine Love.* Edinburgh: Heritage House, 1979.

CHAPTER 22

JÜRGEN MOLTMANN AND WOLFHART PANNENBERG

Theology of Hope

Another theological movement inspired by twentieth-century evil and suffering was the theology of hope, also known as eschatological theology. This theology is closely associated with the writings of German Protestant systematic theologians Jürgen Moltmann (1926–) and Wolfhart Pannenberg (1928–2014). Although the systems of Moltmann and Pannenberg differ in various ways, together these figures stimulated a fresh appreciation for eschatological realism in mainstream Christian theology. Liberal Protestants spoke about the kingdom of God, but they meant a human social order rather than the reign of the transcendent creator of the universe. On the other hand, fundamentalists often conceived of eschatology as a chronology of end-time events and engaged in elaborate speculation about Jesus's return. Both Moltmann and Pannenberg aimed to recover a realistic approach to eschatology completely apart from a social order or a chronology for the end of the world as we know it.

MOLTMANN'S BACKGROUND

Moltmann configures theology along radically eschatological lines whose path is charted by the crucifixion and resurrection of Jesus. Born in Hamburg, Germany, Moltmann was pressed into the German military in 1944. As a young soldier in Hitler's army, Moltmann came to the horrifying realization that he was inadvertently serving evil. When the Allies conquered the Axis powers,

Moltmann became a prisoner of war in Great Britain from 1945 to 1948. While a POW, he fell into despair upon seeing the appalling photographs of the Auschwitz and Belsen concentration camps. His inner torment was broken only when an American chaplain gave him a Bible, as reading the New Testament and Psalms gave him a sense of the reality of God in the midst of suffering. Upon his return to Germany in 1948, Moltmann studied theology at the University of Göttingen. Focusing on the dual themes of suffering and hope, Moltmann launched a theological program that furnishes hope for God's ultimate triumph over evil in the future and momentum for Christian involvement in overcoming suffering in the meantime.

MOLTMANN'S CHRISTOLOGY AND ESCHATOLOGY

As Moltmann tried to make sense of his devastating experience in World War II, he was brought to theological considerations of Jesus's cross and resurrection. He understood these two events dialectically, representing the contradiction between what reality is now in its subjection to sin, suffering, and death, and what God promises to make reality in a new creation. For Moltmann, the future must be linked to the present, such that if Christianity is not about a thoroughgoing eschatology, it has no connection whatsoever with Christ. In his first and most famous book, *Theology of Hope* (1964), Moltmann asserted that genuine hope is necessarily bound up with the resurrection, which is in turn necessarily bound up with eschatology. Hence "from first to last, and not merely in the epilogue, Christianity is eschatology, is hope."[1] Moltmann declared that his theology was not a theology about hope, but a theology out of hope. By eschatology Moltmann means the announcement in temporal history of future possibilities, some of which depend on human beings and some of which God promises will transpire. Since the future is not fixed but is open to possibilities, the theology of hope possesses a here-and-now emphasis that offers hope to the Christ-follower in the present and inspires the Christ-follower with a "passion for what is possible" to actively work to bring about the promised future.[2]

Moltmann argued that Jesus in his death was identified with the world in its godlessness, godforsakenness, and transitoriness. As a result, Jesus's resurrection constitutes God's promise of a new future for all reality in the divine presence eternally. This all-encompassing eschatological perspective supports Moltmann's uncompromisingly holistic perspective on both theology and the mission of the church. Christian hope is not for the spiritual instead of the material, or for the individual instead of the social, or for the personal instead of the political, or for humanity instead of the rest of creation. Nor is Christian hope for another world but for the transformation by God of this present world. All biblical descriptions of Christ not only say who he was but imply statements concerning what is to be currently expected from him. Accordingly, Moltmann's eschatology promotes involvement in the world rather than withdrawal from the world. Out of faithfulness to Jesus, believers must foster change in anticipation of the coming kingdom of God and openness to the future that only God can provide his creation. Believers can rest assured that their work for peace and social justice, albeit inevitably flawed and incomplete, is not in vain but will be perfected and consummated by Jesus himself at his return.

Notwithstanding his theology of hope, Moltmann still bore the painful memory of the Holocaust. He knew he needed to deal with the fundamental problem of suffering and evil in the world. Moltmann turned his attention to the cross, which entailed two dimensions: Jesus's solidarity with sinful humanity, and Jesus's solidarity with the Trinity. In his 1972 *The Crucified God*, Moltmann contended that the divine promise of the resurrection addresses the suffering of the "godless and the godforsaken" by identifying the suffering of Jesus on the cross with the suffering of humanity, which includes both the "oppressed and the oppressors."[3] While Moltmann did not actively abuse Jews or participate in the "final solution," he was keenly aware that he stood on the oppressor's side in World War II. His own spiritual devastation at having aided Hitler provoked the realization that oppressors also suffer in their own way. This weighty insight could only come to someone who had experienced anguish in the depth of one's soul. Hence, for Moltmann, only a suffering God can redeem such suffering sinners.

Moltmann's doctrine of the cross as solidarity with those who are suffering implies a re-visioned concept of God. The cross stands not only as Jesus's solidarity with suffering humanity but also as the Son's solidarity with the Father. Wrestling with the Father's desertion of the Son on the cross, Moltmann claimed that if we are to engage in Christian theology, we "must come to terms with Jesus's cry on the cross. . . . 'My God, why hast thou forsaken me?'"[4] This despairing cry led Moltmann to conclude that not only did Jesus suffer on the cross, but the Father suffered as well. In solidarity with the godforsaken world, the Son voluntarily surrendered himself in love for the world, and the Father voluntarily surrendered his Son in love for the world. At the point of their most painful separation, the Father and Son were united in their love for the world, and this became the precise moment at which the godforsakenness of the world was overcome. For that event of suffering love released the power of the Spirit to overcome all that separated the world from God.

This conception of divine solidarity on the cross prompted Moltmann to revolutionize the doctrine of God in two respects. First, Moltmann expanded on the ancient idea of *perichoresis*, or mutual indwelling of each Trinitarian person in the other two Trinitarian persons. If both the Father and the Son suffer on the cross, then there must exist a profound mutual indwelling of the persons of the Trinity. From this point, Moltmann formulated a Trinitarian history of God with the world, emphasizing the mutual involvement of God and the world. Hence Moltmann enlarged *perichoresis* to describe the unity between God and the world. God experiences a history with the world in which he both affects and is affected by the world. This also constitutes the history of God's own Trinitarian relationships as a community of persons who embrace the world within their love. Moltmann recognizes the Holy Spirit as the immanent presence of God in creation while at the same time recognizing the Spirit's equal role as one divine subject in the completely reciprocal relationships of the Trinity. Accordingly, Moltmann brings the whole of creation and history within the divine experience.

Second, Moltmann championed the doctrine of divine passibility, which holds that God experiences pain and suffering. This runs contrary to the traditional doctrine of God as impassible—that God does not possess or express emotion because emotion necessarily entails change and God cannot change. This doctrine should be rejected, Moltmann asserted, since it is irreconcilable with the love of God. God's love is not simply the unidirectional relationship of active benevolence toward his creation, but a genuinely bidirectional relationship where God is so intimately involved with his creation that he is influenced by it. As Moltmann put it, "God in Auschwitz and Auschwitz in the crucified God— that is the basis for a real hope which both embraces and overcomes the world, and the ground for a love which is stronger than death."[5]

For Moltmann, the cross does not solve the problem of suffering but meets it with the voluntary fellow suffering of love. Theodicy is not a code to be cracked but a demand for the dialectical openness of theology to the suffering of the world until the promise of the resurrection is fulfilled in the eschatological future. Only God's supernatural restoration of the universe gives the universe hope, a fact underscored by the finding of modern cosmology that, absent divine intervention, the universe will suffer extinction in the heat of death. Hence all who trust in a true and everlasting hope for the universe must look beyond the natural for its ground and guarantee. Only God can release the universe from its "bondage to decay" (Rom. 8:21). At this juncture, God will finally take his whole creation beyond evil, suffering, and death and make this universe his home.

MOLTMANN'S THEOLOGY OF PRAXIS

Moltmann's eschatological theology constitutes a theology of praxis centered on action. A true understanding of Jesus's crucifixion and resurrection necessarily entails activism, since the resurrection is "revolutionizing and transforming the present."[6] Jesus's resurrection catalyzes a death-defying opposition to every form of death in every dimension of life, whether social, economic, political, or religious. The theology of hope in the crucified God is thus an activist theology, resisting such powers of death as Hitler and trusting the promises of God. "The crucified God is . . . the God of the poor, the oppressed and the humiliated. The rule of Christ who was crucified for political reasons can only be extended through liberation from forms of rule which make men servile and apathetic. . . . Christians will seek to anticipate the future of Christ according to the measure of the possibilities available to them, by breaking down lordship and building up the political liveliness of each individual."[7]

Consequently, Moltmann's theology strikes an unequivocally political chord. Collaborating with the Roman Catholic theologian Johann Baptist Metz (1928–), Moltmann delineated a political theology of liberation. This theology was not political in the sense of taking up a particular stance, but it was political in the sense of requiring activism from the gospel. The gospel "urges men on towards liberating actions, because it makes them painfully aware of suffering institutions of exploitation, oppression, alienation and captivity."[8] The coming lordship of the risen Jesus cannot be merely hoped for and awaited; it means the historic transformation of life. The Christian life consists not in fleeing and spiritually resigning from the world. Rather, the Christian life is engaged in an attack on the world and a calling in the world. Therefore Moltmann boldly queries, "What are the economic, social, and political consequences of the gospel of the Son of Man who was crucified as a 'rebel'?"[9]

Moltmann finds the answers to this question in the principle of relationality, grounded in the loving and changing relationships of the Trinitarian persons to one another and governing movements and forces in world history. Relationships of mutuality instead of dominance or even hierarchy are therefore mandated for the relationship between the church and world religions, the relationship of persons in society and in the church, the relationship between humanity and other creatures, and the relationship between God and creation. While implicit and explicit modes of unitarianism have, for Moltmann, consistently legitimated human domination of both other humans and nature, social trinitarianism sees God as in himself a fellowship of love and therefore deems relationships of voluntary friendship between humans as most accurately reflecting God and constituting his kingdom. In the political realm, the principle of mutuality demands democracy. In the ecclesiological realm, it demands a model of the church as an open society of friends. In the ecological realm, it demands the interdependence of humanity and the rest of nature.

Moltmann also postulates that these relationships are perichoretic. Regarding God, it is in their *perichoresis*, or mutual indwelling in love, that the three divine persons are both three and one. Likewise, God's relationship to his creation is one of mutual indwelling. Since God is transcendent beyond the world, the world dwells in God; but because, as the Spirit, God is also immanent within the world, God dwells in the world. Employing his dominant notion of the Spirit in creation, Moltmann takes the nonhuman creation as well into his general concept of the Trinitarian history of God. The whole of creation from the beginning is oriented toward the future goal of its glorification through divine indwelling. The Spirit in creation suffers in labor alongside creation through its slavery to decay, keeping creation open to God and to its future with God. The Spirit of God is therefore an eschatological gift, providing an earnest of things to come and binding us to himself to point and direct us to greater pursuits. The eschatological goal of humanity does not raise us out of the material creation but reinforces our solidarity and relatedness with it.

MOLTMANN AND UNIVERSAL SALVATION

Moltmann's doctrine of the glorification of the universe carries with it the doctrine of universal salvation. Rejecting the notion that hell is the necessary consequence of genuine human freedom, Moltmann inquired, "Does God's love preserve our free will, or does it free our enslaved will, which has become un-free through the power of sin? Does God love free men and women, or does he seek the men and women who have become lost?"[10] Moltmann rhetorically asked how children who die early, the severely disabled, victims of geriatric diseases, and persons who have never been confronted with the choice of the gospel will fare if free choice determines our eternal fate. Moreover, if salvation ultimately depends on human free will, then we are being asked "to base the assurance of our salvation on the shaky ground of our own decisions," which abandons us to "a state of uncertainty."[11] Consequently, Moltmann adjudged the doctrine of hell as inhumane.

Going beyond these pastoral considerations, Moltmann argued that the logic of hell is functionally atheistic, as each human being in freedom of choice is her own lord and god. God is simply the accessory that puts human free will into effect. As Moltmann explained, "If I decide for heaven, God must put me there; if I decide for hell, he must leave me there. If God has to abide by our free decision, then we can do with him what we like. Is that 'the love of God'? Free human beings forge their own happiness and are their own executioners. They do not just dispose over their lives here; they decide on their eternal destinies as well. So they have no need of any God at all. . . . Carried to its logical conclusion, the logic of hell is secular humanism, as Feuerbach, Marx, and Nietzsche already perceived a long time ago."[12]

In contrast to the traditional perspective, Moltmann proposes that the Christian doctrine of hell is to be found in what he dubs the gospel of Jesus's descent into hell. Viewing hell as a metaphor for a "God-forsakenness from which there is no way out," Moltmann stipulates that hell is not a place in the afterlife or next world but an experience of desolation by God.[13] Thus Jesus's descent is not his journey to Hades where he preached to the spirits of the dead but "his experience of God-forsakenness from Gethsemane to Golgotha."[14] It is this experience of godforsakenness that furnishes the connection between Jesus and contemporary experience. For Moltmann, the twentieth century "has produced more infernos than all the centuries before us: The gas ovens of Auschwitz and the atomising of Hiroshima heralded an age of potential mass annihilation through ABC [atomic, biological, and chemical weapons]," such that it "is pointless to deny hell."[15] But in relating to Jesus in our hells, we may speak of the gospel of Jesus's descent into hell.

Unlike Dante and the dominant theological tradition, Moltmann posits that a Christian view of hell requires us to proclaim to the entire creation, "Do not abandon hope, all who enter here!"[16] Jesus suffered the godforsakenness that knows no way out so that he could bring God to the godforsaken. Through Jesus, then, hell has been conquered. Moltmann insists that the universality of God's grace cannot be grounded in free will, a grounding that inevitably yields a double outcome of heaven and hell. Instead it is to be grounded in the theology of the cross, which yields universal reconciliation. Since salvation is not based on the shaky ground of our decisions, if we seek ourselves in Christ rather than in ourselves, then our election is made sure. But the fact that there is no double outcome does not entail that there is no judgment. Although judgment is not God's last word—his last word will be "I am making everything new!" (Rev. 21:5)—it is a necessary penultimate word that establishes in the divine righteousness on which the new creation is to be built. Moltmann underscores that from the making new of all things, no one is excepted, not even the mass murderers of world history whom we wish to damn to hell. Provocatively, Moltmann suggests that transforming grace is God's punishment for sinners, as they are deprived of the false freedom they idolatrously desire and given true freedom instead. Thus transforming grace and divine punishment form two sides of the same coin.

For Moltmann, the performance of the good rather than the right to choose defines the reality of human freedom, a notion harking back to Augustine. Distinct from the notion of autonomy, Moltmann believes that freedom consists in choosing what we ought rather than merely choosing what we want. True freedom embodies the will of God. In God's grace, we are all saved from our autonomy for true freedom. This point is especially evident in Moltmann's claim that "no one is excluded or exempt" (*Davon ist niemand ausgenommen oder freiges tellt*) from God's making new of all things.[17] By "no one is excluded," Moltmann meant that no one will be condemned to hell. God's transforming grace is not permissive but requires transformation. This double-edged notion of grace stems from the victory of the cross, which is a victory for all, over all. Hence Moltmann averred, "The message of the new righteousness which eschatological faith brings into the world says that in fact the executioners will not finally triumph over their victims. It also says that in the end the victims will not triumph over their executioners."[18] Moltmann thus offered a picture of universal salvation in which final judgment is central to Christian hope and where the cry for justice is not silenced.

PANNENBERG'S CONCEPT OF REVELATION AS HISTORY

Teaching alongside Moltmann at the University of Wuppertal, Pannenberg burst onto the theological scene in 1964 with the publication of his book *Jesus—God and Man*. In it he emphasized the rational verifiability of the historical event of the bodily resurrection of Jesus, an event dismissed as impossible or mythological by most modern German theologians. Like Moltmann, Pannenberg conceived of Jesus's resurrection as an eschatological event, the anticipation and promise of the future divine kingdom when God will finally reveal his lordship. Fundamental to Pannenberg's theological system, articulated in his three-volume *Systematic Theology*, is the notion that faith is centered in history. Historical events must underlie faith if faith is to be valid. Truth is not to be found, pace Hegel, in inferences from unchanging essences or, pace Schleiermacher, self-authenticating religious experience. Rather, truth is historical in nature and meaning. Christian theology deals not with events that are visible only to the eye of faith, but with public events that take place in the external world. Theology is therefore the public discipline that takes up the quest for universal truth. Pannenberg denounced all attempts to separate faith from fact (including the attempts of Kierkegaard, Wittgenstein, and Bultmann) or to shield the Christian faith from rational inquiry.

In *The Idea of God and Human Freedom* (1973), Pannenberg made the startling claim that "in a restricted but important sense God does not yet exist."[19] This statement must not be misunderstood. For Pannenberg, God exists in and of himself in all eternity, but he is not yet fully present as he will be in the future. In an act of self-limitation, God freely chooses to grant the world its awful freedom until the future kingdom finally and completely breaks into the present. Atrocities like the Holocaust occur because the kingdom of God has not yet come. Nevertheless, God still exercises his lordship from his own futurity by sending Jesus and the Holy Spirit into the present world from the future. God does this both to prove his love and to unleash a spirit of anticipation into human history. In the end, God will come to his world, cancel out all sin and evil, and make the world his home. Holding that God's rule and his being are inseparable, Pannenberg maintained that God will exist in every sense once God has made all things new.

CONCLUSION

The significance of the theological systems of Moltmann and Pannenberg can be captured along six lines. First, they restore the credibility and the necessity of futurist eschatology to contemporary Christian faith. Second, they effectively tackle the problem of post-Holocaust theodicy from the perspective of God's suffering in the cross of Christ. Third, they cultivate an exhaustively Trinitarian understanding of God. Fourth, they construe the God-world relationship as reciprocal and internal to God's own Trinitarian relationships. Fifth, they burst out of the modern paradigm that human history exclusively constitutes reality by emphasizing the reciprocal relationship of humanity and the rest of the natural order. Sixth, they universalize God's righteousness by making it concerned with the justification of life and with the ground of existence of all things, setting each person right with oneself, with all other persons, and with the whole of creation. These six lines converge into an all-inclusive eschatology that expects for the righteousness of God to furnish creation with a new ground of being and a new right to life. In Moltmann's words:

> The cosmic ideas of Christian eschatology are therefore not by any means mythological, but reach forward into the open realm of possibilities ahead

of all reality, give expression to the "expectation of the creature" for a *nova creatio*, and provide a prelude for eternal life, peace and the haven of the reconciliation of all things. They bring to light not only what future means in man's "openness towards the world," but also what future means in the world's "openness towards man" . . . the relation of correspondence between the "expectation of the creature" and the "liberty of the children of God."[20]

FOR FURTHER READING

Primary Sources

Moltmann, Jürgen. "Am Ende ist alles Gottes: Hat der Glaube an die Hölle ausgedient?" *Evangelische Kommentare* 29 (1996): 542–43.

———. *The Church in the Power of the Spirit: A Contribution to Messianic Ecclesiology.* Trans. Margaret Kohl. Minneapolis: Fortress, 1993.

———. *The Crucified God: The Cross of Christ as the Foundation and Criticism of Christian Theology.* Trans. R. A. Wilson and John Bowden. Minneapolis: Fortress, 1993.

———. *God in Creation: A New Theology of Creation and the Spirit of God.* Trans. Margaret Kohl. Minneapolis: Fortress, 1993.

———. "The Logic of Hell." In *God Will Be All in All: The Eschatology of Jürgen Moltmann,* ed. Richard Bauckham, 43–48. Edinburgh: T&T Clark, 1999.

———. *Theology of Hope: On the Ground and the Implications of a Christian Eschatology.* Trans. James W. Leitch. New York: Harper & Row, 1967.

———. *The Trinity and the Kingdom: The Doctrine of God.* Trans. Margaret Kohl. Minneapolis: Fortress, 1993.

Pannenberg, Wolfhart. *The Idea of God and Human Freedom.* Trans. R. A. Wilson. Philadelphia: Westminster, 1973.

———. *Jesus—God and Man.* 2nd ed. Trans. Lewis W. Wilkins and Duane A. Priebe. Philadelphia: Westminster, 1977.

———. *Systematic Theology.* 3 vols. Trans. Geoffrey W. Bromiley. Grand Rapids: Eerdmans, 2009–10.

Secondary Sources

Ansell, Nicholas. *The Annihilation of Hell: Universal Salvation and the Redemption of Time in the Theology of Jürgen Moltmann.* Paternoster Theological Monographs. Milton Keynes, UK: Paternoster, 2013.

Bauckham, Richard. *Moltmann: Messianic Theology in the Making.* Contemporary Christian Studies. Basingstoke, UK: Marshall Pickering, 1987.

Conyers, A. J. *God, Hope, and History: Jürgen Moltmann and the Christian Concept of History.* Macon, GA: Mercer University Press, 1988.

Deane-Drummond, Celia E. *Ecology of Jürgen Moltmann's Theology.* Eugene, OR: Wipf and Stock, 2016.

Meeks, M. Douglas. *Origins of the Theology of Hope.* Minneapolis: Fortress, 1974.

CHAPTER 23

JOHN HOWARD YODER

Current Anabaptist Theology

T he Mennonite theologian and ethicist John Howard Yoder (1927–97) stands as the leading advocate of Christian pacifism in contemporary thought. Bringing the Anabaptist perspective to bear on violence perpetrated in the name of Christ from the time of Constantine to the late twentieth century, Yoder argued that none of this violence could be legitimated by just war theory, even if one granted that theory. Instead of just war theory, Yoder proposed a theory of nonviolent resistance to social evils that he found rooted in the Sermon on the Mount. He first articulated this theory in his most famous book, *The Politics of Jesus* (1972). Throughout his career at Associated Mennonite Biblical Seminary and the University of Notre Dame, Yoder challenged the widespread assumptions that Christians should go to war whenever the government deems it necessary for national security and that Christians should heroize military service.

THE POLITICS OF JESUS

Laboring under harsh Roman occupation, the Jews of Jesus's day expected God to raise up a messiah superior to Moses who would violently drive the Romans out of Israel, make Israel an independent nation-state, restore the borders of Israel to an even greater expanse than enjoyed under David and Solomon, and reign as king on David's throne. Yoder argued that Jesus regarded his Jewish contemporaries' militaristic aspirations as the worst idolatry in Israel's history, namely, attempting to become the people of God by beating the Romans at their own game. The Jewish people thereby found themselves in a far deeper slavery than simply to Rome: they had voluntarily become slaves to the kingdom of the world (*aiōn*), the philosophical system of domination and oppression that the world employs. According to Yoder, in the kingdom of the world one person or group attempts to exercise power over others through the "sword," or the ability to inflict pain on those who threaten and defy one's authority, including but not limited to wielding a literal sword. Functioning as "muscle" for the kingdom of the world, the sword coerces behavior by threats and carries out those threats when necessary.

For Yoder, Scripture teaches that such a "power-over" or "top-down" domination system is ruled by Satan. To illustrate, when Satan tempted Jesus with "all the kingdoms of the world," asserting that "all their authority and splendor . . . has been given to me, and I can give it to anyone I want to" (Luke 4:5–6), Jesus did not dispute this claim. He thereby gave tacit admission to its accuracy, though he refused to succumb to the temptation. Given its sociocultural context, Yoder maintained that worshiping Satan did not mean literally bowing down to the devil or paying him religious homage but attempting to implement the reign of God through the devices of the *aiōn*. Jesus reinforced this point by thrice acknowledging Satan as the *archē* of this world (John 12:31; 14:30; 16:11), where *archē* semantically comes from the domain of politics and denotes the highest ruling authority in a given region. On Yoder's reading, Satan was the highest ruling authority in the *aiōn*, and the Sanhedrin, backed by popular opinion, was chillingly attempting to employ political zeal and military wrath to usher in God's great and final redemption. Thus Jesus contended that Israel had abandoned its original vocation to reach out with open arms to foreign nations and actively display to them God's love.

Yoder saw the Sermon on the Mount as Jesus's challenge to his Jewish hearers to be the light of the world, stressing that the teachings within Jesus's sermon are only validly interpreted against their first-century backdrop of struggle between the Jewish people and the Roman Empire. In its context, the purpose of Jesus's sermon was to promote a countercultural program of nonviolent Jewish resistance against their Roman oppressors, that is, to teach the Jewish people how to respond to the Romans in such a way that they would not overcome evil with evil but conquer evil with good. In other words, any appropriate response to evil must refuse to let the evil define the sufferer (so that the sufferer does not stoop to its level) and must poignantly expose the evil for precisely what it is to the one committing it. But to respond to the Romans through this logic instead of getting involved with the military resistance movement would entail thinking "outside the box." Yoder emphasized that by teaching pacifism, Jesus in no way commanded (or even sanctioned) doing nothing at all against evil; to the contrary, Jesus continually resisted evil with every fiber of his being, such that the Gospels do not record a single instance when Jesus did not resist evil when confronted by it. So when Jesus said, "Do not resist (*antistēnai*) an evil person" (Matt. 5:39), he did not mean, "Let an evil person run all over you without regard for your dignity"; rather, he used the technical term *antistēnai*—which specifically meant "to get involved in the violent resistance movement against Rome"—to say, "Take a stand against evil without resisting violently."

Among the concrete examples Yoder cited to demonstrate the Sermon on the Mount's agenda of nonviolent resistance, three stand out. When Jesus commanded, "If anyone slaps you on the right cheek, turn to them the other cheek also" (Matt. 5:39), he was not telling Jews to be doormats to the Romans. Rather, he was ingeniously exploiting Roman custom to resist Roman oppression without the sword. For Roman custom stipulated that when a Roman citizen got into an argument with an enslaved or oppressed person that became so heated that it resorted to blows, the Roman would give the non-Roman the backhand slap (i.e., slapping on the right cheek), a gesture indicating that the one being slapped was subhuman, unworthy of basic human rights or respect, and vastly inferior in dignity to the fully human one doing the slapping. But when a Roman citizen got into a similar argument with another Roman citizen, one would give the other a forehand slap (i.e., slapping on the left cheek), a gesture indicating that the one being slapped was just as human as, and equal in every respect to, the one doing the slapping; in short, although the two disagreed, they recognized each other as equals in dignity and worth and entitled to the same rights. So Jesus instructed his Jewish audience that if a Roman gives one of them a backhand slap, degrading the Jew as subhuman and inferior in worth to the Roman, "turn to them the other cheek also," entailing that if the Roman slaps again, the Roman will be forced to give the Jew the forehand slap, thereby acknowledging that the Jew is just as much of a human being as he is and equal to him in dignity, worth, and every other respect.

Again when Jesus instructed, "If anyone forces you to go one mile, go with them two miles" (Matt. 5:41), he was making direct reference to Roman martial law. Yoder pointed out that the Roman Empire understood quite well the philosophy of oppression, in which there is one "trade secret" that any oppressor never wants the oppressed to learn: the oppressor has no power in and of himself, but all his so-called power actually comes from those being oppressed. In other words, the oppressor can only accomplish things powered by the oppressed; without the oppressed to build the oppressor's cities, pay the oppressor taxes, and the like, the oppressor would be nothing. Knowing this, martial law was formulated in such a way that soldiers would never do anything to make oppressed peoples aware of the secret. So concerning forced labor, martial law stipulated that a soldier could compel an oppressed person to carry his baggage for a maximum of one mile, since one mile was considered a trivial distance. A distance of one mile or less would preserve the guise that the soldier could have carried his baggage himself, but that he found it beneath him when a lesser individual could do it for him. But if a soldier compelled an oppressed person to carry his baggage for more than one mile, the Roman jurists feared that the oppressed person would start questioning the military's power. For this reason, Jesus advised each of his fellow Jews, when pressed into service by a Roman soldier, to freely carry his baggage an extra mile rather than, as the soldier would anticipate, disgustfully throwing down the baggage at the mile marker. Such an ingenious response would convey two messages to the soldier. First, the Jew would indicate to the soldier, "I am fully aware that you have zero power in and of yourself, but that you can only do what I empower you to do." Second, he would communicate, "In spite of this awareness, I will not violently rebel against you. Instead, forgetting that I'm a Jew and you're a Roman, I will show my love for you by voluntarily carrying your baggage an extra mile."

Finally, Jesus said to a people for whom "enemies" was code for "Romans," "You have heard that it was said, 'Love your neighbor and hate your enemy.' But I tell you, love your enemies and pray for those who persecute you, that you may be children of your Father in heaven" (Matt. 5:43–45). Instead of going to war against Rome—for as Jesus later told Peter, "all who draw the sword will die by the sword" (Matt. 26:52)—the Jews are to pray for the Romans and bless the Romans when the Romans curse them, showing the Romans the love of God that had the power to transform them from the inside out. Therefore Jesus told his audience to be indiscriminate, or perfect, in their love, as God unconditionally loves his enemies as well as his friends (Matt. 5:48).

THE RELATIONSHIP BETWEEN STATE AND CHURCH

Yoder postulated that the civil government or state, while not identical to the kingdom of the world, is dependent for its existence on the kingdom of the world. In other words, the state is literally a "necessary evil," which, in view of wide-scale human subscription to the *aiōn*, forcefully prevents self-seeking individuals from undermining the fabric of society by destroying the conditions necessary for larger groups to thrive and flourish. But if there were no *aiōn* (and thus no one coming under its intoxicating spell of power), then there would be no civil government either. Given its existence, nevertheless, God providentially uses civil government as a servant to maintain basic law and order in the world. According to the apostle Paul, the governmental authorities have been ordered (*tetagmenai*) by God, such that the authorities are the servants of God to execute wrath on evildoers (Rom. 13:1, 4). Yoder spelled out the significance of the verb *tetagmenai* while refuting interpretations of Paul's remarks in Romans 13 as teaching the divine right of rulers and the derivative obligation of supporting one's civil government through military service:

> God is not said to create or institute or ordain the powers that be, but only to order them, to put them in order, sovereignly to tell them where they belong, what is their place. It is not as if there was a time when there was no government and then God made government through a new creative intervention; there has been hierarchy and authority and power since human society existed. Its exercise has involved domination, disrespect for human dignity, and real or potential violence ever since sin has existed. Nor is it that by ordering this realm God specifically, morally approves of what a government does. . . . The librarian does not create nor approve of the book she or he catalogs and shelves. Likewise God does not take responsibility for the existence of the rebellious "powers that be" or for their shape or identity; they already are. What the text says is that God orders them, brings them into line, providentially and permissively lines them up with divine purposes. . . . That God orders and uses the powers does not reveal anything new about what government should be or how we should respond to government. A given government is not mandated or saved or made a channel of the will of God; it is simply lined up, used by God in the ordering of the cosmos. It does not mean that what individuals in government do is good human behavior. . . . The immediate concrete meaning of this text for the Christian Jews in Rome . . . is to call them away from any notion of revolution or insubordination. The call is to a nonresistant attitude toward a tyrannical government. . . . How strange then to make it the classic proof for the duty of Christians to kill.[1]

From the birth of the church at Pentecost until the accession of Constantine to Roman emperorship, the vast majority of Christians did not serve in the Roman military, regarding military service as a clear renunciation of Jesus's lordship and teachings on nonviolence. Standard practice dictated that soldiers would not be admitted into the church unless and until they abandoned their posts. Yoder disclosed that this practice changed when the Roman emperor Constantine (r. 312–37), who almost certainly converted to Christianity for the sake of political expediency, lifted the Roman persecution against Christians and made Christianity virtually the official religion of the Roman Empire. (It would later become the official religion under Constantine's successor Theodosius I in 380.) Yoder regarded the resulting church-state amalgam as the greatest tragedy in church history. From this point forward, Christians assumed the Roman emperor and the Christian God were on the same side and that the Christian God accomplished his aims through the empire. Hence all proscriptions against Christians serving in the military were lifted, and Christians in the Roman and subsequent Byzantine and Holy Roman Empires uncritically supported wars waged by their political leaders over the next millennium. Moreover, during this time it was illegal not to be a Christian. As a result, Yoder noted that the original Christian practice of believers' baptism was replaced by infant baptism, which initiated each person into the church-state amalgam and bestowed upon them their human rights and legal rights of citizenship, marriage, inheritance, and due process. Infant baptism also led many who would never make a personal commitment to follow Jesus as Lord to be regarded as Christian.

Although theologians beginning with Augustine (354–430) tried to defend Christian military participation through just war theory, it remains the case that no pope, bishop, council, emperor, or prince actually used this theory to legitimate the wars they provoked. According to all versions of just war theory, a war can only be entered if each of various conditions is met. Among these conditions are that a perpetuating injustice is being committed by one party against another, whatever injustice is caused by the war itself will be less than the original injustice left unchecked, the war is winnable, and the war is undertaken after all other options have been exhausted. Yoder ingeniously observed that just war theory carries with it a presumption of nonviolence, as war may only be justified as a last resort. But virtually no Christians who participated in war from the fourth through the seventeenth centuries followed just war theory or even knew that there was any such theory. For Yoder, even assuming the validity of just war theory, there has never been a just war in the history of the world, as it has nowhere been the case that all nonviolent alternatives were first exhausted.

Foreshadowed by the twelfth and thirteenth-century Waldensians and the fifteenth-century Czech Brethren, the sixteenth-century Anabaptists pressed for a return to the nonviolent resistance ethic of Jesus and advocated the separation of church and state. Indeed, the separation of church and state coupled with the insistence that only committed disciples should be initiated into the church led the Anabaptists to reinstitute believers' baptism. We will see that, for Yoder, Jesus's repudiation of the political authority offered by the kingdom of the world was undergirded by his proclamation and inauguration of the kingdom of God.

YODER ON THE KINGDOM OF GOD

Yoder maintained that Jesus's conception of the kingdom of God was a two-sided reality. On the one side, it denotes the reign of God over all earthly affairs, whether social, political, economic, aesthetic, or religious; it is the dynamic of God's kingship being applied in a world that is not yet fully under his authority. Wherever God's light-bearing kingdom comes, the evil of darkness is dispelled. On the other side, the reign of God does not look anything like the top-down leadership or the hierarchical authority endemic to the kingdom of the world. Instead of trying to exercise power over others, the kingdom of God functions as a "power-under" or "bottom-up" transformative system that works for the sole purpose of replicating agape (the love that uniquely emanates from God) to all people at all times in all places unconditionally, carrying out the will of God at the probable cost of self-interest. Consequently, Yoder held that the kingdom of God advances when Christians lovingly place themselves under others, serving others at their own expense. Although such underwriting does not imply that Christians conform to others' desires, it does entail that Christians always interact with others with their best interests in view. For Yoder, this altruistic and self-sacrificial love has the power to do what the world and the state can never do: transform the heart and mind of the perceived enemy. While the world and the state are concerned only with coercion, the kingdom of God is concerned only with conversion, namely, a person's voluntarily renouncing the ways of the *aiōn* and voluntarily opening his whole being to God as a dwelling place for his Spirit. Upon this free decision, the Spirit regenerates the person by radically reorienting his fundamental inclinations, desires, and motivations toward the will of God and concern for other people rather than, as before, toward the will of self.

Yoder declared that while the world and state are primarily interested in how people behave, the kingdom of God is primarily interested in what people become, with no interest in regulating behavior as an end in itself. Clearly, when wills and desires are redeemed, transformation of behavior is sure to follow, and without domineering "power-over" force. With this in view, Yoder confronted the question of Christian approaches to politics. A guiding principle employed by

Yoder is that a proper perspective on first-century history ensures that Christians act faithfully today; by contrast, an improper perspective or lack of perspective on first-century history ensures that Christians act unfaithfully today. On this basis, Yoder asserted that, far from conflating any earthly government with the kingdom of God, Jesus's followers must maintain a healthy suspicion toward every government, particularly their own, if they are to avoid nationalistic idolatry. Scripture indicates that however beneficial a particular state may be by worldly standards, it is powerfully influenced by satanic powers. Therefore no member of God's kingdom should either trust in any political ideology or be surprised when state heads or parties behave in contradiction to Jesus's teachings.

Accordingly, Yoder charged that Christians must not put undue stock in politics as the method for solving the world's problems, since politics is itself a department of the world. Therefore politics are impotent to bring about any permanent change, and no political position can lay claim to being "the Christian position" or "the kingdom position," for all political positions are fraught with ambiguities. In other words, for each good any political position can accomplish, there are multiple evils that it accomplishes alongside of that good. Owing to its worldly nature, politics is a matter of attempting to determine the lesser of many evils, which prohibits any clear-cut answers. Yoder opposed Christian endeavors to use politics to compel non-Christians to act in an ethical fashion. He remarked that the social "reformation that we need cannot be imposed from the top, since imposing from the top is part of what is wrong. The error is not that someone is using coercive power toward the wrong end, but that it is used at all."[2] Rather, Christians must realize that the only way to ultimately bring about social change is through Calvary-quality acts of service. These acts often take the form of nonviolent direct action, as exemplified in the American civil rights movement of Martin Luther King Jr. (1929–68) and the South African antiapartheid movement of Desmond Tutu (1931–). Trusting in the power of the kingdom of God, pacifist approaches are not passive but are rather active in resisting evil with suffering love and without lethal force. Ultimately, such approaches are the only ones that are justified and will prevail because the all-loving God is the ruler of the universe: "To say with King, 'love is the most durable power in the world,' or 'there is something in the universe that unfolds for justice' . . . is a confessional or kerygmatic statement made by those whose loyalty to Christ . . . they understand to be validated by its cosmic ground. Suffering love is not right because it 'works' in any calculable short-run way (although it often does). It is right because it goes with the grain of the universe, and that is why *in the long run* nothing else will work."[3]

CONCLUSION

Far from being driven by coercive power, Yoder maintained that human affairs are actually driven by God working in, with, and through the nonviolent, nonresistant community of Jesus's disciples. Yoder dubbed the fourth-century arrangement whereby the state and church supported the goals of each other the "Constantinian mistake." After Constantine, the church came to desire power and political influence, a temptation that Jesus rejected even to the point of suffering ignominious death. Likewise, Yoder contended that Christians must refuse to take over society and impose their convictions and values on people who do not share their faith. Rather, they must "be the church" by not returning evil for evil, living in peace, sharing goods, and performing deeds of charity as opportunities arise. In so doing, they display through the life, teachings, death, and resurrection of Jesus that an alternative to a society based on violence or the threat of violence has been rendered possible.

FOR FURTHER READING

Primary Sources

Yoder, John Howard. *The Politics of Jesus*. 2nd ed. Grand Rapids: Eerdmans, 1994.

———. *The War of the Lamb: The Ethics of Nonviolence and Peacemaking*. Ed. Glen Stassen, Mark Thiessen Nation, and Matt Hamsher. Grand Rapids: Brazos, 2009.

Secondary Sources

Finger, Thomas N. *A Contemporary Anabaptist Theology: Biblical, Historical, Constructive*. Downers Grove, IL: IVP Academic, 2004.

Friedmann, Robert. *The Theology of Anabaptism*. Scottdale, PA: Herald, 1973.

MacGregor, Kirk R. *A Molinist-Anabaptist Systematic Theology*. Lanham, MD: University Press of America, 2007.

Murray, Stewart. *The Naked Anabaptist: The Bare Essentials of a Radical Faith*. Harrisonburg, VA: Herald, 2010.

Nation, Mark Thiessen. "John Howard Yoder: Mennonite, Evangelical, Catholic." *Mennonite Quarterly Review* 77, no. 3 (2003): 1–13.

CHAPTER 24

LIBERATION
THEOLOGY

A phenomenon of the late twentieth and early twenty-first century, liberation theology is most closely associated with Latin America and the social struggles of African Americans. In essence, it is a movement designed to involve the church in positive action on behalf of the poor of the developing world and other oppressed peoples. Emerging from discrete instances of social injustice as well as political and economic oppression, liberation theology is highly contextual and calls for a reconceptualization of the church and its doctrine. Liberation theologians argue that any doctrinal system that covertly or overtly permits the exploitation of the poor or socially marginalized is not the doctrinal system of Jesus. While granting the sinfulness of humanity, liberation theologians principally identify sin as social, economic, and political injustice. As an activist theology, liberation theology deliberately manifests itself in social and political spheres.

TENDENCIES AMONG LIBERATION THEOLOGIANS

Foundational to liberation theology is the demand that theological reflection follows praxis. In other words, theology is a second, theoretical enterprise critically reflecting on the first, practical enterprise of commitment to and solidarity with the oppressed. The first enterprise is stimulated by the principle that God has a preferential love for the poor and oppressed. Accordingly, theology is not construed essentially as a system of doctrinal principles logically derived from scriptural texts. Rather, theology is construed essentially as an activist program with social and political manifestations. Another important tendency among liberation theologians is to view salvation within a social framework instead of individualistically. They contend, based on the message of the biblical prophets, that God sides with the oppressed and actively strives to liberate them from every form of bondage, slavery, and inequality. Hence the church is divinely summoned to identify with oppressed and marginalized people and not to identify with wealthy, powerful, and privileged people. In Latin America, liberation theologians focus on freeing the poor from structural poverty and political injustice. In North America, they focus on freeing the victims of oppression and racism.

Other streams leading into the river of liberation theology are Hegel's dialectical theology, the social teachings of Jesus, and the doctrine of redemption found in the Hebrew Bible. Among the architects of liberation theology is the Peruvian Dominican priest Gustavo Gutiérrez (1928–). In his most famous work, *A Theology of Liberation* (1971; 2nd ed., 1988), Gutiérrez appropriates Hegel's sense of history as a dialectical process between masters and slaves; only through this process can humanity realize full actualization in freedom. Neither the master nor the slave is completely free, as the identity of each is determined by its relation to the other. If humanity is to advance, it must advance in such a way that master-slave relations are finally overcome.

The social composition of the original Christian community possesses normative religious value for liberation theology. Underscored by the observations that Jesus and his disciples were workers and in some cases outcasts and that Jesus himself underwent persecution culminating in crucifixion, liberation theologians insist that the meaning of Jesus's teachings—particularly the Beatitudes in the Sermon on the Mount—can be fully recognized only by persons who are meek, oppressed, and suffering. The marginal status of Jesus's disciples is an integral part of the gospel message, and only by identifying with that marginalized ancient audience can one grasp the significance of that message. Hence the poor of Latin America display a profound kinship with disoriented Jews under Roman domination in Palestine, meaning that the New Testament message speaks across the cultures and becomes as powerful a force in the lives of Latin American Christians as it had been for first-century Jews. For liberation theologians, the inversion of the power structure, causing the first to be last and the last to be first, is identical in both cases. While the dominant class of Europeans in South America held all the economic and political power, for this very reason they held no spiritual power. By contrast, the indigenous peoples were excluded from the power structure and therefore possessed the spiritual knowledge that constituted true power. Moreover, since God is still the author of history, the reversal of the world's order is an eventual certainty.

In its doctrine of redemption, liberation theology offers a bold new under-standing of God's action in history that reinforces the vitality of the biblical narrative. Liberation theologians only partially identify redemption with the cross, a symbol that primarily represents divine solidarity with the oppressed and the willingness of the incarnate deity to suffer at the hands of a cruel temporal force. Consequently, the crucifixion is just as much a form of reassurance to those who suffer as a liberating act itself. An equally if not more important redemptive event in liberation theology was the exodus. Like Judaism, liberation theology regards God's redemptive work as completely realized in history. The parting of the Red Sea and the liberation of the Jews from Egypt, followed nine centuries later by the restoration of the Jews to Jerusalem after the Babylonian exile, illustrate how God redeems the faithful. Since the Christian faith is con-tinuous with the Jewish witness, it follows for liberation theologians that God still acts in redemptive ways within the course of human affairs. So whenever and wherever the righteous are oppressed and enslaved to such a degree that they cannot authentically worship God, divine intervention overthrows the oppressors and restores the people to optimal conditions for the pious life. To the liberation theologians of Latin America, faith in a redemptive God furnishes hope for another miraculous victory over their European masters. In Gutiérrez's provocative expression, political liberation is tied to God's creative work as the "self-creation" of humanity.[1]

LATIN AMERICAN LIBERATION THEOLOGY

In the mid-twentieth century, a group of Roman Catholic priests in Latin America grew convinced that the crippling poverty they witnessed was caused by social and economic injustice. This awareness led to the establishment in 1955 of the *Consejo Episcopal Latinoamericano* (CELAM or Latin American Episcopal Conference). After Vatican II, CELAM held two conferences—the first in 1968 at Medellín, Colombia, and the second in 1979 in Puebla, Mexico—that were instrumental in the formation of Latin American liberation theology. The Medellín conference formulated the slogan "preferential option for the poor," representing a conception of theology from the perspective of those on the underside of history. This conception maintains that Jesus was a revolutionary whose theology surfaced from a class struggle against the religious and political oppressors of his day. The primary source of Latin American liberation theol-ogy is Gutiérrez's personal experience of poverty in the barrios of Lima, Peru. Gutiérrez was a *mestizo* (part Spanish and part native Latin American) who suffered extreme poverty and social ostracism as a member of this oppressed ethnic group. His experience was not exceptional but shared with more than half of his countrymen.

It should be emphasized that Gutiérrez lived through the era when Latin American dictators and military governments held power, and right-wing death squads terrorized the populace. One of the most appalling instances of such brutality was the assassination of Archbishop Óscar Romero (1917–80) of El Salvador while he celebrated Mass one day after he publically demanded Salvadoran soldiers to disobey military orders to kill fellow citizens. Against this backdrop, Gutiérrez asserted, "Poverty is not fate, it is a condition; it is not a misfortune, it is an injustice. It is the result of social structures and . . . cultural categories."[2]

Gutiérrez conceives of liberation as a threefold process. At a first, primary level, liberation "expresses the aspirations of oppressed peoples and social classes, emphasizing the conflictual aspect of the economic, social, and political process which puts them at odds with wealthy nations and oppressive classes."[3]

At a second, deeper level, liberation can be applied to an understanding of history:

Humankind is seen as assuming conscious responsibility for its own destiny. This understanding provides a dynamic context and broadens the horizons of the desired social changes. In this perspective the unfolding of all the dimensions of humanness is demanded—persons who make themselves throughout their life and throughout history. The gradual conquest of true freedom leads to the creation of a new humankind and a qualitatively different society. This vision provides, therefore, a better understanding of what in fact is at stake in our times.[4]

At the third, deepest level, liberation is rooted christologically in the ministry of Jesus. Jesus the Savior "liberates from sin, which is the ultimate root of all disruption of friendship and of all injustice and oppression. Christ makes humankind truly free, that is to say, he enables us to live in communion with him; and this is the basis for all human fellowship."[5]

Gutiérrez emphasizes that these three levels are not chronologically successive processes but rather interdependent facets of a single, complex process that finds its metaphysical ground and full realization in Jesus's saving work. By considering these levels simultaneously, two pitfalls will be avoided. One consists of idealist or spiritualist approaches, which Gutiérrez sees as nothing but ways of evading a harsh and demanding reality. The other consists of programs with short-term effect, which Gutiérrez deems as shallow analyses initiated under the pretext of meeting immediate social needs.

Gutiérrez may be understood as offering a summons to the Roman Catholic Church to reclaim its mission to the poor and disenfranchised. He castigates the church for having too often affiliated with the decadent, militaristic governments that afflicted their citizens. For Gutiérrez, this denunciation is grounded in the consistent witness of Scripture: "The entire Bible, beginning with the story of Cain and Abel, mirrors God's predilection for the weak and abused of human history."[6] Preference for the poor does not indicate God's lack of love for the wealthy; it simply means that the poor are to be given priority in terms of urgency. Thus "preference implies the universality of God's love, which excludes no one. It is only within the framework of this universality that we can understand the preference, that is, what comes first."[7] Gutiérrez encapsulates his summons in this stark soteriological assertion: "To know God is to work for justice. There is no other path to reach God."[8] Thinking of salvation as something with merely religious value for the soul, stresses Gutiérrez, is inadequate; salvation directly contributes to concrete human life here and now.

The potential for conflict between Latin American liberation theology and the Roman Catholic Church is obvious. Gutiérrez indicts the Catholic Church of the Spanish and Portuguese colonists as a coconspirator in oppression, while the Catholic Church of the Natives comprises the one true Israel awaiting God's liberating deed. The Catholic Church—and the Iberian and Roman establishments to which it is linked—did not respond favorably to being identified with the Egyptians of Moses's time. In fact, to the extent that it viewed liberation theology as a subversive movement, the Catholic Church condemned it more vehemently as false doctrine. Under the auspices of Cardinal Joseph Ratzinger (1927–), later Pope Benedict XVI, the Congregation for the Doctrine of the Faith (CDF)—the Vatican's office for doctrinal orthodoxy—issued denunciations of liberation theology. The CDF cautioned that liberation theology has served as an incubator of violence, citing the Catholic priest turned guerrilla Camilo Torres Restrepo (1929–66) as a prime example. A staunch socialist, Torres came to believe that violent struggle was justified to procure justice for the poor. Infamously concluding that "if Jesus were alive today, He would be a *guerrillero*," Torres joined a guerilla organization (the National Liberation Army) and was slain in battle with the Colombian military.[9] Although Gutiérrez never condoned violence, he declares that violence may be justified in certain oppressive conditions: "We cannot say that violence is all right when the oppressor uses it to maintain or preserve 'order,' but wrong when the oppressed use it to overthrow this same order."[10]

Featuring a chorus of voices, Latin American liberation theologians encompass Catholic theologians Leonardo Boff (1938–) of Brazil, Juan Luis Segundo (1925–96) of Uruguay, and Jon Sobrino (1938–) of El Salvador as well as Protestant theologians José Míguez Bonino (1924–2012) of Argentina and Emilio Castro (1927–2013) of Uruguay. Moreover, the poor on whose behalf these thinkers write experience the effect of their theology in their lives. In several parts of Latin America—but particularly in El Salvador, Nicaragua, and Colombia—Catholic priests and lay leaders of the liberation movement have created base communities, or parishes that address the economic and spiritual needs of the people. These base communities are structured along socialist lines but order each day around the Mass and Catholic devotions. Many base community leaders have suffered to the same degree as the people they serve. Within these groups, certain symbols exert a power that they rarely display in secular and bourgeois cultures. The slavery of the Israelites under Pharaoh, the Psalter's expressions of faithfulness amid desolation, and the prophetic sayings of Jesus regarding the meek and the persecuted are regarded by the poor of Latin America as truer and more real than their own earthly sufferings. To furnish a contemporary voice to their experience, Latin American writers have created a vast corpus of poetry and song, portraying both piety and hope.

BLACK LIBERATION THEOLOGY

Emerging from the social struggles of African Americans for freedom and equality in the United States, black liberation theology marked the increasing dissatisfaction among younger African Americans with the nonviolent methodology of Dr. Martin Luther King Jr. during the 1960s. In 1966 the National Committee of Negro Churchmen (consisting of fifty-one African American pastors) issued a "Black Power" statement in the *New York Times*, declaring that their message issued from their faithfulness to the Christian gospel. They were ethically obliged as Christians to tackle the "gross imbalance of power and conscience between Negroes and white Americans," a cause "more important than who gets to the moon or the war in Vietnam."[11]

But the Black Power statement proved tame in comparison to the "Black Manifesto" issued by the Black Economic Development Conference in 1969. Coming exactly one year after the assassination of King and four years after the murder of Malcolm X, the manifesto signaled a new militancy: "No oppressed people ever gained their liberation until they were ready to fight, to use whatever means necessary, including the use of force and the power of the gun."[12] The manifesto ordered white America—particularly white religious groups—to pay reparations to the African American community. "White America has exploited our resources, our minds, our bodies, our labor. For centuries we have been forced to live as colonized people inside the United States, victimized by the most vicious, racist system in the world. . . . We are therefore demanding of the white Christian churches and Jewish synagogues . . . that they begin to pay reparations to black people in this country. We are demanding $500,000,000. . . . This total comes to 15 dollars per [African American]."[13] On May 4, 1969, James Forman (1928–2005), the primary author of the manifesto, interrupted Sunday services at New York City's historic (and white Protestant) Riverside Church to demand reparations. The Black Manifesto tied reparations to repentance, a connection with the twofold advantage of identifying with an essential Christian doctrine and posing a physical if not spiritual threat.

One month later, in June 1969, the National Committee of Black Churchmen published a historic document on "black theology," specifically tying the gospel of Jesus to black liberation. "Black Theology is a theology of black liberation. It seeks to plumb the black condition in the light of God's revelation in Jesus Christ. . . . It affirms the humanity of white people in that it says No to the encroachment of white oppression. The message of liberation is the revelation of God as revealed in the incarnation of Jesus Christ. Freedom IS the gospel. Jesus is the Liberator!"[14]

Significantly, these statements of escalated militancy came primarily from the African American church. It was not until the work of James H. Cone (1938–) that the academic world started to codify the black liberation theology first expressed in the church. As the Charles Augustus Briggs Distinguished Professor of Systematic Theology at Union Theological Seminary in New York, Cone employed his academic standing to amplify the urgent problems facing African Americans. His academic standing coupled with his personal experience as a young African American man raised in Bearden, Arkansas, uniquely qualified Cone to address these problems.

With a population of four hundred blacks and eight hundred whites, Bearden was saturated with racism, including segregated schools and restaurants as well as political and economic inequality. In Cone's words, the whites in Bearden "tried to make us believe that God created black people to be white people's servants."[15] These encounters led Cone to radical black power movements that taught a significantly different approach to conquering racism than that taken by King. Cone demarcates three stages in the formulation of black liberation theology. From 1966 to 1970 the movement centered on African American churches. From 1970 to 1977 the movement centered on academic institutions and systematic development. Since 1977 the movement has established partnerships with global liberation movements such as the Ecumenical Association of Third World Theologians, an organization of theologians from third world countries dedicated to the liberation of oppressed peoples.

Cone rose to prominence with the publication of two groundbreaking and extremely controversial books justifying African American activism: *Black Theology and Black Power* (1969) and *A Black Theology of Liberation* (1970). He indicts the theologians he studied in graduate school of failing to provide meaningful solutions to the plight of African Americans: "What could Karl Barth possibly mean for black students who had come from the cotton fields of Arkansas, Louisiana, and Mississippi, seeking to change the structure of their lives in a society that had defined *black* as non-being?"[16] Hence Cone proffers a more radical theology organized around black liberation from white racism. Cone explicitly defines black theology in liberation terms: "It is a *rational study* of the being of God in the world in light of the existential situation of an oppressed community. . . . Liberation is not only consistent with the gospel, but is the gospel of Jesus Christ."[17] For Cone, the overarching theological concept that informs all doctrinal rubrics is blackness, such that "God is black" and divine revelation "is a black-event."[18] By this Cone means that God identifies with the marginalized of society and that revelation goes beyond God's self-disclosure to God's promise of liberation. Appealing to the exodus narratives and gospel accounts of Jesus's declaration that he had come "to proclaim good news to the poor" and "to set the oppressed free" (Luke 4:18), Cone identifies the "essence of biblical revelation" as God's "emancipation from death-dealing political, economic and social structures of society."[19] In light of this observation, Cone issues the looming threat that African American patience has run out, and if white America does not participate in God's emancipation, "then a bloody, protracted civil war is inevitable."[20] Accordingly, Cone's theology is rooted in the phenomenon of black anger.

Among the most provocative aspects of Cone's understanding of Jesus is that Jesus was and is literally black. Contrasting modern American images of Jesus with the historical Jesus, Cone writes, "The 'raceless' American Christ has a light skin, wavy brown hair, and sometimes—wonder of wonders—blue eyes. For whites to find him with big lips and kinky hair is as offensive as it was for the Pharisees to find him partying with tax collectors. But whether whites want to hear it or not, Christ is black, baby, with all of the features which are so detestable to white society."[21] For Cone, the resurrection of the black Jesus is a historical event symbolizing universal freedom for all who are bound. Far from a heavenly compensation for earthly ills, resurrection hope focuses on the earthly future in such a way that it precludes African Americans from putting up with current inequities. Indeed, Cone goes so far as to allege that Jesus's blackness is essential to the significance of his life and resurrection: "The importance of Jesus must be found in his blackness. If he is not black as we are, then the resurrection has little significance for our times. . . . In a society that defines blackness as evil and whiteness as good, the theological significance of Jesus is found in the possibility of human liberation through blackness. Jesus is the black Christ!"[22] Any charge for African Americans to focus on heaven, asserts Cone, amounts to a disingenuous effort by whites to preclude African Americans from the goal of real liberation in the here and now.

CONCLUSION

Liberation theologians of all stripes reject a universal theology that is valid for every person everywhere. Rather, theology must be freshly contextualized in each unique set of sociocultural circumstances and then concretized through a commitment to justice in those circumstances. Every oppressed group must possess the liberty to engage critically with the Bible vis-à-vis their particular circumstances and choose for itself how best to interpret and apply the gospel message. Hence theology is not primarily the endeavor to provide an accurate description of God's attributes or actions but the endeavor to articulate the action of faith, the shape of liberating activity realized in obedience. In short, theology must quit explaining the world and start transforming it.

FOR FURTHER READING

Primary Sources

Black Economic Development Conference. "Black Manifesto." *New York Review of Books* (July 10, 1969).
Bonino, José Míguez. *Doing Theology in a Revolutionary Situation*. Philadelphia: Fortress, 1975.
Cone, James H. *Black Theology and Black Power*. New York: Seabury, 1969.
———. *A Black Theology of Liberation*. Philadelphia: J. B. Lippincott, 1970.
———. *God of the Oppressed*. New York: Seabury, 1975.
———. "The White Church and Black Power." In *Black Theology: A Documentary History*, 2 vols., ed. James H. Cone and Gayraud S. Wilmore, 1:66–85. Maryknoll, NY: Orbis, 1979.

Gutiérrez, Gustavo. *Essential Writings*. Ed. James B. Nickoloff. Minneapolis: Fortress, 1996.
———. *The Power of the Poor in History*. Trans. Robert R. Barr. Maryknoll, NY: Orbis, 1983.
———. *A Theology of Liberation*. Trans. Sister Caridad Inda and John Eagleson. 2nd ed. Maryknoll, NY: Orbis, 1988.
National Committee of Black Churchmen. "Black Theology" (June 13, 1969). In *Black Theology: A Documentary History*, 2 vols., ed. James H. Cone and Gayraud S. Wilmore, 1:37–39. Maryknoll, NY: Orbis, 1979.
National Committee of Negro Churchmen. "Black Power." *New York Times*, July 31, 1966.
Restrepo, Camilo Torres. *Revolutionary Priest: The Complete Writings and Messages of Camilo Torres*. Ed. John Gerassi. New York: Random House, 1971.

Secondary Sources

Cooper, Thia, ed. *The Reemergence of Liberation Theologies: Models for the Twenty-First Century*. New York: Palgrave Macmillan, 2013.
Hopkins, Dwight N. *Being Human: Race, Culture and Religion*. Minneapolis: Fortress, 2005.
Leech, Kenneth. *Race: Changing Society and the Churches*. London: SPCK, 2005.
Rowland, Christopher, ed. *The Cambridge Companion to Liberation Theology*. 2nd ed. Cambridge Companions to Religion. Cambridge: Cambridge University Press, 2007.
Sugirtharajah, R. S. *Postcolonial Reconfigurations: An Alternative Way of Reading the Bible and Doing Theology*. London: SCM, 2003.

---| CHAPTER 25 |---

FEMINIST
THEOLOGY

Similar to liberation theology in Latin America and the African American community, feminist theology is a contextual theology with powerful political dimensions, emerging from a grave sense of continuing injustice and oppression in North American cultural and church life. Feminists view the North American situation as a further expression of a longstanding history of patriarchy in the Christian tradition. While particular women and individual movements have challenged cultural and ecclesiastical patriarchy, none was effective in overcoming patriarchal propensities until the twentieth-century North American suffragette movement. The women's liberation movement of the 1960s gave rise to a theological movement in which the experience of women is the controlling subtext underlying doctrinal construction. Three broad categories of feminist theology can be distinguished: post-Christian, revisionist, and ethnic.

POST-CHRISTIAN FEMINIST THEOLOGY

Among the most radical feminist theologians was the Boston College professor Mary Daly (1928–2010). Equipped with three doctorates in religion, theology, and philosophy, Daly passed through a brief liberal Catholic phase on the way to becoming decisively "feminist postchristian."[1] In her book *The Church and the Second Sex* (1968), Daly proposed as an alternative to Simon de Beauvoir's rejection of Christianity the "commitment to radical transformation of the negative, life-destroying elements of the Church," upheld by the conviction that women and men "will with God's help mount together toward a higher order of consciousness and being."[2] Quickly thereafter, she abandoned such

244

"unimaginative reform." In 1971 Daly became the first woman to preach at the Harvard Memorial Church, staging an exodus from the church after delivering the sermon to symbolize her renunciation of Christianity. This renunciation was predicated on her contentions that Christianity is a leading cause of women's oppression and that the teachings of the Bible constitute the means by which women are subjected to patriarchy and male control.

In her second book, *Beyond God the Father* (1973), Daly condemned Christianity itself and denounced as misogynist the ultimate authority of the Bible. Daly addressed the implications of the biblical pronouns used for God and the meaning of the Christian idea that God took human form as a man. She rejected the maleness of God (in the form of Jesus) in favor of an alternative religion in which the "Goddess" becomes the projection of a feminine ideal. As Daly famously put it, "If God is male, then the male is God."[3] In other words, the patriarchal and androcentric images of the Bible and Christianity necessarily perpetuate sexist attitudes and behavior, leading Daly to "call for the castration of sexist religion."[4] Lamenting that "there is no way to remove male/masculine imagery from God," Daly explained that "when writing/speaking 'anthropo-morphically' of ultimate reality, of the divine spark of be-ing, I now choose to write/speak gynomorphically. I do so because God represents the necrophilia of patriarchy, whereas Goddess affirms the life-loving be-ing of women and nature."[5] Desertion of Christianity put Daly on a new course of formulating a "feminist theology of Be-ing," whose central factor is "the deep connection between women's becoming and the unfolding of cosmic process."[6] Many feminist theologians have followed Daly in embracing process theology as a tool to critique the perceived hopelessly patriarchal and essentialist assumptions of traditional systematic theology.

For Daly, the Christian tradition and Scriptures are laced with a religiously legitimated and therefore exceedingly harmful form of patriarchy. Accordingly, women were blamed for the sin of Adam and the fall of the human race, and women's reproductive capacities were believed to be more animalistic and less spiritual than those of men. Concurring with the 1960 *Journal of Religion* article by Valerie Saiving (1921–92) that criticized Reinhold Niebuhr's analysis of sin as pride, Daly argued that women are tempted not so much to pride as they are to give themselves away in self-sacrifice and self-effacement, and the church has aided and abetted this often destructive sacrifice of women's selves. Further, by historically precluding women from leadership roles and consigning wives to the socially constructed gender role of submission to their husbands, the church has abnegated women's dignity. Ironically, then, the church afflicts women with sin, which Daly construed as dependence on others for one's self-definition and thus underdevelopment or negation of the self.

To counteract these ecclesiastical tendencies, Daly crafted her own theological anthropology based on what it means to be a woman. In so doing, she developed a rubric that separates the intellectual realm into the world of false images that create oppression (the foreground) and the world of communion in true being (the background). Identifying the foreground as the realm of patriarchy and the background as the realm of woman, Daly regarded the foreground as a distortion of true being that, since it possesses no energy in and of itself, survives by draining the "life energy" of women inhabiting the background.[7] Hating all living things, the foreground is necrophilic and generates a host of poisons that contaminate natural life. By contrast, the background is the space where all living things connect. To destroy the foreground and cultivate the background, Daly employed rhetorical theory in carrying out a feminist reversal of traditional conceptual canons. In her *Pure Lust: Elemental Feminist Philosophy* (1984) and *Websters' First New Intergalactic Wickedary of the English Language* (1987), Daly presented an alternative rhetoric that plays on old words, creates new words, invents new ways of writing words, explores metaphorical and etymological meanings, and recovers abusive terms for women from their patriarchal bias. Hence it is the task of women to disclose the freeing nature of such terms as "hag," "witch," and "lunatic." To that end, Daly furnished definitions and even chants that can be used by women to liberate themselves from the patriarchal domination that has "gang raped" their minds.[8]

In later writings, Daly grew increasingly more radical. Going beyond a critique of patriarchy, she advocated a reversal of power between the genders in which women rule over men. Moreover, planetary subsistence demands a decline in the male population: "If life is to survive on this planet, there must be a decontamination of the Earth. I think this will be accompanied by an evolutionary process that will result in a drastic reduction of the population of males."[9]

REVISIONIST FEMINIST THEOLOGY

From the outset, feminist theologians have resisted traditional Christianity on the grounds that its depiction of normative human experience amounted to exclusively male experience. Feminists felt voiceless and neglected in a religious sphere socially, sexually, and ecclesiastically constructed by men. Despite the recognition by traditional theology that God is neither male nor female, the story of Christianity has been primarily told by men and from their perspective. Unlike

Daly, several feminist theologians have attempted to revise Christianity while preserving their Christian identification. The American applied theologian Rosemary Radford Ruether (1936–) is especially notable for constructing a feminist systematic theology. In her *Sexism and God-Talk: Toward a Feminist Theology* (1993), Ruether poses the traditional christological dictum "*Quod non est assumptum non est sanatum*" (What is not assumed is not saved) to the following question: "Can a male savior save women?"[10] Since femaleness is not assumed by a male savior, Ruether's answer is no. Using as a springboard Tillich's concept of the new being in Jesus as the Christ, Ruether presents Jesus as the liberator and representative of the new egalitarian humanity, such that Jesus inaugurated but did not complete the identity of the Christ: "Christ is not to be encapsulated 'once for all' in the historical Jesus. The Christian community continues Christ's identity."[11] Since the Christian community encompasses females, the Christ assumes and therefore saves women as well as men. Also adapting Tillich's concept of God as the ground of being, Ruether speaks of God as the "primal Matrix" or "God/ess" and thus stresses divine immanence.

Ruether charges that Scripture is so thoroughly patriarchal that women must transcend the doctrine of biblical authority to formulate a meaningful theology; as a result, "many aspects of the Bible are to be frankly set aside and rejected."[12] For instance, "texts of terror" expose a deep-seated misogyny and violent patriarchy, such as the accounts of Lot (Gen. 19:4–8) and the old man at Gibeah (Judg. 19:22–26) offering up daughters and a concubine to a mob for gang rape in order to protect male houseguests.[13] Nevertheless, Scripture does contain a valuable "prophetic-liberating" stream whose female-affirming texts comprise a "canon within a canon."[14] Hence the Bible remains a theological resource, though not an infallible one that can be drawn on indiscriminately. In addition, church history must be rewritten so as to capture the contributions of women, thus recovering their "lost memory."[15]

Ruether possesses an ongoing interest in justice issues, especially in Palestine. In her *Beyond Occupation: American, Jewish, Christian, and Palestinian Voices for Peace* (1990), Ruether issues scathing criticism of Israel's current policies in the Israeli-Palestinian conflict. Working for Palestinian human rights, Ruether has traveled to Israel and Palestine and endeavored to foster dialogue between Israelis and Palestinians and between American Jews and Christians. Ruether synthesizes themes of recovering women's experience, justice, and the environment in her *Gaia and God* (1994). Here she offers an "ecological-libertarian" worldview that affirms insights from liberal, Marxist, and romantic environmentalists while accepting finitude and limits.[16] Her worldview is premised on the following three problems: the earth cannot sustain infinite expansion; it is impossible to return to a mythic age of innocence; and we must not tolerate a static-state society that sanctions current social inequalities. As a solution, Ruether stipulates a model of conversion: "We need a fundamentally different model of human hope and change. I suggest conversion rather than either infinite growth or a final revolution."[17] Ruether grounds her model in the biblical Jubilee, God's periodic restoration of harmony to a social world out of balance. Based on new environments and technologies, Ruether aims to expose the ubiquitous need to work for justice within ever-changing historical circumstances.

Arguably the most prolific feminist theologian now writing is Elisabeth Schüssler Fiorenza (1938–), the Krister Stendahl Professor of Divinity at Harvard Divinity School. Her most famous book, *In Memory of Her: A Feminist Theological Reconstruction of Christian Origins* (1984), attempts to retrieve the unnoticed contributions of women in the early Christian church and contests the inevitability of patriarchy in the formative stage of early Christianity. Fiorenza portrays Jesus as a liberator who defied the androcentric domination system of his day to protect and enhance the rights of women and the poor. Accordingly, Fiorenza construes sin in terms of social structures that alienate and exploit the disenfranchised. She exchanges the image of God the Father for the image of God as Spirit or as the Ground of Being. Rejecting the idea that the biblical text contains any divine revelation, Fiorenza situates the spring of divine revelation in the women-church community, "the hermeneutical center of feminist theology."[18] Therefore the worshiping community of women serves as the channel and arbiter of theological truth.

Another leading revisionist feminist theologian is Vanderbilt Divinity School professor Sallie McFague (1933–). Defining metaphor as a word used in an unfamiliar context to provoke insight, McFague constructed a theological method dubbed "metaphorical theology," which she developed in four books. In *Speaking in Parables* (1975), she points theologians to the centrality of Jesus's parables, understood as extended metaphors, in the Gospels and promotes the replacement of systematic theology with narrative theology. In *Metaphorical Theology: Models of God in Religious Language* (1982), McFague denounces the patriarchal model of God as unable to communicate the doctrine of grace and as oppressive to women. Nevertheless, she preserves the monarchical model of God in her emphasis that Christianity's root metaphor is the kingdom of God. McFague furnishes a mini–systematic theology in her *Models of God: Theology for an Ecological, Nuclear Age* (1987), premised on the conviction that the task of theologians is not merely to interpret biblical metaphors for the present but also to create new metaphors. Thus McFague modifies the doctrine of the Trinity so as to encompass the following three models of God: God as mother, God as lover, and God as friend. Such "remythologizing" facilitates the liberation of groups of persons who are excluded by traditional models. Employing the metaphor of mother, McFague stresses the close relationship between God and the world, which she understood panentheistically as God's body. She applies this organic model of the world to the environmental crisis in *Body of God: An Ecological Theology* (1993). For McFague, ecofeminist theology ought to bring about increased care for the entire earth community.

ETHNIC FEMINIST THEOLOGY

The rising presence of minority women constituted the single most important development in feminist theology at the close of the twentieth century. Although concurring that the experiences of women represented an indispensable theological resource, African American and Latina women saw a world of difference between their experiences and those of the white middle-class developers of feminist theology. These minority voices contended that the dominance of white women in the feminist movement reflects the dominance of white culture. Writing out of their own ethnic backgrounds, African American and Latina feminists constructed their own unique brand of theology.

Employing black theology and revisionist feminist theology as springboards, African American women have accepted the novelist Alice Walker's (1944–) term "womanist." Womanist theology is a theological perspective founded on the experience of African American women and concentrates equally on liberation and survival. Hagar in the Old Testament is portrayed as a model for all women who venture out into the world to earn a living for themselves and their children. Indicting white feminist theology for concentrating on women alone, womanist theology is also forged by a concern for family and community. In her *White Women's Christ and Black Women's Jesus: Feminist Christology and Womanist Response* (1989), seminal womanist theologian Jacquelyn Grant (1948–) locates a primary source of authority in the history of African American women and their faith. It should be noted that womanist theologians do not reject biblical authority, since the Bible has served African American women as a source of strength and comfort throughout their history. For African American women, Jesus was the divine cosufferer and a wellspring of power during the civil rights movement. But the corporate experience of African American women constitutes a source of theological authority equal to Scripture.

Cuban-American theologian Ada María Isasi-Díaz (1943–2012) devised the term *mujerista*, based on the Spanish word for woman (*mujer*) and the womanist community of African American women, to emphasize Latina experiences as a source for feminist theology. In her *Mujerista Theology: A Theology for the 21st Century* (1996), Isasi-Díaz attacked the patriarchal machismo that often typifies Hispanic culture. The suffering Jesus is a credible source of encouragement to Latina women who have been oppressed. Isasi-Díaz redefined sin as acquiescence in the face of oppression and reluctance to dream of a better future. She challenged Latina women to build bridges among themselves while denouncing sectarianism and divisive tactics. *Mujeristas* must recognize that their task is to gather the hopes and expectations of the people about justice and peace. For Isasi-Díaz, in *mujeristas* (but not exclusively so) God chooses once again to revindicate the divine image and likeness. *Mujeristas* are called to gestate new women and new men—Latino people willing to work for the good of the people, cognizant that such work demands the renunciation of all destructive sense of self-denial. *Mujerista* theology may be understood as a process of enablement for Latina women that develops a strong sense of moral agency and exposes the importance and value of who they are, what they think, and what they do. *Mujerista* theology empowers Latinas to understand the many oppressive structures that almost completely determine their daily lives. It defines the goal of their struggle not as participating in and benefiting from these structures but as changing them radically. Accordingly, *mujerista* theology helps Latinas discover and affirm the presence of God in the midst of their communities and the revelation of God in their daily lives. Moreover, it exposes Latinas to the reality of structural evil and ways of combating it because it effectively hides God's ongoing revelation from them and from society at large.

CONCLUSION

The women's liberation movement of the 1960s possessed strong religious overtones. The former Catholic theologian and then radical feminist philosopher Mary Daly, the church historian Rosemary Radford Ruether, and the biblical scholar Elisabeth Schüssler Fiorenza broke into the privileged ranks of Protestant male academics and built their lives' work around exposing the misogyny of the dominant society. From these pioneers have come a number of other radical theological schools, including womanist theology and *mujerista* theology. Most of these schools affirm the existence of a liberating strand within the biblical tradition and an egalitarian first-century Jesus community, but they are highly adept in eradicating patriarchy and androcentrism in all their disguises from Scripture, tradition, and church. Feminist theology invites the church to acknowledge how culturally dependent and partisan are many of its proclamations of "truth," and to listen to those often clandestine aspects of the Christian tradition that have declared the full humanity of women and other oppressed groups, thereby revealing God's ever-creating Spirit.

FOR FURTHER READING

Primary Sources

Daly, Mary. *Beyond God the Father*. Boston: Beacon, 1973.
———. *The Church and the Second Sex: With a New Feminist Postchristian Introduction by the Author*. Boston: Beacon, 1975.
———. *Gyn/ecology: The Metaethics of Radical Feminism*. Boston: Beacon, 1990.
———. *Pure Lust: Elemental Feminist Philosophy*. Toronto: Women's Press, 1984.
———. *Websters' First New Intergalactic Wickedary of the English Language*. Boston: Beacon, 1987.
Fiorenza, Elisabeth Schüssler. *Bread Not Stone: The Challenge of Feminist Biblical Interpretation*. Boston: Beacon, 1984.
———. *In Memory of Her: A Feminist Theological Reconstruction of Christian Origins*. New York: Crossroad, 1984.
Grant, Jacquelyn. *White Women's Christ and Black Women's Jesus: Feminist Christology and Womanist Response*. Atlanta: Scholars, 1989.
Isasi-Díaz, Ada María. *Mujerista Theology: A Theology for the 21st Century*. Maryknoll, NY: Orbis, 1996.
McFague, Sallie. *Body of God: An Ecological Theology*. Minneapolis: Fortress, 1993.
———. *Metaphorical Theology: Models of God in Religious Language*. Minneapolis: Fortress, 1982.
———. *Models of God: Theology for an Ecological, Nuclear Age*. Minneapolis: Fortress, 1987.
———. *Speaking in Parables: A Study of Metaphor and Theology*. Minneapolis: Fortress, 1975.
Ruether, Rosemary Radford. *Gaia and God: An Ecofeminist Theology of Earth Healing*. San Franciso: HarperOne, 1994.
———. *Sexism and God-Talk: Toward a Feminist Theology*. Boston: Beacon, 1993.
———. *To Change the World: Christology and Cultural Criticism*. New York: Crossroad, 1989.
Ruether, Rosemary, and Marc H. Ellis, eds. *Beyond Occupation: American, Jewish, Christian, and Palestinian Voices for Peace*. Boston: Beacon, 1990.

Secondary Sources

Bridle, Susan. "No Man's Land." *What Is Enlightenment?* (Fall–Winter 1999): 16.
Briggs, Sheila, and Mary McClintock Fulkerson, eds. *The Oxford Handbook of Feminist Theology*. Oxford Handbooks. Oxford: Oxford University Press, 2014.
Parsons, Susan Frank, ed. *The Cambridge Companion to Feminist Theology*. Cambridge Companions to Religion. Cambridge: Cambridge University Press, 2002.
Pui-lan, Kwok. *Postcolonial Imagination and Feminist Theology*. Louisville: Westminster John Knox, 2005.
Williams, Delores S. *Sisters in the Wilderness: The Challenge of Womanist God-Talk*. Maryknoll, NY: Orbis, 2013.

CHAPTER 26

EVANGELICAL COMPLEMENTARIANISM AND EGALITARIANISM

I n response to feminist theology, evangelical theologians separated into two camps. Represented by the Council on Biblical Manhood and Womanhood (founded in 1987 by John Piper, Wayne Grudem, Wayne House, Dorothy Patterson, James Borland, Susan Foh, and Ken Sarles), the first camp articulated the complementarian view, which affirms that both men and women are created in God's image but have different roles and functions. In the home, men are viewed as the spiritual leaders, and wives are to submit to the husband's authority. In the church, women's gifts must be exercised under male authority and are generally encouraged in women's and children's ministries. Formal governing and teaching roles, however, are restricted to men.

Represented by Christians for Biblical Equality (founded in 1988 by Gilbert Bilezikian, W. Ward Gasque, Stanley Gundry, Gretchen Gaebelein Hull, Catherine Clark Kroeger, Jo Anne Lyon, Roger Nicole, and Alvera Mickelsen), the second camp articulated the egalitarian view, which affirms that when correctly interpreted, the Bible teaches the full equality of men and women in ontology and function, such that all ministry roles are equally available to men and women. Egalitarians find grounding in the conviction that all humans bear equal responsibility in the home and church to exercise their gifts in service to God. Both complementarians and egalitarians are committed to the inerrancy of Scripture, yet each view interprets particular texts differently in support of their positions.

252

THE THEOLOGICAL BASIS OF COMPLEMENTARIANISM

Complementarianism is based on the creation theology expressed in Genesis 1–2, where distinctions in masculine and feminine roles are ordained by God as part of the created order. Contrary to the assertion of egalitarians, complementarians emphasize that Adam's headship in marriage was established by God before the fall and was not a result of sin. When egalitarians claim that Adam's pre-fall headship would violate the intrinsic equality of men and women—an equality on which complementarians insist—complementarians respond that egalitarians can only make their argument at the price of denying the intrinsic equality of the Father and the Son during the period that Christ was incarnate on earth, if not eternally. Complementarians assert, with the ecumenical councils of the historic Christian church, that the Father, the Son, and the Holy Spirit are *homoousios* and therefore equally God. However, during Jesus's earthly life, there were differences in roles between the Father and the Son. The Son fully submitted to the Father, not vice versa. At the same time, the Father and the Son possessed equality in personhood, deity, and significance. Some complementarians maintain that there are eternally fixed differences in roles between the members of the Trinity, even as these members eternally exhibit equality in personhood, deity, and significance. For these complementarians, God the Father has always been the Father and has always related to the Son as a Father relates to his Son. Possessing a leadership role among the members of the Trinity that the Son and the Holy Spirit lack, the Father has greater authority than the Son or the Holy Spirit. In creation, the Father speaks and initiates, but the work of creation is completed through the Son and preserved by the continuing presence of the Holy Spirit. In redemption, the Father sends the Son into the world, and the Son obeys the Father and dies for the sins of humanity. After the Son's ascension, the Holy Spirit obeys the Father and the Son by equipping and empowering the church. However, differences in roles or authority between the members of the Trinity are entirely consistent with their equal personhood, deity, and significance. So if human beings are made in the *imago Dei*, then there may be analogous differences in roles between male and female. Complementarians believe that Scripture reveals the existence of such differences.

In their 1991 coedited book *Recovering Biblical Manhood and Womanhood: A Response to Evangelical Feminism*, complementarian leaders John Piper (1946–) and Wayne Grudem (1948–) argue that just as God the Father has authority over the Son (at least during Jesus's earthly ministry) while the two are equal in deity, the husband has authority over the wife while the two are equal in personhood. For this position, they cite 1 Corinthians 11:3 as their primary evidence: "But I want you to realize that the head of every man is Christ, and the head of the woman is man, and the head of Christ is God." Accordingly, the man's role parallels that of God the Father, and the woman's role parallels that of God the incarnate Son. For Piper and Grudem, the difference in authority between men and women is part of God's original plan for creation that predates the fall. They furnish eight arguments in support of this inference.

First, the fact that God created Adam first, then after a period of time created Eve, indicates that God viewed Adam as holding a leadership role in his family. As Grudem notes, "No such two-stage procedure is mentioned for any of the animals God made, but here it seems to have a special purpose. The creation of Adam first is consistent with the Old Testament pattern of 'primogeniture,' the idea that the firstborn in any generation in a human family has leadership in the family for that generation."[1] Second, Eve was created as a helper for Adam, such that God made Eve for Adam and not Adam for Eve (Gen. 2:18; 1 Cor. 11:9). Third, Adam named Eve, and the right to name someone depicts authority over that person (Gen. 2:23). Fourth, God named the human race "man," not "woman" (Gen. 5:2). Denominating the human race with a term that also referred to Adam in particular or man in distinction from woman implies a leadership role belonging to the man. Fifth, the serpent came to Eve first (Gen. 3:1), while God spoke to Adam first (Gen. 2:15–17). This reversal implies that Satan was attempting to undercut the pattern of male leadership that God had ordained in the marriage. Sixth, even though Eve sinned first, God came first to Adam and called him to account for his actions. Hence God regarded Adam as the leader of his family, the one to be held responsible for what happened. Seventh, Adam, not Eve, represented the human race. Although Eve sinned first, each human is counted sinful because of Adam's sin (Rom. 5:15; 1 Cor. 15:22). Eighth, New Testament commands regarding marriage, which presuppose Christ's reversal of the fall, affirm the subjection of wives to their husbands (Col. 3:18–19; Titus 2:5; 1 Peter 3:1–7).

EFFECTS OF COMPLEMENTARIANISM IN HOME AND CHURCH

Complementarians maintain that home relations should be structured along the lines of Ephesians 5:22–24, "Wives, submit [hypotassō] yourselves to your own husbands as you do to the Lord. For the husband is the head of the wife as Christ is the head of the church, his body, of which he is the Savior. Now as the church submits [*hypotassō*] to Christ, so also wives should submit [*hypotassō*] to their husbands in everything." Complementarians insist that *hypotassō* entails a relationship of submission to an authority. Grudem reasons that this entailment is evident in the uses of *hypotassō* throughout the New Testament and extrabiblical literature:

> It is used elsewhere in the New Testament of the submission of Jesus to the authority of his parents (Luke 2:51); of demons being subject to the disciples (Luke 10:17—clearly the meaning "act in love, be considerate" cannot fit here); of citizens being subject to government authorities (Rom. 13:1, 5; Titus 3:1; 1 Peter 2:13); of the universe being subject to Christ (1 Cor. 15:27; Eph. 1:22); of unseen spiritual powers being subject to Christ (1 Peter 3:22); of Christ being subject to God the Father (1 Cor. 15:28); of church members being subject to church leaders (1 Cor. 16:15–16 [see 1 Clem. 4:24]; 1 Peter 5:5) . . . of servants being subject to their masters (Titus 2:9; 1 Peter 2:18); and of Christians being subject to God (Heb. 12:9; James 4:7). *None of these relationships is ever reversed.* . . . In fact, the term is used outside the New Testament to describe the submission and obedience of soldiers in an army to those of superior rank.[2]

Accordingly, when wives feel rebellious, indignant toward their husband's leadership, or when they vie with their husbands for family leadership, they ought to recognize that this is a sinful consequence of the fall. Wives seeking to live in conformity to God's plan ought rather to be submissive to her husband and rejoice in his leadership of the home.

Nevertheless, complementarians deny that submission is entirely passive, insisting that wives should not fail either to contribute to the decision-making process of the family or to speak words of correction to her husband when he is doing wrong. For complementarians, submission to the husband's authority does not entail agreeing with everything the husband says or recommends. Uncritical acquiescence is not what it means to submit to the authority of an employer, of government officials, or of church officers—we can certainly differ with each of them yet still submit to them. Likewise, a wife can still be subject to her husband even though she may disagree with some of his decisions. Husbands should strive for supremely loving, considerate, and thoughtful leadership in their families and avoid the errors of being physically or emotionally absent from the home and of spending their time almost entirely on other concerns. Complementarians insist that the love husbands show their wives must be utterly self-sacrificial, just as

Jesus's love for the church entailed his self-sacrifice on the cross: "Husbands, love your wives, just as Christ loved the church and gave himself up for her" (Eph. 5:25). When wives and husbands steer clear of passivity and follow a biblical structure, complementarians contend that they will respectively discover true womanhood and true manhood in all of their noble dignity and reflect more accurately the *imago Dei* in their lives.

Complementarians declare that the Bible does not permit women to serve in the role of pastor, elder, or other functionally equivalent roles in churches that do not have pastors or elders. Four biblical passages are typically adduced in support of this declaration. First, 1 Timothy 2:11–14 states, "A woman should learn in quietness and full submission. I do not permit a woman *to teach* or *to assume authority* over a man; she must be quiet. For Adam was formed first, then Eve. And Adam was not the one deceived; it was the woman who was deceived and became a sinner" (emphasis added). Complementarians insist that Paul is here addressing the church when it is assembled and that "to teach" and "to assume authority" represent the unique functions carried out by pastors or elders. For complementarians, the present tense of Paul's prohibition (*ouk epitrepō*, lit. "I am not permitting") requires the gnomic or timeless sense of proverbial instruction. Hence complementarians maintain that 1 Timothy 2:11–14 represents a command applicable to all Christians at all times. If egalitarians deny the timeless applicability of this text and others like it, complementarians warn that such a denial presupposes a process of interpreting Scripture that will quickly nullify the authority of Scripture in the lives of Christians today.

Second, 1 Corinthians 14:34–35 exhorts, "Women should remain silent in the churches. They are not allowed to speak, but must be in submission, as the law says. If they want to inquire about something, they should ask their own husbands at home; for it is disgraceful for a woman to speak in the church." Complementarians concede that Paul cannot be forbidding all public speech by women in the church, since he earlier permits them to pray and prophesy in church (1 Cor. 11:5). Hence complementarians judge it best to understand this passage as referring to the speech examined in the immediate context, namely, the spoken assessment of prophecies in the congregation (1 Cor. 14:29). So although Paul allowed women to prophesy in church, he did not allow them to speak up and critique the prophecies that had been uttered, as this would be a ruling or governing function with respect to the church. Consequently, Paul was concerned to preserve male leadership in church teaching and governance.

Third and fourth, both 1 Timothy 3:1–7 and Titus 1:5–9 presuppose that overseers are going to be men. An overseer must be "faithful to his wife"

(1 Tim. 3:2; Titus 1:6) and "must manage his own family well and see that his children obey him, and he must do so in a manner worthy of full respect" (1 Tim. 3:4).

Based on these texts, complementarians see egalitarianism as a false teaching that God allows to exist in the church to test whether his people will be faithful to his Word or not. Will Christians obey God's Word on matters of manhood and womanhood, complementarians ask, or will they capitulate to a secular culture that blurs divinely ordained gender distinctions?

THE THEOLOGICAL BASIS OF EGALITARIANISM

Egalitarianism is based on the new covenant theology expressed by Paul in Galatians 3:26–29, "So in Christ Jesus you are all children of God through faith, for all of you who were baptized into Christ have clothed yourself with Christ. There is neither Jew nor Gentile, neither slave nor free, nor is there male and female, for you are all one in Christ Jesus. If you belong to Christ, then you are Abraham's seed, and heirs according to the promise." On the egalitarian view, Paul here contended that since the salvific identity of Christians is in Jesus alone, it is contrary to the gospel to assign status or privilege in the church (i.e., "in Christ Jesus") based on ethnicity, class, or gender. In terms of cultural context, Galatians 3:28 renounces the notions conveyed by the daily Jewish prayer thanking God for not being born a Gentile, a slave, or a woman, as these groups lacked the privilege of studying Torah. Hence Paul's renunciation of these distinctions must imply the opposite, namely, affirmation of the equal standing in the life of the church of each of these groups, who are one in Christ. Moreover, egalitarian scholar Mimi Haddad, president of Christians for Biblical Equality, notes that the three statements in Galatians 3:28 about the new creation's transcendence of ethnicity (lit. "no longer Jew *or* Gentile"), class (lit. "no longer slave *or* free"), and gender (lit. "no longer male *and* female") are not exactly parallel in the Greek text. The grammatical shift from "or" to "and" reflects both that women and men need each other and that traditional feminine-masculine social roles represent a continuum on which individuals may locate themselves comfortably and without fear of reprisal.

In his 2009 book *Man and Woman, One in Christ*, egalitarian leader Philip B. Payne maintains that 1 Corinthians 11:11 ("Nevertheless, in the Lord woman is not independent of man, nor is man independent of woman"), like Galatians 3:28, explicitly asserts that women and men are equals in church life. Payne points out that 1 Corinthians 11:11 occurs in the context of affirming that women, like men, may lead the central activities in public meetings of the church, namely, prayer (the vertical dimension of worship) and prophecy (the horizontal dimension of worship), so long as they do so in ways that neither renounce marriage nor Christian morality. Accordingly, Paul's denial of independence between women and men "in the Lord" must at minimum pertain to these activities of church leadership.

Egalitarian leader Kevin Giles argues that the Greek word *kephalē*, which anatomically refers to the head but carries the metaphorical meaning of either "source" or "authority over," denotes "source" in 1 Corinthians 11:3. For Paul could not say, on pain of contradiction, that man is authority over woman and then immediately say in 1 Corinthians 11:5 that both women and men can lead in church by praying and prophesying. Nor could Paul have said in 1 Corinthians 11:10 that women have "authority" on their heads if authority were reserved to men. Accordingly, "the head (*kephalē*) of the woman is man" means that man/Adam is the source of woman (Gen. 2:21–23), an interpretation confirmed by 1 Corinthians 11:12, "For as woman came from man, so also man is born of woman." As a result, "the head (*kephalē*) of Christ is God" means that the Father is the source of Jesus Christ in either his incarnation or his eternal generation from the Father.

EFFECTS OF EGALITARIANISM IN HOME AND CHURCH

Egalitarians underscore 1 Corinthians 7, Paul's most thorough treatment of marriage, as delineating precisely the same conditions, opportunities, rights, and obligations for the wife as for the husband in ten distinct areas. In each, Paul regarded husbands and wives as equals. Egalitarians view this as a nonexhaustive list of examples that implies that wives have the same conditions, opportunities, rights, and obligations as husbands in all areas. Paul's symmetrically balanced wording emphasizes equality: husbands and wives mutually possess each other (1 Cor. 7:2); they have mutual conjugal rights (1 Cor. 7:3); they have mutual authority over the other's body (1 Cor. 7:4); they have mutual sexual obligations (1 Cor. 7:5); both are told not to separate or divorce (1 Cor. 7:10–13); both consecrate the other and sanctify their children (1 Cor. 7:14); both possess freedom if deserted (1 Cor. 7:15); both hold a potentially saving influence on the other (1 Cor. 7:16); both are free to marry (1 Cor. 7:28); both may focus on pleasing the other in marriage (1 Cor. 7:33–34). Paul even commanded that "the husband does not have authority over his own body but yields it to his wife" (1 Cor. 7:4). In an age where the sexual union between husband and wife was a matter of the husband's having it his way, the mutuality Paul championed stands unparalleled in the literature of the ancient world. As New Testament scholar Richard Hays observes, "Paul offers a paradigm-shattering vision of marriage as a relationship in which the partners are bonded together in submission to one another."[3]

Likewise, egalitarians contend that the instruction of Ephesians 5:22–24 for wives to submit to their husbands falls under the umbrella of Ephesians 5:21, directed at both husbands and wives: "Submit (*hypotassō*) to one another out of reverence for Christ." Hence the wife's submission is explicitly one facet of mutual submission, where husband and wife each voluntarily yield to the other in love. Neither the husband nor the wife has an authority over their partner that their partner lacks. On the egalitarian view, Paul called both husbands and wives to defer to and nurture each other. When Paul claimed that "the husband is the head (*kephalē*) of the wife as Christ is the head (*kephalē*) of the church" (Eph. 5:23), egalitarians contend that *kephalē* again means "source," as seen by Paul's focus on Christ as the source of love and nourishment of the church (Eph. 5:25, 29). In addition, the Bible approves women leading in the home. Paul treated husbands and wives equally in relation to their children (Eph. 6:1–2; Col. 3:20) and instructed wives "to manage their homes" (*oikodespotein*, lit. "to be house despots"; 1 Tim. 5:14).

Affirming the right of women to serve in the roles of pastor, elder, and every other ecclesiastical office, egalitarians offer different interpretations of the texts complementarians believe preclude women from these roles. In 1 Timothy 2:12, egalitarians emphasize that the meaning of the key verb *authentein* means "to assume a stance of independent authority," claiming that every documented occurrence of this verb denotes unauthorized assumption of authority. They proceed to argue that Paul did not prohibit two activities—women teaching *and* assuming authority over men—but prohibits one thing: women assuming, without ecclesiastical authorization, authority to teach men. As is standard with Paul's use of the conjunction *oude*, "to teach" plus *oude* plus "to assume authority" conveys a single idea. On the egalitarian reading, Paul identified two reasons for this prohibition. First, for women to assume authority to teach men without recognized authorization by the church was disrespectful to men, whom they ought to respect since man was the source from whom woman came (1 Tim. 2:13). Second, some women in Ephesus were deceived by false teachers—whom Paul had already barred from teaching (1 Tim. 1:3)—to follow after Satan (1 Tim. 2:14). As a result, egalitarians argue that Paul in 1 Timothy 2:12 did not prohibit women from having authority over men but rather prohibited women from unauthorized assumption of authority over men because of the present crisis of false teaching in Ephesus.

Egalitarians posit two interpretations of 1 Corinthians 14:34–35, that "women should remain silent in the churches. . . ." First, some egalitarians (most notably Philip Payne and Gordon Fee) contend on the basis of textual criticism that the passage is an interpolation into the text of 1 Corinthians and therefore does not stand as part of Scripture. Second, some egalitarians contend that the passage, though penned by Paul, constitutes a quotation of the Judaizing Corinthian men's position from the letter the Corinthians had sent Paul and which Paul proceeded to refute. This stance is based largely on the remark immediately following the alleged quotation: "Or did the word of God originate with you? Or are you the *only people* (*monous*, masculine plural) it has reached?" (1 Cor. 14:36; emphasis added). For egalitarians, Paul is telling the men who apparently want to restrict women that such an attitude is not to be tolerated since they, the men, did not originate God's word, and that they are therefore not the only ones to whom God's word has come.

Egalitarians claim that 1 Timothy 3:1–7 and Titus 1:5–9 do not presuppose that all overseers be men, maintaining that it is simply Greek convention to employ grammatically masculine forms when describing groups of people including men and women. Hence egalitarians state that "faithful to his wife" (1 Tim. 3:2; Titus 1:6) is a generic idiom that means "monogamous." In fact, egalitarians insist that Paul encouraged every believer to aspire to be an overseer: "Here is a trustworthy saying: Whoever (*tis*) aspires to be an overseer desires a noble task" (1 Tim. 3:1). In Greek, "whoever" or "anyone" (*tis*) is a gender-inclusive word, indicating to egalitarians an open door to women and men alike. For egalitarians, Paul clearly indicated that "anyone" was his continuing subject by repeating "anyone" (1 Tim. 3:5) and identifying *tis* as the subject of the parallel list for overseer qualifications in Titus 1:6. Egalitarians note that, contra most translations, the Greek does not contain a single masculine pronoun in any of the qualifications of church leaders in 1 Timothy 3:1–13 or Titus 1:5–9.

Finally, egalitarians highlight Romans 16:1–16 as a celebration of women in ministry. Out of the ten people Paul greets by name as his ministry colleagues, seven are women: "Phoebe, a deacon of the church in Cenchreae" (Rom. 16:1); "Junia . . . outstanding among the apostles" (Rom. 16:7); "Priscilla . . . my [coworker] in Christ Jesus" (Rom. 16:3); "Mary," "Tryphena and Tryphosa," and "Persis," who "worked very hard in the Lord" (Rom. 16:6, 12). First Corinthians 16:16 exhorts believers "to submit to . . . everyone who joins in the work and labors at it," and 1 Thessalonians 5:12 identifies "those who work hard among you" as those "who care for you in the Lord and who admonish you." Hence egalitarians insist that Paul denominates these women not simply as believers but also as ministry leaders. Egalitarians contend that Paul's naming of such a high proportion of women leaders in an open society is without parallel in the entire history of ancient Greek literature and implies a level of female leadership in the early church exceptional for its culture.

CONCLUSION

As evangelicals, both complementarians and egalitarians are committed to the final authority of Scripture, yet each group emphasizes different biblical texts in support of their position and interpret pivotal biblical texts divergently. While the Christian church has historically been complementarian rather than egalitarian, egalitarians have gained considerable ground in North American evangelicalism. Several evangelical denominations affirm the ordination of women, and most complementarian seminaries admit women to their master of divinity programs, even if women are excluded from certain classes like preaching. On the other hand, within those evangelical and nonevangelical denominations that ordain women, ordained women often find it quite difficult to obtain positions as senior pastors of larger churches. Statistics reveal that ordained women generally find positions as assistant pastors, associate pastors, interim pastors, and pastors of small congregations. Sadly, there are also cases of discrimination on the egalitarian side. Some complementarian men are prevented from becoming pastors in their denominations because they cannot conscientiously participate in what they regard as their denominations' cultural relativizing of the God-ordained gender roles according to which men and women were created.

FOR FURTHER READING

Primary Sources

Giles, Kevin. *Jesus and the Father: Modern Evangelicals Reinvent the Doctrine of the Trinity.* Grand Rapids: Zondervan, 2006.

Grudem, Wayne. *Systematic Theology: An Introduction to Biblical Doctrine.* Grand Rapids: Zondervan, 1994.

Payne, Philip B. *Man and Woman, One in Christ: An Exegetical and Theological Study of Paul's Letters.* Grand Rapids: Zondervan, 2009.

Pierce, Ronald W., and Rebecca Merrill Groothuis, gen. eds. and Gordon D. Fee, contributing. ed. *Discovering Biblical Equality: Complementarity without Hierarchy.* Downers Grove, IL: IVP Academic, 2005.

Piper, John, and Wayne Grudem, ed. *Recovering Biblical Manhood and Womanhood: A Response to Evangelical Feminism.* Wheaton, IL: Crossway, 1991.

Secondary Sources

Achtemeier, Paul J., Joel B. Green, and Marianne Meye Thompson. *Introducing the New Testament: Its Literature and Theology.* Grand Rapids: Eerdmans, 2001.

Beck, James R., gen. ed.; Stanley N. Gundry, ser. ed. *Two Views on Women in Ministry.* Rev. ed. Grand Rapids: Zondervan, 2005.

Bilezikian, Gilbert. *Beyond Sex Roles: What the Bible Says about a Woman's Place in Church and Family.* 3rd ed. Grand Rapids: Baker Academic, 2006.

Hays, Richard B. *First Corinthians.* Louisville: Westminster John Knox, 1997.

MacArthur, John. *Divine Design: God's Complementary Roles for Men and Women.* Colorado Springs: David C Cook, 2011.

CHAPTER 27

REFORMED EPISTEMOLOGY

he secular culture that delivered the "Death of God" movement has been
successfully challenged by a new cadre of Christian philosophers. Their
undisputed leader is Alvin Plantinga (1932–), the John A. O'Brien, professor of philosophy emeritus at the University of Notre Dame and the inaugural
holder of the Jellema Chair of Philosophy at Calvin College. More than anyone
else, Plantinga has rehabilitated belief in God and made theism respectable again
among philosophers of all stripes. Agnostic philosophers may still claim they do
not know there is a God, but they can no longer sneer at the idea of God without
looking foolish. Plantinga's philosophical work is voluminous and groundbreaking. Challenging theological rationalism (or evidentialism), Plantinga worked
with Yale philosopher Nicholas Wolterstorff (1932–) and Syracuse philosopher
William Alston (1921–2009) to develop a new epistemology, or theory of knowledge, rooted in insights from the Reformed tradition. Reformed epistemology is
nonevidentialist, as it maintains that evidence is not necessary for a person's
faith to be rational. This chapter elucidates the details of Reformed epistemology, including such key concepts as properly basic beliefs, justification, warrant,
the *sensus divinitatis*, and the internal instigation of the Holy Spirit.

PLANTINGA'S DEFENSIVE REPLY TO THE EVIDENTIALIST OBJECTION

Arising with the advent of modernity, evidentialism is the stance that one can
only rationally believe in a claim to the degree that it is supported by evidence.
According to the evidentialist objection to theism, belief in God is unjustified or

264 Contemporary Theology

unwarranted because there is insufficient evidence that God exists. Evidentialists typically construe "evidence" narrowly as propositional—a matter of good argument—rather than broadly as anything a person has access to that is relevant to the truth of some proposition. While not granting the point that the arguments for God's existence are insufficient, Plantinga contends that belief in God can be justified and warranted even if there is no good argument for the existence of God. Plantinga points out that the evidentialist objection is a de jure objection to theism, which aims to undermine the rationality of belief in God even if God does exist. It is not a de facto objection to theism, which aims to show that God in fact does not exist. De facto objections are metaphysical, having to do with the way reality is, whereas de jure objections are epistemic, having to do with the requirements for beliefs to be rational.

To show that no good reason exists to think we need arguments to be justified in believing in God, Plantinga employs a two-pronged cumulative defense against the evidentialist objection. First, it is false that every belief must be justified by argument. If every rational belief requires an argument, then the premises of that argument would also need to be established by a second argument. But then the premises of that second argument would have to be established by a third argument, and so on *ad infinitum*. In this case, we couldn't believe anything because we don't have an infinite amount of time to construct arguments. Moreover, there are clear examples of things we are justified in believing without arguments. For instance, when we have a headache we experience the pain and, on that basis alone, we form the justified belief that we have a headache. Hence at least some beliefs are justified even if they are not based on arguments. That gives us two categories of justified beliefs: those justified independently of arguments and those justified by arguments. So in which category is belief in God?

Second, people have assumed belief in God falls in the second category because of the influence of a historically important epistemological theory—classical foundationalism, which arose with Descartes. But Plantinga reasons that classical foundationalism is self-referentially incoherent, or self-refuting. Classical foundationalism holds that all justified beliefs must be either properly basic (held in an immediate way, apart from argument) or logically derived from properly basic beliefs. Classical foundationalists allege that only three types of beliefs are properly basic. First are *incorrigible beliefs*, or beliefs about which it is logically impossible to be mistaken. Examples include the belief that one is in pain or that one seems to be seeing something as yellow. Second are *self-evident beliefs*, or beliefs that are obviously true considered in themselves. Consider the belief that "2 + 2 = 4" or "all bachelors are unmarried." One sees immediately that these beliefs are true simply by understanding them. Third are *perceptual beliefs*, or beliefs evident to one or more of the five senses. Perceptual beliefs include seeing a tree or smelling a fresh daisy. At this juncture, Plantinga delivers what he takes to be the *coup de grace* against classical foundationalism. Its own criterion states, "A belief is rational only if it is incorrigible, self-evident, perceptual, or derived from beliefs that are one of the three." But is that criterion itself "incorrigible, self-evident, perceptual, or derived from beliefs that are one of the three"? It certainly seems not! Hence classical foundationalism cannot even meet its own criterion for rationality. It is self-stultifying. One cannot rationally affirm the criterion without also denying it. Because the view that belief in God must be justified by argument presupposes classical foundationalism, and classical foundationalism is inherently self-contradictory, there remains no good reason to think belief in God must be justified by argument.

PLANTINGA'S MODEST, REIDIAN FOUNDATIONALISM

Although Plantinga rejects classical foundationalism, he insists that the foundationalist axiom that rationally justified beliefs must either be properly basic or derived from properly basic beliefs is correct. In fact, Plantinga thinks that something like the foundationalism of the Scottish philosopher Thomas Reid (1710–96) is correct. Reid argued for an expansion of properly basic beliefs to include those generated by other belief-producing mechanisms of the mind, such as reflection, memory, and inference. Concerning any belief like "I am the same person I was five years ago," "I skipped lunch this afternoon," or "My friend is in pain," Plantinga notes, "In the typical case I do not hold this belief on the basis of other beliefs; it is nonetheless not groundless. My having that characteristic sort of experience . . . plays a crucial role in the formation of that belief. It also plays a crucial role in its justification."[1] Given mental beliefs, memory beliefs, ascriptions of mental states to others, and the like, Plantinga defines justification as follows:

> Let us say that a belief is *justified* for a person at a time if (a) he is violating no epistemic duties and is within his epistemic rights in accepting it then and (b) his noetic structure is not defective by virtue of his then accepting it. Then my being appeared to in this characteristic way (together with other circumstances) is what confers on me the right to hold the belief in question; this is what justifies me in accepting it. We could say, if we wish, that this experience is what justifies me in holding it; this is the ground of my justification, and, by extension, the ground of the belief itself.[2]

Thus justification involves two main components: epistemic obligation and introspective awareness.

Epistemic obligation means we have an obligation to try our best to make sure everything we believe is true. This general obligation gives rise to other epistemic obligations. To illustrate, if we have a duty to try to believe only true things, then we might be obligated not to form beliefs about a person who is a long distance away in the dark. We might have a duty not to believe that we had white cake on our third birthday if the memory is quite vague. Accordingly, we should at least try to temper beliefs formed from seeing things from a distance in the dark or based on very distant recollections. Epistemic obligation entails internalism, the view that the ability to reflect on the reasons for believing something is essential to justification. If we have obligations about how to form beliefs, then we must be able to examine the reasons for our beliefs introspectively to ensure they do not flout any duties. In sum, for Plantinga a belief is justified if it meets two conditions: it was formed without disregarding our epistemic duty to try our best to ensure that what we believe is true, and we can reflect inwardly on the factors that confer justification.

But justification is not the only element that turns true belief into knowledge. We are justified in claiming we know something if we mentally performed our duty to reflect on the reasons for our true belief. But do we always have such firm control over what we choose to believe? Plantinga suspects we do not, and he argues that warrant rather than justification is a more promising candidate for turning our true beliefs into knowledge. Plantinga alleges that a belief has warrant if the belief is produced by cognitive faculties that are properly functioning and are functioning in circumstances in which those faculties are designed to operate. Thus Frank's belief that his car is in the driveway is warranted if it is formed by his properly functioning visual system (e.g., not by optical illusions, hallucinations, or other malfunctions) in conditions in which it was designed to operate (e.g., proper lighting and distance). Here we see that, on Plantinga's view, warrant does not depend on the fulfilling of epistemic duties but on the reliability of the cognitive processes that produced the belief. So Plantinga's account of warrant centers on properly functioning cognitive processes rather than obligations and duties. Moreover, warrant is externalistic, not internalistic. A belief can possess warrant even if the individual has no conception of what gives the belief warrant. Frank doesn't have to know that his eyes are functioning properly or that they are operating in the circumstances for which they were designed for his belief to possess warrant.

Though Plantinga prefers the externalist concept of warrant—note the title of perhaps his most influential book is *Warranted Christian Belief*—he maintains that belief in God is both justified and warranted. Since the concepts are different, he offers two arguments, one for justification and the other for warrant.

JUSTIFICATION OF BELIEF IN GOD

According to Plantinga, it is fairly obvious that belief in God is justified in the sense of epistemic obligation, for the believer needs only fulfill her epistemic duty to try to ensure that what she believes is true. Suppose a believer does her level best to make sure her belief about God's existence is true. She open-mindedly reads the standard atheist arguments against the existence of God. She mulls over the problem of evil and alleged inconsistencies in the nature of God. She also reads Nietzsche's, Freud's, and Marx's critiques of religious beliefs. Alternatively, she reads the arguments for the existence of God but does not believe in God because of them. The believer has had religious experiences in which she took God to be comforting, loving, and encouraging her. During worship services, prayer, or Bible reading sessions, she has a strong sense of the majesty and awe of God. The believer may sometimes even feel as if she is in God's very presence. She might feel what she takes to be the Holy Spirit enlightening her as previously bewildering passages of Scripture suddenly become perfectly clear.

The believer assesses her experiences:

> After long, hard, conscientious reflection, this all seems to her more convincing than the complaints of the critics. Is she then going contrary to duty in believing as she does? Is she being irresponsible? Clearly not. There could be something defective about her, some malfunction not apparent on the surface. She could be mistaken, a victim of illusion or wishful thinking, despite her best efforts. She could be wrong, desperately wrong, pitiably wrong. . . . Nevertheless, she isn't flouting any discernible duty. She is fulfilling her epistemic responsibilities; she is doing her level best; she is justified.[3]

Hence the believer has considered the arguments and experiences pro and con, and she has introspective access to that which she takes to confer justification, her rich spiritual life. As a result, she legitimately concludes that God exists; as Plantinga puts it, "How can she possibly be blameworthy or irresponsible, if she thinks about the matter as hard as she can, in the most responsible way she can, and she still comes to these conclusions?"[4] Plantinga observes that many people hold their theistic beliefs in this way.

WARRANT OF BELIEF IN GOD

But don't theists need to prove their belief in God? No more than we need to prove that other people have minds or that our memory beliefs are true before we believe in them. I cannot prove what I ate for breakfast this morning, but I am warranted in holding that memory as a properly basic belief. Belief in God is sort of like that. Based on the philosophical and theological views of Thomas Aquinas (1225–74) and John Calvin (1509–64), Plantinga proposes the A/C (Aquinas/Calvin) model and the extended A/C model of religious epistemology. The A/C model applies if humans are not cognitively damaged by sin; the extended A/C model applies if humans are cognitively damaged by sin.

Regarding the A/C model, both Aquinas and Calvin contend there is a kind of natural knowledge of God. Calvin called this the *sensus divinitatis* (divine sense), by which he meant an innate tendency to see the hand of God in nature. While the capacity for this natural knowledge is present since birth (just as the capacity for mathematical knowledge is present since birth), the functioning of the *sensus divinitatis* requires some maturity. Plantinga identifies the *sensus divinitatis* as a cognitive mechanism that outputs a belief in God given the correct sort of input. If the mechanism is functioning properly, then the input of seeing majestic mountains, starry heavens, or the eyes of one's newborn child may "trip our trigger" and generate the output of belief in God. Religious experience, worship, or Bible study may also trigger the *sensus divinitatis* to yield theistic belief. Likewise, one may be aware of God's disapproval after committing some sin, or one may sense God's forgiveness upon repentance and confession.

Plantinga emphasizes that the deliverances of the *sensus divinitatis* are not inferential beliefs. They do not come by way of argument. One does not view a beautiful sunset and infer that "only God could have created all of this." Rather, beliefs formed by the *sensus divinitatis* parallel the way perceptual beliefs are formed. Upon seeing a pine tree capped with snow on a moonlit night, one does not infer from that perceptual experience that "I am being appeared to in a way characteristic of a pine tree capped with snow on a moonlit night." Instead, upon perceiving the tree, snow, and moonlight, the pertinent belief arises spontaneously and immediately. Hence the beliefs of the *sensus divinitatis* are properly basic; they are both psychologically and epistemologically direct. Indeed, they are properly basic with regard to warrant; they are formed by a cognitive faculty functioning properly, aimed at truth, and in an appropriate cognitive environment.[5]

On the condition that humans are cognitively damaged by sin, Plantinga offers the extended A/C model, which builds on the A/C model and encompasses God's plan of salvation in Christ. God makes humans aware of his plan of salvation via the inward work of the Holy Spirit (which Plantinga calls the "internal instigation of the Holy Spirit") and Scripture.[6] Through the internal instigation of the Holy Spirit, we come to see that the Bible contains divine testimony. Moreover, the primary work of the Holy Spirit is the generation of faith, something that fallen humans cannot produce on their own. Plantinga quotes Calvin approvingly that "faith is a firm and certain knowledge of God's benevolence towards us, founded on the truth of the freely given promise in Christ, both revealed to our minds and sealed upon our hearts through the Holy Spirit."[7] Consequently, faith includes an explicitly cognitive element, as having faith is to believe that it is true that God exists, that God has a plan of salvation, and so forth. But faith also includes the will and the affections. Plantinga quotes Aquinas approvingly that "the Holy Spirit makes us lovers of God."[8] In sum, through the work of the Holy Spirit, the person with faith not only *believes that* God exists but also *believes in* God (coming to trust, love, and serve God).

Plantinga argues that the extended A/C model furnishes a possible way that Christian belief, and not merely theistic belief, possesses warrant. The relevant beliefs are not generated by any of humanity's original cognitive faculties, including the *sensus divinitatis*. They "come instead by way of the work of the Holy Spirit, who gets us to accept, causes us to believe, these great truths of the gospel. These beliefs don't come by way of the normal operation of our noetic faculties; they are a supernatural gift."[9] Here we observe a significant difference between the *sensus divinitatis* and the internal instigation of the Holy Spirit. While the *sensus divinitatis* is part of humanity's cognitive equipment as created, the internal instigation of the Holy Spirit—whereby we come to affirm the great truths of the gospel—is a supernatural gift bestowed by God that accompanies salvation and forms part of the process designed to generate faith. Though not a human cognitive faculty, it is functionally equivalent to a cognitive faculty. Thus beliefs "will be produced . . . by a belief-producing process that is functioning properly in an appropriate cognitive environment (the one for which they were designed), according to a design plan successfully aimed at the production of true beliefs."[10] As a result, not only is the believer completely justified in her beliefs (she is flouting no epistemic duties as to gaining and preserving her beliefs), these beliefs are also warranted and, if true, thereby constitute knowledge.

So is the A/C and/or extended A/C model true? Plantinga claims that if Christianity is true, then one of these models or something extremely similar to them is true. Notice that Plantinga is not making the trivial claim that if

Christianity is true, then God exists. Rather, he is claiming that if Christianity is true, belief in God is warranted and properly basic. Critics of theistic belief have long charged that whether or not Christianity is true, there exists no good reason to believe that God exists, such that belief in God is in any case unwarranted and certainly not properly basic. Plantinga's proposal refutes this type of de jure objection. On Plantinga's proposal, the truth of Christianity carries with it the mechanism for warranted theistic belief. Hence if Christianity is true, then belief in God is warranted. This means that for the critic to show that belief in God is unwarranted, the critic would have to prove that, in fact, Christianity is false. In other words, no de jure objections to theistic belief can succeed, as they collapse into de facto objections. Therefore Plantinga demonstrates that whether belief in God is warranted depends on whether Christianity is true.

DISMANTLING DE FACTO OBJECTIONS: EVIL AND EVOLUTION

Plantinga recognizes that the two most prevalent de facto objections to theism are the problem of evil and the notion that evolution supports atheism. Accordingly, Plantinga argues that neither evil nor evolution supply good reason to believe that God does not exist.

Evil

Regarding the problem of evil, Plantinga points out that the propositions "God exists" and "Evil exists" are not explicitly contradictory to each other, as one is not the negation of the other. So if God's existence is falsified by evil, the atheist must be making hidden assumptions that would serve to bring out the force of the contradiction and render it explicit. Plantinga surmises that there are two such assumptions:

1. If God is all-powerful, then God can create a world without evil.
2. If God is all-loving, then God prefers a world without evil.

Given that God, if he exists, would be both (1) able and (2) willing to prevent evil, and that evil exists, it would follow that God does not exist. Plantinga notes that both (1) and (2) must be necessarily true in order for evil to disprove God; if either (1) or (2) is possibly false, then any logical version of the problem of evil fails. For the datum that God may be either unable or unwilling to prevent evil would show that God's existence is not contradicted by evil. Moreover, if either (1) or (2) is probably false, then any probabilistic version of the problem of evil fails. For the datum that God is either probably unable or probably unwilling to prevent evil would show that evil does not render God's existence improbable.

As for (1), Plantinga observes that the only limits on God's power are logical limits, for omnipotence means not the ability to do anything but rather the ability to do anything that is logically possible. But suppose God desires to create angelic and human persons with libertarian free will, possessing both the unconstrained ability to choose anything on the moral spectrum from the greatest goods to the worst evils and also the unimpeded power to actualize their choices. If God indeed creates such persons, God voluntarily places himself under the logical constraint of being unable to stop those creatures either from choosing anything on the moral spectrum or from carrying out those choices. Given that at least human libertarian creatures exist, God's being all-powerful does not guarantee that the world God created contains no evil. In fact, the existence of such creatures would render it probable that the world would contain a balance between good and evil, which is precisely what we find. Hence (1) is not only possibly false but probably false, thus evacuating the force of the logical and probabilistic versions of the problem of evil. Plantinga fittingly dubbed his refutation the "free will defense."[11]

Although this suffices to refute both versions of the problem of evil, Plantinga pushes his analysis further to consider the plausibility of (2). Plantinga finds (2) unlikely on the grounds that even if there were worlds of libertarian free creatures without evil that God could create, those worlds may well have other overriding deficiencies that make them less preferable. To illustrate, suppose that God, in his omniscience, knows that there are creatable (or feasible) worlds where creatures always choose good, but that all such worlds have only a few people in them, say, two. And God knows that if he were to create a world with any more persons, then evil would result. Does God's being all-loving compel him to choose one of these vastly underpopulated worlds to a world in which multitudes of persons find salvation—the ultimate good—even though various evils obtain? In Plantinga's estimation, the answer is obviously not. Hence (2) is not necessarily true, and the only way it could be rendered probably true is for the atheist to show that it is likely that there exists a feasible world with at least as much knowledge of God and his salvation as the actual world but with less evil. But that scenario is sheer speculation and so could never be rendered likely. Thus Plantinga deems the logical and probabilistic versions of the problem of evil to be doubly invalid, as each of the critical assumptions on which they rely are both possibly and probably false.

Evolution

Plantinga does not dispute the truth of biological evolution but provocatively argues that it can only be rationally affirmed on theism. In other words, Plantinga proposes an evolutionary argument against naturalism, according to which the conjunction of naturalism (the view that no immaterial realities, such as God, exist) and evolution is self-refuting. For if evolution occurred in a naturalistic universe, then our cognitive faculties would not be geared toward acquiring true beliefs but only toward acquiring beliefs that enable us to survive. Survival advantage is not the same thing as "aimed at truth," and this is why naturalistic evolution lacks one of the criteria for warrant. To illustrate, suppose that we need to attain tiger-avoidance behavior in a naturalistic universe. So long as we develop cognitive faculties productive of a belief that gets us away from tigers, it matters not to evolution whether that belief is true or false. Statistically speaking, there are far more false beliefs that could cause us to start running in the opposite direction when we see a tiger than the single true belief that the tiger is trying to eat us and being eaten is aversive. We could just as well believe that the tiger is a regularly recurring illusion signaling that we need to run a mile at top speed to get our weight down, that the tiger is the starting signal in a 1,600 meter race that we want to win, that being eaten is a good thing but, when we see a tiger, we should run off looking for a better prospect on the grounds that it is unlikely that the tiger we see will eat us, and so forth. Hence the probability that evolution will select for our cognitive faculties to generate a true tiger-avoidance belief is low. For Plantinga, the same goes for all our other beliefs. And this, of course, includes our belief in the conjunction of naturalism and evolution. So in self-refuting fashion, if evolution occurred in a naturalistic universe, then our belief that evolution occurred in a naturalistic universe could never be justified or warranted since our belief-forming mechanisms would yield a far greater proportion of false beliefs than true ones, thus short-circuiting epistemic obligation. As a result, Plantinga holds that the only way we can possess either justified or warranted belief in evolution is for it to have occurred in a theistic universe where God superintends the evolutionary process to ensure that it selects for cognitive faculties aimed at the production of true beliefs.

THE MODAL ONTOLOGICAL ARGUMENT FOR GOD'S EXISTENCE

Not content simply to rest on the affirmation that there are no successful de facto objections to God's existence, Plantinga offers a refurbished version of the ontological argument first proposed by Anselm (1033–1109). This version is modal (dealing with the logic of possibility, impossibility, and necessity) and so avails itself of the concept of possible worlds, where a possible world is a complete description of the way reality could be. Based on Anselm's definition of God as that than which nothing greater can be conceived, Plantinga conceives of God as a being who is maximally excellent in every possible world. Plantinga construes maximal excellence to include all great-making properties, such as omniscience, omnipotence, and moral perfection. A being who possesses maximal excellence in every possible world would possess maximal greatness. With this in mind, Plantinga argues:

1. It is possible that a maximally great being exists.
2. If it is possible that a maximally great being exists, then a maximally great being exists in some possible world.
3. If a maximally great being exists in some possible world, then it exists in every possible world.
4. If a maximally great being exists in every possible world, then it exists in the actual world.
5. If a maximally great being exists in the actual world, then a maximally great being exists.
6. Therefore a maximally great being exists.

In this argument, (2) through (5) are relatively uncontroversial. Premise (2) is true by the definition of "possible world," as the possible existence of something means that it constitutes part of some complete description of the way the world could be. Premise (3) is true by the definition of a maximally great being, as the existence in some possible world of a being who possesses maximal excellence in every possible world transitively guarantees its existence in every possible world. Premise (4) is obviously true since the actual world is the complete description of the way the world could be, or possible world, that in fact obtains. Premise (5) is true by definition of "actual world," since a maximally great being's inclusion in the complete description of the way the world is entails the existence of a maximally great being.

The controversial premise in the modal ontological argument is therefore (1). Here Plantinga notes that by "possible" he does not mean epistemically possible, or possible so far as we know. Rather, by "possible" he means broadly logically possible, such that the concept of a maximally great being violates no law of logic or other metaphysical principle and therefore may exist. Intuitively, it seems evident that the concept of a maximally great being is logically coherent and otherwise metaphysically coherent. This intuitive insight is corroborated by the fact that no atheistic attempt to show the incoherence of the concept of a maximally great being has succeeded. Accordingly, Plantinga insists that we have good reason to believe (1), and given the truth of (2) through (5), (6) follows inescapably. If Plantinga is correct, the modal ontological argument proves the existence of a maximally great being, namely, God.

CONCLUSION

Plantinga has enriched the philosophy of religion with sophisticated epistemic views. He has succeeded in undercutting forms of evidentialism that were once standard in the modern philosophy of religion and in exposing the gratuitous preference for inferential ways of knowing. As a result, Plantinga has shown that, all things being equal, belief in God, like belief in the existence of other minds or memory beliefs, does not require argument or other propositional evidence to be justified or warranted and so to be rational. Plantinga is therefore fond of boldly asserting that belief in God is in the same epistemic boat as other common beliefs like the belief in the external world. Moreover, Plantinga has furnished excellent arguments that typically offered defeaters of theistic belief, such as evil and evolution, are unsuccessful. Finally, Plantinga has devised a provocative and powerful argument for the existence of God that can only be refuted by demonstrating a logical or metaphysical incompatibility in the concept of God.

FOR FURTHER READING

Primary Sources

Plantinga, Alvin. *God and Other Minds: A Study of the Rational Justification of Belief in God.* Rev. ed. Ithaca, NY: Cornell University Press, 1990.
———. *God, Freedom, and Evil.* Grand Rapids: Eerdmans, 1974.
———. *Warrant: The Current Debate.* Oxford: Oxford University Press, 1993.
———. *Warrant and Proper Function.* Oxford: Oxford University Press, 1993.
———. *Warranted Christian Belief.* Oxford: Oxford University Press, 2000.
Plantinga, Alvin, and Nicholas Wolterstorff, eds. *Faith and Rationality: Reason and Belief in God.* Notre Dame, IN: University of Notre Dame Press, 1991.

Secondary Sources

Baker, Deane-Peter, ed. *Alvin Plantinga.* Cambridge: Cambridge University Press, 2007.
Beilby, James K. *Epistemology as Theology: An Evaluation of Alvin Plantinga's Religious Epistemology.* Burlington, VT: Ashgate, 2005.

Crisp, Thomas M., Matthew Davidson, and David Vander Laan, eds. *Knowledge and Reality: Essays in Honor of Alvin Plantinga*. Dordrecht: Springer, 2006.

Kvanvig, Jonathan L., ed. *Warrant in Contemporary Epistemology: Essays in Honor of Plantinga's Theory of Knowledge*. Lanham, MD: Rowman and Littlefield, 1996.

McLeod, Mark S. *Rationality and Theistic Belief: An Essay on Reformed Epistemology*. Ithaca, NY: Cornell University Press, 1993.

Stairs, Allen, and Christopher Bernard. *A Thinker's Guide to the Philosophy of Religion*. New York: Pearson Longman, 2007.

CHAPTER 28

AFRICAN CHRISTOLOGY

Healer and Ancestor

C hristological deliberation was first roused by Jesus himself when he raised the question, "Who do you say I am?" (Mark 8:29). In the nineteenth and early twentieth centuries, the evangelical missionary movement brought the gospel to other continents, including Africa. Initially the missionaries unwittingly imposed their Western theology on the new converts. Thus African Christians were not encouraged to deliberate on this question for themselves but were instead urged to faithfully copy what the missionaries had taught them. As a result, they were answering the question, "Who do *the missionaries* say I am?" But as the number of African Christians swelled and theological analysis intensified, many Africans started to feel Jesus asking them as Africans, "Who do *you* say I am?" This question has sparked an entire generation of African Christians—women and men, educated and illiterate—to develop an indigenous African Christology. African Christology thus furnishes the response to the query posed by John V. Taylor: "Christ has been presented as the answer to the questions a white man would ask, the solution to the needs that Western man would feel, the Savior of the world of the European world-view, the object of adoration and prayer of historic Christendom. But if Christ were to appear as the answer to the questions that Africans are asking, what would he look like?"[1] Hence this chapter outlines indigenous African Christology as it has taken shape under representative African theologians John Mbiti (1931–), Bolaji Idowu (1913–93), Charles Nyamiti (1931–), Kwame Bediako (1945–2008), and Akintunde Akinade (1968–).

CENTRAL THEMES IN AFRICAN CHRISTOLOGY

African Christology exhibits at least four distinctive features. First, its starting point and central concern is "from below," or from the African perspective on Jesus's person and work, rather than "from above," or from the divine perspective of God's initiative in becoming human. Thus African theologians are not as preoccupied with the ontology of Christ and the relationship of his deity and his humanity as Western theologians have been. By contrast, African Christology is more holistic in its integration of the person and work of Christ. Its understanding of the person of Jesus is perpetually informed by what Jesus has accomplished in history and what Jesus continues to accomplish in the world. Showing how the person and work of Jesus pertain to the entirety of African life, African Christology discloses that Jesus is no stranger to the practical realities of poverty, illiteracy, ethnic tensions, colonialism, dictatorship, illness, disenfranchisement, and suffering, which form the "multiheaded hydra" of Africa.[2] Moreover, since the traditional African worldview draws no distinction between the visible and invisible worlds, African preaching about Jesus must present him as Lord of the crops, protector during dangerous journeys, and facilitator of the safe birth of newborn infants.

Second, African Christology is consciously aware and highly respectful of traditional Western christological formulations, seeking to provide an additional vantage point to the ecumenical confessions rather than an alternative to them. Employing the analogy of a puzzle, Timothy Tennent explains that "the Africans are not seeking so much to take out past pieces that fit well and have served the church. Rather, they are simply seeking to add some additional pieces that have not yet been properly accounted for in christological discussions to date."[3]

Third, African Christology emphasizes the power and victory of Christ. Thus African preachers typically focus on Jesus's victory over the devil, his works of healing and demonic deliverance, his proclamation of deliverance for the captives, his triumphal entry into Jerusalem, and his resurrection. Such focal points are consistent with African colonial history, the tragic legacy of slavery, the traditional African stress on the presence of spiritual powers, the strong belief in the demonic, and the incidence of such devastating physical diseases as AIDS. Mbiti observes that Jesus commands attention "first and foremost as the Victor over the forces which have dominated African life from time immemorial," the one who conquered the "multiheaded hydra" of Africa.[4] For African theologians, the greatest need of the African peoples is to know and experience Jesus as conqueror over the problems from which Africa perceives no means of deliverance.

Fourth, African Christology connects Jesus to Africa's pre-Christian past, particularly to the three-tiered religious system of African traditional religion. At the system's highest tier is a Supreme Being who superintends the entire cosmology. Mediating God and humanity, the second tier is inhabited by a pantheon of various divinities—including divinized ancestors and nonhuman divinities—and generally constitutes the focus of African religious life. African traditional religion senses no fundamental contradiction between a supreme deity and a pantheon of divinities, since a "deity" possesses innate powers while a "divinity" possesses merely derived powers. The third tier is the earthly realm where various expressions of ritualized power occur to preserve harmony, balance, and order, giving rise to a broad scope of religious functionaries, including traditional healers, herbalists, chiefs, and priests. African Christians view Jesus as the fulfillment of the hopes embodied by the belief in ancestors.

We shall now survey the two major African Christologies, one of which stresses Christ's power and victory (feature three) and the other of which stresses the link between Jesus and Africa's pre-Christian past (feature four).

JESUS AS HEALER

The imagery of Jesus as Healer conveys several circles of meaning, each linked with the next and each furnishing deeper understandings of Jesus. This christological portrait begins with the acknowledgment that Jesus spent a tremendous amount of time in his earthly ministry caring for people with diverse sicknesses. Hence the first circle of meaning related to Jesus as Healer pertains to physical healing and underscores Jesus's care for Africa's suffering, malnutrition, and the AIDS pandemic. The Jesus of the Gospels, who was "despised and rejected by mankind" (Isa. 53:3), comes as the Healer to persons who, more than any other races on earth, have also been despised and rejected by others. In the nineteenth century, the "great chain of being" relegated the peoples of Africa to the very bottom, ethnically, culturally, and religiously. Far from a distant stranger, Jesus enters Africa as a fellow "man of suffering, and familiar with pain. Like one from whom people hide their faces he was despised, and we held him in low esteem" (Isa. 53:3). At the same time, Jesus enters as the Great Physician who promises, "I have come that they may have life, and have it to the full" (John 10:10). The Gospel of John is replete with metaphors that supply grounding for the image of a life-giving Christ. Jesus is the "living water" (John 4:10), "the bread of life" (John 6:35), "the light of the world" (John 8:12; 9:5), and "the resurrection and the life" (John 11:25).

The christological portrait of Jesus as Healer is not restricted to his satisfying physical needs (the first circle of meaning). Linked to the physical first circle, the second circle of meaning portrays Jesus's role in spiritual healing. African theologians see spiritual healing not as a separate work of Jesus but as an extension of his work of physical healing. This integration is illustrated in the account of the crippled beggar being healed through the name of Jesus. The physical healing furnished concrete, public proof of Peter's claim to the bystanders that Jesus is "the author of life" (Acts 3:15). The miracle thus opened the door for Peter to apply Jesus's healing power in regenerating sinful hearts (Acts 3:19). As Diane Stinton reveals through her fieldwork, the holistic understanding of Jesus's healing work constitutes the nucleus of much of African Christology. Accordingly, Stinton quotes the Ghanaian pastor Aboagye-Mensah: "Jesus is the healer, one who heals not only our sicknesses, but our deeply wounded souls."[5] Likewise, Stinton quotes the Kenyan laywoman Marcy Muhia:

> When Christ comes into your life, something fundamental happens within you, and he begins a process of restoration. . . .But, more and more, I think I'm understanding what it means for Christ to really heal, that there's a restoration of the inner man that is taking place as well. We're broken: we're broken in our sinfulness, broken in our relationships because of that sinfulness, broken in our emotions because of unhealthy patterns of life. Those things have brought about a brokenness in us. And I think Christ is able to heal that, to heal very completely.[6]

Interestingly, Africans seamlessly connect the spiritual healing Jesus brings with the rebuilding of a broken community. On the African view, the work of Jesus entails not only bringing individuals into saving relationship with God but also fostering the spiritual healing of relationships between individuals. Spiritual healing is therefore both individual and corporate. Christ extends his healing within the wider context of social reintegration into the community.

Reflecting the full cosmic dimensions of the African worldview, the third circle of meaning enveloped by Jesus as Healer concerns cosmic healing over Satan and the principalities. Jesus grants us victory over Satan: while Satan "comes only to steal and kill and destroy," Jesus comes that we "may have life, and have it to the full" (John 10:10). Consequently, the life of Christ must extend into the entire cosmos, overthrowing Satan and the principalities and powers that rule in "the present evil age" (Gal. 1:4). Stinton records the description of Aboagye-Mensah concerning the importance of Jesus's defeating the forces of spiritual darkness in his pastoral work: "Related to this is Jesus as the victor, one who is victorious over the spiritual forces, whether it's in the powers of darkness, principalities and powers and so on. These are some of the areas that most people, when they come to you, want solace and prayer for, because they believe that Jesus has overcome these powers of darkness and therefore can set them free from those."[7]

To sum up, the Christology of Jesus as Healer presents Jesus as the provider of physical healing, the spiritual healing of the community, and the cosmic healing over Satan and the principalities. In this way, African Christology merges soteriology, ecclesiology, and eschatology. Soteriologically, Jesus saves his people. Ecclesiologically, Jesus restores the community by building his church. Eschatologically, Jesus is the *Christus Victor* over the spiritual powers of evil in the heavenly realms and the one who progressively repairs the universe, a renovation consummated at his second coming. Undoubtedly the portrait of Jesus as Healer represents a powerful expression of the good news of the gospel in the context of Africa. As Elizabeth Amoah and Mercy Oduyoye point out, the defining trait of the African Independent Churches, the fastest-growing movement in African Christianity, is that "Christ, the great Healer, is seen as the center of the Christology of these charismatic churches."[8]

JESUS AS ANCESTOR

African writers commonly recognize the dominant role of ancestors in the African religious consciousness. Many African cultures hold that an individual should never approach God directly; rather, this should be done via mediation. Functioning as supernatural mediators, the ancestors also serve as liturgical companions, guardians of particular clans, and paragons of virtuous behavior. According to the Tanzanian scholar Charles Nyamiti, an ancestor is "a relative of a person with whom he has a common parent, and of whom he is mediator to God, archetype of behavior, and with whom—thanks to his supernatural status acquired through death—he is entitled to have regular sacred communication."[9] For any individual to be declared an ancestor, they should be widely recognized as having lived a righteous life that sustained the moral fiber of the clan, they should have left descendants who commemorate them, and they should have "died well," living to an old age and not dying an unnatural or untimely death.

Once persons are pronounced ancestors, some operate as "family" or "clan" ancestors and are venerated only by the specific families who descend from their line. Other ancestors become "glorified" and are venerated by an entire people, including myriad clans who have no direct blood tie or familial link with that ancestor.[10] Bediako observed that ancestors of all kinds are designated the "living-dead" because, despite their physical death, they "remain united in affection and in mutual obligations with the 'living-living.'"[11]

By reflecting deeply on Jesus Christ against the African backdrop, many African laypeople and theologians conceived of the ancestor imagery as a bridge rather than a hindrance to the expansion of the gospel in their continent. Africans believed the image of ancestor could uniquely facilitate explanation of such indispensable facets of Jesus's person and work as the relation of his humanity and deity, his role as the sole and final mediator between God and humanity, and his standing as Lord of the church, the community of the redeemed. Jesus as Ancestor represents an ascending Christology, which begins with Jesus as a man in real history and gradually establishes that the deeds he performed could only be possible if he was more than a man. In fact, sustained reflection on his deeds proves that Jesus is the unique Son of God the Father, completely sharing the Father's essence and attributes. African theologians contend that this approach is basically the path for christological development exemplified in the Gospels, as the disciples meet Jesus as a man in history, gradually embrace his messiahship, and finally, as eyewitnesses of his resurrection, come to acknowledge his ultimate identity as the second person of the Trinity.

Contextualizing to African views of ancestorship, the Christology of Jesus as Ancestor maintains that Jesus entered into Africa as a man, participating fully in the suffering and pain that is paradigmatic to African humanity. As the second Adam, Jesus becomes the proto-Ancestor, the head of the entire human family who thereby fulfills and transcends the traditional role of the ancestor. African theologian John Pobee comments, "On account of his humanity, Christ's Ancestorship is linked with Adam. This fact renders Christ a member of our race and gives his Ancestorship a transcendental connotation in virtue of which it transcends all family, clanic, tribal, or racial limitations."[12] Further, an assessment of the life and teachings of Jesus plainly demonstrate that he is the archetype of righteous action and the mediator between God and humanity. While Jesus's crucifixion initially seemed a catastrophic halt to his work and an untimely, shameful death, Jesus's resurrection proved that he continues as the Living One, conquering even death itself. The New Testament proclaims that Jesus actually died well since his death atoned for the sin of the world and "disarmed the powers and authorities," making "a public spectacle of them" (Col. 2:15). Owing to his death and resurrection, Jesus is certified as possessing supernatural status. He is not only the "firstborn" of the living but "the first-born over all creation" (Col. 1:15) as the Lord of all the redeemed. Just as Jesus proclaimed that the God of the Israelite patriarchs "is not the God of the dead, but of the living, for to him all are alive" (Luke 20:38), so Jesus's triumph over death and his ascension into "the realm of spirit-power" exalts him to the status of "Supreme Ancestor."[13]

Africans who employ ancestor Christology appeal to three major theological anchors. First, the Gospel of John's use of *logos* constitutes precedent for applying a nonbiblical term to Jesus. John's first-century readers would have seen *logos* as a philosophical term designating a rational capacity or generative principle present throughout nature. The prologue to John's Gospel ingeniously employs the philosophical term *logos* as a starting point but equates it with the divine, spoken word that in Genesis brings the entire universe into existence. It should be understood that in its Hellenistic context, since *logos* denoted an impersonal, all-pervading force, its semantic origin was actually nearer to a Hindu worldview than to orthodox Christianity. Nonetheless, John rooted the term in biblical revelation when he proclaimed that the *logos* "became flesh and made his dwelling among us" (John 1:14). Based on the Johannine use of *logos*, African theologians maintain that a nonbiblical term like "ancestor" can be oriented toward Christian purposes and rooted in biblical revelation.

Observing that Ghanians regularly pray to *Nana Yesu* (Ancestor Jesus), Bediako argued that "the reality and actuality of Jesus as intended in the Christian affirmation inhabit[s] the Akan world of Nana in the same way that it . . . inhabit[ed] the Greek world of *logos*."[14] Bediako makes a profound theological point here: John was divinely inspired to use the *logos* concept both to convey the significance of Jesus to the Greek world and to model an interpretive method that must be applied to other languages and cultures as the church spreads around the world. Therefore John's use of *logos* demonstrates the theological translatability of the gospel across the globe and trains Christians today to more effectively communicate the gospel within their own linguistic and cultural milieus. As a result, many African theologians locate in the Johannine *logos* a monumental precedent summoning Africans to take what is true from non-Christian cultures by appropriating the notion of ancestor and applying it to Jesus.

A second theological anchor linking ancestors to Jesus is the biblical role of Christ as mediator: "For there is one God and one mediator between God and mankind, the man Christ Jesus" (1 Tim. 2:5). Mediation between heaven and earth constitutes the primary role of the ancestors and the rationale for all ancestor veneration in Africa. African theologians purport that "mediator" is the most important christological picture in the New Testament because only a proper doctrine of Jesus as Mediator resolves the apparent tension between the humanity and deity of Christ.

A third theological anchor is the scriptural relationship between the life and death of the Christian community. The Apostles' Creed professes that we believe in "the communion of the saints." However, Nyamiti charges that traditional Western Christology focused on Christ "without consideration of his mystical relationship to his members . . . with the result that one does not duly investigate the theological implications which Christ's mystical union with his members have on his resurrection."[15] Every biblical metaphor of Christology implies this connection; in Tennent's words, "There can be no kingship without subjects of a kingdom; there can be no shepherd without sheep; there can be no head without a body."[16] The African interlock between communities and their ancestral head affords them a powerful sense of their connectedness beyond earthly life. Because of Christ, Bediako observed that natural "ancestors are cut off as a means of blessing and we lay our power-lines differently."[17] Bediako perceived among the advantages of ancestor Christology its correct positioning of the natural ancestors under Jesus's rule: "By making room among the 'living dead' for the Lord, the judge of both the living and the dead, it becomes more evident how they relate to Him, and He to them."[18]

All in all, various points of contact between Jesus and the traditional African worldview regarding ancestors deserve emphasis. Jesus serves as the mediator between God and humanity. Jesus is the creator and head of the redeemed community. As the risen Lord, Jesus plays the continuing role of directing and guiding the community's life. Jesus bestows identity on and communicates life to his community. Therefore for Jesus to genuinely dwell in the African religious consciousness, it seems necessary that his person and work be overtly shown to execute and fulfill the vital functions traditionally carried out by ancestors, lest Jesus enter Africa as a foreigner.

CONCLUSION

The christological images of Jesus as Healer and Jesus as Ancestor transcend particular tribal identities and can thereby unify African Christians. Several African countries, including those with very high percentages of Christian affiliation, have been plagued by tribal conflict, ethnic tensions, and genocide. This is because the African kinship system forges, on the one hand, a strong sense of solidarity and belonging among persons of common ethnicity and, on the other hand, a palpable hostility toward outsiders. However, if Jesus is received by African Christians as Healer and Ancestor—and therefore head—of the whole body of Christ, encompassing peoples from all tribes and languages, such reception has the potential to engender an authentic spirit of African solidarity.

FOR FURTHER READING

Primary Sources

Bediako, Kwame. *Christianity in Africa—The Renewal of a Non-Western Religion.* Maryknoll, NY: Orbis, 1995.

———. "The Doctrine of Christ and the Significance of Vernacular Terminology." *International Bulletin of Missionary Research* 22, no. 3 (1998): 110–11.

Fabella, Virginia, and Mercy Amba Oduyoye, eds. *With Passion and Compassion: Third World Women Doing Theology.* Maryknoll, NY: Orbis, 1988.

Idowu, Bolaji. *Towards an Indigenous Church.* Oxford: Oxford University Press, 1965.

Nyamiti, Charles. *Christ as Our Ancestor: Christology from an African Perspective.* Gweru, Zimbabwe: Mambo, 1984.

Pobee, John S., ed. *Exploring Afro-Christology.* New York: Peter Lang, 1992.

Stinton, Diane. *Jesus of Africa: Voices of Contemporary African Christology.* Maryknoll, NY: Orbis, 2004.

Secondary Sources

Lawson, Thomas. *Religions of Africa.* New York: Harper & Row, 1984.

Schreiter, Robert J., ed. *Faces of Jesus in Africa.* Maryknoll, NY: Orbis, 2005.

Taylor, John V. *The Primal Vision: Christian Presence and African Religion.* London: SCM, 1963.

Tennent, Timothy C. *Theology in the Context of World Christianity: How the Global Church Is Influencing the Way We Think about and Discuss Theology.* Grand Rapids: Zondervan, 2007.

Vicedom, Georg F., ed. *Christ and the Younger Churches.* London: SPCK, 1972.

| CHAPTER 29 |

POSTMODERN
THEOLOGY

I n Europe and America, a philosophical and theological reaction to modern thought is underfoot. Modernity was rooted in the quest to find overarching philosophies (e.g., Hegelianism, existentialism, and process thought) or theologies (e.g., Protestant liberalism, neo-orthodoxy, and Tillich's systematics) that explained the totality of human experience. But following such postmodern continental philosophers as Jacques Derrida (1930–2004), Emmanuel Levinas (1906–95), and Philippe Lacoue-Labarthe (1940–2007), postmodern theologians reject all metanarratives, or grand, overarching accounts of the world. Any metanarrative "is a global or totalizing cultural narrative schema which orders and explains knowledge and experience."[1] As postmodern philosopher Jean-François Lyotard (1924–98) explained, the hallmark of postmodernism is its "incredulity toward metanarratives" and demand for their replacement by local narratives, each of which operates according to its own culturally relative Wittgensteinian language game.[2] Using a meticulous method of reading known as deconstruction, which is designed to unearth the presuppositions and values implied by a text, postmodern theologians question the ideal of knowing things exactly as they are and argue that the mediation of knowledge by language makes such an idea impossible. Hence our knowledge of objects is constantly mediated by linguistic signs that act as a supplement for that which cannot be purely present to consciousness. Thus theological language presents us not with things in their fullness but with only traces of them.

Troubled by religious violence in the contemporary world, postmodern theologians aver that dominant contemporary expositions of theology are inherently ideological, totalizing, and militant. This chapter illustrates the postmodern

285

nondogmatic, perspectival approach in thinking about theology from a deconstructive viewpoint. As John Caputo (1940–), Gianni Vattimo (1936–), and Slavoj Žižek (1949–) propose, the resulting "weak theology" expresses itself through acts of interpretation, foremost among which is the notion of the weakness of God. Postmodernists believe it is mistaken to view the paradigm of God as an overwhelming metaphysical force. They prefer instead an idea of God as an "unconditional claim without force" or an "entity beyond being" that does not intervene in nature. Placing an emphasis on the "weak" human virtues of forgiveness, hospitality, openness, and receptivity, weak theology emphasizes the responsibility of humans to act in this world here and now.

GOD AS EVENT

Several postmodern theologians contend that God is an event rather than an entity, a claim rather than a causal actor, and an incitement or promise rather than a presence. This event is what Derrida called the "weak force" of the unconditional that lacks sovereignty.[3] For Derrida, the unconditionality of an unconditional claim—such as the call of and for justice to come—is categorically distinct from sovereign power, by which he meant the raw power to enforce whatever one is calling for, whether it be just or unjust. Disputing the notion that an omnipotent God is the *archē* (ruler) of the cosmos, postmodern theologians argue instead that God is a weak force that brings form to indeterminate and uncertain elements that are thereby redeemed through the powerless power of God's Son. The weakness of God is an expression of God's vulnerable love and faithful justice that Derrida contrasts with an almighty warrior who slaughters all enemies. Nevertheless, God still lays an unconditional claim on the lives of all humans. In biblical terminology, postmodern theologians identify the weak force as the "kingdom of God," while the forces that conspire to stop the event comprise the "world." Designating himself as a postmodern anarchist because he believes that God's weakness produces anarchy, Caputo attempts to get to "the root" of the kingdom of God.[4] Thus Caputo contends that the kingdom of God is not a rule of holy law, but a sacred anarchy that is embodied in acts of love, forgiveness, and hospitality.

The postmodern interpretation of the kingdom of God is a field or coalition of weak forces for justice. This anarchic field of reversals and displacements undermines traditional hierarchies of the church and the world. Through holy disarray, the high and mighty are supplanted by the least of these. Such virtues of weakness as forgiveness and hospitality are what reign in this kingdom. Vattimo views forgiveness as a weak force because it represents an ethical claim made on us rather than a physical force. By refusing to trade strong force for strong force, the weakness of forgiveness can break the lethal and otherwise endless chain of physical retribution. As a community of weakness, the kingdom of God stands in mocking defiance to the sheer strength of empire that desires to consume it. Hence the powerless power of the kingdom of God constitutes the earthly and human correlate of the weakness of God. Postmodern theologians find God's weak power advantageous in responding to the problem of natural and moral evil, as God is simply not in a position to intervene in the affairs of the universe: "God does not prevent evil in advance, nor can God . . . retroactively remove evil after the fact."[5] Hence the human community must take responsibility for gratuitous suffering in the world. The weakness of God's kingdom, then, paradoxically screams out for us to bring the event of justice to the world.

For postmodern theologians, Jesus both teaches and embodies the spirit of sacred anarchy that animates God's kingdom. By shaking up the religious and political systems of his day, Jesus illustrated that an ethic of hospitality and forgiveness necessitates a radical openness to the claims and concerns of the other. Following Martin Luther's theology of the cross, postmodern theologians find the helpless, human body of Jesus crucified on a Roman cross as the ultimate symbol of God's powerless power. As Caputo writes:

> On the classical account of strong theology, Jesus was just holding back his divine power in order to let his human nature suffer. He freely chose to check his power because the Father had a plan to redeem the world with his blood. . . . That is not the weakness of God that I am here defending. God, the event harbored by the name of God, is present at the crucifixion, as the power of the powerlessness of Jesus, in and as the protest against the injustice that rises up from the cross, in and as the words of forgiveness, not a deferred power that will be visited upon one's enemies at a later time. God is in attendance as the weak force of the call that cries out from Calvary and calls across the epochs, that cries out from every corpse created by every cruel and unjust power. The logos of the cross is a call to renounce violence, not to conceal and defer it and then, in a stunning act that takes the enemy by surprise, to lay them low with real power, which shows the enemy who really has the power. That is just what Nietzsche was criticizing under the name of *ressentiment*.[6]

Such a colorful Christology pronounces judgment against those traditional constructions that interpret Jesus and the kingdom in masculine, militaristic, and capitalistic categories. In line with liberation theology, postmodern theologians declare that Jesus stands in solidarity with the excluded and marginalized.

GOD AS ENTITY BEYOND BEING

While concurring with the aforementioned analysis of the kingdom of God and Christology, some postmodern theologians are uncomfortable denying that God is an entity. They therefore affirm God as entity while maintaining that God is a wholly different type of reality than others, transcending all rational thought. Among the most prominent postmodern theologians taking this line is Jean-Luc Marion (1946–), who writes from a Catholic sacramental perspective. In his book *God without Being* (1991), Marion reflects on what kind of talk about God is appropriate. Considering that God can never be fully present to consciousness, Marion maintains that our claims to knowledge of God always threaten to place a conceptual schema on God that creates God in our own image. Since Marion contends that God is above even "being" (such that God is not, per Anselm, the greatest conceivable being), he affirms the God of faith instead of the God of the philosophers.[7] Distinguishing between idols and icons, Marion defines idols as our pictures or concepts of God that reflect us rather than God, while icons point us beyond ourselves to God. For Marion, any concept of God that pretends to present us with the divine fullness is idolatrous, as God perennially escapes human grasp. By contrast, icons furnish us with a "trace" of God, who is the ultimate "saturated phenomenon" in the sense that there is such an inundation of divine presence that no concepts could "capture" him.[8] According to Marion, God "exists," but not as we exist: his existence is love, and he lies beyond the realm of being and predication.[9] Marion endeavors to forge a *media via* between "bad silence" (when all God-talk is stifled) and imprudent babble.[10] A wise silence recognizes the limitations of language and tries to speak only what one can legitimately utter, the question being not so much "what" one says of God but "how."[11] Marion asserts that the Eucharist is central to theology, as we meet Christ in the breaking of the bread. Here Christ is present to us as a gift of which we are not the originators and which we do not possess.

By memorializing Christ's passion, the Eucharist underscores the role of suffering in the history of God himself. Insisting on the importance of a suffering God, Žižek maintains that God is a life, not merely a being, and that all life has a fate and is subject to suffering and becoming. Like the suffering Christ on the cross, Žižek's God is agonized and assumes the burden of suffering in solidarity with human misery. Deeply influenced by the Holocaust, Žižek asserts the literal truth of the claim that the unspeakable suffering of six million Jews is also the voice of the suffering of God, as the very excess of this suffering over any normal human measure renders it divine. Žižek conceives of the coming of the Holy Spirit after Christ's ascension as this suffering power that manifests itself in an egalitarian community bound by love. By not thinking about God as a metaphysical force but instead as a suffering power that lays an unconditional claim on us, Žižek hopes to provide the kingdom of God with theological resources to subvert the sovereign aspirations of nation-states, global economic systems, and religions that often legitimate their power projects in the name of God.

WEAK THEOLOGY

In the view of those postmodern theologians for whom the name of God is the name of an event, theology is the hermeneutics of that event that simultaneously triggers the event and restrains the forces that attempt to preclude the event. Moreover, Caputo and Vattimo insist on a deliteralization of the event harbored in the name of God. On the grounds that a name never measures up to the event that lives within it, Caputo and Vattimo demand that confessional theology be replaced by theopoetics, which they use to describe the event by depicting its dynamics, tracing its style, and managing its unintended consequences through suitable tropes. In theopoetics, the event is the subject matter not of a confession but of a "circumfession," in which "we 'fess up' to being cut and wounded by something wondrous."[12] Theopoetics is also embraced but put to a different use by postmodern theologians who believe that God is an entity. According to Marion and Žižek, theologians should try to find God through poetic articulations of their lived experiences rather than formulating a quasi-scientific theory of God, as systematic theology pretends to do. On all uses of theopoetics, theologians are asked to accept reality as a legitimate source of divine revelation and to view both the divine and the real as mysterious, or irreducible to literalist dogmas or scientific proofs.

Postmodern theologians assume that if theological content is "strong" or "thick" (by which they mean convictional), this necessarily leads to violence in the world. For postmodern theologians, confessional, doctrinal, and metaphysical postures of churches across the ecumenical spectrum are ipso facto militant. Thus the theological answer to gratuitous suffering is, through theopoetics, to construct a weak theology that is better able to promote peace and justice. Moreover, the weakness of God mandates the weakness of theology, or theology that is nonconfessional, nondogmatic, pluralistic, and tolerant. Caputo and

Vattimo argue that weak theology is not a "sorry spinelessness," but a robust nonfoundationalist and nonfundamentalist bearing of testimony to God as a coming reality of justice.[13] On the theopoetic basis that theology is more akin to poetry than science, weak theology makes profound use of radical and ontological metaphors to fashion a more fluid referent for the divine. Opposing the imposition of the logical principle of bivalence on God-language, weak theology takes an allegorical position on scriptural and creedal utterances and insists that they can be continuously reinterpreted. Hence theopoetics maintains that just as a poem can assume new meaning based on the context in which the reader interprets it, texts and experiences of the divine can and should assume new meaning based on the changing situation of the individual or society.

Weak theology supplies a new basis for humans to accept the paradoxes of life's "risky business," including the alleged paradox of creation itself.[14] Catherine Keller (1953–) proposes the concept of *creatio ex profundis* (creation out of the depth or creation out of chaos), in which creation is a concert of fluid and free-floating forces that shape preexisting elements into a new and good life. Resembling Derrida's *khora*, or space between being and non-being, the preexisting elements are "mythologemes" of uncertainty and undecidability.[15] Postmodern theologians hold that these mythologemes bear prophetic testimony to the open-endedness and riskiness of human and divine life. Creation represents an ongoing process demanding faith. Since absolute meaning is impossible, indecision is inescapable. Thus we always live somewhere between absolute certainty and absolute doubt and must constantly negotiate risk. Caputo thus depicts the "beautiful risk" of creation as the right way to think about the relationship between God and the world, where the two function interdependently as the ebb and flow of two salsa dancers.

CONSTRUCTING NEW SPIRITUAL PATHWAYS

Postmodern theologians reject a correspondence theory of truth—according to which a statement is true if and only if it corresponds with reality—in favor of the constructivist theory of truth. According to the constructivist theory, truth is an artifact whose fundamental design we often have to alter rather than something delivered by God or nature. Truth is not "out there" at all; rather, truth, whether religious or scientific, is nowhere until we use language to give it substance and location. Here we note that unlike the correspondence view that truth and fact are synonymous, postmodern theologians (following Wittgenstein) draw a distinction between truth and fact. While fact corresponds with reality, truth essentially refers to that which works for a given purpose. In the religious sphere, that purpose is to generate meaningful, morally life-transforming spiritual experience.

Employing the constructivist theory of truth, postmodern theologians urge contemporary Christians to construct their own spiritual pathways that fulfill this purpose. Any such spiritual pathway should be shaped by four contours that have proven effective over the course of the history of religions. First, spiritual pathways must be simple; for, in the words of medieval spiritual theologian Bernard of Clairvaux (1090–1153), God is "pure simplicity."[16] This does not mean a simplistic faith in which there is zeal without knowledge, literalist understanding of Scripture, little historical perspective, and the fervent belief that one has all the truth and those who differ are heretical. As postmodern theologian Duncan S. Ferguson (1937–) puts it, "We must avoid the worst forms of fundamentalism that suffers from ignorance, arrogance, and intolerance. We must guard against our own intellectual, moral, and cultural pride which claims that our way is the only right way."[17] A simple pathway is pure and uncluttered, not ideologically narrow and provincial. It is a deep and profound personal understanding of the divine way that seeks the truth, lives in love, and pursues justice. A faith arising out of this pathway embraces what Ferguson calls "second naiveté," the first naiveté having vanished in what is mythically called the trip east of Eden.[18] It is a faith, having been born in humanity's original state of innocence, hardened in the give and take of a violent and rapidly changing world, and now come full circle to a fresh purity and integrity.

Second, spiritual pathways must be open and thoughtful, seeking new directions and possessing an intellectually credible basis. They are simultaneously grounded in truth, love, and justice and realize that they may stake no claim on the absolute definition and expression of truth, love, and justice. An open and thoughtful pathway is a way of being acutely aware that our understanding of the spiritual center is limited by our historical time and place, culture, and language. Moreover, it acknowledges that our faith constructs and metaphors constitute approximations that participate in divine truth and enable us to truly meet God, but nevertheless do not contain the whole truth about God.

Third, spiritual pathways must be in dialogue and in transition. Informed by the Scripture and tradition of the Christian faith family and by association with others who seek the will and way of God, spiritual pathways must also be informed by other cultures, traditions, and faith families. Postmodern theologians insist that spiritual pathways listen to others and engage in constant conversation with the infinitely complex world they inhabit. Further, spiritual pathways must be strong enough to doubt current constructs, to develop as life unfolds, and to intersect with an ever-changing world.

Fourth, spiritual pathways must be ethical, rooted in a spiritual center that cares for this world and all of its creatures. Ethical spiritual pathways lead to courageous love, challenge all forms of injustice, and seek peace for all. Ethical spiritual pathways engender a faith grounded in agape, or unlimited, unconditional, and active love, freely given for the good of one's neighbor. Ferguson argues that agape embodies the attributes of extensiveness, intensiveness, endurance, purity, and adequacy. By extensiveness, Ferguson means that agape reaches into every nook and cranny where human suffering and need are present. By intensiveness, Ferguson denotes that agape compassionately conjoins doing good deeds and having a presence. Thus it is essential to challenge and transform the infrastructure that discriminates against classes of people and to support those agencies that improve the condition of others. But it is equally essential to prove by word and touch that one truly cares for the needy and suffering. By endurance, Ferguson signifies that agape lasts across time, resistance, and fatigue, even when there is no one acknowledging the effort or extending gratitude. By purity, Ferguson indicates that agape offers help solely for the welfare of the other without thought of personal gain. By adequacy, Ferguson claims that agape appropriately meets the needs of the other rather than manipulatively attempting to change the other according to our preferences.

Summing up these contours, postmodern theologians demand that contemporary Christian spiritual pathways embody life-giving characteristics and avoid life-denying characteristics. Ferguson lists as indispensable the following five life-giving characteristics:

1. The spiritual pathway *empowers* the person or the group to behave in constructive ways that lead to love, compassion, understanding, and acceptance.
2. The spiritual pathway *guides* the person or group to be socially responsible and concerned about creating a more just and humane world. It guards against being taken over by a political point of view.
3. The spiritual pathway is intellectually credible and *encourages* the person or group to be open and responsive to new ideas and challenges.
4. The spiritual pathway helps the individual or group to *flourish* and *integrate* the beliefs and practices into a life of coherence, conviction, serenity, and integrity.
5. The spiritual pathway offers guidance and practices that *sustain* the individual and group in times of difficulty and challenge.[19]

By contrast, life-denying characteristics include sectarianism, zealotry, and inculcation of fear, mistrust, and intolerance. Hence postmodern theologians insist that spiritual pathways must never be captured by political ideologies that use the ends to justify the means. Likewise, spiritual pathways must not confine and control their followers by asking for blind obedience, as such a tactic imprisons rather than liberates.

CONCLUSION

Affirming that God is either an event or an entity beyond being, postmodern theology endeavors to shift the theological enterprise into a nonfoundationalist, nonsystematic mode, a mode that it finds more conducive to the "weak values" exemplified by the kingdom of God. The logical strictures of classical theology are therefore replaced by the fluid categories of theopoetics, which allow for the same theological affirmation to validly assume a limitless supply of meanings in relation to the differing perspectives of various individuals and cultures. Postmodern theologians call individuals on a quest to forge their own life-affirming spiritual pathways predicated on a constructivist, not correspondence, theory of truth. Postmodern theology has also given rise to radical orthodoxy, a Christian theological and philosophical school of thought that attempts to reclaim theology as the queen of the sciences. For proponents of radical orthodoxy like John Milbank (1952–), the alleged postmodern discovery that truth has no absolute grounding or certainty actually orients the finite toward the eternal, thus subordinating the study of finite realities to the study of God.

FOR FURTHER READING

Primary Sources

Caputo, John D. *The Weakness of God: A Theology of the Event*. Bloomington, IN: Indiana University Press, 2006.

Ferguson, Duncan S. *Exploring the Spirituality of the World Religions: The Quest for Personal, Spiritual, and Social Transformation*. London: Continuum, 2010.

Lyotard, Jean-François. *The Postmodern Condition: A Report on Knowledge*. Trans. Geoff Bennington and Brian Massumi. Minneapolis: University of Minnesota Press, 1984.

Marion, Jean-Luc. *God without Being*. Trans. Thomas A. Carlson. Chicago: University of Chicago Press, 1991.

Vattimo, Gianni. *After Christianity*. New York: Columbia University Press, 2002.

Žižek, Slavoj, and Boris Gunjevic. *God in Pain: Inversions of Apocalypse*. New York: Seven Stories, 2012.

Secondary Sources

Heltzel, Peter Goodwin. "The Weakness of God." Review of *The Weakness of God: A Theology of the Event*, by John D. Caputo. *Journal for Cultural and Religious Theory* 7, no. 2 (2006): 96–101.

Riggs, John W. *Postmodern Christianity: Doing Theology in the Contemporary World*. London: Trinity Press International, 2003.

Smith, James K. A. *Who's Afraid of Postmodernism? Taking Derrida, Lyotard, and Foucault to Church*. Grand Rapids: Baker Academic, 2006.

Snider, Phil. *Preaching after God: Derrida, Caputo, and the Language of Postmodern Homiletics*. Eugene, OR: Cascade, 2012.

Stephens, John, and Robyn McCallum. *Retelling Stories, Framing Culture*. New York: Garland, 1998.

CHAPTER 30

OPEN THEISM

Starting in the late 1980s, several evangelical theologians— calling themselves "open theists" —have challenged the traditional position that God exhaustively knows the future, including the free future actions of humans and other free moral agents. This position made its entry into mainstream Christian thought in 1994 with the publication of the watershed collection of essays *The Openness of God*. Among the most prominent open theists are William Hasker (1935–), Clark Pinnock (1937–2010), Richard Rice (1944–), David Basinger (1947–), John Sanders (1956–), and Gregory A. Boyd (1957–). Open theists concur with their fellow evangelicals that God has complete and perfect knowledge of the past and present. Moreover, open theists maintain that God knows part of the future, namely, the part that he himself has freely fixed. But there are other future events that God does not know, all of which involve creaturely freedom. This notion is quite controversial, since many other evangelicals maintain that God can and does know future events involving creaturely freedom. We will see a proposal for how God can and does know such events in the next chapter. However, the present chapter surveys the results of the open view in the realms of biblical exegesis, divine omniscience, and divine providence.

BIBLICAL EXEGESIS

On the basis of passages where God declares, "I make known the end from the beginning, from ancient times, what is still to come" (Isa. 46:10; cf. 48:3–5), open theists proclaim God the sovereign Lord of history. However chaotic the world may seem, God is navigating history toward his intended goal. God's overall plan for creation cannot fail, and his eternal purpose for each individual life is secure (Job 42:2; Isa. 14:27; Rom. 8:28; Eph. 1:11). This theme entails that God has settled a good deal of the future ahead of time, and in this way he foreknows it. Indeed, God can fix whatever he wants to fix about the future. Over against Molinism and Arminianism, open theism concurs with Calvinism that the sole fashion in which God can know anything about the future is by predetermining it. In other words, God knows what will happen because he has decided to make it happen. Cognizant of the intentions of his will and his almighty power, God knows that all he has foreordained shall be accomplished. But open theism disagrees with Calvinism concerning the extent of the future that God has predetermined. While Calvinism alleges that God has predetermined the future in its entirety, open theism postulates that God has predetermined only parts of the future, leaving those parts he desires to be determined by free creaturely decisions presently undetermined, such that, in Boyd's words, "the future is partly open and partly settled."[1]

Open theists protest against the typical inference that because Scripture proves that many future events are settled in God's mind, all future events are settled in God's mind. Rather, they offer a two-pronged argument for the coherence of a partly open and partly settled future. First, we are acquainted with this truth whenever we deliberate about something, as deliberation presupposes that the future is partly up to us to decide and partly decided for us. Boyd illustrates: "Suppose I am deliberating about whether or not to purchase a new edition of Kant's *Critique of Pure Reason* tomorrow. My act of deliberation presupposes that it lies within my power either to purchase this book or to not. It illustrates my conviction that at least this much of my future is up to me to decide. But my deliberation also presupposes that much of the future is not up to me to decide. I couldn't deliberate about this particular purchase if it were up to me to decide whether, say, the bookstore would exist or whether money would have any value tomorrow."[2] Thus to deliberate about any particular matter, we must be freed from deliberating about every matter. Assuming that much of the future is already settled, our sense of freedom must always occur within the parameters of things we do not choose. So, open theists insist, we live as though the future is partly settled and partly open, and open theism is the only view that confirms the reality of this experienced perspective.

Second, a partly settled and partly open future is being corroborated in many branches of contemporary science. For example, physics has shown that we can accurately predict the general behavior of a group of quantum particles—yielding the regularity of the phenomenological world—but that we cannot in principle predict the precise behavior of any individual particle. Hence the phenomenological world is settled while the world of quantum particles is somewhat open. Likewise, chaos theory has demonstrated that all predictable facets of reality incorporate unpredictable facets and vice versa. Consequently, open theists allege that there should be no difficulty conceiving how God could predetermine and so foreknow that a particular event was going to occur (such as Israel's four-century-long captivity in Egypt) without predetermining or foreknowing every detail surrounding this event.

Boyd appeals to six categories of scriptural passages that open theists regard as definitive evidence that the future is partially open. While each of these six categories has been traditionally understood as expressing anthropomorphisms, or metaphors depicting God in human terms, open theists protest that it is impossible on the anthropomorphic reading to identify any literal truths to which these passages point, thereby evacuating the texts of any substance. To avoid nonsensicality, any metaphor must have a literal truth at its core, which it figuratively expresses, and open theists believe no such literal truth exists on the anthropomorphic understanding.

The first category depicts God confronting the unexpected. In Isaiah, God portrayed Israel as his vineyard and himself as its loving owner. He expected the vineyard to produce good grapes, only to shockingly find that it produced exclusively bad grapes: "What more could have been done for my vineyard than I have done for it? When I looked for good grapes, why did it yield only bad?" (Isa. 5:4). Similarly, three times in Jeremiah God expressed his surprise at Israel's actions by saying his people were doing things "I did not command or mention, nor did it enter my mind" (Jer. 19:5; cf. 7:31; 32:35). For Boyd, the phrase "nor did it enter my mind" obviates the possibility that the Israelites' idolatrous deeds were eternally certain in God's mind. On the same score, God stated concerning Israel's inexcusable obduracy, "I thought that after she had done all this she would return to me but she did not. . . . I thought you would call me 'Father' and not turn away from following me. But like a woman unfaithful to her husband, so you, Israel, have been unfaithful to me" (Jer. 3:7, 19–20).

The second category depicts God experiencing regret for decisions he himself made. After recounting the utter depravity and violence of humanity before the flood, Scripture reports, "The LORD regretted that he had made human beings on the earth, and his heart was deeply troubled" (Gen. 6:6). Another instance of God's regret surrounds his decision to make Saul king of Israel. At first, God sincerely intended to establish Saul's kingdom over Israel forever (1 Sam. 13:13). But when Saul forsook God's ways and pursued his own agenda, God removed him from his appointed office and rescinded the blessing. Thus God lamented,

"I regret that I have made Saul king, because he has turned away from me and has not carried out my instructions" (1 Sam. 15:11; cf. 15:35).

The third category depicts God expressing frustration toward people who intractably resist his purposes for their lives. At one point in Israel's rebellion, God declared, "I looked for someone among them who would build up the wall and stand before me in the gap on behalf of the land so I would not have to destroy it, but I found no one" (Ezek. 22:30). Open theists posit that God could not have sincerely looked for someone to intercede if he had foreknown that there would be no one. God also displayed his frustration at the fact that not everyone he creates accepts his invitation to eternal life. Peter revealed that the Lord delays his return because he does not want "anyone to perish, but everyone to come to repentance" (2 Peter 3:9). In the Hebrew prophets, God literally pleaded with the wicked Israelites to repent, an overture that open theists insist would have been pointless if God foreknew that they would not repent: "Do I take any pleasure in the death of the wicked? declares the Sovereign LORD. Rather, am I not pleased when they turn from their ways and live? . . . Repent! Turn away from all your offenses; then sin will not be your downfall. Rid yourselves of all the offenses you have committed, and get a new heart and a new spirit. Why will you die, people of Israel? For I take no pleasure in the death of anyone, declares the Sovereign LORD. Repent and live!" (Ezek. 18:23, 30–32; cf. 33:11).

The fourth category depicts God speaking in conditional terms of what might or might not happen. When God attempted to convince Moses to be his representative to the Israelite elders, Moses asked, "What if they do not believe me or listen to me and say, 'The LORD did not appear to you'?" (Ex. 4:1). God first demonstrated a miracle "so that they may believe that the LORD . . . has appeared" to Moses (Ex. 4:5). When Moses remained unconvinced, God demonstrated a second miracle and remarked, "If they do not believe you or pay attention to the first sign, they may believe the second" (Ex. 4:8). Moreover, God offered Moses a third miracle in case the second miracle did not persuade the elders. Boyd comments:

> If the future is exhaustively settled, God would have known exactly how many miracles, if any, it would take to get the elders to believe Moses; and this means that the meaning of the words he chose (*may* and *if*) could not be sincere. . . . This passage demonstrates that God is perfectly confident in his ability to achieve his desired results (viz., getting the elders of Israel to listen to Moses) even though he works with free agents who are, to some extent, unpredictable. He is able to declare to Moses the conclusion of his plan from

the time he first announces it (cf. Is 46:10, "the *end* from the *beginning*") without controlling every variable in between. *That* the Israelites will get out of Egypt is certain; *how many miracles* it will take to pull this off depends on the free choices of some key people. This is a picture of a God who is as creative and resourceful as he is wise and powerful.[3]

Although God often portrays his future plans as certainties, there are also times in Scripture when God portrays his desires for the future as possibilities. Thus God told Ezekiel to symbolically enact Judah's exile as a warning so that "perhaps they will understand, though they are a rebellious people" (Ezek. 12:3), and Judah did not understand. Likewise, God commanded Jeremiah to stand in the courtyard of the temple and preach to the Judeans, assuring him: "Perhaps they will listen and each will turn from their evil ways. Then I will relent and not inflict on them the disaster I was planning because of the evil they have done" (Jer. 26:3). Scripture discloses God's inner thoughts and motives regarding his decision not to lead the Israelites near the Philistines: "If they face war, they might change their minds and return to Egypt" (Ex. 13:17). In the garden of Gethsemane, Jesus prayed, "My Father, if it is possible, may this cup be taken from me" (Matt. 26:39). Open theists contend that this prayer is unintelligible if Jesus thought the entire future was eternally settled in the Father's mind; rather, Jesus must have believed there was at least a chance another course of action could be taken at the last minute.

The fifth category depicts God testing people to know their character. When Abraham successfully passed God's test by proving his willingness to sacrifice Isaac, God proclaimed, "Now I know that you fear God, because you have not withheld from me your son, your only son" (Gen. 22:12). The Bible says that God tested Hezekiah "to know everything that was in his heart" (2 Chron. 32:31). Likewise, Moses told the Israelites that God led them forty years in the wilderness to "test you in order to know what was in your heart, whether or not you would keep his commands" (Deut. 8:2; cf. 8:21). Moses gave the same rationale for why God sometimes allowed false prophets to be correct: "The Lord your God is testing you to find out whether you love him with all your heart and with all your soul" (Deut. 13:3). Likewise, God left Israel's enemies in place "to test the Israelites to see whether they would obey the Lord's commands" (Judg. 3:4).

The sixth category depicts God changing his mind. Hence God told Jeremiah, "If at any time I announce that a nation or kingdom is to be uprooted, torn down and destroyed, and if that nation I warned repents of its evil, then I will relent and not inflict on it the disaster I had planned. And if at another time I announce that a nation or kingdom is to be built up and planted, and if it does evil in my sight and does not obey me, then I will reconsider the good I had intended to do for it" (Jer. 18:7–10). When the priests and officials of Judah heard Jeremiah's prophecy and wanted to kill him, Jeremiah replied: "Now reform your ways and your actions and obey the LORD your God. Then the LORD will relent and not bring the disaster he has pronounced against you" (Jer. 26:13). Some of the elders came to Jeremiah's defense by reminding the priests and officials that when Hezekiah and the people of Judah repented, God changed his mind about the judgment Micah prophesied against them (Jer. 26:17–19).

Summarizing these categories of biblical passages, Boyd contrasts them with such obvious anthropomorphisms as God's possession of physical features: "Expressions like 'the right hand of God' or 'the eyes of the Lord,' for example, communicate something true of God's strength and knowledge. But what does the concept of God's changing his mind communicate, for example, if indeed it is an anthropomorphism? If God in fact never changes his mind, saying he does so doesn't communicate anything truthful: it is simply inaccurate."[4] The open view of God entails redefinitions of the traditional divine attributes of omniscience and providence, to which we shall now turn.

DIVINE OMNISCIENCE

Open theists construe omniscience as knowing all truths that are logically possible to know. They proceed to maintain that counterfactuals of creaturely freedom (CCFs)—propositions of the form "if person P were in currently unrealized circumstances C, P would freely do action A"—are logically unknowable for two reasons. First, the future does not yet exist, rendering future circumstances and actions a vista of endless possibilities. Only that which exists may logically be known. Second, if someone were to know a CCF before it occurred, then P's action would not be free but would rather be predetermined to occur by virtue of the unalterability or unchangeability of the past. Therefore not even God, whom open theists regard as omniscient, can know CCFs. This is no indictment on God's omniscience, as God indeed knows everything that is logically possible to know. Hence open theists insist that the difference between their view and the traditional view is not over the nature of God at all but over the nature of the future and the type of world God has chosen to create.

Because of divine love—the central attribute and arguably the very essence of God—God has chosen to create a world where human creatures can love him in return. This entails God's creating them as libertarian free agents, able not only to love and obey him but also to do the very opposite. God will not force his children to love or obey him. But on the grounds that God's knowledge of what persons will do would deem it impossible for them to do otherwise, God's decision to make them as libertarian free agents was also a decision to be logically unable to foreknow what they will choose. Despite this freely chosen limitation (though not an imperfection), God possesses superior abilities of analysis and inference, which enable God to predict with amazing accuracy what actually will occur.

DIVINE PROVIDENCE

In his 1998 book *The God Who Risks*, Sanders offers a "risk" model of divine providence that stands in contrast to the traditional "no-risk" model that "no event ever happens without God's specifically selecting it to happen. Nothing is too insignificant for God's meticulous and exhaustive control."[5] Characterizing providence as "the adequacy of God's wisdom and power to the task with which he has charged himself," Sanders claims that God freely chose to be affected by his creatures, such that there is contingency in God's relation with creation.[6] Further, God is "the sovereign determiner of the sort of sovereignty he will exercise. God is free to sovereignly decide not to determine everything that happens in history. He does not have to because God is supremely wise, endlessly resourceful, amazingly creative and omnicompetent in seeking to fulfill his project."[7]

While the divine goal for creation is settled, the path to its actualization is flexible. Accordingly, God neither foreordains everything that happens nor exercises exhaustive control. Instead, he gives humans libertarian freedom that creates the potential for individual instances of gratuitous evil—evil that does not contribute to any greater good. On Sanders's conception, God's choice to create this kind of world possesses a high chance of success and small chance of failure while concurrently entailing a great amount of risk in the sense that it matters profoundly to God how things transpire. Sanders holds that his view of providence enjoys advantages to other views with respect to salvation, suffering and evil, prayer, and divine guidance. He encapsulates his risk-taking view of divine providence as follows:

> First, God loves us and desires for us to enter into reciprocal relations of love with him and with our fellow creatures. . . . In this we would freely come

to collaborate with God toward the achievement of God's goals. Second, God has sovereignly decided to make some of his actions contingent on our requests and actions. . . . Hence there is conditionality in God, for God truly responds to what we do. Third, God chooses to exercise general rather than meticulous providence, allowing space for us to operate and for God to be creative and resourceful in working with us. Fourth, God has granted us the libertarian freedom necessary for a truly personal relationship of love to develop. In summary, God freely enters into genuine give-and-take relations with us. This entails risking on his part because we are capable of letting God down.[8]

CONCLUSION

Open theists allege that their view enjoys greater explanatory power to account for the full range of biblical evidence than Calvinism, Molinism, or Arminianism and carries with it a number of other theological and practical advantages. To illustrate, it proposes an answer to why God creates people who inflict horrifying suffering on others and damn themselves: God does not foreknow that they will engage in such destructive behavior. By making intelligible the evil in the world, open theism inspires Christians to pursue an aggressive stance in combating it. Open theism is purportedly most consistent with the portrait of reality emerging from contemporary science. Open theism celebrates the power of prayer, as prayer not only changes us but may well change God's mind and therefore the course of history. Finally, open theism proffers a model of sovereignty apparently best compatible with the revelation of God in Christ. Critics of open theism deny these advantages, and many charge that open theism is an evangelical revision of process theology because God changes over time by constantly acquiring new knowledge and modifying his plans in response to creatures.

FOR FURTHER READING

Primary Sources

Boyd, Gregory A. *God of the Possible: A Biblical Introduction to the Open View of God*. Grand Rapids: Baker, 2000.

———. *Satan and the Problem of Evil: Constructing a Trinitarian Warfare Theodicy*. Downers Grove, IL: IVP, 2002.

Cobb, John B., and Clark Pinnock, eds. *Searching for an Adequate God: A Dialogue between Process and Free Will Theists*. Grand Rapids: Eerdmans, 2000.

Pinnock, Clark. *Most Moved Mover: A Theology of God's Openness*. Grand Rapids: Baker, 2001.

Pinnock, Clark, Richard Rice, John Sanders, William Hasker, and David Basinger. *The Openness of God: A Biblical Challenge to the Traditional Understanding of God*. Downers Grove, IL: IVP, 1994.

Sanders, John. *The God Who Risks: A Theology of Providence*. Downers Grove, IL: IVP, 1998.

Secondary Sources

Beilby, James K., and Paul R. Eddy, eds. *Divine Foreknowledge: Four Views*. Downers Grove, IL: IVP, 2001.

Erickson, Millard J. *What Does God Know and When Does He Know It? The Current Controversy over Divine Foreknowledge*. Grand Rapids: Zondervan, 2003.

Geisler, Norman L., and Wayne H. House. *The Battle for God: Responding to the Challenge of Neotheism*. Grand Rapids: Kregel, 2001.

Jowers, Dennis W., gen. ed.; Stanley N. Gundry, ser. ed. *Four Views on Divine Providence*. Grand Rapids: Zondervan, 2011.

Ware, Bruce. *God's Lesser Glory: The Diminished God of Open Theism*. Wheaton, IL: Crossway, 2000.

CHAPTER 31

PHILOSOPHY OF RELIGION AND ANALYTIC THEOLOGY

O ver the past half century, a renaissance in Anglophone philosophy of religion has defended Christian truth claims and engendered arguably the most creative developments in contemporary theology. Prominent in this renaissance of philosophical apologetics are William Lane Craig (1949–), Richard Swinburne (1934–), J. P. Moreland (1948–), Stuart C. Hackett (1925–2012), Robin Collins (1961–), Michael Rea (1968–), and Alexander Pruss (1973–). This chapter explores these thinkers' major contributions to the project of analytic theology, or the synthesis of analytic philosophy, systematic theology, biblical studies, and the sciences. Today analytic theology flourishes through such professional societies as the Evangelical Philosophical Society (founded 1977) and the Society of Christian Philosophers (founded 1978).

THE LEIBNIZIAN COSMOLOGICAL ARGUMENT

Craig, Pruss, and Swinburne have revivified the argument of philosopher and mathematician Gottfried Wilhelm von Leibniz (1646–1716) for the existence of God based on the universe's existence. This Leibnizian cosmological argument possesses the advantage of making no assumption regarding whether the universe had a beginning or is eternal in the past, such that even a proponent of an eternal universe must take the argument seriously. It centers on the simple question: Why does the (possibly eternal) universe exist instead of just nothing? The question deserves to be asked because the universe is contingent—that is, it doesn't have to exist and it could possibly pass out of existence. As one surveys the universe, none of the things that make it up, whether stars, planets, galaxies, dust, or radiation, exist necessarily. They could all fail to exist and, in fact, none of them did exist at some point in the past when the universe was extremely dense. These things are made of matter, which is composed of subatomic particles that cannot be further broken down. The universe simply is the collection of all these particles arranged in different ways. But none of these particles exists necessarily, and a different collection of fundamental particles could have existed; indeed, scientists regularly theorize about other possible universes.

With this in mind, the Leibnizian cosmological argument runs as follows:

1. Everything that exists has an explanation of its existence, either in the necessity of its own nature or in an external cause.
2. If the universe has an explanation of its existence, that explanation is an external cause that transcends the universe.
3. The universe exists.
4. Therefore the universe has an explanation of its existence.
5. Therefore the explanation of the existence of the universe is an external cause that transcends the universe.

Two features of this argument deserve further note. First, (1) does not exempt God from having an explanation of his existence. God certainly has an explanation of his existence in the necessity of his own nature, just as many philosophers think that the laws of logic and many mathematicians think that numbers have an explanation of their existence in the necessity of their own nature. It is simply impossible for any of these entities not to exist. But one cannot say that the universe has an explanation of its existence in the necessity of its own nature, for its nature is contingent. Thus the explanation of the universe's existence lies in an external cause that transcends it. Second, since the universe is, by definition, all time, space, matter, and energy, the external cause posited by (2) and deduced by (5) must transcend all time, space, matter, and energy. As the cause of time, it must be timeless, at least sans the universe. As the cause of space and matter, it must be immaterial. As the cause of energy, it must be enormously powerful.

But Swinburne and Craig are not content to let the conclusion rest here. They continue the argument by insisting that this cause is demonstrably personal. Swinburne observes that there are two types of causal explanation: scientific explanations in terms of laws and initial conditions, and personal explanations in terms of agents and their wills. However, the existence of the universe itself cannot have a scientific explanation, since laws and initial conditions constitute features of the universe. The universe's existence can thus only be accounted for in terms of an agent and his volitions, namely, a personal explanation. Moreover, Craig maintains that the personhood of the cause of the universe's existence is implied by its timelessness and immateriality. The only entities identified by philosophers as possibly being timeless and immaterial are minds and abstract objects. But abstract objects, like laws of logic and numbers, do not stand in causal relations, as the inability to cause anything is part of what it means to be abstract. Hence the cause of the universe's existence must be a mind. To sum up, the Leibnizian cosmological argument gives us a timeless, immaterial, enormously powerful, and personal cause of the universe's existence, which, as Thomas Aquinas laconically remarked, all people call "God."

THE *KALĀM* COSMOLOGICAL ARGUMENT

One of the two projects for which Craig is best known is his refurbishing of the *kalām* cosmological argument, first proposed by the Islamic theologian al-Ghazali (1058–1111). Unlike the Leibnizian cosmological argument, the *kalām* cosmological argument is based on the insight that the universe had a beginning. It can be stated in this way:

1. Whatever begins to exist has a cause.
2. The universe began to exist.
3. Therefore the universe has a cause.

Craig argues that (1) is a self-evident first principle of metaphysics. For if, *per impossibile*, something could begin to exist without a cause, that is logically equivalent to its coming into being from nothing. And such a suggestion is literally worse than magic. For consider what nothing is—the complete absence of anything; it has no properties, no potentialities, and no powers. At least when the magician pulls the rabbit out of the hat, there is the magician, not to mention the hat. But out of nothing, nothing comes.

Craig contends that (2) is certified on philosophical and scientific grounds. Philosophically, a beginningless universe entails an actually infinite number of previous events. Now while a potentially infinite number of things can exist (where infinity serves merely as an ideal limit that is never reached), an actually infinite number of things cannot exist (where a collection is not growing toward infinity as a limit but is already complete). By *reductio ad absurdum*, then, the universe cannot be beginningless. Scientifically, in 2003 the cosmologists Arvind Borde, Alan Guth, and Alexander Vilenkin proved a theorem (appropriately dubbed the Borde-Guth-Vilenkin theorem) revealing that any universe that has, on average, been expanding throughout its history cannot be infinite in the past but must have a past space-time boundary. All scientifically tenable models of the universe to date—such as the Big Bang *simpliciter* and the Big Bang generated in the multiverse—propose a universe that has, on average, expanded throughout its history. Thus Vilenkin pulls no punches as to the implications of the Borde-Guth-Vilenkin theorem: "It is said that an argument is what convinces reasonable men and a proof is what it takes to convince even an unreasonable man. With the proof now in place, cosmologists can no longer hide behind the possibility of a past-eternal universe. There is no escape: they have to face the problem of a cosmic beginning."[1]

From (1) and (2) it follows that (3) the universe has a cause. Conceptually unpacking the attributes of this cause in the same way as with the Leibnizian cosmological argument, Craig finds that the cause of the universe is timeless, immaterial, and enormously powerful. Drawing on its properties of being timeless and immaterial, Craig points out that this cause is either personal or impersonal and then proceeds to eliminate the option of impersonality. Suppose this timeless, immaterial cause were impersonal. Then the cause could never exist without the effect. If an impersonal cause is timelessly present, then the effect must be timelessly present as well. To illustrate, the timeless, immaterial, impersonal cause of water's freezing is the temperature being below zero degrees Celsius. Now if the temperature were below zero timelessly, then any water around would be frozen timelessly. It would be impossible for the water to just begin to freeze a finite time ago! In exactly the same way, if the timeless, immaterial cause of the universe were impersonal, then the universe would exist timelessly. There would be no such thing as time! But this we know to be false from philosophy and cosmology. Therefore it follows that the timeless, immaterial cause of the universe is personal. Such a personal being would be endowed with freedom of the will and so have the ability to create a new effect without any prior determining conditions. Again, such a being is identifiable with what theists mean by God.

THE TELEOLOGICAL ARGUMENT

Robin Collins maintains that God is the best explanation for the fine-tuning of the universe for life in any form. It should be observed here that "fine-tuned" does not mean designed. Rather, "fine-tuning" refers to the fact that, in the last forty years, scientists have been stunned by the discovery that the existence of life depends on a delicate balance of the laws of nature, the constants of nature, and the initial conditions present in the first split second (the first $10-4^3$ second) of the universe. If any of these laws, constants, or conditions were altered by even a hair's breadth, the universe would be life prohibiting, and life simply would not exist. We now know that life-prohibiting universes are vastly more probable than any life-permitting universe like ours. Hence we may reason:

1. The laws of nature are fine-tuned for the existence of life.
2. The constants of nature are fine-tuned for the existence of life.
3. The cosmic initial conditions are fine-tuned for the existence of life.
4. The fine-tuning of the universe is due to either necessity, chance, or design.
5. The fine-tuning of the universe is not due to necessity.
6. The fine-tuning of the universe is not due to chance.
7. Therefore the fine-tuning of the universe is due to design.

Regarding (1), Collins points out that the law of gravity, the law of electromagnetism, the strong nuclear force, the principle of quantization, and the Pauli exclusion principle must assume precisely the forms they do for life to exist. Regarding (2), Collins illustrates that if the gravitational constant were altered by as little as one part in 10^{34}, even single-celled organisms could not exist. Likewise, if the cosmological constant were altered by as little as one part in 10^{50}, the universe would either collapse or expand too rapidly for galaxies and stars—and thus life—to exist. Regarding (3), Collins highlights that the initial distribution of mass-energy at the universe's inception was fine-tuned to 1 part in 10 to the power of 10 to the power of 123, a precision so mind-defying that calling it astronomical would be a gross understatement. To illustrate, the precision of the universe's initial explosion must be far greater than that needed to blow up a pile of rubble and obtain a fully formed building filled with desks, tables, chairs, and computers. Point (4) simply lists the live options for explaining the remarkable fine-tuning of (1) through (3). Point (5) is established by the fact that the laws of nature, established in the first $10-4^3$ second of the universe, are clearly not necessary; prior to that point the laws simply did not exist. Moreover, the constants and initial conditions of the universe are independent of the laws of nature. Thus, even on the mistaken assumption that the laws of nature were necessary, the constants and initial conditions could have assumed a vast range of values. Point (6) is demonstrated by the fact that the odds of a life-permitting universe are simply so infinitesimal that they cannot be reasonably faced. To illustrate, imagine a lottery that randomly selects one ball from one white ball and a trillion trillion trillion black balls. Each black ball represents a life-prohibiting universe, and the white ball represents a life-permitting universe. It is overwhelmingly more probable that whichever ball rolls down the chute, it will be black rather than white. Thus our getting the white ball of a life-permitting universe cries out for the explanation that the lottery was rigged to permit life. From (1) through (6) it follows that (7) the universe was designed to permit life, entailing an intelligent designer of the cosmos.

THE AXIOLOGICAL ARGUMENT

Stuart Hackett and William Lane Craig furnish an axiological, or moral, argument for the existence of God based on the existence of objective moral values. To say that a moral value is objective means that it holds independently of human consciousness. As with laws of logic or mathematical truths, it does not depend on what anyone thinks, believes, or feels. Thus the assertion "The Holocaust was objectively evil" means that the Holocaust was evil even though the Nazis who carried it out thought that it was good, and it would still be evil even if the Nazis had won World War II and succeeded in exterminating or brainwashing everyone who disagreed with them. So even if everyone on planet Earth believed the Holocaust was good, it would still be evil; everyone would simply be mistaken. Likewise, the assertion "Love is objectively good" means that love is good even if everyone on the earth believed that love was evil and all earthly governments passed laws forbidding love. Now the crucial notion is that if God does not exist, then moral values are not objective in the aforementioned sense. Hence we may proffer this argument:

1. If God does not exist, then objective moral values do not exist.
2. Objective moral values exist.
3. Therefore God exists.

In support of (1), let us assume that sociobiological evolution occurred and ask, What is the status of moral values on theism versus on atheism? On theism, humans in the course of evolution come to gradually and fallibly apprehend a realm of objectively existing moral values flowing necessarily from the all-good character or nature of God, just as humans in the course of evolution come to gradually and fallibly apprehend a realm of objectively existing physical objects. Thus evolution, on theism, is the vehicle through which objective moral values are *discovered*. But on atheism, there is no transcendent source of objective moral values, such that sociobiological evolution becomes the means through which moral values are *created*. This is easy to see: had sociobiological evolution taken a different turn, it would have churned out a completely different set of moral values for humans. As Charles Darwin himself noted, "If . . . men were reared under precisely the same conditions as hive-bees, there can hardly be a doubt that our unmarried females would, like the worker-bees, think it a sacred duty to kill their brothers, and mothers would strive to kill their fertile daughters; and no one would think of interfering."[2]

Thus the agnostic philosopher of science Michael Ruse poignantly writes, "Morality is a biological adaptation no less than are hands and feet and teeth. . . . Considered as a rationally justifiable set of claims about an objective something, ethics is illusory. I appreciate that when somebody says, 'Love thy neighbor as thyself,' they *think* they are referring above and beyond themselves. . . . Nevertheless . . . such reference is truly without foundation. Morality is just an aid to survival and reproduction . . . and any deeper meaning is illusory."[3]

To sum up, if God exists, then actions like love, equality, generosity, and self-sacrifice are objectively good and would still be good even if humans never existed. Similarly, actions like rape, cruelty, discrimination, and child abuse are objectively evil. Humans simply discover these moral facts. But if God does not exist, then we just happened to evolve the notions of love, equality, generosity, and self-sacrifice as good and the notions of rape, cruelty, discrimination, and child abuse as evil through sociobiological pressures. These values are not objectively true like $2 + 2 = 4$, but are rather dependent for their existence on the evolutionary process and the descent of humanity. So it seems unquestionable that if God does not exist, then objective moral values do not exist.

As for (2), we can discover through introspection that objective moral values exist. As the atheistic ethicist Walter Sinnott-Armstrong points out, introspection is the standard way of doing ethical theory: "The most common way to choose among moral theories is to test how well they cohere with our intuitions or considered judgments about what is morally right and wrong, about the nature or ideal of a person, and about the purpose(s) of morality."[4] Virtually everyone perceives that at least some things are objectively good and at least some things are objectively evil. The moral skeptic who cannot see the objectivity of at least some moral values is analogous to the colorblind person who cannot see the objectivity of colors; thus the presence of moral skeptics does nothing more to undermine the objectivity of values than the presence of colorblind people does to undermine the objectivity of colors. Accordingly, the atheistic ethicist

Louise Antony concedes, "Any argument for moral skepticism will be based upon premises which are less obvious than the existence of objective moral values themselves."[5]

Thus it seems that (1) and (2) are true; if so, it follows deductively that God exists.

THE ARGUMENT FOR THE RESURRECTION OF JESUS

The second project for which Craig is best known is developing an interdisciplinary argument for the historicity of Jesus's resurrection. In view of the arguments for God's existence, Craig combines history and philosophy to argue:

1. Historical criticism establishes the truth of four facts surrounding Jesus's fate.
   a. After his death, Jesus was buried in a tomb by Joseph of Arimathea.
   b. On the Sunday following the crucifixion, Jesus's tomb was found empty by a group of his women followers.
   c. On multiple occasions and under various circumstances, different individuals and groups of people believed they saw Jesus alive after his death.
   d. The original disciples came to believe in Jesus's resurrection from the dead despite having every predisposition to the contrary.
2. The best explanation of these four facts is that God resurrected Jesus from the dead.

Concerning (1), Craig insists that (a) is demonstrated by the description of Jesus's burial in the pre-Pauline creed (*terminus ante quem* AD 35) quoted by Paul in 1 Corinthians 15:3–7, the account of Jesus's burial by Joseph in the pre-Markan passion narrative (*terminus ante quem* AD 37), the embarrassing attribution of Jesus's burial to a Sanhedrist (the Sanhedrin was, in the eyes of the early Jesus movement, responsible for the judicial murder of Jesus), the simplicity of the pre-Markan burial account, and the lack of any competing burial account. Craig maintains that (b) is evinced by the empty tomb account in the pre-Markan passion narrative, the implication of the empty tomb in the pre-Pauline creed, the simplicity of the pre-Markan empty tomb account, the embarrassing discovery of the empty tomb by women (who in the first century were regarded misogynistically as so unreliable that they could not even serve as witnesses in a Jewish court of law), and the Sanhedrin's acknowledgment of the empty tomb in their charge that the disciples had stolen Jesus's body. Craig holds that (c) is verified by the list of eyewitnesses to Jesus's postmortem appearances in the pre-Pauline creed, the multiple independent accounts of Jesus's post-mortem appearances in the Gospels, and the earmarks of historical credibility in specific appearance narratives. Craig asserts that (d) is corroborated by the multiple independent New Testament reports that the first disciples believed in Jesus's resurrection notwithstanding the facts that Jews had no belief in a dying, much less rising, Messiah, Jesus's crucifixion in Jewish thought exposed him as a heretic accursed by God, Jewish beliefs about the afterlife precluded anyone's resurrection from the dead before the end of the world, and no belief in or accounts of resurrection existed in Greco-Roman thought.

Concerning (2), Craig employs the standard historical tests for determining the best explanation for a given set of historical facts. These include explanatory scope, explanatory power, plausibility, not being *ad hoc* (i.e., contrived), accordance with accepted beliefs, and outstripping its rival theories in meeting the afore listed criteria. As for explanatory scope and power, the resurrection hypothesis explains all four facts and explains each fact well. In light of Jesus's radical personal claims to be the unique divine Son of God, God's resurrecting Jesus would constitute the vindication of those claims and so stand as plausible. The resurrection hypothesis is not *ad hoc* because it requires only one additional datum—that God exists—for which argument has already been given. Moreover, the hypothesis "God resurrected Jesus from the dead" does not in any way conflict with the accepted belief that people do not resurrect naturally from the dead. Finally, the resurrection hypothesis far outstrips the hallucination hypothesis, the apparent death hypothesis, the displaced body hypothesis, and other rival theories in meeting the relevant historical criteria. Therefore the rational person ought to believe in the historicity of Jesus's resurrection.

THE CASE FOR THE EXISTENCE OF THE SOUL

J. P. Moreland argues that humans possess an immaterial soul or mind distinct from the physical brain, where the soul causes changes in the brain and the brain causes changes in the mind. We shall highlight seven grounds on which Moreland posits the existence of the soul. The first six are based on the logical law of identity (also known as Leibniz's law of the indiscernibility of identicals), which states that for any entities x and y, x and y are the same entity if and only if whatever is true of x is true of y and whatever is true of y is true of x. Accordingly, if there is even one thing true of x that is not true of y or true of y that is not true of x, then x and y are not the same entity. So the strategy of the first six grounds is to show that there are things true of the brain but false of the mind or true of the mind but false of the brain, thus establishing that the mind and brain are not the same entity. Since the brain is a material substance, the mind must therefore be an immaterial substance (i.e., a soul).

First, Moreland points to the distinctiveness of mental events and brain events. Some events of the mind lack properties that their corresponding events of the brain possess and some events of the mind possess properties that their corresponding events of the brain lack. Mental events include episodes of thought, feelings of pain, and episodes of having sensory experience (e.g., a picture of a ball in my mind). Brain events can be described exhaustively using terms of chemistry, physics, and biology. For example, my thought of Kansas City (a mental event) is not ten centimeters long; it does not weigh anything; it does not have an electrical current; it is not located anywhere (it is not two inches from my left ear). But the brain event correlated with this thought has a neuronal length, a weight, an electrical current, and is located somewhere within my head. Similarly, my afterimage of a ball (the impression of the ball in my mind when I close my eyes) is pink. But nothing in my brain is pink. Therefore the mind and brain cannot be the same entity.

Second, Moreland calls attention to the private access of the mental. My thoughts and mental processes are known by me in a way unavailable to anyone else; but the corresponding brain events are not known by me in a way unavailable to anyone else. Mental events are privately accessible; brain events are publicly accessible. So it is possible for a neurosurgeon to know far more about my brain than I do, looking into it and knowing its operations far better than I do. But the neurosurgeon cannot know my mental life, including those mental aspects associated with the brain operations we both can see. The only way the neurosurgeon can know what I think, believe, feel, fear, and so forth is to ask me. So the mind is distinct from the brain.

Third, Moreland observes the incorrigibility—or logical impossibility of being mistaken—about some mental events, while it is quite possible to be mistaken about the corresponding brain events. Suppose I am experiencing what I take to be a green rug. It is possible that the rug is not there or that the light is poor and the rug is really gray. I could be mistaken about the rug itself. But it is logically impossible for me to be mistaken that I am experiencing what I take to be a green rug right now. However, I could easily be mistaken about the brain state associated with my experience of the green rug. Hence the mind and brain cannot be the same entity.

Fourth, Moreland emphasizes the experience of first-person subjectivity. The character of subjective mental events cannot be captured in physicalist terms; but the corresponding brain events can be captured in physicalist terms. Consider the following thought experiment. Suppose a deaf scientist became the world's leading expert on the neurology of hearing. It is possible for him to know and describe everything there is to know about the brain processes involved in hearing, since they can be captured in physicalist terms. But it is impossible for him to know and describe the experience of what it is like to hear, since that cannot be captured in physicalist terms. Moreover, a brain does not have first-person, subjective states, but a mind does. The brain is not happy or sad, but a mind can be happy or sad. Certain neurons firing in my brain may well cause my mind to be happy or sad, but those neuronal firings are not the same as the experience of happiness or sadness. Accordingly, the mind is distinct from the brain.

Fifth, Moreland underscores the intentionality, namely, the about-ness, for-ness, or of-ness, of the mind. Mental states point beyond themselves to other objects even if those objects do not exist. But the brain does not possess intentionality; brain states do not point beyond themselves to other objects. To illustrate, my mind thinks *about* my wife, my mind hopes *for* a new car, and my mind dreams *of* a unicorn. But no physical event happening in my brain is *about* my wife, *for* a new car, or *of* a unicorn. The mind has the ability to transcend itself and be *of* or *about* something else; this about-ness is not a property of anything physical, like the brain. So the mind is not the physical brain.

Sixth, Moreland stresses personal identity over time. My mind does not lose old parts or gain new ones and is therefore the same throughout time. But my brain loses old parts and gains new ones. In fact, every seven years my brain cells are entirely replaced. So my brain is not literally the same throughout time. Hence the mind and the brain cannot be the same reality.

Seventh, Moreland contends that our possession of libertarian free will is only possible if we have a soul. He furnishes the following syllogism:

1. If I am simply my brain, then everything I do is determined by my genetic makeup and the input of my five senses (i.e., I don't have libertarian free will).
2. But I do have libertarian free will.
3. Therefore I am not simply my brain.
4. I am either my brain or an immaterial mind (soul) embodied.
5. Therefore I am an immaterial mind (soul) embodied.

THE MOLINIST RESPONSE TO OPEN THEISM

While some analytic theologians are open theists, the majority are Molinists (i.e., indebted in their understanding of omniscience to the sixteenth-century Spanish Catholic reformer Luis de Molina) who attempt to reveal the shortcomings of open theism. Regarding the six categories of divine relational changeability texts (texts portraying God as changing his mind or learning truths due to his relationship with humans), Molinist analytic theologians affirm that they are anthropomorphisms and, contra open theists, point to a literal truth. This truth is that God's sovereignty does not consist of arbitrary decrees functioning irrespective of free human choices. Rather, the divine decrees take into account and are conditioned by what God middle-knows the free acts of creatures would be in all worlds possible for God to create given libertarian freedom. Middle knowledge is God's prevolitional knowledge of all counterfactual truths, including counterfactuals of creaturely freedom (CCFs). Thus, by his middle knowledge, God knows what each possible libertarian agent would freely do in any possible set of circumstances. Such a reality is expressed anthropomorphically from the human vantage point in terms of God's changing his mind, regretting previous actions, disappointment, frustration, learning about creatures, or relenting on planned action.

Affirming with open theists that the future does not yet exist, Molinist analytic theologians deny that the nonexistence of the future renders it logically unknowable. The only property that a proposition p must meet to be logically knowable is truth, and future tense as well as counterfactual propositions possess truth values. This is seen, as Craig observes, in the fact that we often know the truth value of CCFs: "If I were to offer my wife a plate of liver and onions and a plate of chocolate-chip cookies, I know which one she would choose as certainly as I know almost anything!"[6] So, if humans, with our finite intelligences and finite knowledge of the essences of some actual individuals, can know what they would freely do in some sets of circumstances, it seems eminently reasonable to hold that God, with his infinite intelligence and infinite knowledge of the essences of all possible individuals, can know what each of them would freely do in any set of circumstances in which they find themselves. Hence, even on the open theist's definition of omniscience as knowing all truths logically possible to know, it is logically possible for God to possess middle knowledge and therefore future knowledge of libertarian free decisions. Indeed, God must have such knowledge by virtue of his omniscience.

Molinist analytic theologians challenge the open theistic notion that the unchangeability of the past makes God's foreknowledge inevitable, as there is nothing we can now do to alter it. For, as open theists note, backward causation is impossible. Nevertheless, this impossibility is relevant only if there does not exist any functional equivalent to backward causation by which present and future actions can render the past different than it would have been otherwise, and such a functional equivalent is readily provided by middle knowledge. On the Molinist view, it lies within the power of every individual to freely perform any action A such that if A occurred, God's middle knowledge, and derivatively his foreknowledge, would have been different than it in fact was. To illustrate, suppose that God has always known that I would submit a proposal to speak at the 2017 American Academy of Religion Annual Meeting. Up until the submission deadline arrives, I possess the ability to avail or disavail myself of the opportunity. If the deadline passes without my writing a proposal, then the past would have included God's foreknowledge of my nonsubmission, rather than my submission, of the proposal. That God, in the past, would have held different foreknowledge than he in fact held results from the fact that different counterfactual propositions, which God would have discerned via his middle knowledge, would have been true. So while God's foreknowledge of human decisions is chronologically prior to those decisions, the truth of propositions concerning the decisions of creatures that God could potentially create is logically prior to God's foreknowledge of those decisions.

CONCLUSION

Analytic theology has furnished contemporary Christians with powerful arguments for the central Christian truth claims that God exists and has decisively revealed himself to humanity in the person of Jesus of Nazareth. Moreover, analytic theologians have made a strong case for the existence of the human soul, and those analytic theologians who are Molinists have given good reason that libertarian human freedom is consistent with God's exhaustive foreknowledge. Many of the most innovative projects in contemporary theology are currently coming out of analytic circles. Such projects include but are not limited to delineating the relationships between God and time, between God and abstract objects, between Christianity and other world religions, as well as explicating the justice of the atonement.

FOR FURTHER READING

Primary Sources

Craig, William Lane. *The Only Wise God: The Compatibility of Divine Foreknowledge and Human Freedom*. Grand Rapids: Baker, 1987.

———. *Reasonable Faith: Christian Truth and Apologetics*. 3rd ed. Wheaton, IL: Crossway, 2008.

Craig, William Lane, and J. P. Moreland, eds. *The Blackwell Companion to Natural Theology*. Malden, MA: Wiley-Blackwell, 2012.

Moreland, J. P. *The Soul: How We Know It's Real and Why It Matters*. Chicago: Moody, 2014.

Moreland, J. P., and William Lane Craig. *Philosophical Foundations for a Christian Worldview*. 2nd ed. Downers Grove, IL: IVP Academic, 2017.

Pruss, Alexander R. *The Principle of Sufficient Reason: A Reassessment*. Cambridge: Cambridge University Press, 2006.

Swinburne, Richard. *The Existence of God*. Rev. ed. Oxford: Clarendon, 1991.

Secondary Sources

Copan, Paul, ed. *Will the Real Jesus Please Stand Up?* Grand Rapids: Baker, 1998.

Crisp, Oliver D., and Michael C. Rea, eds. *Analytic Theology: New Essays in the Philosophy of Theology*. Oxford: Oxford University Press, 2009.

Garcia, Robert K., and Nathan L. King, ed. *Is Goodness without God Good Enough? A Debate on Faith, Secularism, and Ethics*. Lanham, MD: Rowman and Littlefield, 2009.

MacGregor, Kirk R. *Luis de Molina: The Life and Theology of the Founder of Middle Knowledge*. Grand Rapids: Zondervan, 2015.

McCall, Thomas H. *An Invitation to Analytic Christian Theology*. Downers Grove, IL: IVP Academic, 2015.

Meister, Chad. *Introducing Philosophy of Religion*. New York: Routledge, 2009.

CHAPTER 32

CHINESE ESCHATOLOGY

I t is projected that by the year 2025, China will be sending out more foreign missionaries than any other nation.[1] As this chapter reveals, the mission impulse
of Chinese Christians is inextricably tied to the indigenous eschatology they
have developed since the Cultural Revolution (1966–76). In the words of prominent Chinese house church leaders Brother Yun (1958–), Peter Xu Yongze
(1940–), and Enoch Wang (1954–), "We believe God has given us a solemn
responsibility to take the fire from his altar and complete the Great Commission
by establishing his kingdom in all of the remaining countries and people groups
in Asia, the Middle East, and Islamic North Africa. When this happens, we
believe that the Scripture says the Lord Jesus will return for his bride."[2] The
resultant missionary phenomenon is known among Chinese Christians as the
Back to Jerusalem movement. This chapter will trace the history of the Back to
Jerusalem movement and explore its central theological motifs.

HISTORY OF THE BACK TO JERUSALEM MOVEMENT

The birth of the Back to Jerusalem movement occurred in 1942 at the Northwest
Bible Institute in Shaanxi Province. Vice Principal Mark Ma and a host of students felt burdened for the salvation of the Muslim people groups residing in
the province of Xinjiang in Northwest China. Quickly Ma and his students
inferred that Xinjiang was not only a mission field but also the groundwork
for a major missionary project back across the ancient Silk Road, directly into
such central Asian Islamic countries as Kazakhstan, Kyrgyzstan, Tajikistan,
Afghanistan, and Pakistan. In 1943 Ma reported receiving a direct call from

God to complete the Great Commission. Ma proposed that the center of the missionary movement throughout history had moved from its starting point in Jerusalem to Antioch to Western Europe to North America and eventually arrived at China at the eastern and southern coastal port cities of Shanghai, Macau, and Guangzhou. To circumnavigate the globe and so fulfill the Great Commission, Ma argued the gospel must continue into Northwestern China, across central Asia, and back to Jerusalem. Upon its return to Jerusalem, the Second Coming will occur. Brother Yun summarizes this vision: "We believe the farthest the gospel can travel from Jerusalem is to circle the entire globe and come all the way back to where it started—Jerusalem! When the fire of the gospel completes its circuit of the whole globe, the Lord Jesus will return!"[3]

In 1946 a small band of Chinese Christians took up the vision, focusing on all the Islamic countries in central Asia and North Africa as well as the Jews in Palestine. However, the vision was stifled by the political upheaval in China, climaxing in the Communist rise to power in 1949. The Communists vehemently opposed all missionary activity, imprisoned the leaders of the Back to Jerusalem movement, and drove the movement underground. The most important of these early leaders was Simon Zhao (1918–2003), who survived over forty years of imprisonment. Zhao kept the movement alive and bestowed it on the current leadership of China's house church networks in the early 1990s.

During the fifty-year gap between Ma's original vision and the release of Simon Zhao from prison, the Chinese church had profoundly changed in three ways. First, the number of Chinese Christians had mushroomed from a few million to over seventy million. Although it is hard to count the number of Christians in a largely underground church, it can be safely estimated that today the number stands at over ninety million. Second, this phenomenal growth sparked a sense of confidence about the divine eschatological role the Chinese church has been called to accomplish. Third, fifty years of Communist rule specially equipped Chinese Christians to work in Islamic contexts. Learning how to work and flourish in a hostile environment and to persist and keep their witness in the face of persecution and beatings, Chinese Christians believed (and continue to believe) there was nothing that any Muslim, Buddhist, or Hindu country could inflict on them that they had not already experienced and overcome in China. Chinese Christians also learned how to coordinate outreach apart from the costly and complex administrative structures prevalent in the West. The Back to Jerusalem movement garnered significant momentum through a number of strategic gatherings of house church leaders between 1996 and 2002.

On November 26, 1998, churches engaged in the Back to Jerusalem movement embraced a common Confession of Faith. The confession denounces various heresies (such as the Oriental Lightning movement, which holds that Christ has returned as a thirty-five-year-old Chinese woman named Mrs. Deng), delineates why the member churches refuse to affiliate with the Three-Self Patriotic movement (the Communist governmental body overseeing Chinese religion), and professes the commitment to preserve the faith encapsulated in the classic Christian creeds. The confession affirms biblical inspiration and freedom from error, the Trinity, and the incarnation, death, and bodily resurrection of Jesus. Celebrating the priesthood of all believers, the confession significantly rejects any use of political power to accomplish its goals: "We are opposed to the expansion of the church by relying on political power, whether domestic or international."[4] The confession affirms premillennialism but not a pretribulational rapture. In 2002 the Beijing Forum began to coordinate the strong Chinese missionary thrust with several international efforts to reach central Asia, the Islamic world, and Israel with the gospel. Currently the Back to Jerusalem movement has dispatched more than a hundred thousand Chinese missionaries for the task, a missionary force twice as large as any mobilized by North America.

Nevertheless, the Chinese church plans for the majority of these missionaries to be self-supporting, employing their skills and vocations to relocate all along the ancient Silk Road. This strategy will enable the missionaries to integrate into their host cultures without suspicion and circumvent the monetary and administrative obstacles that frequently hinder Western missions organizations. Yongze has dubbed the "grandiose strategies" of the West "elephant plans," since elephants make a tremendous amount of noise and are nearly impossible to hide. But like the mustard seed in Jesus's parable, Yongze views the Back to Jerusalem movement as a quiet, grassroots organization akin to an "army of insects" and the gradual, persistent, yet quiet work of "termites."[5] Via these means, Yun proclaims that the movement will "pull down the world's last remaining spiritual strongholds—the house of Buddha, the house of Muhammad, and the house of Hinduism—and ... proclaim the glorious gospel to all nations before the Second Coming of our Lord Jesus Christ."[6]

CENTRAL THEOLOGICAL MOTIFS

At this point, we turn to an exposition of the four dominant theological motifs governing the Back to Jerusalem movement.

Premillennial Global Advance

The Back to Jerusalem movement anticipates a massive global advance of the gospel prior to the millennium. In missiologist Timothy Tennent's words, the movement repudiates "the notion that the inauguration of the millennium will be preceded by nothing but apostasy, despair, and calamity for the church."[7] For the movement, the preeminent sign that will herald the end of the age is neither wars nor natural disasters nor the consolidation of the nation of Israel, but the accomplishment of Matthew 24:14: "This gospel of the kingdom will be preached in the whole world as a testimony to all nations, and then the end will come." From the Chinese perspective, it looks as though wherever one turns—to the city or the country, to the intellectuals or the peasants—people are coming to Jesus and new churches are cropping up. Yun has gone so far as to say that "in thirty years *all* of China will know the Lord."[8] Yongze emphasizes that the Back to Jerusalem movement will soon spread the gospel throughout the entire 10/40 window—the region located between 10 and 40 degrees north of the equator (including central Asia and Israel) which corresponds to the most unreached people groups in the world—thus making missions a "race towards the finish line" of "the return of our Lord Jesus Christ."[9] Wang concurs with this assessment that the Great Commission is nearly complete: "Let's rush to the front line one more time for our King and Christ will come! We can have a holiday for 1,000 years when it is all finished!"[10]

The Stronghold of Islam, Judaism, and Other World Religions

The Back to Jerusalem movement is deeply aware of the challenges posed by non-Christian religions in the fulfillment of the Great Commission. Chinese eschatology is distinguished by the commitment, in Yun's words, to "tear down the world's last remaining spiritual strongholds" and to bring the gospel "to the nations that lie between China and Jerusalem, the place where the fire of the gospel first started to spread."[11] Chinese Christians interpret this development as transpiring in definite stages: first the Muslim groups in Northwest China, then the Muslims of Central Asia, and finally the Jews in Israel. While the early church started with a "first to the Jews and then to the Gentiles" approach, Chinese Christians expect a "first to the Gentiles and then to the Jews" finale. Given their alliance with international missions groups, Chinese Christians also anticipate that African Christians will evangelize and plant churches throughout sub-Saharan Africa.

Persecution of the People of God in the Last Days

The dawn and the later revivification of the Back to Jerusalem movement is inextricably intertwined in Chinese thought with the persecution of Zhao, who took part in the nascent vision and, following more than forty years in prison, revitalized the vision in a new generation of house church leaders. Since each of the movement's pioneers spent decades in prison, its hymnody echoes a suffering church. Rich in their profundity, many Back to Jerusalem hymns draw heavily on images of persecution as Chinese Christians proclaim the good news all the way to Jerusalem. In one hymn, their tear-filled eyes are uplifted to the harvest while blood pours from their chests; because of their dedication to the harvest, they take up their crosses and advance toward Jerusalem. Chinese Christians envisage thousands of martyrs, and they implore the house church warriors to pen their testimonies with their own blood. Yongze describes the rationale behind this anticipation: "The devil, who has kept Muslim, Buddhist and Hindu nations captive for thousands of years, will not surrender without a strong and bloody fight."[12] Yun anticipates that of the more than one hundred thousand missionaries sent out thus far into the mission field, ten thousand will be martyrs in the next decade. Contrary to Western ministerial preparation, the training of Chinese missionaries includes lessons and coaching on how to be an effective witness in prison as well as in death. Hence by comprehending the eschatological significance of suffering, Chinese Christians discover a source of strength to cope with suffering while engaging in the task of evangelization.

Role of Prayer in Missions and Millennial Preparation

Using agricultural imagery, the Back to Jerusalem movement maintains that following a long period of labor, a compacted period of harvest will transpire when the fruit is ingathered. Such a season of ingathering will be quickened and aided by prayer, since God achieves his providential purpose in response to the intercessions of his saints. Appealing to the book of Revelation, Chinese Christians view "the prayers of God's people" as the heavenly "golden bowls full of incense" (Rev. 5:8), which go "up before God from the angel's hand" (Rev. 8:4) immediately prior to the actualization of the seventh and final seal. Because it is viewed as the key that unlocks the door of the millennium, prayer epitomizes Chinese churches. As Carl Lawrence and David Wang point out, "The distinguishing feature of the present day church growth in China is the disciplined prayer life of every believer."[13] Insisting on the supreme power that emanates from the mixture of prayer and fasting, members of the Back to Jerusalem movement employ this combination to press for the advance of the gospel in China, the collapse of the spiritual strongholds of Islam, and significantly, that Western seminaries and Bible colleges will remain faithful to the Word of God. Prayer plus fasting, according to a senior movement pastor in Gwangwashi, constitutes the sole divinely given vehicle for ensuring "that everyone in Beijing knows Jesus and that Jesus will be known in the whole country and that China will be a country from which the gospel is spreading to the rest of the world."[14] Hence the movement stipulates the symbiotic relationship between devoted prayer plus fasting and the eschatological fulfillment of Matthew 24:14.

CONCLUSION

The Back to Jerusalem movement centers on the essential link between eschatology and global missions. The movement understands eschatology not as mostly speculation about future events but as the framework for interpreting the inbreaking of the work of God today. Further, eschatology encompasses the movement's trenchant denunciation of the entire structure of Communist China. Eschatology requires a *telos* to human history that consumes atheistic sociopolitical ambitions in the fire of God's wider redemptive plan in the world. The movement has sparked an extraordinary increase in the number of people embracing the lordship of Jesus without the assistance of paid staff, experts, monetary resources, or complicated programs. This kingdom influx is taken to be part of the last great missiological endeavor before the earth is "filled with the knowledge of the glory of the LORD as the waters cover the sea" (Hab. 2:14). As a result, the movement sees the overall future of the church and the expectations of the gospel in the world as tremendously positive while it excitedly awaits the dawn of the millennium.

FOR FURTHER READING

Primary Sources

Hattaway, Paul, and Liu Zhenying. *The Heavenly Man. The Remarkable True Story of Chinese Christian Brother Yun.* Grand Rapids: Kregel, 2004.

Jin, Mingri. *Back to Jerusalem with All Nations: A Biblical Foundation.* Eugene, OR: Wipf and Stock, 2016.

Kwak, Sun-Hee. *Eschatology and Christian Mission.* Seoul: Data World, 2000.

Yiwu, Liao. *God Is Red: The Secret Story of How Christianity Survived and Flourished in Communist China.* Trans. Wen Huang. San Francisco: HarperOne, 2011.

Yun, Brother, Peter Xu Yongze, and Enoch Wang, with Paul Hattaway. *Back to Jerusalem: Three Chinese House Church Leaders Share Their Vision to Complete the Great Commission.* Downers Grove, IL: IVP, 2003.

Secondary Sources

Aikman, David. *Jesus in Beijing: How Christianity Is Transforming China and Changing the Global Balance of Power*. Washington, DC: Regnery, 2003.

Bush, Luis, Brent Fulton, and a Christian worker in China. *China's Next Generation: New China, New Church, New World*. Orange, CA: ChinaSource, 2014.

Lawrence, Carl, and David Wang. *The Coming Influence of China*. Artesia, CA: Shannon, 2000.

Tennent, Timothy C. *Invitation to World Missions: A Trinitarian Missiology for the Twenty-First Century*. Grand Rapids: Kregel, 2010.

———. *Theology in the Context of World Christianity: How the Global Church Is Influencing the Way We Think about and Discuss Theology*. Grand Rapids: Zondervan, 2007.

CHAPTER 33

POSTLIBERAL THEOLOGY

Postliberal theology designates a theological method associated with Yale Divinity School that aims to reverse modern Christianity's accommodation to culture by cultivating the distinctive language of the Christian community. According to this so-called "Yale School," theology amounts to Christian self-description, not substantiation by or correlation with some universal religious experience. Postliberal theology locates itself as a third path between liberal and conservative theology. Postliberals agree with liberal theology that the Bible is not inerrant and that higher biblical criticism is both legitimate and necessary. Postliberals concur with evangelical theology that scriptural revelation holds a position of primacy, that the biblical canon comprises a unified whole, and that Jesus Christ is the unique Savior. Originally formulated by Yale theologians Hans Frei (1922–88) and George Lindbeck (1923–), postliberal theology was first given its moniker by Lindbeck in his classic work *The Nature of Doctrine* (1984). Frei's emphasis on the narrative structure of the Bible gave rise to another descriptor: narrative theology. The students of Frei and Lindbeck, especially Stanley Hauerwas (1940–) and William Placher (1948–2008), have further developed and refined the movement's central ideas. Since the mid-1980s, postliberal theology has posed arguably the most significant theological challenge to mainline Protestant liberalism.

FREI'S NARRATIVE THOUGHT

In 1974 Frei published his seminal text *The Eclipse of Biblical Narrative* (1974), which launched the postliberal movement. Frei began by depicting the erosion of the premodern view of Scripture, where the biblical narrative crafted the world in which Christians lived and worshiped. With the advent of modernity and its skepticism, theologians became preoccupied with Scripture's credibility and therefore endeavored to comprehend the Bible through the possibilities of meaning dictated by their contemporary intellectual worlds. This strategy engendered two divergent hermeneutical pathways whereby modern theologians discovered scriptural meaning. On the one hand, liberal theologians searched for the real meaning of Scripture in the religious experience shared by all humanity and otherwise deconstructed the biblical text into historical-critical pieces. On the other hand, conservative theologians pursued the literal meaning of Scripture—stressing the intention of its original human authors and the historical facticity of its stories—and as a result, turned the Bible into a sourcebook for doctrinal propositions. Both pathways, insisted Frei, displaced the primacy of the biblical narrative and its unique semiotic system, replacing it with a foreign and extratextual world of meaning.

Frei was therefore convinced that both modern liberal and conservative approaches to the Bible missed the point of Scripture by locating its meaning in something other than the overarching biblical narrative itself. He worried that biblical hermeneutics had undergone a "great reversal" in which "interpretation was a matter of fitting the biblical story into another world with another story rather than incorporating that world into the biblical story."[1] Frei stipulated that the subject matter of the Bible cannot be expressed without the biblical narrative. For any other hermeneutical strategy threatens the integrity of Scripture's grand narrative of God's words and deeds focused centrally on the person of Jesus Christ. For Frei, the biblical narrative is indispensable to Jesus's identity as Redeemer; without it, Jesus becomes little more than a symbol for our religious desires. What is important, maintained Frei, is not whether the gospel accounts are historically accurate but how the accounts reveal the character of Jesus. Thus the scriptural narrative must be given a normative function. Frei pointed out that the early Christians made sense of their lives by viewing themselves as related to and participating in the story told by Scripture.

While disclaiming apologetics because its veracity rests on the shifting sands of historical investigation, Frei affirmed the bodily resurrection of Jesus, repudiating the notion that it serves as a myth. While Frei did not believe the Gospels are necessarily historically accurate, he did find their claim that Jesus resurrected from the dead to be credible on various metaphysical grounds. Hence Frei wrote, "We should ask, then, if the Gospel account of the resurrection can be understood to be a myth. . . . The resurrection account (or, better, the passion-resurrection

account as an unbroken unity) is a demythologization of the dying-rising savior myth. For, in contrast to the substance of myth, the passion-resurrection
account concerns an unsubstitutable individual whose mysterious identity is
not ineffably behind the story but is inseparable from the unsubstitutable events
constituting it, with the resurrection as its climax."[2] Frei contended that the
reference and truth of the resurrection cannot be asserted on any ground other
than faith. At the same time, however, Frei offered a quasi-ontological argument
for Jesus's resurrection: "What the accounts are saying, in effect, is that the
being and identity of Jesus in the resurrection are such that his nonresurrection
becomes inconceivable."[3] In other words, the very concept of "Jesus" analytically
contains the idea of existence with us now, so Jesus cannot be conceived as not
present. To think of Jesus is to think of a person who is not dead but alive, who is
not absent but always with us.

LINDBECK'S LINGUISTIC THOUGHT

Supplementing Frei's insistence on the primacy of scriptural narrative for
theology, Lindbeck emphasized the primacy of language over experience and
furnished a theory of religion as a cultural-linguistic medium. Frei appealed to
Wittgenstein's analysis of language and the cultural anthropology of Princeton
professor Clifford Geertz (1926–2006) in mapping out three broad theories of
Christian doctrine. First, the "propositionalist" theory underscores the cognitive
aspects of religion, holding that doctrines constitute truth claims. Most often
identified with evangelical theology, this theory considers the biblical text as
"informational propositions or truth claims about objective realities."[4] Lindbeck
argues that this theory depends on the false assumption that it is possible to
express the objective truth about God absolutely, comprehensively, and timelessly in propositional form. Second, the "experiential-expressive" theory interprets doctrines as noncognitive symbols of inner feelings, attitudes, or existential
orientations.[5] Most often identified with liberal theology, this theory alleges
that there is a common universal religious experience that Christian doctrine
endeavors to provoke or summon through language. For Lindbeck, this theory
is ultimately unverifiable and therefore problematic. Moreover, it seems *prima
facie* false: Christians worship God in a distinctively Trinitarian manner that
does not appear similar to other religions. Consequently, Lindbeck pronounces
that both the propositional theory and the cultural-linguistic theory that have
dominated theology throughout the modern age have failed.

In contrast to these options, Lindbeck proposes a new, third approach called the "cultural-linguistic" theory.[6] This view holds that the essence of religion consists in living within a specific historical religious tradition and adopting its concepts and values. For Lindbeck, religious traditions are historically shaped and controlled by internal norms. In the Christian tradition, Lindbeck declares with Frei that biblical narrative shapes the cultural-linguistic world of the Christian community. On Lindbeck's analysis, Christian doctrines are neither objectively true propositions nor calls to a universal religious experience but are akin to grammatical rules that govern the way we employ language to depict the world. Becoming a member of the Christian community, claimed Lindbeck, means learning a new language. Further, the meaning of Christian language can be found only within the Bible. Rather than attempting to translate Scripture into extratextual categories (the purported error of liberals and conservatives alike), Lindbeck devised an intratextual approach. In his words, "Religious communities are likely to be practically relevant in the long run to the degree that they do not first ask what is either practical or relevant, but instead concentrate on their own intratextual outlooks and forms of life."[7] So for Christians, the story of the Bible must become their own story.

Hence Christianity resembles a culture with its own distinctive language, practices, and system of meaning. The church's language and practices (e.g., preaching, exhortation, prayer, and worship) represent the first-order enterprise. Doctrines represent the second-order enterprise, namely, the rules or grammar of the faith that govern Christian life. They reflect the cultural-linguistic medium that facilitates the Christian's particular description of reality, experience, and action. Lindbeck insists that being a Christian means living out of the community's vision of reality narrated in the Bible as centered on Jesus Christ and becoming an adept practitioner in this way of life. It follows from this contention that Christian catechesis is a more suitable emphasis for churches than the assorted modern approaches to make Christianity reasonable, attractive, or relevant. On Lindberg's account of early Christianity, most converts did not partake of Christian teaching intellectually and then opt to become Christians. Rather, they were drawn by what they perceived of the faith and practices of Christian communities, and only later did they cognitively receive Christian teaching, typically after a lengthy period of catechetical instruction.

POSTLIBERAL THEMES

Four essential themes characterize postliberal theology: a sociocommunitarian view of human life, a nonfoundationalism that permits the particularity of the

Christian revelation to create the context for cognition and praxis, an intratextual approach to the Bible underscoring the primacy of its narratives, and the absorption of the universe into the biblical world.

Sociocommunitarian View of Human Life

Postliberal theologians insist that humans are fundamentally social and cultural beings who are formed by the communities within which they reside. As opposed to the universal reason of propositionalism and the universal experience of experiential-expressivism, our language and tradition mold our experience and understanding of the most basic aspects of reality. Just as the Newtonian view of mechanics differs from the Einsteinian view, the Christian position on the human condition and our redemption conflicts with the Buddhist position. Various linguistic systems facilitate their respective beliefs and actions. The reality of sin as rebellion against God and salvation in Jesus Christ can be grasped only within the Christian cultural-linguistic system, the church.

This analysis carries profound consequences for ethics, as Stanley Hauerwas reveals. Rather than following Enlightenment reflexes by grounding morality in terms of individuals, reason, isolated facts, and deeds, Hauerwas contends that virtues are grounded in a particular narrative. In *The Peaceable Kingdom* (1991), Hauerwas depicts ethics as learning God's story of the world as God's gift, our sinfulness, and our standing as convicted and forgiven sinners. Hence Christian ethics is unique to its story, such that Hauerwas rejects continuity between Christian and non-Christian morality. Narrative is pivotal to addressing the topic of character, and character is most sufficiently evidenced within communities shaped by the biblical narrative. Such distinctive Christian practices as peacemaking and hospitality function as the conditions for understanding within the church. Accordingly, a medieval crusader who shouts "Christ is Lord" with a raised sword disqualifies his own claim. Hauerwas thus calls for the church to be faithful as the church, acknowledging that culture cannot be evaded but that the church must live a displaced or alien existence within culture.

Nonfoundationalism

Embracing various trends in postmodern philosophy and theology, postliberal theologians repudiate the Enlightenment endeavor to locate a universal standard of rationality that constitutes the objective foundation for public life. According to postliberal theology, such a neutral, theory-free viewpoint has yet to be discovered. Moreover, postliberals reject foundationalism on two theological grounds. First, following Barth's denunciation of natural theology, postliberals claim that foundationalism subordinates the particular Christian story to a foreign framework that inescapably misrepresents and impedes revelation. Second, postliberals regard foundationalism as a form of epistemological Pelagianism. In view of its so-called modern turn to the subject, contemporary foundationalism renders human subjectivity, not God's action, as the first principle of theology. This reduces God's contingent and prevenient grace to an anthropological given.

While postliberalism possesses no objective criteria for adjudicating between the truth-claims of different religious narratives, it holds that the biblical narrative furnishes its own criteria of truth. Although these criteria are not universally accepted, postliberal theologians assert that this hardly makes truth relative any more than a hung jury implies the defendant was both guilty and innocent. For postliberal theologians, true beliefs are not limited to those that are objectively justified, as the issue of justification is separate from the issue of truth.

Narrative Intratextual Interpretation

Instead of a supposedly universal foundation, postliberal theologians start with the Bible, read as an overarching story and realistic narrative that defines its own conceptual world. They interpret Scripture as history-like literature, not as a mythical account representing a universal human experience. The category of narrative reaffirms God's primacy for theology because the biblical story portrays the deeds that comprise God's identity in Jesus Christ. Since Jesus stands as the hermeneutical key to this story, the biblical text is read intratextually, namely, as a self-referential, self-interpreting unified whole. The biblical narrative is world-constructing, furnishing the categories for the understanding and practice of every facet of life. Nevertheless, postliberal theologians disclaim biblical foundationalism, as the Bible does not create this world *ex nihilo*. Although the believing community prizes the text as Scripture, its ostensibly clear meaning is determined by the community's cultural context. While rules exist for distinguishing Christian doctrine, such as textual faithfulness and christological consistency, Christian beliefs are fallible and so able to be reformed, leading to a host of theological positions within the worldwide Christian community.

Absorption of the Universe into the Biblical World

The biblical world provides the conceptual framework within which believers aim to live and comprehend reality. As a result, the role of theology is to expose and remedy distortions in the community as well as to assist the community's internalization of Christian faith and praxis, and so improve Christian life and identity. Although the narrative of Scripture shapes the world of believers,

William Placher maintained this Christian world is neither autonomous nor totally insulated. Placher insisted the logic of the gospel entails the precisely opposite conclusion—the universe must be absorbed into the biblical world. Hence Placher's program aimed to construct a comprehensive vision that makes Christian sense out of the world, especially its negative features. Placher posited that the contrary apologetic strategy of translating Christianity into extratextual categories both devalues the particularity of the faith and represents a futile attempt to keep up with an ever-shifting culture. As Placher declared, the postliberal approach of retaining the particularity and internal logic of the Christian religion models the philosophical-theological ideal of *fides quaerens intellectum* (faith seeking understanding).

CONCLUSION

Postliberal theology presents a third path between liberal and conservative theology. The postliberal emphasis on each religion's intrasystemic world of meaning poses a strong challenge to the pluralistic assumption that all religions are, in the end, pointing to the same ultimate reality. Hence postliberal theology dissents from the thesis of Christian pluralist John Hick (1922–2012) that everyone devoted to a theistic religion worships the true God, albeit in different ways. Diagnosing our Pelagian culture, postliberal theologians endeavor to rehabilitate the scriptural concepts of God's revelation and sovereignty. As Hauerwas illustrates, moreover, the Christian life as shaped by the story of Jesus Christ in the church furnishes an alternative and prophetic moral vision to contemporary society.

FOR FURTHER READING

Primary Sources

Frei, Hans W. *The Eclipse of Biblical Narrative: A Study in Eighteenth and Nineteenth Century Hermeneutics*. New Haven, CT: Yale University Press, 1974.

———. *The Identity of Jesus Christ: The Hermeneutical Bases of Dogmatic Theology*. Philadelphia: Fortress, 1975.

Hauerwas, Stanley. *Character and the Christian Life: A Study in Theological Ethics*. Notre Dame, IN: University of Notre Dame Press, 1994.

———. *The Peaceable Kingdom: A Primer in Christian Ethics*. Notre Dame, IN: University of Notre Dame Press, 1991.

Lindbeck, George A. *The Nature of Doctrine: Religion and Theology in a Postliberal Age*. Louisville: Westminster John Knox, 1984.

Placher, William C. *Unapologetic Theology: A Christian Voice in a Pluralistic Conversation.* Louisville: Westminster John Knox, 1989.

Secondary Sources

Goldberg, Michael. *Theology and Narrative: A Critical Introduction.* Harrisburg, PA: Trinity Press International, 1991.

Green, Joel B., and Michael Pasquarello III, ed. *Narrative Reading, Narrative Preaching: Reuniting New Testament Interpretation and Proclamation.* Grand Rapids: Baker Academic, 2003.

Harink, Douglas. *Paul among the Postliberals: Pauline Theology beyond Christendom and Modernity.* Grand Rapids: Brazos, 2003.

Phillips, Timothy R., and Dennis L. Okholm, eds. *Nature of Confession: Evangelicals and Postliberals in Conversation.* Downers Grove, IL: IVP, 1996.

Stroup, George W. *The Promise of Narrative Theology: Recovering the Gospel in the Church.* Louisville: John Knox, 1991.

CHAPTER 34

THEOLOGY AND
THE ARTS

he Thomas A. Langford Research Professor of Theology at Duke Divinity
School, British theologian and pianist Jeremy Begbie (1957–) has spearheaded a flourishing theology of the arts movement that aims to discover
and demonstrate ways in which the arts can facilitate the renewal of Christian
theology. Notable contributors to this movement include Steven Guthrie
(1967–), Carol Harrison (1961–), Joyce Irwin (1945–), Daniel Chua (1966–),
and Catherine Pickstock (1971–). The theology of the arts movement offers
churches a middle way between what Begbie dubs "word-obsessed Protestantism"
and "floating aestheticism."[1] In this middle way, art reveals the possibility of
transformation through the interplay of tradition and innovation and of order
and disorder. This chapter explores the major theses of Begbie's movement and
their application in the works of his followers. Privileging cognitive to noncognitive theories of emotion, Begbie charts a course through which the emotions
elicited by art redirect humans to the God worthy of all praise and reorient
believers in love to one another as the people of God.

MUSIC AND EMOTION

Begbie observes that music's emotional power is likely its single most controversial attribute. Philosophers, psychologists, and music theorists robustly debate
exactly how music affects our emotions. Many in the church fear the ability
of music to get inside us, especially in worship. For these critics, writes Begbie,
"music all too easily turns into a device of manipulation, a tool of moral harm,
all the more dangerous because it can work its charms without our being aware

of it."[2] By contrast, others in the church dismiss such worries as betraying an inflated suspicion of anything not subject to rational control. It is commonly held that some basic emotions are universal to all human beings, encompassing variants of happiness, sadness, anger, fear, and disgust. Begbie reports that the presence of these emotions is standardly gleaned from three kinds of evidence: self-reports (how people report they feel), overt behavior (how people act), and physiological phenomena (how their bodily systems behave). This has prompted a fairly typical way of portraying emotional states as involving an interplay between the members of the "classic triad" of conscious experience, expressive bodily behavior, and physiological activation.[3] Begbie finds substantial evidence that our emotional involvement in music entails all three. Nonetheless, Begbie argues that the classic triad must be expanded to include an element that plays a role in occurrent emotional states: cognition. A good deal of recent discussion has surrounded Begbie's proposal, thus leading to a distinction between noncognitive and cognitive accounts of emotion.

Noncognitive theories view emotion as categorically distinct from, and actually opposed to, the rational and intellectual, and therefore having virtually nothing to do with the mind's pursuit and acquisition of truth. Emotions are essentially irrational physical reactions, temporary bursts of affect quite unrelated to cognition. Hence accounts of affective experiences can be explained fully in terms of physiological changes and external bodily movements. Begbie notes that noncognitivism is sometimes tied to a theological anthropology that opposes the "lower," "animal," bodily nature with the "higher," mental faculties.[4]

Begbie perceives that noncognitive views of emotion frequently predominate in conversations about worship. Many laypeople and practical theologians are instinctively wary of songs that range over emotional extremes, preaching that stresses the emotions, and enthusiastic bodily expression. They fear that we will lose our grip on reality, grow too consumed with the body, and expose ourselves to manipulation by church leaders. Accordingly, songs should be focused on intellectually graspable truth and only secondarily, if at all, with emotionally stirring us; preaching should be offered first to the mind and only then to the emotions; and bodily movement should be kept to a minimum. Despite the ecclesiastical dominance of noncognitivist theories, Begbie argues against them on three primary grounds. First, one cannot satisfactorily distinguish emotions from one another if they are interpreted exclusively in terms of bodily changes and movements. Second, noncognitivism fails to account for the way emotions serve as motives for behavior. Thus we do not say, "I ran away because my heart suddenly beat faster," but "I ran away because I was scared of the mugger with the knife."[5] Third, the dichotomy between emotion and cognition cannot be supported from a neuroscientific perspective.

Accordingly, Begbie advocates a cognitive view of emotion that stresses the integral role of cognition in emotional experience. Cognitive theories highlight that what we take to be full-fledged emotions depend on beliefs about the world or oneself. One's fear of falling off a five-hundred-foot cliff is based on the belief that one will die if one falls. While beliefs may be true or false, rational or irrational, profound or superficial, they are necessary for emotions to arise. No beliefs, no emotions. Begbie asserts that beliefs in turn comprise the basis of evaluation or appraisal. Various people have different emotional responses to the same situation because they interpret it differently. In Begbie's estimation, the evaluative factor constitutes the best tool for specifying and distinguishing emotions; consequently, we need to ascertain how the subject of an emotion is appraising a situation to accurately identify the emotion being experienced.

Begbie goes on to propose the object-oriented character of emotions: if emotions necessarily entail beliefs and judgments, they will be oriented toward objects. As Begbie puts it, "I am not angry in the abstract, but angry *about* something or angry *at* someone. Fear arises because something has threatened me, joy because I have encountered something that is good, beautiful, or whatever."[6] Therefore emotions are *of* or *about* or *at* some particular object. Since emotions have this directional character, arising from beliefs about and evaluations of an object or objects, Begbie contends that they can be appropriate or inappropriate. A person who jumps on a desk screaming wildly when a mouse crawls into the room has an inappropriate fear, while a person who hides under a desk and shakes uncontrollably when a masked man runs into the room wielding an AK-47 has an appropriate fear.

Since emotions entail beliefs and evaluations about states of affairs and can thus be appropriate or inappropriate, Begbie deduces, against noncognitivist theories, that emotions must not be regarded as intrinsically opposed to truthful perception. Rather, emotions are capable of advancing and assisting our grasping for the truth and may therefore work in tandem with reason. In support of Begbie's inference, many philosophers have recently argued that emotions are critical for decision making, as they validly guide action in contexts where our knowledge is incomplete and we are confronted with multiple, conflicting goals. Moreover, since emotions involve belief and evaluation, they are usually motivators to action, as one acts *out of* happiness, fear, and so forth. Begbie specifies that emotions become motivators to action when they contain desire, either conscious or unconscious, as part of their occurrent states.

EMOTION AND FAITHFUL CHRISTIAN WORSHIP

Begbie attempts to situate his cognitive account of emotion within a theology of Christian worship. Significantly, Begbie gives a Trinitarian definition of worship as "those regular occasions when the church is gathered by the triune God to receive and celebrate its corporate identity in a focused, concentrated way."[7] In sum, worship reorients us to God and so constitutes the opposite of sin. Whereas sin is a rejection of our calling to honor God and serve one another, worship redirects us to God and reorients us in love to one another, thereby building us up as God's people and reorienting our mission in God's world. Begbie identifies the indwelling agent of this reorientation as the Holy Spirit and its mediator as Jesus Christ. Such worship will be faithful as it fulfills Begbie's fivefold checklist of the emotions therein.

First, Begbie's conception of worship is faithful insofar as it is properly oriented—"primarily to God, and, in the power of the Spirit, to others with whom we worship, and to the world we represent and to which we are sent."[8] As a result, emotion is rightly directed, rendering our worship appropriate to God, others, and the world. Regarding emotion in worship, Begbie discerns that the danger lies not in emotion per se, but in emotion that is either improperly directed or inappropriate or both. To illustrate, if someone is more captivated by the sound of the choir than by the God they praise, their emotion is misdirected; if someone spends the whole service trembling and recoiling in fear of God, their emotion is inappropriate.

Second, faithful worship occurs with and through Jesus, and Jesus ensures its proper orientation: in the Holy Spirit and to God the Father, propelling us to reach out to fellow worshipers and the larger world. Moreover, Jesus guarantees that worship is appropriate, specifically in its truthfulness to God's nature and purpose. Owing to this theocentric reflection, worship empowers us to love fellow worshipers and the larger world. Central to Begbie's vision of worship is the "vicarious humanity of Christ."[9] As fully human, Jesus embodies and enables faithful worship: "He is 'faith-ful,' full of faith in the Father, not only in his earthly life of loving and obedient self-offering to the Father, culminating in crucifixion, but also in his continuing risen life—he is now the human High Priest who, on the ground of his atoning work, leads us in our worship (Heb. 2:12; 4:14; cf. Rom. 8:34). In him, our humanity has been taken, and through the Holy Spirit re-formed, re-turned to God, so that now with him we can know his 'Abba, Father' as *our* Abba, Father."[10] Hence the church's worship is united with the uniquely perfect worship of the incarnate Son, namely, his once-for-all offering of worship on the cross. This unity is facilitated through the same Spirit who empowered Jesus's own earthly self-offering. Worship is therefore "a sharing by the Spirit in the Son's communion with the Father by the Spirit."[11] Conceived in this way, worship is an invitation to be rehumanized, as we grow in the image of Christ. For Begbie, here the traditional christological dictum *quod non est assumptum non est sanatum* (what is not assumed is not saved) applies, as Jesus assumed our full humanness, including our emotions, in order to redeem us. Emotions are neither inherently fallen nor unessential to our humanity, but part of what God longs to transform, especially in worship. Accordingly, Begbie provocatively stipulates that worship should be, in part, a school for the emotions: "Whether confessing with heavy Lenten hearts, or shouting Easter acclamations, we learn to become emotionally mature, to become (so to speak) a little less adolescent."[12]

Third, faithful worship is a truthful activity. For Begbie, in worship we apprehend through the Spirit and with the Son such truths as a new dimension of the Father's love for us, the unspoken need of the individual in the pew adjacent to us, or another facet of evil in an act of terror. When this happens, our emotions—far from hampering our grasp of truth—empower a clearer discernment of truth.

Fourth, faithful worship is a uniting activity. To be directed to the Father through the Son by the Spirit is to find the love that is eternally given and received between Father and Son, the love whereby we should be bound together (John 17:21). Begbie declares that all worship in the Spirit builds up the body of Christ and promotes unity (1 Cor. 14:5, 12, 26). Although emotions can destroy relationships, they can also be instrumental in creating and sustaining extremely strong ties between people and thereby serve the Spirit's work of accomplishing the reconciled unity available through Jesus's atoning death.

Fifth, faithful worship is an ex-centric activity, whereby our being snatched up in the life of the Trinitarian God involves being thrown out into the world as agents of change. On Begbie's view, worship occurs in the rhythm of adoration and action. Since emotions generally produce tendencies to action, they play a pivotal role in stirring the desire to do God's will and so mobilizing God's people for mission.

A BIBLICAL HIERARCHY OF THE ARTS

Synthesizing Begbie's analysis with the thought of Augustine (354–430) and Thomas Aquinas (1225–74), Begbie's fellow aesthetic theologians have formulated a biblical hierarchy of the arts. This hierarchy is governed by the logical principle that an art concerned with the end for which something is ordained is higher than an art concerned with its means. These means then subdivide into further means produced by lesser arts. The supreme end of biblical cosmology is the restoration of the faithful, body and soul, to God at the general resurrection, as well as the reconciliation of the entire cosmos. Jesus is not only the means through which the restoration is partially transpiring and will fully transpire but also the only person who applied his free choice with unfailing constancy to the achievement of this ultimate goal. It follows from these considerations of Jesus's humanity as well as the fact of Jesus's deity that the artistic hierarchy is inescapably headed by Jesus. Thus Jesus, as the artist who is concerned with the end, is the principal or master artist. By virtue of this hierarchy, all human arts are providentially directed by Jesus, regardless of whether their creaturely artists realize or even approve of it. Aesthetic theologians reason that the Spirit enables all persons, both believers and nonbelievers, to participate in the Christocentric creativity, thus affording each person the opportunity to become an artist. In other words, a share in the artistic dimension is divinely granted to every person as a result of common grace.

Such a concept carries great significance for the ontological, and perhaps parasacramental, status of every artwork. Aquinas defined the term *image* as the likeness a piece of art bears to the ideal, or perfect conceptual form, in the mind of the artist.[13] However, aesthetic theologians maintain that any such ideal is rooted in the divine essence and is only apprehended by the artist via general revelation. In addition, every person is an image of its respective ideal, or individual essence, in the divine mind. Each artwork, then, shares in the reality and participates in the being of the perfect concept or immaterial form that it symbolizes, thereby constituting a channel of grace (here understood as divine empowerment) linking the material and immaterial realms. Hence works of art, on the aesthetic theologian's view, literally possess a parasacramental quality, that is, the quality of being points of contact with God. Ascending one level on the hierarchy, artists perform a twofold capacity: to increasingly mediate a unique facet of the divine intelligence as they progress in sanctification; and to be carried along, in a qualitatively lower manner than the scriptural authors (2 Peter 1:21), by the divine intelligence through the act of artistic production. In these ways, the artist incarnates and so reveals the transcendentals of beauty, goodness, and truth to humanity via an active receptivity that discovers all forms through sustained personal communion with God, who in turn enables the artist's involvement with them.

Following the Augustinian premise that evil is not a substance but rather a *privatio boni* (a privation of good) of a preexisting substance, aesthetic theologians characterize sin as a departure of a work from its end. In the human artistic endeavor, therefore, it follows that sin can occur in two ways. First, artists may depart from the particular end of the artwork. Such a sin is "proper to" the artwork and "directly against" the artwork.[14] Second, the artist may depart from the general end of human life—the reconciliation of humanity with God—which departure is then reflected in both the original intent and the completion of the artwork. Far more severe, the latter sin commits a brazen act of treason against God by misappropriating Christ's own creative power contrary to its previsioned salvific end. The following comparison illustrates the relationship between art and ethics. If an artist intends to create a particular object but through shoddy or otherwise defective work produces an object that fails to meet the artist's standard, then the artist has sinned against her art. However, if the artist intends and proceeds to create an object that will hinder the divine-human relationship, then no matter how precisely the created object conforms to its image in the mind of the artist, the artist has blasphemed God.

The preceding considerations facilitate a method for determining artistic quality, whether it be a musical piece, a painting, or the like. For aesthetic theologians, the goal of art is to foster relational union with the Trinitarian God by clearly mediating to an audience the Christ-centered forms on which it is metaphysically grounded. Hence the quality of any piece of art is directly proportional to how well it performs this goal. Beautiful art therefore demands a total response of the artist's being to the creativity emanating from the Holy Spirit and is marked by lucidity, intelligibility, and illumination of Christ in one of his infinite aspects. By contrast, artistic ugliness is spawned under conditions of depravity, in which the artist's whole self, for moral or religious reasons, is unable to participate in the Spirit's inspiration. Hence ugly art fails to convey something of Christ's essence. It is vague, manipulates the flesh instead of engaging the Spirit, and substitutes the impotent acquaintance between an "I" and some particular "It" for the beholder's personally transformative relationship with the universal Thou.

CONCLUSION

Begbie and his fellow aesthetic theologians champion the twin notions that theology illuminates the arts and that the arts illuminate and enrich our theology, particularly the theology of worship. In worship, Begbie insists that the emotional capacities of music in particular are linked with the body and must be celebrated. Bodily renewal forms part of the divine intention for humanity: even now life is given to our mortal bodies by the Spirit of the Father who resurrected Jesus from the dead in anticipation of the Spirit-filled life of the new heavens and new earth (Rom. 8:11). Worship in the Spirit, through Jesus, will "by its very nature be caught up in this body-transforming momentum."[15] In view of the fact that music embodies emotionally significant bodily movements in a concentrated form, it has the power to represent us and concentrate us emotionally as we are drawn into its being. Begbie affirms that remarkable correspondence exists between the dynamics of musical emotion and the dynamics of worship. A parallel case can be made for the other fine arts. Hence aesthetic theologians proclaim that the arts are particularly well suited to serving as vehicles of emotional renewal in worship and powerful instruments through which the Holy Spirit can gradually remake and transform us into the image of the incarnate Jesus, the ultimate worshiper.

FOR FURTHER READING

Primary Sources

Begbie, Jeremy. *Beholding the Glory: Incarnation through the Arts.* Grand Rapids: Baker Academic, 2000.

———. *Music, Modernity, and God: Essays in Listening.* Oxford: Oxford University Press, 2015.

———. *A Peculiar Orthodoxy: Reflections on Theology and the Arts.* Grand Rapids: Baker Academic, 2018.

———. *Resounding Truth: Christian Wisdom in the World of Music.* Grand Rapids: Baker Academic, 2007.

———. *Voicing Creation's Praise: Towards a Theology of the Arts.* London: T&T Clark, 1991.

Begbie, Jeremy, and Steven R. Guthrie, eds. *Resonant Witness: Conversations between Music and Theology.* Grand Rapids: Eerdmans, 2011.

Secondary Sources

Brown, Frank Burch. *Religious Aesthetics: A Theological Study of Making and Meaning.* Princeton, NJ: Princeton University Press, 1989.

Dow, Jamie. *Engaging Emotions: The Need for Emotions in the Church.* Cambridge: Grove, 2005.

MacGregor, Kirk R. "Aquinas, Christology, and Art." *Bridges: An Interdisciplinary Journal of Theology, Philosophy, History, and Science* 14, no. 3–4 (2007): 233–50.

Nussbaum, Martha C. *Love's Knowledge: Essays on Philosophy and Literature.* Oxford: Oxford University Press, 1992.

Torrance, James. *Worship, Community and the Triune God of Grace.* Carlisle: Paternoster, 1996.

CHAPTER 35

A NEW PERSPECTIVE ON PAUL AND JUSTIFICATION

The new perspective on Paul is a school of thought in New Testament scholarship that aims to reinterpret Paul and his epistles in light of his first-century Jewish context. Among the movement's principal proponents are Duke New Testament scholar E. P. Sanders (1937–), Durham New Testament scholar James D. G. Dunn (1939–), and St. Andrews New Testament scholar N. T. Wright (1948–). The movement is a reaction to the Reformation perspective on Paul, which depicts him as arguing against a legalistic Jewish culture that seeks to earn salvation by works. The new perspective on Paul contends that Paul has been misread, claiming that Paul was actually combating Jews who believed in *sola gratia* (grace alone) and, rather than asserting that their works earned their salvation, boasted that their works identified them as the covenant people of God. Thus ramifications of the new perspective on Paul affect our understanding of the Protestant doctrine of *sola fide* (justification by faith alone).

BREAKING THE PARADIGM OF LEGALISTIC JUDAISM

Since the time of Martin Luther (1483–1546), Paul's insistence that we are saved by *pistis Christou*—a phrase that can either be translated "faith in Christ" or "the faithfulness of Christ"—and not by the works of the law (Gal. 2:16) has been interpreted as an indictment of legalistic efforts to merit favor before God. According to the new perspective on Paul, this view was understandable in light of the works-centered and merit-based late medieval Catholicism that incited the Protestant Reformation, but it caricatured the Judaism of Jesus's day in the late medieval Catholic mold. From the sixteenth century until recent times, then, Judaism has been regarded as legalistic. However, new perspective scholars point to twentieth-century historical studies that purport to show that first-century Jews did not conceive Torah (the law of Moses) as a burden that produced self-righteousness; rather, the law was itself a gift from a merciful and forgiving God. The doctrine of merit was formulated by medieval Catholic theologians and simply did not exist in first-century Judaism.

In 1977 Sanders published *Paul and Palestinian Judaism*, which new perspective thinkers see as driving the final nail into the coffin of the traditional Christian caricature of Judaism. Sanders employed the Tannaitic literature, the Dead Sea Scrolls, the Apocrypha, and the pseudepigrapha to describe and define Palestinian Judaism on its own terms. He coined a now well-known phrase to describe the character of first-century Judaism: "covenantal nomism."[1] Covenantal nomism is the notion that human obedience is not construed as the means of entering into God's covenant. That cannot be earned; inclusion within the covenant body is by the grace of God. Rather, obedience is the means of maintaining one's status within the covenant. As Sanders summarizes, "one's place in God's plan is established on the basis of the covenant and . . . the covenant requires as the proper response of man his obedience to its commandments, while providing means of atonement for transgression."[2] With its emphasis on divine grace and forgiveness, Sanders maintains that Judaism was never a religion of legalism.

SANDERS AND TRANSFER TERMINOLOGY

Soteriologically, Sanders argues that Paul worked backward from solution to plight rather than from plight to solution. In other words, Paul first became convinced that salvation comes to all, both Jews and Gentiles, through Christ; as a result, it cannot come through Torah. For Sanders, the Judaizing conflict, as evidenced in Galatians, was an issue between Jews and Gentiles rather than a philosophical debate about human freedom and divine sovereignty. On this score Sanders writes:

> The dispute in Galatians is not about "doing" as such. Neither of the opposing factions saw the requirement of "doing" to be a denial of faith. When Paul makes requirements of his converts, he does not think that he has denied faith, and there is no reason to think that Jewish Christians who specified different requirements denied faith. The supposed conflict between "doing" as such and "faith" as such is simply not present in Galatians. What was at

stake was not a way of life summarized by the word "trust" versus a mode of life summarized by "requirements," but whether or not the requirement for membership in the Israel of God would result in there being "neither Jew nor Greek." . . . There was no dispute over the necessity to trust God and have faith in Christ. The dispute was about whether or not one had to be Jewish.[3]

Sanders holds that Paul's language of justification is "transfer terminology."[4] Thus to be justified is to enter into the covenant people. The distinction between "getting in" and "staying in" is important in this regard. The debate between faith and law, maintains Sanders, is a debate about entry requirements, not about life following conversion. Paul excludes the law as an entry requirement into the body of those who will be saved; entrance must be by faith apart from the law. Once Gentiles are "in," however, they must behave appropriately and fulfill the law in order to retain their status. However, Paul discards elements of the law that create social distinctions between Jews and Gentiles, such as circumcision, Sabbath-keeping, and food laws, for he realizes that social distinctions and hence the regulations that engender them have been annulled by Christ.

DUNN AND THE WORKS OF THE LAW

Expanding on the work of Sanders, Dunn argues that the language of justification is more than simply transfer terminology, as there exist continual and future elements of justification besides the initial act of acceptance. Dunn goes on to claim that it was not the law itself that Paul criticized but rather its misuse as a social barrier. For Dunn, this abuse of the law is what Paul means by the phrase "the works of the law" (Gal. 2:16):

> "Works of law," "works of the law" are nowhere understood here, either by his Jewish interlocutors or by Paul himself, as works which earn God's favor, as merit-amassing observances. They are rather seen as badges: they are simply what membership of the covenant people involves, what mark out the Jews as God's people. . . . In other words, Paul has in view precisely what Sanders calls "covenantal nomism." And what he denies is that God's justification depends on "covenantal nomism," that God's grace extends only to those who wear the badge of the covenant.[5]

The "badges" or "works" specifically at issue comprised circumcision and food laws, not human efforts to do good.

As Dunn observes, the implications of this observation for traditional Protestantism are sweeping: "More important for Reformation exegesis is the corollary that 'works of the law' do not mean 'good works' in general, 'good works' in the sense disparaged by the heirs of Luther, works in the sense of achievement."[6] Dunn also underscores the implications for the traditional dichotomy between faith and works: "We should not let our grasp of Paul's reasoning slip back into the old distinction between faith and works in general, between faith and 'good works.' Paul is not arguing here for a concept of faith which is totally passive because it fears to become a 'work.' It is the demand for a particular work as the necessary expression of faith which he denies."[7]

WRIGHT AND GOD'S RIGHTEOUSNESS

In his 1997 book, *What Saint Paul Really Said*, Wright focuses on Paul's understanding of the gospel vis-à-vis his doctrine of justification. Wright asserts that the essence of Paul's gospel was not justification by faith, but the death and resurrection of Jesus and his exaltation as Lord. For Wright, the overarching thesis of the book of Romans is the gospel proclamation of Jesus as Lord, the Messiah who fulfilled Israel's expectations. Contrary to Reformation theology, Wright holds that the core of Paul's message to the Roman church is Romans 1:1–4 ("the gospel of God . . . regarding his Son, who as to his earthly life was a descendant of David, and who through the Spirit of holiness was appointed the Son of God in power by his resurrection from the dead: Jesus Christ our Lord"), not Romans 1:17 ("For in the gospel the righteousness of God is revealed—a righteousness that is by faith from first to last, just as it is written, 'The righteous will live by faith'").

Accordingly, Wright maintains that justification is not the center of Paul's thought but an outworking of it:

> The doctrine of justification by faith is not what Paul means by "the gospel." It is implied by the gospel; when the gospel is proclaimed, people come to faith and so are regarded by God as members of his people. But "the gospel" is not an account of how people get saved. It is, as we saw in an earlier chapter, the proclamation of the lordship of Jesus Christ. . . . Let us be quite clear. "The gospel" is the announcement of Jesus' lordship, which works with power to bring people into the family of Abraham, now redefined around Jesus Christ and characterized solely by faith in him. "Justification" is the doctrine which insists that all those who have this faith belong as full members of this family, on this basis and no other.[8]

Wright proceeds to explain what "justification" (*dikaiosynē*)—a term bound up with legal terminology, eschatology, and God's faithfulness to God's covenant— meant in Paul's Jewish context. Justification denotes the verdict of God himself as to who really is a member of his people. The criterion for this verdict is Jesus the Messiah: hence "the Messiah and his faithfulness unto death, the death to which he gave himself to 'set us free from the present evil age' (Galatians 1:4, echoed in the 'giving of himself' in 2:20), are the basis on which God makes the declaration 'Here are my people.'"[9] Moreover, Wright emphasizes that *dikaiosynē* in the Hebrew law court setting denotes the status that someone possesses when the court has found in their favor. But since in Romans 3 Paul demonstrates that the entire human race stands guilty before the judgment seat of God, our *dikaiosynē* necessarily entails acquittal—the granting of the status of "righteous" to those who had been on trial—and, since we were in fact guilty, "forgiveness."[10]

Wright attempts to refute the notion that the pre-Christian Saul was a pious, proto-Pelagian moralist seeking to earn his individual entrance to heaven. Underscoring Paul's autobiographical confessions (including his assertion of blamelessness under the law in Philippians 3:6), Wright demonstrates that Saul was a zealous Jewish nationalist whose motivating concern was to cleanse Israel of Gentiles as well as Jews who had negligent attitudes toward the law. Hence Wright contends, "Jews like Saul of Tarsus were not interested in an abstract, ahistorical system of salvation. They were not even primarily interested in, as we say, 'going to heaven when they died.' (They believed in the resurrection, in which God would raise them all to share in the life of the promised renewed Israel and renewed world; but that is very different from the normal Western vision of 'heaven.') They were interested in the salvation which, they believed, the one true God had promised to his people Israel."[11] When Saul became a Christian, Wright asserts, he maintained the Jewish shape of his doctrine but filled it with new content. The zeal of Saul the Pharisee was now the zeal of Paul the apostle. God's covenant faithfulness—"the righteousness of God" (Rom. 1:17)—had indeed been fulfilled in the death and resurrection of Jesus the Messiah.

Wright holds that as a Christian, Paul continued to challenge paganism by taking the moral high ground of the Jewish monotheist who maintained that God was creator of and moral lawgiver to all. The doctrine of justification was not what Paul preached to the Gentiles as the main point of his gospel; it was rather "the thing his converts most needed to know in order to be assured that they really were part of God's people" after responding to the gospel.[12] Even while taking the gospel to the Gentiles, Paul continued to critique Judaism from within as he had as a zealous Pharisee. But while his previous mission was to eliminate those with negligent attitudes toward the law, now his mission was to prove that God's covenant faithfulness or righteousness had already been revealed in Jesus.

At this juncture, Wright analyzes Paul's use of the phrase "the righteousness of God" (*dikaiosynē theou*), unpacking his meaning against the legal backdrop of the Jewish concept of justification. The righteousness of God and the righteousness of the party who is justified cannot be confused because the term bears different connotations for the judge than for the plaintiff or the defendant. The judge is "righteous" (*dikaios*) if his judgment is fair and impartial; the plaintiff or defendant is "righteous" (*dikaios*) if the judge rules in the respective favor of the plaintiff or defendant. For Wright, this observation refutes the Protestant doctrine of imputed righteousness whereby God imparts his own righteousness to sinners:

> If we use the language of the law court, it makes no sense whatsoever to say that the judge imputes, imparts, bequeaths, conveys or otherwise transfers his righteousness to either the plaintiff or the defendant. Righteousness is not an object, a substance or a gas which can be passed across the courtroom. For the judge to be righteous does not mean that the court has found in his favor. For the plaintiff or defendant to be righteous does not mean that he or she has tried the case properly or impartially. To imagine the defendant somehow receiving the judge's righteousness is simply a category mistake. That is not how the language works.[13]

Specifically, God's righteousness (*dikaiosynē theou*)—his fairness and impartiality—denotes his faithfulness to the covenant he made with Abraham in Genesis 12 and 15 to bless the whole world through Abraham's family.

Wright uses his insights to provide what he regards as a contextually sensible interpretation of Galatians and Philippians. The "works of the law" in these epistles are not proto-Pelagian efforts to earn salvation, but rather Sabbath-keeping, food laws, and circumcision. It was around circumcision that the controversy in Galatia revolved:

> Despite a long tradition to the contrary, the problem Paul addresses in Galatians is not the question of how precisely someone becomes a Christian, or attains to a relationship with God. . . . The problem he addresses is: should his ex-pagan converts be circumcised or not? Now this question is by no means obviously to do with the questions faced by Augustine and Pelagius, or by Luther and Erasmus. On anyone's reading, but especially within its first-century context, it has to do quite obviously with the question of how

you define the people of God: are they to be defined by the badges of Jewish race, or in some other way? Circumcision is not a "moral" issue; it does not have to do with moral effort, or earning salvation by good deeds. Nor can we simply treat it as a religious ritual, then designate all religious ritual as crypto-Pelagian good works, and so smuggle Pelagius into Galatia as the arch-opponent after all. First-century thought, both Jewish and Christian, simply doesn't work like that.[14]

Therefore, on Wright's view the first-century debate about justification was far more about ecclesiology than soteriology. Wright observes with irony that this doctrine, which was primarily concerned with unity and acceptance in the body of Christ regardless of social barriers, has constituted one of the most divisive doctrines in the history of Christianity, especially between Catholics and Protestants who have traditionally interpreted it as a question of exactly how salvation is to be attained.

One of the most controversial tenets of the new perspective on Paul is that Paul taught salvation by grace and final judgment according to works. This raises two vexing issues. First, is this not simply another way of saying that salvation is, in the end, by works? Second, could a person be justified—admitted into the company of God's people—and in the end be lost? For Wright, the answer to both questions lie in Paul's doctrine of sanctification. Through sanctification, the Holy Spirit so transforms and empowers us spiritually that we naturally perform the works God desires. Ultimately, then, "it is God who works in you to will and to act in order to fulfill his good purpose" (Phil. 2:13). So salvation is not by works but by faith, where the Spirit responds to that faith with such a grace that its recipient unfailingly does the will of God. Hence justification is the decision of the final judgment announced in advance: no one whom God has declared justified, and therefore forgiven, will in the end be lost. Indeed, in justification God is authoritatively stating that those in whose favor he finds will proceed to do works of righteousness and so, by the time of the final judgment, show themselves by their actions to be the very people of God he has already declared them to be. As Paul declared, "those [God] justified, he also glorified" (Rom. 8:30).

CONCLUSION

Drawing together the threads of the new perspective, a re-visioned covenant theology emerges in which the Creator God called Abraham's family into covenant with him so that through his family all the world might escape from the curse of sin and death and enjoy the blessing and life of the new creation. This theology occurs amid the continuing metaphor of the law court. Through this metaphor, Paul develops the biblical understanding that God must judge the world in the sense of putting the world right at the end, and as Wright explains, "that God has brought this judgment into the middle of history, precisely in the covenant-fulfilling work of Jesus Christ, dealing with sin through his death, launching the new world in his resurrection, and sending his Spirit to enable human beings, through repentance and faith, to become little walking and breathing advance parts of that eventual new creation."[15] According to this judgment, the verdict announced through Jesus's death and resurrection is that all who are in Jesus are reckoned to have died and been raised with him, so that from God's perspective their sins are no longer accounted against them and they stand on resurrection ground, finally liberated to live as genuine human beings. The present verdict, issued on the basis of faith alone, furnishes the assurance that the future verdict will match it, and the Spirit gives the power through which that future verdict will be evidenced in accordance with the lives believers have lived.

FOR FURTHER READING

Primary Sources

Dunn, James D. G. *Jesus, Paul, and the Law: Studies in Mark and Galatians*. Louisville: Westminster John Knox, 1990.

Sanders, E. P. *Paul, the Law, and the Jewish People*. Minneapolis: Fortress, 1983.

———. *Paul and Palestinian Judaism: A Comparison of Patterns of Religion*. Minneapolis: Fortress, 1977.

Wright, N. T. *Justification: God's Plan and Paul's Vision*. Downers Grove, IL: IVP Academic, 2009.

———. *Paul and the Faithfulness of God*. Minneapolis: Fortress, 2013.

———. *What Saint Paul Really Said: Was Paul of Tarsus the Real Founder of Christianity?* Grand Rapids: Eerdmans, 1997.

Secondary Sources

Carson, D. A., Peter T. O'Brien, and Mark A. Seifrid, eds. *Justification and Variegated Nomism*. 2 vols. Grand Rapids: Baker Academic, 2004.

Garlington, Don. *In Defense of the New Perspective on Paul: Essays and Reviews*. Eugene, OR: Wipf and Stock, 2005.

Gathercole, Simon J. *Where Is Boasting? Early Jewish Soteriology and Paul's Response in Romans 1–5*. Grand Rapids: Eerdmans, 2002.

Thielman, Frank. *Paul and the Law: A Contextual Approach*. Downers Grove, IL: IVP Academic, 1995.

Westerholm, Stephen. *Justification Reconsidered: Rethinking a Pauline Theme*. Grand Rapids: Eerdmans, 2013.

CHAPTER 36

THEOLOGICAL INTERPRETATION OF SCRIPTURE

E ndeavoring to return to the church-based, transformative study of the Bible that characterized pre-Enlightenment Christians, scholars such as Kevin Vanhoozer (1957–), Daniel Treier (1972–), Francis Watson (1956–), and Stephen Fowl (1959–) have led the theological interpretation of Scripture movement. The movement attempts to repair the "ugly ditches" between exegesis and theology in modern biblical interpretation and between exegesis and ideology in postmodern biblical interpretation. Theological interpreters insist that scriptural interpretation must cultivate personal spirituality, as the Bible cannot merely be seen as a historical puzzle to be solved but must be recognized as a word from God to his people. Since biblical interpretation is fundamentally in and for the church, the movement respects external theological parameters, such as the *regula fidei* (the "rule of faith," or early Christian summary of fundamental beliefs), as legitimate guides for interpretation. This chapter outlines the main contours of the movement, emphasizing the seminal contributions of Vanhoozer.

CLEARING UP MISCONCEPTIONS

Vanhoozer notes that many observers may be initially skeptical of a movement that criticizes modern and postmodern exegesis, fearing that it constitutes a retreat to precritical interpretation of Scripture. To clear up any misconceptions, Vanhoozer finds it helpful to define theological interpretation of Scripture in terms of what it is not before either justifying the movement or defining the movement in terms of what it is.

Exponents of theological interpretation of Scripture insist that their movement is not a superimposition of a theological system or confessional grid onto the text of the Bible. Readers are not urged to read their theologies into the text. However, theological interpreters hold that it is impossible to perform exegesis without theological presuppositions. They presuppose the ecumenical consensus of the church through the centuries and across confessional lines that the Bible should be read as a unified whole and a narrative testimony to the identity and deeds of the Trinitarian God revealed in Jesus Christ. Nevertheless, theological interpreters claim they are not doing what dogmatic theologians before the rise of historical criticism did in using the Bible to support their particular doctrinal positions. Such precritical interpretations are susceptible to three weaknesses: failure to take the text seriously in its historical context, failure to integrate the text into the theology of the Old Testament or New Testament as a whole, and unawareness and hence uncritical acceptance of their own presuppositions.

Theological interpreters point out that theological interpretation of Scripture is not the superimposition of a general hermeneutic onto the text of the Bible, as if the Bible could be read like any other book. As Vanhoozer puts it, "There is something left for interpreters to do after reading the Bible like any other book."[1] Properly theological questions, such as the relationship between the Old and New Testaments, require more than a general hermeneutic can provide. Hence there are some interpretive questions that require theological rather than hermeneutical answers. Those theological answers can, in turn, inform general hermeneutics.

Moreover, theological interpretation of Scripture is not simply a form of historical, literary, or sociological criticism focused on the world "behind," "of," or "in front of" the text of the Bible.[2] Theological interpreters will incorporate into their exegesis whatever valid insights may be mined from the historical, literary, and sociological approaches depicting the ancient world behind the text, the plot and literary form of the text, and the ways in which readers receive and react to the text. While theological interpretation is more than historical, literary, or sociopolitical criticism, it is certainly not less, since God works in history, in the composition of the text of Scripture, and in the establishment of his redeemed people. But each of these approaches, auxiliary to the venture of interpreting the church's Scripture, brackets any consideration of divine action and so cannot constitute a properly theological criticism.

THE NECESSITY OF THEOLOGICAL INTERPRETATION

Theological interpreters of Scripture are responding to two crises respectively engendered by Enlightenment and postmodern developments in biblical interpretation. The Enlightenment created the schism between biblical studies and theology that plagues modern interpretation, and postmodernism has proliferated "advocacy" approaches to reading Scripture in which each interpretive community follows its own distinctive standards.[3] For the movement's proponents, theological interpretation of Scripture is needed to furnish biblical interpreters with a paradigm of best interpretive practice and to recover biblical studies as a properly theological discipline.

The critical approach to biblical interpretation that presently dominates modern Scripture study in the university and many seminaries was formulated to rescue the Bible from its alleged "dogmatic captivity" to confessional and theological traditions.[4] For the last two centuries, Christian faith has not been regarded as either necessary or relevant in attempting to decipher what the Bible meant. Consequently, theology became only marginally important for biblical studies as practiced in university and many seminary settings. Indeed, Vanhoozer laments that "modern biblical studies has become a virtual 'theology-free zone.' Even scholars who identify themselves as Christians have to check their theological convictions at the door when they enter the academy."[5] The schism between biblical studies and theology was nothing less than Gotthold Ephraim Lessing's (1729–81) broad, ugly ditch between reason in the form of publicly accessible history and faith in the form of privately valued belief. Hence the goal of biblical studies for the typical modern scholar is to comprehend the texts as merely human products of particular times and cultures. As a result, the Bible has been widely viewed as evidence of a historically developing religion—how ancient Israelites as well as Jesus and his followers thought about God, the world, and themselves—rather than as evidence of a divinely revealed theology—God's mighty deeds performed in human history.

While modern biblical scholarship laudably reconstructed historical contexts and the history of Scripture's composition, theological interpreters locate its fundamental flaw in its treatment of the biblical texts as sources for reconstructing human history and religion rather than as sources that testify to God's presence and actions in history. Theological interpreters therefore indict modern critics as working with an overly "thin," or reductionist, conception of history as a sequence of purely naturalistic cause and effect. However, the Bible gives a "thick" description of history, proclaiming events that participate in the fullness of time accomplished by divine as well as human agency in which the future breaks in from above.[6] Nontheological biblical criticism is therefore analogous to music criticism by the deaf and art criticism by the blind.

Theological interpreters concur with the postmodern verdict that there can be no objective, neutral, and value-free reading of biblical texts or any other texts; hence the critical approach only pretends to display these attributes. In fact, the critical approach is itself a confessional tradition that assumes faith in naturalism coupled with reason's evenhanded capacity to ascertain truth. However, theological interpreters declare that postmodernism has gone too far in denying that we can escape our social location, or our historical, cultural, class, and gender statuses. According to postmodernism, any reading of Scripture will be decisively shaped by the social location of the interpreter. Thus the goal of interpretation is to ascertain what the Bible means to one's own community, to those with one's own interpretive interest. But no particular interest can assert more authority than another. As Vanhoozer observes, this situation "gives rise to a pluralism of interpretative approaches and hence to a legitimation crisis: Whose interpretation of the Bible counts, and why?"[7] On postmodern approaches, then, interpretation of Scripture is reduced to thinly veiled echoes of the interpreter's own voice with no basis in fact.

POSITIVELY CHARACTERIZING THEOLOGICAL INTERPRETATION

Theological interpretation of Scripture is defined by a governing interest in God, God's word and deeds, and by a governing interest to engage in what may be termed "theological criticism."[8] Advocates of the movement point out that a theological interpretation is more likely to be critical of readers than of scriptural authors or scriptural texts. This is not because textual and other forms of criticism perform no task; it is because of the final goal of reading. Theological interpreters ultimately desire to hear the word of God in the Bible and therefore to be transformed by the renewing of their minds (Rom. 12:2). Accordingly, God must not be an afterthought in biblical interpretation; rather, God is prior to the community and to the biblical texts themselves. A properly theological criticism aims to do justice to the priority of the living and active Trinitarian God, guarding against the idolatry of interpretive communities crafting their own images of God.

Theological interpreters affirm that the principal interest of Scripture's authors, of the text itself, and of the original community of readers was theological. Hence reading the Bible meant coming to hear God's Word and to know God better. Vanhoozer explains, "Our aim therefore is not to impose yet another agenda or ideology onto the Bible, but rather to recover the Bible's original governing interest. On this view, biblical interpretation takes the form of a *confession* or acknowledgment of the word and work of God in and through Scripture."[9] Theological interpreters insist that scholarly tools and methods must not be abandoned. Instead, modern and postmodern tools and methods are helpfully utilized in theological interpretation to the degree that they are oriented to illuminating the text itself and not to something that lay "behind" or "before" it.[10] At the same time, theological interpretation challenges the autonomy of nature and so the autonomy of purportedly critical approaches to reading Scripture that often treat the natural world as all there is. From the vantage point of Christian theology, neither nature nor knowledge is religiously neutral, for nature is the creation of God and knowledge is inseparable from some type of faith. For theological interpreters, the challenge is to employ critical methods critically, as critical methods must play a ministerial and not magisterial role in biblical interpretation.

Theological criticism is controlled by the persuasion that God speaks in and through the biblical texts and by the conviction that only through adopting this persuasion can an interpreter do justice to the subject matter of Scripture. Thus Vanhoozer writes, "Because biblical texts are ultimately concerned with the reality of God, readers must have a similar theological interest. . . . Theological *text* genres (e.g., Gospels, prophecies, apocalyptic, etc.) call for theological *reading genres*, for styles of reading that proceed from faith and yet seek theological understanding. To read the biblical texts theologically is to read the texts as they wish to be read, and as they should be read in order to do them justice."[11]

Since all Christians bear the responsibility of reading Scripture as it was intended to be read, theological interpretation is therefore not the exclusive province of biblical scholars but the shared responsibility of all the theological disciplines and of the entire people of God. In short, theological interpretation is a distinctive fruit of the community of believers. Theological interpreters note that the current confusion over what the Bible means and how to read it represents a crisis for the church. Because church history is fundamentally the history of biblical interpretation, the study of church history is a theological discipline that enables the current church to learn from previous ways of interpreting Scripture. On this score, Vanhoozer underscores that "one reason for the increased interest in theological interpretation of the Bible is the recent rehabilitation of the reputation of the church fathers as profound exegetes."[12]

Theological interpreters insist that biblical studies is essentially a theological discipline for five reasons. First, biblical scholars need theology in order to make sense of the Bible's principal subject matter, God. Interpretations restricted to the historical, literary, or sociological levels lack the power to explain what the scriptural texts are truly about. Second, biblical studies requires the theological analysis of contemporary culture to understand the aims, intentions, and assumptions that readers inescapably bring to the scriptural texts. Third, biblical studies needs theology to furnish a sufficient rationale for the academy's continued engagement with Scripture. Only the conviction that Scripture says something of unique and profound significance can ultimately justify the depth of the interpreter's engagement. Fourth, since presuppositionless exegesis is impossible and some of the exegete's presuppositions regard the nature and activity of God, biblical interpretation is always inherently theological. Thus a person's view of God will affect which biblical statements about God she considers literal and which statements she considers figurative. Moreover, in both the academy and the church, readers with theological interests inevitably desire to go beyond describing what others have said or thought about God and hence want to know, based on Scripture and in view of contemporary concerns, what they should say and think about God. Fifth, practical theology participates in biblical interpretation when it investigates how the people of God should respond to Scripture. Arguably the most important mode of theological interpretation is how the church witnesses through its language and life.

Theological interpretation of Scripture designates a broad ecclesial concern that embraces a variety of complementary academic approaches. Currently three such approaches stand out. The first approach focuses on reading the Bible in terms of divine authorship or as divinely appropriated human discourse. Interpreting Scripture as divine discourse unlocks fascinating possibilities for discovering the unity among the diversity of biblical books and for relating the Old and New Testaments. Theological presuppositions about God's participation in the production of Scripture play a significant role in the way interpreters construe the text, understand thematic developments, and deal with apparent historical inconsistencies.

The second approach focuses on the final form of the Bible, stressing that the Bible as a completed literary work or narrative constitutes the prime theological witness. One learns who God is, in Vanhoozer's words, "by indwelling the symbolic world of the Bible."[13] This second approach endeavors to understand Scripture on its own terms, such as narrative and canon. Theology carefully unfolds the world of the text in order to enter the ongoing theodrama of God's words and deeds on the stage of history that climaxes in Jesus Christ. Hence the

God-world relation portrayed in Scripture becomes the paradigm for understanding the contemporary world.

The third approach focuses on theodramatic participation in the believing community today. The work of the Holy Spirit is equally present now as in the past, and biblical interpretation must constitute a vehicle for living before God and worshiping faithfully. Indeed, theological interpretation is biblical interpretation oriented toward knowing God. Hence theological interpretation recovers the symbiosis between biblical studies, theology, and spirituality in pursuit of the knowledge of God that historically prevailed from the early church to the Reformation era.

Vanhoozer draws together the threads of these three approaches in enabling readers of Scripture to know and love God:

> Knowing God, like theological interpretation of the Bible itself, is at once an intellectual, imaginative, and spiritual exercise. To know God as the author and subject of Scripture requires more than intellectual acknowledgment. To know God is to love and obey him, for the knowledge of God is both restorative and transformative. The saving knowledge of God results in the transformation of the reader into the likeness of Jesus Christ. In the final analysis, theological interpretation of the Bible may be less a matter of knowing God than of engaging with the living God and being known by God (Gal. 4:9).[14]

Hence theological interpretation of Scripture achieves its goal when readers enter into the world of the text with faith, hope, and love. When readers allow God's thoughts to become their thoughts and God's Word to become their word, they participate in the theodrama of divine redemption. As a result, readers know the Trinitarian God by experiencing the Trinitarian presence and love and taking part in the Trinitarian mission to creation.

CONCLUSION

For those disillusioned with the historical-critical method, biblical theology, principles of interpretation, and ideologically driven interpretation as ends in themselves, theological interpretation of Scripture is in many ways a rejection of the status quo. Recent scholarly work on the Bible either leaves theology in the cerebral realm or does not read Scripture as do followers of Jesus who encounter God in the words of the Bible. Practitioners of theological interpretation of Scripture emphasize confessing Christians as participants and the audience of interpretation. Accordingly, interpretation must take place in the church and for the church. Appreciating the narrative story line of Scripture, practitioners approach Scripture not primarily as a set of propositions but as the story of the living God and his saving revelation of himself to wayward humans. The language of theodrama is seen as a powerful metaphor for God's story in Scripture and the ongoing participation of Christians today in God's work in the world.

FOR FURTHER READING

Primary Sources

Fowl, Stephen E. *Theological Interpretation of Scripture.* Eugene, OR: Cascade, 2009.

Vanhoozer, Kevin J. *The Drama of Doctrine: A Canonical-Linguistic Approach to Christian Theology.* Louisville: Westminster John Knox, 2005.

——, gen. ed.; Craig G. Bartholomew and Daniel J. Treier, assoc. eds. *Theological Interpretation of the Old Testament: A Book-by-Book Survey.* Grand Rapids: Baker Academic, 2008.

——, gen. ed.; Daniel J. Treier and N. T. Wright, assoc. eds. *Theological Interpretation of the New Testament: A Book-by-Book Survey.* Grand Rapids: Baker Academic, 2008.

Watson, Francis. *Text and Truth: Redefining Biblical Theology.* Grand Rapids: Eerdmans, 1997.

Secondary Sources

Bartholomew, Craig, Colin Greene, and Karl Möller, eds.; Craig Bartholomew, ser. ed. *Renewing Biblical Interpretation.* Vol. 1. Grand Rapids: Zondervan, 2000.

Davis, Ellen F., and Richard B. Hays, eds. *The Art of Reading Scripture.* Grand Rapids: Eerdmans, 2003.

Jeanrond, Werner G. *Text and Interpretation as Categories of Theological Thinking.* Trans. Thomas J. Wilson. New York: Crossroad, 1986.

Levering, Matthew. *Participatory Biblical Exegesis: A Theology of Biblical Interpretation.* Notre Dame, IN: University of Notre Dame Press, 2008.

Plummer, Robert L. *40 Questions about Interpreting the Bible.* Grand Rapids: Kregel, 2010.

CHAPTER 37

EVOLUTIONARY CREATION

Deeming the "evolution versus creation" debate a false dichotomy, scientists and biblical scholars associated with the BioLogos Foundation, established in 2007 by geneticist and National Institutes of Health Director Francis Collins (1950–), have proposed evolutionary creation as the most faithful way to understand both science and Scripture. Evolutionary creation asserts that the Father, Son, and Holy Spirit created the universe and life through an ordained, sustained, and design-reflecting evolutionary process. This view of origins claims to fully embrace both the religious beliefs of biblical Christianity and the scientific theories of cosmological, geological, and biological evolution. It contends that the Creator established and maintains the laws of nature, including the mechanisms of a teleological evolution. Humans evolved from prehuman ancestors, and over a period of time the *imago Dei* and human sin were gradually manifested. A key question for many Christians concerning evolutionary creationism is how it can be squared with the teachings of Genesis 1–3. Since evolutionary creation represents a fast-moving stream of thought, I am limiting myself in this chapter to a snapshot of the movement taken through the lenses of one of its most notable representatives. This chapter focuses on the seminal efforts of Old Testament scholar John Walton (1952–) to show that there is no contradiction or even tension between the grammatico-historical exegesis of Genesis 1–3—namely, the meaning of the creation narrative originally intended by its author and originally understood by its ancient Israelite audience—and the theory of evolution.

GENESIS I AS FUNCTION-ORIENTED, TEMPLE-INAUGURATING ANCIENT COSMOLOGY

Walton maintains that as the Word of God, Genesis is written *for* us, but it was not written *to* us. It was written to ancient Israel, such that we are, in effect, reading someone else's mail. To correctly understand Genesis, Walton asserts that we must not only translate the language but also enter the ancient Near Eastern culture. We can enter the culture by becoming familiar with its literature. For Walton, this is not a circular claim, since we possess far more ancient Near Eastern literature than just the Old Testament. Moreover, Walton avers that any given ancient Near Eastern culture was more similar to other ancient Near Eastern cultures than any of them are to American or European culture, as ancient Near Eastern cultures had a common conceptual worldview. In the ancient Near East, Walton maintains that no dichotomy existed between the natural and the supernatural. Since Genesis 1 belongs to the genre of ancient cosmology, we must interpret it in light of the numerous other examples of ancient cosmology, including Egyptian, Babylonian, and Sumerian, that we have at our disposal.

According to Walton, the ancient Near Eastern evidence reveals that ancient cosmology is function oriented, or based on the roles things play, rather than materially oriented. This is because ancient Near Easterners possessed a functional ontology rather than the material ontology that characterizes Western culture. To grasp the difference between these ontologies, we must ask the question, "What does it mean for something to exist?" A material ontology would reply, "It exists by virtue of its physical properties and its ability to be experienced by the senses." But a functional ontology would reply, "It exists by virtue of its having a function in an ordered system."[1] For example, we may consider a house and ask when it began to exist. Contemporary Westerners, due to their material ontology, would reply that it began to exist when its material construction was finished. But Walton maintains that ancient Near Easterners, due to their functional ontology, would say that even when its material construction was finished, it still did not exist. Rather, it began to exist at the moment that it started serving as a home for a person or persons, thus fulfilling its function. Walton points out that this leads to the question: What did ancient Israelites mean by creation? Walton argues that they meant giving something a function in an ordered system in relation to society and culture. Unless persons (human or divine) are there to benefit from functions, existence is not achieved. Hence we should strongly suspect that in Genesis 1, God's creative acts amount to his assigning already materially present things their functioning roles in an ordered system.

Walton contends that this suspicion is confirmed by linguistic analysis of the Hebrew verb *bārā'*, "to create," employed throughout Genesis 1. Examining its usage elsewhere in Hebrew literature, *bārā'* always takes God as its subject (either explicitly or implicitly), and it takes objects that either demand functions, suggest functions, or are ambiguous. However, *bārā'* never takes objects that demand anything material. For Walton, it follows from these observations that the literal meaning of *bārā'* is to functionally create, not to materially create. Hence Walton proposes that Genesis 1:1 ("In the beginning God created the heavens and the earth") originally meant, "In the initial period, God created by assigning functions throughout the heavens and the earth, and this is how he did it."[2] Just as one creates a committee by assigning functions to people who were previously materially present, so God creates in Genesis 1 by assigning functions to entities (impersonal and personal) that were previously materially present.

It is important to note that Walton believes, on the basis of New Testament texts that come out of a Greek culture that held largely to a material ontology, that God did materially create the universe *ex nihilo*. This is affirmed, for instance, by Hebrews 11:3—"By faith we understand that the universe was formed at God's command, so that what is seen was not made out of what was visible" (cf. Heb. 1:2; John 1:3; Col. 1:16–17). However, Walton insists that Genesis 1 is simply not the story of God's creating the universe *ex nihilo* but a different story altogether. Indeed, Genesis 1 opens with material already present, specifically the earth and the waters. The earth is described as *tōhû* and *bōhû*, a phrase that Walton contends from the usage of these words elsewhere (Isa. 45:18; 49:4; 59:4; Jer. 4:23) means "unproductive."[3] Thus the creation account begins with no functions relative to beings rather than no material.

Walton contends that the first three days of creation establish functions. On day one, God calls light "day" rather than "light" (Gen. 1:5); by metonymy, light therefore means "period of light." Hence God says, in effect, "Let there be a period of light," followed by a period of light (Gen. 1:3), thereby establishing the function of time.[4] Day two employs the terms of ancient cosmic geography to depict space where people could live complete with a mechanism to control precipitation, thereby establishing the function of weather. Day three, according to Walton, is marked by the absence of even the possibility of material creation, but soil, water, and seed bearing are discussed. Taken together, these elements establish the function of food. Walton declares that his reading is confirmed by Genesis 8:22, which reestablishes in reverse order these same three functions after the great flood: "As long as the earth endures, seedtime and harvest [food], cold and heat, summer and winter [weather], day and night [time] will never cease."

Linked respectively with the first three days of creation, the second three days of creation, on Walton's interpretation, establish functionaries. Tied to day one, day four depicts God giving celestial bodies the task of separating day and night and serving as signs, markers for festival celebrations, days, and years. Tied to day two, day five depicts God giving sea creatures and birds the task of being fruitful and multiplying in the cosmic spaces they inhabit. Tied to day three, day six depicts God giving humans three extremely important tasks, one relative to God, one relative to themselves, and one relative to their terrestrial space. Relative to God, humans are to perform the function of serving in God's image. Relative to each other, humans are to perform the function of living as male and female. Relative to their terrestrial space, humans are to perform the function of being fruitful and multiplying. Moreover, Walton claims that the repeated refrain "it was (very) good" (Gen. 1:4, 10, 12, 18, 21, 31) means that everything described was functioning properly.

The pinnacle of the days of creation, emphasizes Walton, is day seven; without it the cosmos is literally pointless and in functional terms does not exist. Day seven features God resting, and in the ancient Near East divine rest occurred by definition in a temple. Far from disengaging with the tasks of life, rest in the ancient Near East entailed "engagement in the normal activities that can be carried out when stability has been achieved. . . . For deity this means that the normal operations of the cosmos can be undertaken."[5] This is borne out by the terminology used in Genesis 2:2 and its commentary in Exodus 20:11: "By the seventh day God had finished the work he had been doing; so on the seventh day he rested (*šābat*) from all his work" (Gen. 2:2), and "For in six days the Lord made the heavens and the earth, the sea, and all that is in them, but he rested (*nûḥa*) on the seventh day" (Ex. 20:11). *Šābat*, from which "Sabbath" is derived, denotes the completion of activity with which one had been occupied and subsequent transition into a new state. Here the new state is *nûḥa*, which refers to a position of safety, security, and stability. Hence day seven sees God "move in" to the universe by making it his cosmic temple, a temple in which human beings serve as the guests of honor and where the universe's functions serve our needs (as God has no needs). Once God "moves in," rendering the universe his home, the universe fulfills its intended purpose and so functionally begins to exist. Moreover, temple inaugurations in the ancient Near East typically took seven days. Accordingly, the whole of Genesis 1 depicts the functional cosmic temple inauguration.

Walton insists that his reading is confirmed by the two Jerusalem temples, constructed to serve as pointers to the ultimate temple, namely, the cosmos.

As the Jewish historian Josephus (AD 37–100) described the objects in the temple, "Every one of these objects is intended to recall and represent the universe."[6] Moreover, 1 Kings 7 arranges the horizontal axis of the temple in the same order as the vertical axis of the cosmos. The temple courtyard represented the elements outside the organized cosmos (the pillars of the earth and cosmic waters); the temple antechamber represented the organized cosmos with the menorah (light), bread of the presence (food provided by God), and altar of incense with its sweet-smelling cloud (weather); the temple veil represented the firmament separating the heavenly sphere (where God dwells) from the earthly sphere (where humans dwell); and the holy of holies represented the heavenly dwelling place of God.

Since on Walton's reading Genesis 1 is a functional creation account depicting the inauguration of the already materially present universe as God's temple, an inauguration that entailed assigning already materially present entities in the universe like plants, animals, and humans their temple roles, Walton judges Genesis 1 to say nothing about the material origins of the universe or entities therein. Accordingly, Genesis 1 is entirely consistent with cosmological, geological, and biological evolution. Walton summarizes his view of Genesis 1 by explaining what happened before, during, and after the seven days (which he takes to be literal, twenty-four-hour days). Before the seven days, the material phase was under development for long eras (which correspond to the prehistoric ages). The sun was shining, plants were growing, and animals and humans were present; all of this was like the rehearsals leading up to the performance of a play. These rehearsals were preparatory and necessary, but they are not the play. During the seven days (analogous to the play), the functions of the universe are decreed by God to serve the purposes of humanity, humanity is given the function to serve in God's image, and God takes up residence (i.e., rests) in his cosmic temple. After the seven days, the cosmos is God's residence, humans serve him as vice regents in the world that has been made for them, and the cosmos is finally a fully functioning temple.

GENESIS 2–3: ADAM AND EVE AS OUR PRIESTLY REPRESENTATIVES IN SACRED SPACE

Walton commences his exegesis of Genesis 2–3 by proposing that it is a sequel to Genesis 1 rather than a recapitulation of day six in Genesis 1. The second creation account is introduced by a *toledot* ("this is the account of") formula: "This is the account of the heavens and the earth when they were created, when the LORD God made the earth and the heavens" (Gen. 2:4). *Toledot* occurs here and ten other times in Genesis; it is one of the formal characteristics of the book. In all the other occurrences, the formula introduces either a narrative of someone's sons, someone's relative, or a genealogy of that person's descendants. It therefore tells what came after that person and what developed from that person. Using the same logic, we would conclude that the section introduced in Genesis 2:4 is going to talk about what came after the creation of the heavens and the earth in the seven-day account and what developed from it, that is, a sequel to the seven-day account.

If Genesis 2–3 were instead a recapitulation of day six, avers Walton, then several features of the narrative do not make sense. Genesis 2:5–6 states that there were no plants when God created humans, yet plants come on day three and humans on day six in Genesis 1. In Genesis 2, Adam is formed before the animals; in Genesis 1, God created the animals first and then humans on day six. That the events of Genesis 2–3 could all take place in a twenty-four-hour day (among them, Adam's naming all the animals) stretches credulity. But if Genesis 2–3 is indeed a sequel, then a very important consequence arises: there are other people in the image of God in Genesis 2–4, not just Adam and Eve and their family. This consequence is quite advantageous when reading Genesis 4. For Cain has a wife (Gen. 4:17); Cain fears that "whoever finds me will kill me" (Gen. 4:14) when he is driven from Yahweh's presence; and Cain builds a city (*'iyr*), a term that denotes a settlement of some size for many people (Gen. 4:17).

Walton suggests that the garden of Eden is sacred space, the significance of which has more to do with divine presence than human paradise. Genesis 2 describes Eden as featuring waters that bring fertility and a kind of arboretum filled with all sorts of animals. This depiction, explains Walton, is common to ancient Near Eastern gardens that adjoin temples:

> This parklike environment is well known in the ancient world. The motif of flowing rivers (four is common) is connected to sacred space early and often. The same motif can be seen in Ezekiel 47, and there are allusions to it throughout the Psalms and the Prophets. Gardens were constructed adjoining sacred space as evidence of the fertility that resulted from the presence of God. They were not vegetable gardens or fields of crops; they were beautifully landscaped parks. . . . Thus, the text of Genesis can be seen to describe a garden, a park landscaped with exotic trees and stocked with wildlife. These were common accoutrements to temples.[7]

At this juncture Walton draws several comparisons between the first creation account and the second creation account. Just as the first creation account began with a state of nonorder in the larger cosmos, the second creation account begins with a state of nonorder in the terrestrial realm. The second creation account explains how humans function in sacred space and on its behalf, in contrast to the first creation account, which addressed how sacred space functions for humanity. The second creation account locates the center of sacred space—the garden—in contrast to the first creation account, which only indicates that the cosmos was set up to be sacred space.

While Walton insists that Adam and Eve were real, historical individuals, he posits that Adam often serves as an archetype for humankind. An archetype is an individual who embodies all others in the group. To determine whether the treatment of Adam in the text focuses on him primarily as an individual or as an archetype, Walton suggests a test question: Is the text describing something that is uniquely true of Adam, or is it describing something that is true of all humanity?

Walton then tackles the question of whether Genesis 2 tells us anything about the material origins of Adam or Eve. Regarding Genesis 2:7, "Then the LORD God formed (*yatsar*) a man from the dust (*'aphar*) of the ground and breathed into his nostrils the breath of life, and the man became a living being," Walton argues that *yatsar* does not describe a material act. Most of the forty-two instances of *yatsar* in the Old Testament are shown by context to be unrelated to material and could easily be translated by alternatives like "prepare," "ordain," or "decree."[8] Hence *yatsar* in Genesis 2:7 should be read the same way. Since all humanity is formed from dust (Ps. 103:14) and have the breath of life that comes from God (Job 27:3; 32:8; 33:4; 34:14–15; Isa. 42:5), Genesis 2:7 is treating Adam primarily as an archetype and only secondarily as an individual. In stating that Adam was formed from the dust (*'aphar*) of the ground, the ancient Israelite author, alleges Walton, was not thinking about chemistry and therefore had some other purpose in mind. And if it were chemistry, it would be bad chemistry, as dust is not the primary ingredient of the human body. Neither was the author thinking about craftsmanship, as the term used in craftsmanship contexts is "clay" (*chomer*). Dust is impervious to being shaped by its very nature. Rather, Genesis 3:19 furnishes the meaning of *'aphar*: "for dust you are and to dust you will return." Hence dust refers to mortality. Walton observes that this association would make sense to an Israelite reader who was well acquainted with a corpse that was laid out on the slab in the family tomb and deteriorated to merely a pile of bones and the dust of the desiccated flesh within a year. It also makes sense of why God provided humans in the garden a Tree of Life, which would have been needless for immortal persons. So Walton stipulates that Genesis 2–3 does not teach that humans were created immortal but rather teaches that because of their sin, humans lost the antidote for their mortality.

Concerning Eve, Walton asks whether Adam thought of Eve as having been built from his rib and answers no: "This is now bone of my bones and flesh of my flesh" (Gen. 2:23). More than a rib is involved because Eve is also flesh of Adam's flesh. The term in Genesis 2:21–22 traditionally translated "rib"—*sela*—is used forty times in the Old Testament and is not an anatomical term in any other passage. Rather, *sela* is used architecturally in passages describing either the tabernacle or the temple, referring to one side or the other. Thus we would have to conclude that God took one of Adam's sides, cutting Adam in half, and from one side built the woman.

But now Walton queries: Would Israelites naturally think of surgery, believing that Adam was anesthetized when God put Adam in a deep sleep? This is ruled out on the grounds that Israelites knew nothing of the use of anesthesia. Instead, the term "deep sleep" (*tardema*) means "when someone has become unresponsive to the human realm in order to receive communication from the divine realm"; such sleep blocks all perception in the human realm.[9] *Tardema* denotes the sleep that accompanies a visionary dream in Genesis 15:12; Job 4:13; Daniel 8:18; and Daniel 10:9. In the Septuagint, the Greek term used to translate *tardema* is *ekstasis* (vision, trance, ecstasy). So Walton maintains that the description of Adam being cut in half and the woman being built from the other half refers not to something Adam physically experienced but to something he saw in a vision. Hence Genesis 2 does not describe the material origin of Eve, but rather concerns her identity as ontologically related to the man. On this score, Genesis 2:24 offers an observation that is true of all mankind and all womankind: "That is why a man leaves his father and mother and is united to his wife, and they become one flesh." Walton alleges that, in other words, marriage is being rejoined and recovering humanity's original state. Genesis 2:24 is responding to the question of why a person would leave the closest biological relationship (parents to children) to forge a relationship with a biological outsider. Its answer is that marriage goes beyond biology to recover an original ontological state; ontology trumps biology.

Given that the second creation narrative is a sequel to the first creation narrative, Walton argues that Adam and Eve were likely not among the humans described in Genesis 1. Given that the second creation narrative says nothing about the material origins of Adam or Eve, we should also assume that each of them was born of a woman. However, Walton contends that Genesis 2–3 depicts Adam and Eve as the first theologically significant humans in salvation history, as they are divinely elected to priestly roles and are the first humans God placed in the center of sacred space. This is supported by the terms "work" (*'abad*) and "take care of" (*samar*) in Genesis 2:15, which refer to priestly tasks. For Walton, then, God chose Adam and Eve to represent the human race as his priests in the garden of Eden. Moreover, Walton notes that the priestly role of Adam and the identification of Eden as sacred space is supported by the intertestamental book of Jubilees and the commentaries of Origen. In ancient Near Eastern thought, the main role of a priest was caring for sacred space. Sacred space was the center of order because order emanates from God. Hence caring for sacred space was a way of upholding creation; by preserving order, nonorder was held at bay. Maintaining order made one a participant with God in the ongoing task of sustaining the equilibrium God had established in the cosmos. A priest cared for sacred space by instructing the people what sacred space required of them, keeping out anything that would compromise or corrupt its sanctity, and serving as mediators who made the benefits of sacred space available to the people and assured that the gifts of the people got to God.

Walton declares that the serpent in ancient Near Eastern thinking was viewed as a chaos creature from the nonordered realm, promoting disorder. By following the serpent's suggestion and eating from the Tree of Knowledge of Good and Evil, Adam and Eve chose to place themselves instead of God as the center of order and source of wisdom, thereby readmitting disorder into the cosmos (the disorder that existed prior to Genesis 1) and violating their role as priests. Because of the disorder in the world, all people are now subject to sin and death.

CONCLUSION

Walton's functional cosmic temple interpretation of Genesis 1 and his archetypal interpretation of Genesis 2–3 are quite provocative and, if true, may eliminate a great deal of tension between mainstream science and the opening chapters of Genesis. Against those who charge him with hermeneutical innovation, Walton insists that his interpretations recover the literal reading of the text, namely, the reading intended by its ancient Israelite author and understood by its ancient Israelite audience. For Walton, the universe is the place of God's presence. Adam and Eve were commissioned as priests to serve in the center of sacred space mediating revelation of God and access to God. Tragically, they failed to realize life and wisdom because they opted to place themselves, instead of God, as the locus of order, a sin that now epitomizes the fallen human condition.

FOR FURTHER READING

Primary Sources

Lamoureux, Denis O. *Evolutionary Creation: A Christian Approach to Evolution*. Eugene, OR: Wipf and Stock, 2008.

Walton, John H. *Ancient Near Eastern Thought and the Old Testament: Introducing the Conceptual World of the Hebrew Bible*. Grand Rapids: Baker Academic, 2006.

———. *Genesis 1 as Ancient Cosmology*. Winona Lake, IN: Eisenbrauns, 2011.

———. *The Lost World of Adam and Eve: Genesis 2–3 and the Human Origins Debate*. Downers Grove, IL: IVP Academic, 2015.

———. *The Lost World of Genesis One: Ancient Cosmology and the Origins Debate*. Downers Grove, IL: IVP Academic, 2009.

Secondary Sources

Barrett, Matthew, and Ardel B. Caneday, gen. eds.; Stanley N. Gundry, ser. ed. *Four Views on the Historical Adam*. Grand Rapids: Zondervan, 2013.

Blocher, Henri. *In the Beginning: The Opening Chapters of Genesis*. Downers Grove, IL: IVP, 1984.

Halton, Charles, gen. ed.; Stanley N. Gundry, ser. ed. *Genesis: History, Fiction, or Neither? Three Views on the Bible's Earliest Chapters*. Grand Rapids: Zondervan, 2015.

Stump, J. B., ed.; Stanley N. Gundry, ser. ed. *Four Views on Creation, Evolution, and Intelligent Design*. Grand Rapids: Zondervan, 2017.

Van Till, Howard J., ed. *Portraits of Creation: Biblical and Scientific Perspectives on the World's Formation*. Grand Rapids: Eerdmans, 1990.

CHAPTER 38

POSTCONSERVATIVE
THEOLOGY

Primarily because of the popular media, many Americans identify evangelicalism with the so-called Religious Right or a conservative political agenda centered on abortion and homosexuality. Evangelical social ethicists including Tony Campolo (1935–), Ronald Sider (1939–), and Jim Wallis (1948–) have argued that it is possible to be genuinely evangelical while being liberal politically, especially on issues of poverty, war, and capital punishment. Similarly, evangelical theologian Roger Olson (1952–), professor at the Truett Theological Seminary of Baylor University, has argued that it is possible to be genuinely evangelical while disclaiming theological conservatism. Foreshadowed by the work of evangelical theologian Stanley Grenz (1950–2005), Olson's resultant movement is known as postconservative theology, expounded in his 2007 book, *Reformed and Always Reforming: The Postconservative Approach to Evangelical Theology* and his 2008 book, *How to Be Evangelical without Being Conservative*. This chapter delineates the essential threads making up the fabric of postconservative theology, a movement that continues to encompass larger numbers of evangelical theologians.

SCRIPTURE, TRADITION, AND EVANGELICALISM

The postconservative style of doing theology moves beyond unbending adherence to the "received evangelical tradition" in its willingness to subject any doctrine or practice to scrutiny in light of the Word of God.[1] Adherents of *sola scriptura* (Scripture alone) or *prima scriptura* (Scripture first and above all else), postconservative theologians are open to new ways of thinking about anything insofar

367

as the ongoing faithful interpretation of Scripture demands. As Olson observes, "That is why it is possible to be more evangelical by being less conservative: insofar as 'conservative' denotes firm adherence to tradition and unwillingness to consider new theological ideas even in the light of fresh and faithful interpretation to Scripture, being conservative is contrary to the spirit of evangelical faith, which elevates the Bible above tradition."[2] Postconservative theology is therefore an evangelical reaction against the essence of conservatism—the determined adherence to the tradition of what has always been believed by Christians in general or by evangelicals in particular.

For postconservative theologians, being evangelical means commitment to the normative value of Scripture in the Christian life, the necessity of conversion, the recognition of Jesus Christ as the sole mediator between God and humanity, the imperative of evangelism, and adherence to traditional evangelical doctrines when not in conflict with the Bible. Postconservative theologians therefore indict their conservative brethren of both adhering to a school of traditional evangelical orthodoxy (usually Princeton theology) even when it conflicts with the Bible and reading the Bible through the lenses of that orthodox school so that any potential conflict between the two never comes to light.

MARKS OF THE POSTCONSERVATIVE STYLE

Postconservative theologians regard the primary purpose of revelation as transformation instead of information. They do not reject the propositional, factual, and informational aspects of divine revelation, but they emphasize that God gives revelation mainly to redeem humans through personal encounter and relationship, an endeavor in which nonpropositional aspects of revelation prove effective. Many postconservative theologians champion narrative theology—as seen in postliberal theology and the theological interpretation of Scripture—stressing the power of story to transform persons in a way propositions cannot. They wish to avoid reducing revelation to communication of information, a view they deem to be truncated. Postconservative theologians fear that conservative theology is too enamored by the notion of cognitive Christianity to the neglect of Christianity as, in Olson's words, "a personally transforming and personally involving relationship, rooted in revelation as God's self-giving by means of a complex of dramatic actions, including but not limited to communication of truths."[3]

The postconservative vision of what theology is all about amounts to a pilgrimage and a journey, not the discovery and conquest epitomizing the fundamentalist-modernist controversy. Hence the constructive task of theology is always open; there are no closed, once-and-for-all theological systems. Postconservative theologians argue that it is deceptively easy for those who believe themselves in possession of God's inerrant Word to transfer some of that inerrancy to themselves and thus to respond to anyone who challenges any aspect of their received doctrinal paradigms with righteous anger and vehement rejection. In contrast to this approach, postconservative theologians claim it is no sin to take risks in theological construction via thought experiments. They promote appreciation for the role of imagination in theological work. Far from being the devil's playground, imagination is God's gift employed by the biblical authors (in, for instance, poetry and parables) and beneficial to theologians whose job is to pick up where the Bible leaves off, looking both at and along the scriptural path. Evangelical theology, insist postconservative theologians, needs to rediscover and rehabilitate imagination's function in faithfully improvising on the dramatic themes of scriptural revelation. Accordingly, theology is not so much "thinking God's thoughts after him" or erecting timeless and impregnable fortresses of thought but creative performance based on the "dramatic script" of scriptural revelation supplemented by the Great Tradition of Christianity.[4]

Postconservative theologians evince an uneasiness and dissatisfaction with the dependence of conservative evangelical theology on Enlightenment and modern modes of thought. This is highly ironic because most conservative theologians denounce the Enlightenment and modernity, laying most of the blame for evangelicalism's slide into pluralism and lack of prophetic voice at the feet of these forces. However, several historians of evangelicalism have observed how strongly the movement is influenced by the Enlightenment and modernity. Some conservative theologians operate under the Enlightenment-inspired philosophical method known as classical foundationalism (encountered in chapter 27), which in the eyes of postconservative theologians treasures rational certainty and puts propositions and coherent systems on practically an idolatrous pedestal. Springing from the philosophical influences of Enlightenment thinkers René Descartes (1596–1650) and John Locke (1632–1704), classical foundationalism considers dubious all claims to knowledge except for those based on self-evident truths of reason or evidences of the senses. It therefore precludes truth claims based on faith and revelation stemming from the inner testimony of the Holy Spirit through spiritual experience. Raising red flags over this issue, postconservative theologians insist that evangelical theology must be freed from the Enlightenment and that some aspects of postmodern thought can aid in that liberation. Postconservative theologians fear that "conservative foundationalism and propositionalism" elevate something foreign to revelation above revelation as the criterion of truth, thus demoting Christianity to a philosophy insofar as Enlightenment-inspired methods and commitments steer evangelical thinking.[5]

The concept of evangelicalism held by postconservative theologians amounts to a centered set category instead of a set having boundaries. Conservative evangelicals tend to limit the boundaries of genuine evangelicalism. This, for example, was the purpose of the 1989 Evangelical Affirmations conference and document sponsored by the National Association of Evangelicals and Trinity Evangelical Divinity School. From 2000 to 2003, the Evangelical Theological Society took up the issue of evangelical boundaries by considering whether to divest two open theists of their membership status, although in the end they were permitted to retain their memberships. Thus Olson charges, "Who is 'in' and who is 'out' is an obsession with some conservative evangelicals. For many of them the 'tent' of authentic evangelicalism is small, even if the 'tent' of the evangelical subculture is too large."[6]

By contrast, postconservative theologians maintain that the question is not over who is "in" and "out" but over who is closer to the center and who is departing from it. Olson declares that "authentic evangelicalism is defined by its centrifugal center of powerful gravity and not by outlying boundaries that serve as walls or fences."[7] The center is Jesus Christ, the gospel, and the five core commitments of biblicism, conversionism, crucicentrism (emphasis on Jesus's saving work on the cross), activism in missions and social transformation, and respect for historic Christian orthodoxy as a secondary norm only to be corrected by the primary norm of Scripture. Individuals gathered around the center or moving toward it are genuinely evangelical; individuals departing from it or with their backs turned against it possess doubtful evangelical status. But there is no evangelical magisterium to determine who is "in" or "out."

Some conservative critics have wondered how there can be a center without a circumference. Postconservative theologians reply that many centers without circumferences exist in nature, mathematics, and other realms of reality. Olson suggests the following analogy:

> Who is an American? Any and every US citizen is an American. America is not a movement but a definite organization even if nobody knows for sure exactly how many members it has and even if at times problems arise in identifying certain people as either members or not members (e.g., children of citizens born in other countries who must be nationalized even though that is a formal process). By contrast, who is a Westerner? Not all Europeans

or Americans are truly Westerners culturally and many people living in Asia are Westernized. Some people stand out as paragons of Western culture, but others are mixtures and hybrids of that and other cultures.[8]

The same applies to the term *evangelical*. While there is no office or litmus test that determines exactly who is an evangelical, it is apparent to postconservative theologians that not everyone who claims the label does so justifiably. Thus evangelicalism is a definite movement with no boundaries but a strong center that suffices for defining it.

Postconservative theologians desire to bypass debates about biblical inerrancy and focus instead on the instrumental use of Scripture, which they see as more in line with Jesus's own use. Unlike the rabbis and Essenes, Jesus purportedly did not view his task as exegeting Scripture for its own sake. Rather, for Jesus Scripture served as a means for different ends, such as expressing an awareness of fulfillment, provoking new forms of behavior, grounding doctrinal positions, and founding ethics. Regarding fulfillment, Scripture imparts knowledge of God's eschatological action, which Jesus experienced as being fulfilled in the present and which he could interpret with Scripture's aid. Hence Jesus interpreted the miracles he performs as a fulfillment of prophetic statements about the time of salvation (Matt. 11:4–5). Regarding provocation of new behavior, Jesus employed scriptural passages or motifs to shock his hearers into carrying out conduct appropriate to the kingdom of God. The confrontation of skeptical observers with biblical examples of pious Gentiles (Matt. 13:54–58), the messianic banquet (Matt. 8:10–11), the vineyard of Israel (Mark 12:1–9), and the hardening of Israel (Mark 4:12) all functioned to move his audience to repentance. Regarding doctrine, Jesus appealed to Scripture to support the general resurrection (Mark 12:18–27) and to repudiate divorce (Mark 10:2–12), in the latter case even playing one less relevant passage of Scripture (Deut. 24:1) against another more relevant passage (Gen. 2:24). Regarding ethics, Jesus utilized Scripture to sum up the whole moral duty of humanity: to love God maximally and to love one's neighbor as oneself (Mark 12:29–31). On this foundation, we can affirm the objective goodness and rightness of love, equality, generosity, and self-sacrifice, and we can condemn as objectively evil all hatred, abuse, discrimination, and oppression. In all these cases, postconservative theologians point out, Scripture is applied rather than defended.

Postconservative theologians are more interested in doing theology for the church than for the academy. For postconservative theologians, theology since Schleiermacher has been devoted to the mistaken task of trying to satisfy

372   Contemporary Theology

modernity's expectation of proper scientific knowledge and has thereby undercut the true work of theology in the service of the church. Instead of considering the fallenness of humanity and hence the limitations of human knowledge, classical foundationalism exalted human sentiments over God's Word. Theology's adherence to classical foundationalism thus yields an anthropocentric rather than a theocentric approach to the knowledge of God. Postconservative theologians endeavor to reverse this trend, basing theological epistemology on Scripture and employing Scripture for the edification and spiritual vitality of the body of Christ.

Postconservative theologians conceive the enduring essence of Christianity—and therefore the true identity of evangelical faith—as personal relationship with Jesus Christ rather than as doctrinal belief. Many other evangelicals deny that these two can be validly separated. The roots of postconservative theology in Pietism, the seventeenth-century Lutheran movement that stressed the experiential aspects of Christianity over the intellectual aspects, prove abundantly apparent here. This is also the point where conservatives raise some of their most trenchant criticism because of the seeming similarity to the theology of Friedrich Schleiermacher (1768–1834), the founder of liberal theology. We recall from chapter 2 that Schleiermacher's method centered on God-consciousness as the heart and essence of religion, including Christianity. Postconservative theologians contend that evangelicalism is a form of the Christian faith expressed first and foremost in a distinctive spirituality that may be dubbed "convertive piety."[9] As Grenz put it, "To be truly evangelical, right doctrine, as important as it is, is not enough. The truth of the Christian faith must become personally experienced truth."[10] Hence the doctrinal language of Christianity is second-order language; it is the communal expression of the experience of God in Christians' encounter with Jesus Christ.

A key difference between Schleiermacher and postconservative theologians resides in their varying conceptions of "experience." Schleiermacher regarded the experience of general God-consciousness as a universal a priori, residing in some measure in every human being regardless of religious persuasion or lack thereof. But postconservative theologians regard the experience that defines genuine evangelical faith as the supernatural and uniquely Christian work of God that converts believers and results in a transformed life of commitment and devotion to Jesus Christ grounded in the authoritative and inspired Word of God.

Although holding lightly to recent evangelical tradition, postconservative theologians respect the Great Tradition of Christian belief. Postconservative theologians decry the "virtual elimination of tradition" in much contemporary

Protestant theology.[11] However, the Great Tradition serves a ministerial rather than a magisterial role in theology, receiving "a vote but never a veto in matters of doctrinal examination and reconstruction."[12] Following the Protestant dictum of *reformata et semper reformanda* (reformed and always reforming), the Great Tradition must not commandeer the position of Scripture itself.

CONCLUSION

We may draw together the threads of postconservative theology in seven "beyond" moves. First, postconservatism aims to move beyond the agenda of the fundamentalist-modernist controversy toward a more holistic theology. Second, postconservatism aims to move beyond classical foundationalism toward alternative epistemologies. Third, postconservatism aims to move beyond concentration on rationalism toward incorporating additional ways of knowing. Fourth, postconservatism aims to move beyond the fear of liberalism toward a selective yet critical appropriation of postmodern insights. Fifth, postconservatism aims to move beyond debates over inerrancy toward an instrumental use of Scripture. Sixth, postconservatism aims to move beyond academic theologizing toward ecclesial and community-oriented thinking. Seventh, postconservatism aims to move beyond gatekeeping on boundary-setting doctrinalism toward a generous orthodoxy rooted in Pietism.[13]

FOR FURTHER READING

Primary Sources

Campolo, Tony. *Red Letter Christians: A Citizen's Guide to Faith and Politics.* Ventura, CA: Regal, 2008.

Grenz, Stanley J. *Revisioning Evangelical Theology: A Fresh Agenda for the 21st Century.* Downers Grove, IL: IVP Academic, 1993.

Olson, Roger E. *How to Be Evangelical without Being Conservative.* Grand Rapids: Zondervan, 2008.

———. *Reformed and Always Reforming: The Postconservative Approach to Evangelical Theology.* Grand Rapids: Baker Academic, 2007.

Sider, Ronald J. *The Scandal of the Evangelical Conscience: Why Are Christians Living Just Like the Rest of the World?* Grand Rapids: Baker, 2005.

Wallis, Jim. *God's Politics: Why the Right Gets It Wrong and the Left Doesn't Get It; A New Vision for Faith and Politics in America.* San Francisco: HarperSanFrancisco, 2006.

Secondary Sources

Balmer, Randall. *Thy Kingdom Come—How the Religious Right Distorts the Faith and Threatens America: An Evangelical's Lament.* New York: Basic, 2006.

Boyd, Gregory A. *The Myth of a Christian Nation: How the Quest for Political Power Is Destroying the Church.* Grand Rapids: Zondervan, 2007.

———. *The Myth of a Christian Religion: Losing Your Religion for the Beauty of a Revolution.* Grand Rapids: Zondervan, 2009.

Gasaway, Brantley W. *Progressive Evangelicals and the Pursuit of Social Justice.* Chapel Hill, NC: University of North Carolina Press, 2014.

Gushee, David P., and Glen H. Stassen. *Kingdom Ethics: Following Jesus in Contemporary Context.* 2nd ed. Grand Rapids: Eerdmans, 2016.

Sherman, Steven B. *Revitalizing Theological Epistemology: Holistic Evangelical Approaches to the Knowledge of God.* Princeton Theological Monograph Series 83. Eugene, OR: Pickwick, 2008.

NOTES

Chapter 1: Philosophical Backgrounds

1. Immanuel Kant, *Critique of Pure Reason*, trans. Norman Kemp Smith (New York: St. Martin's, 1965), 1.2.1.2.3.
2. Ibid.
3. Ibid.
4. Immanuel Kant, *Religion within the Limits of Reason Alone*, 2nd ed., trans. Theodore M. Greene and Hoyt H. Hudson (New York: Harper, 1960), 11.

Chapter 2: Friedrich Schleiermacher

1. Friedrich Schleiermacher, *On Religion: Addresses in Response to Its Cultured Critics*, trans. Terrence N. Tice (Richmond: John Knox, 1969), 12.
2. Keith W. Clements, *Friedrich Schleiermacher: Pioneer of Modern Theology* (London: Collins, 1987), 7.
3. Friedrich Schleiermacher, *The Christian Faith*, ed. H. R. Mackintosh and J. S. Stewart (1928; repr., Edinburgh: T&T Clark, 1960), 194.
4. Ibid., 33.
5. Ibid., 739.
6. Ibid., 593.
7. Ibid., 608.
8. Ibid., 599.
9. Ibid., 610–11.
10. Ibid., 183.
11. Ibid., 385.
12. Ibid., 387.
13. Ibid., 383.
14. Ibid., 381.
15. Ibid., 425.
16. Ibid., 720.
17. Ibid., 156.
18. Ibid., 158.

19. Ibid., 161.
20. Ibid., 168–69.
21. Ibid., 169.
22. Ibid., 350.
23. Ibid.
24. Ibid., 715–16.
25. Ibid., 720–21.
26. Ibid., 722.

Chapter 3: G. W. F. Hegel

1. G. W. F. Hegel, *Phenomenology of Spirit*, trans. A. V. Miller, analysis and foreword by J. N. Findlay (Oxford: Oxford University Press, 1977), §17.
2. Ibid., §438.

Chapter 4: Søren Kierkegaard

1. Søren Kierkegaard, *Concluding Unscientific Postscript*, ed. and trans. Howard and Edna Hong (Princeton, NJ: Princeton University Press, 1992), 540.
2. Ibid., 189.
3. Søren Kierkegaard, *Training in Christianity and the Edifying Discourse Which 'Accompanied' It*, trans. Walter Lowrie (Princeton, NJ: Princeton University Press, 1944), 68.
4. Kristen K. Deede, "The Infinite Qualitative Difference: Sin, the Self, and Revelation in the Thought of Søren Kierkegaard," *International Journal for Philosophy of Religion* 53, no. 1 (2003): 25.

Chapter 5: Early Dispensationalism

1. John Nelson Darby, *The Collected Writings of J. N. Darby*, ed. William Kelly, 34 vols., repr. ed. (Sunbury, PA: Believers Bookshelf, 1972), 11:125.
2. Ernest R. Sandeen, *The Roots of Fundamentalism: British and American Millenarianism, 1800–1930* (Chicago: University of Chicago Press, 1970), 65–67.
3. Darby, *Collected Writings*, 11:153–54.
4. Ibid., 11:155.
5. Ibid., 11:162.
6. Ibid., 2:378.

Chapter 6: Princeton Theology

1. Justo González, *A History of Christian Thought*, vol. 3, *From the Protestant Reformation to the Twentieth Century*, rev. ed. (Nashville: Abingdon, 1987), 276.
2. Ibid., 278.
3. Charles Hodge, *Systematic Theology*, 3 vols. (Grand Rapids: Eerdmans, 1973), 1:10.
4. Ibid., 1:170.
5. Ibid.
6. Ibid., 1:128.
7. Ibid., 1:179.
8. Ibid., 2:196–97.

9. Ibid., 2:520.

10. Ibid., 2:541.

11. Benjamin Breckinridge Warfield, *The Inspiration and Authority of the Bible*, ed. Samuel G. Craig (Philadelphia: Presbyterian and Reformed, 1948), 160.

12. Ibid., 158.

13. Ibid., 114.

14. Ibid., 181.

15. Benjamin Breckinridge Warfield, in *Evolution, Scripture, and Science*, ed. Mark A. Noll and Daniel N. Livingstone (Grand Rapids: Baker, 2000), 165, 130.

16. Ibid., 217–18.

17. Hodge, *Systematic Theology*, 1:114.

Chapter 7: Charles Haddon Spurgeon

1. Charles Haddon Spurgeon, *The Complete Works of C. H. Spurgeon* (Harrington, DE: Delmarva, 2013), sermon 2685.

2. Ibid., sermon 303.

3. Tom Nettles, *Living by Revealed Truth: The Life and Pastoral Theology of Charles Haddon Spurgeon* (Fearn, Scotland: Mentor, 2013), 179.

4. Charles Haddon Spurgeon, *The Sword and the Trowel* (London: Passmore & Alabaster, 1869), 349.

5. Ibid., 351.

6. Charles Haddon Spurgeon, *Sermons of Rev. C. H. Spurgeon*, 20 vols. (New York: Funk & Wagnalls, 1857–92), 2:201–2.

7. Charles Haddon Spurgeon, in *The Christian World*, June 8, 1878, 4.

8. Ibid.

9. Charles Haddon Spurgeon, *The Autobiography of Charles H. Spurgeon*, 2 vols. (Chicago: Revell, 1899), 2:248.

10. Charles Haddon Spurgeon, in *The Daily Telegraph*, September 23, 1874.

11. Charles Haddon Spurgeon, *"Till He Come": Communion Meditations and Addresses* (London: Passmore & Alabaster, 1896), 69.

12. Spurgeon, *Complete Works*, sermon 3338.

13. Spurgeon, *"Till He Come,"* 17.

14. Ibid.

15. Spurgeon, *Complete Works*, sermon 3338.

16. Spurgeon, *Sermons*, 2:352.

17. Ibid., 1:238.

18. Charles Haddon Spurgeon, *Metropolitan Tabernacle Pulpit* (London: Passmore & Alabaster, 1861–92), 507.

19. Spurgeon, *Sermons*, 1:300.

20. J. C. Carlile, *Charles H. Spurgeon: An Interpretative Biography* (London: Religious Tract Society, 1933), 237.

21. Charles Haddon Spurgeon, *Spurgeon's Expository Encyclopedia*, 15 vols. (Grand Rapids: Baker, 1977), 2:442.

22. Spurgeon, *Metropolitan Tabernacle Pulpit*, 509.

23. Charles Haddon Spurgeon, *The Sword and the Trowel* (London: Passmore & Alabaster, 1887), 399.

24. Ibid., preface.

25. Ibid., 558.

26. Carlile, *Charles H. Spurgeon*, 267.

27. Spurgeon, *Metropolitan Tabernacle Pulpit*, 171.

28. Spurgeon, *The Sword and the Trowel*, 344.

29. Spurgeon, *Sermons*, 4:71.

Chapter 8: Vatican I and Neo-Thomism

1. Vatican Council, Section IV, in *Documents of the Christian Church*, 4th ed., ed. Henry Bettenson and Chris Maunder (Oxford: Oxford University Press, 2011), 277.

2. Ralph Keen, *The Christian Tradition* (Lanham, MD: Rowman and Littlefield, 2008), 328.

3. Leo XIII, *Aeterni Patris* 18, 22, Papal Encyclicals Online. http://www.papalencyclicals.net/Leo13/l13cph.htm.

Chapter 9: Revivalist Theology

1. George Needham, *Recollections of Henry Moorhouse, Evangelist* (Chicago: Revell, 1881), 118.

2. Stanley L. Gundry, "The Three Rs of Moody's Theology," *Christian History* 25 (1990): 16.

3. Dwight L. Moody, *Moody's Latest Sermons* (Chicago: BICA, 1900), 1–2.

4. Stanley L. Gundry, *Love Them In: The Life and Theology of D. L. Moody* (Chicago: Moody, 1999), 215.

5. Ibid., 106.

6. Ibid., 91.

7. Ibid., 92.

8. Ibid.

9. Ibid., 93.

10. Dwight L. Moody, *New Sermons, Addresses and Prayers* (St. Louis: N. D. Thompson, 1877), 334.

11. Ibid., 258–59.

12. Ibid., 173.

13. Ibid., 147.

14. Ibid., 149–50.

15. Ibid., 151.

16. Ibid., 158.

17. Gundry, *Love Them In*, 133.

18. Ibid., 157.

19. Ibid., 70.

Chapter 10: The Social Gospel

1. Walter Rauschenbusch, *A Theology for the Social Gospel* (New York: Macmillan, 1917), 1.

2. Ibid., 140.

3. Ibid., 139–40.

4. Ibid., 40.

5. Ibid., 214.
6. Ibid., 53.
7. Ibid., 66.
8. Ibid., 43.
9. Ibid., 139.
10. Ibid., 143.
11. Ibid., 140.
12. Ibid., 5.
13. Ibid., 248, 258.

Chapter 11: Christian Fundamentalism

1. J. Gresham Machen, *Christianity and Liberalism* (Grand Rapids: Eerdmans, 1985), 8.
2. Ibid., 53.
3. Martin E. Marty and R. Scott Appleby, ed., *The Fundamentalism Project*, 5 vols. (Chicago: University of Chicago Press, 1991–95), 1:814–40.
4. Roger E. Olson, *The Story of Christian Theology: Twenty Centuries of Tradition and Reform* (Downers Grove, IL: IVP, 1999), 567.
5. George W. Dollar, *A History of Fundamentalism in America* (Greenville, SC: Bob Jones University Press, 1973), 281.

Chapter 12: Karl Barth and Neo-Orthodoxy

1. Karl Barth, *The Word of God and the Word of Man*, trans. Douglas Horton (Gloucester, MA: Peter Smith, 1958), 43.
2. Karl Barth, *Church Dogmatics*, 4 vols. (Edinburgh: T&T Clark, 1936–62), I/1, 222.
3. Ibid., II/2, 191–92.
4. Ibid., I/1, 241.
5. Ibid., II/1, 263.
6. Ibid., II/1, 260.
7. Ibid., II/1, 281.
8. Ibid., II/2, 163, 167.
9. Ibid., II/2, 319, 346.

Chapter 13: Christian Realism

1. Reinhold Niebuhr, "Ten Years That Shook My World," *Christian Century*, April 26, 1939, 542.
2. H. Richard Niebuhr, "Religious Realism in the Twentieth Century," in *Religious Realism*, ed. Douglas Clyde Macintosh (New York: Macmillan, 1931), 419.
3. Reinhold Niebuhr, "The Blindness of Liberalism," *Radical Religion* 1 (Autumn 1936): 4–5.
4. Reinhold Niebuhr, *Moral Man and Immoral Society: A Study in Ethics and Politics* (New York: Scribner, 1932), xxxiv.
5. Reinhold Niebuhr, *Man's Nature and His Communities: Essays on the Dynamics and Enigmas of Man's Personal and Social Existence* (New York: Scribner, 1965), 24.
6. Reinhold Niebuhr, *Nature and Destiny of Man*, 2 vols. (New York: Scribner, 1941, 1943), 1:174.
7. Ibid., 1:xiii.

8. H. Richard Niebuhr, "The Grace of Doing Nothing," *Christian Century* 49 (March 30, 1932): 379.
9. Reinhold Niebuhr, "Must We Do Nothing?" *Christian Century*, March 30, 1932, 416.
10. H. Richard Niebuhr, *The Kingdom of God in America* (Chicago: Willett, Clark & Company, 1937), 193.
11. H. Richard Niebuhr, *The Meaning of Revelation* (New York: Macmillan, 1941), 45.
12. H. Richard Niebuhr, *Radical Monotheism and Western Culture* (New York: Harper & Row, 1960), 32.
13. H. Richard Niebuhr, *The Responsible Self* (New York: Harper & Row, 1963), 56.

Chapter 14: Pentecostalism and Latin American Pneumatology

1. Cecil M. Robeck Jr., "Pentecostals and Apostolic Faith: Implications for Ecumenism," *Pneuma: The Journal of the Society for Pentecostal Studies* 9 (1987): 64.
2. Timothy C. Tennent, *Theology in the Context of World Christianity: How the Global Church Is Influencing the Way We Think about and Discuss Theology* (Grand Rapids: Zondervan, 2007), 167.
3. Lesslie Newbigin, *Honest Religion for Secular Man* (Philadelphia: Westminster, 1966), 137.
4. Tennent, *Theology in the Context of World Christianity*, 182.
5. Orlando Costas, *Theology of the Crossroads* (Amsterdam: Editions Rodopi, 1976), 19.
6. Gamaliel Lugo Morales, "Moving Forward with the Latin American Pentecostal Movement," *International Review of Mission* 87 (1998): 505–6.
7. Tennent, *Theology in the Context of World Christianity*, 184.
8. Paul A. Pommerville, *The Third Force in Missions* (Peabody, MA: Hendrickson, 1985), 75.

Chapter 15: Ludwig Wittgenstein, Picture Theory, and Language Games

1. Ludwig Wittgenstein, *Tractatus Logico-Philosophicus* (New York: Harcourt, Brace & Company, 1922), §6.5.4.
2. Ibid., §7.

Chapter 16: The Birth of Contemporary Evangelicalism

1. Harold John Ockenga, "Can Fundamentalism Win America?" *Christian Life and Times* 2 (June 1947): 15.
2. Harold John Ockenga, in *The Annals of America, Vol. 16: 1940–1949*, ed. Mortimer J. Adler and Charles Van Doren (New York: Encyclopædia Britannica, 1968), 118.
3. John D. Woodbridge and Frank A. James III, *Church History*, vol. 2, *From Pre-Reformation to the Present Day* (Grand Rapids: Zondervan, 2013), 806.
4. Carl F. H. Henry, *The Uneasy Conscience of Modern Fundamentalism* (Grand Rapids: Eerdmans, 1947), 3.
5. Carl F. H. Henry, *Confessions of a Theologian: An Autobiography* (Waco, TX: Word, 1986), 55.
6. Carl F. H. Henry, *Evangelicals at the Brink of Crisis* (Waco, TX: Word, 1967), 16.
7. "Doctrinal Basis," The Evangelical Theological Society, http://www.etsjets.org/about.
8. Carl F. H. Henry, "Reaction and Realignment," *Christianity Today* 20 (July 2, 1976): 30.

9. Ibid.
10. J. Gresham Machen, *Christianity and Liberalism* (Grand Rapids: Eerdmans, 1985), 75.
11. "Statement of Faith," Fuller, http://fuller.edu/about/mission-and-values/statement-of-faith/.
12. Harold Lindsell, *The Battle for the Bible* (Grand Rapids: Zondervan, 1976), 210.
13. The Chicago Statement on Biblical Inerrancy, in *Inerrancy*, ed. Norman L. Geisler (Grand Rapids: Zondervan, 1990), 496.
14. Ibid., 495–96.
15. Ibid., 500.
16. Ibid., 500–1.
17. Ibid., 501.
18. William Randolph Hearst, quoted in Woodbridge and James, *Church History*, 811.
19. Mark A. Noll, *American Evangelical Christianity: An Introduction* (Hoboken, NJ: Wiley-Blackwell, 2000), 48–49.
20. Woodbridge and James, *Church History*, 811.
21. Billy Graham, quoted in Basyle Tchividdjian and Aram Tchividdjian, *Invitation: Billy Graham and the Lives God Touched* (Colorado Springs: Multnomah, 2008), 49.

Chapter 17: Rudolf Bultmann

1. Rudolf Bultmann, *Jesus Christ and Mythology* (New York: Scribner, 1958), 56.
2. Ibid., 57.
3. Rudolf Bultmann, *Theology of the New Testament*, 2 vols., trans. Kendrick Grobel (New York: Scribner, 1951–55), 1:3.
4. Bultmann, *Jesus Christ and Mythology*, 18.
5. Bultmann, *Theology of the New Testament*, 1:295.
6. Bultmann, *Jesus Christ and Mythology*, 81–82.
7. Ibid., 82.

Chapter 18: Paul Tillich

1. Paul Tillich, *Systematic Theology*, 3 vols. in 1 (Chicago: University of Chicago Press, 1967), 1:4.
2. Ibid., 1:9.
3. Ibid., 1:11.
4. Ibid., 1:12.
5. Ibid., 1:14.
6. Ibid., 1:16.
7. Ibid., 1:50.
8. Ibid., 1:211.
9. Ibid., 1:235.
10. Ibid., 1:239.
11. Ibid., 1:236.
12. Ibid., 2:20–21.
13. Ibid., 1:248.
14. Ibid., 2:31.
15. Ibid., 2:27.
16. Ibid., 2:95.

17. Ibid., 2:177.
18. Ibid., 2:178.
19. Ibid., 3:414.

Chapter 19: Death of God Theologies

1. Paul M. Van Buren, *The Secular Meaning of the Gospel: Based on Analysis of Its Language* (New York: Macmillan, 1963), 82.
2. Ibid.
3. Ibid., 84.
4. Thomas J. J. Altizer, *The Gospel of Christian Atheism* (Philadelphia: Westminster, 1966), 67.
5. Ibid., 83–84.
6. Ibid., 71.

Chapter 20: Roman Catholic Theology from Vatican II to the Present

1. Massimo Faggioli, *Vatican II: The Complete History* (New York: Paulist, 2015), 57.
2. Pope Paul VI, *Ecclesiam suam* 50, Papal Encyclicals Online. http://www.papalencyclicals.net/Paul06/p6eccles.htm.
3. *Unitatis Redintegratio*, in *Vatican Council II, The Basic Sixteen Documents: Constitutions, Decrees, Declarations* (Northport, NY: Costello, 1996), 508.
4. Ibid., 503.
5. Secretariat for Christian Unity, *Reflections and Suggestions Concerning Ecumenical Dialogue*, in *Diversity and Communion*, by Yves Congar (London: SCM, 1984), 128.
6. *Nostra Aetate*, in *Vatican Council II, The Basic Sixteen Documents*, 569–74.
7. Congar, *Diversity*, 135.
8. The Lutheran World Federation and the Roman Catholic Church, *Joint Declaration on the Doctrine of Justification* (Grand Rapids: Eerdmans, 2000), 43.
9. Ibid., 26.
10. Karl Rahner, *Theological Investigations*, 23 vols. (New York: Herder, 1965–92), 6:390.

Chapter 21: Process Theology

1. Alfred North Whitehead, *Process and Reality: An Essay in Cosmology* (New York: Harper Torchbooks, 1929), 348.
2. Ibid., 85.
3. Charles Hartshorne, *A Natural Theology for Our Time* (La Salle, IL: Open Court, 1967), 6.
4. Whitehead, *Process and Reality*, 351.
5. Norman Pittenger, *The Lure of Divine Love* (Edinburgh: Heritage House, 1979), 131.
6. Hartshorne, *Natural Theology for Our Time*, 147.
7. Pittenger, *Lure of Divine Love*, 144.

Chapter 22: Jürgen Moltmann and Wolfhart Pannenberg

1. Jürgen Moltmann, *Theology of Hope: On the Ground and the Implications of a Christian Eschatology*, trans. James W. Leitch (New York: Harper & Row, 1967), 16.
2. Ibid., 20.

3. Jürgen Moltmann, *The Crucified God: The Cross of Christ as the Foundation and Criticism of Christian Theology*, trans. R. A. Wilson and John Bowden (Minneapolis: Fortress, 1993), 276, 25.

4. Ibid., 4.

5. Ibid., 278.

6. Ibid., 258.

7. Ibid., 329.

8. Ibid., 317.

9. Ibid.

10. Jürgen Moltmann, "The Logic of Hell," in *God Will Be All in All: The Eschatology of Jürgen Moltmann*, ed. Richard Bauckham (Edinburgh: T&T Clark, 1999), 44.

11. Ibid., 45.

12. Ibid.

13. Ibid., 44.

14. Ibid., 46.

15. Ibid.

16. Ibid.

17. Jürgen Moltmann, "Am Ende ist alles Gottes: Hat der Glaube an die Hölle ausgedient?" *Evangelische Kommentare* 29 (1996): 543.

18. Moltmann, *Crucified God*, 178.

19. Wolfhart Pannenberg, *The Idea of God and Human Freedom*, trans. R. A. Wilson (Philadelphia: Westminster, 1973), 53, 110.

20. Moltmann, *Theology of Hope*, 214–15.

Chapter 23: John Howard Yoder

1. John Howard Yoder, *The Politics of Jesus*, 2nd ed. (Grand Rapids: Eerdmans, 1994), 201.

2. John Howard Yoder, *The War of the Lamb: The Ethics of Nonviolence and Peacemaking*, ed. Glen Stassen, Mark Thiessen Nation, and Matt Hamsher (Grand Rapids: Brazos, 2009), 149.

3. Ibid., 62, emphasis original.

Chapter 24: Liberation Theology

1. Gustavo Gutiérrez, *A Theology of Liberation*, trans. Sister Caridad Inda and John Eagleson, 2nd ed. (Maryknoll, NY: Orbis, 1988), 135.

2. Ibid., 166.

3. Ibid., 24.

4. Ibid., 24–25.

5. Ibid., 25.

6. Ibid., xxvii.

7. Gustavo Gutiérrez, *Essential Writings*, ed. James B. Nickoloff (Minneapolis: Fortress, 1996), 145.

8. Gutiérrez, *A Theology of Liberation*, 110.

9. Camilo Torres Restrepo, *Revolutionary Priest: The Complete Writings and Messages of Camilo Torres*, ed. John Gerassi (New York: Random House, 1971), vii.

10. Gustavo Gutiérrez, *The Power of the Poor in History*, trans. Robert R. Barr (Maryknoll, NY: Orbis, 1983), 28.

11. National Committee of Negro Churchmen, "Black Power," *New York Times*, July 31, 1966.

12. Black Economic Development Conference, "Black Manifesto," *New York Review of Books*, July 10, 1969.

13. Ibid.

14. National Committee of Black Churchmen, "Black Theology," June 13, 1969, in *Black Theology: A Documentary History*, 2 vols., ed. James H. Cone and Gayraud S. Wilmore (Maryknoll, NY: Orbis, 1979), 1:38.

15. James H. Cone, *God of the Oppressed* (New York: Seabury, 1975), 2.

16. Ibid., 3, emphasis in original.

17. James H. Cone, *A Black Theology of Liberation* (Philadelphia: J. B. Lippincott, 1970), 185, emphasis in original.

18. Ibid., 5.

19. Ibid., 48.

20. James H. Cone, *Black Theology and Black Power* (New York: Seabury, 1969), 143.

21. James H. Cone, "The White Church and Black Power," in *Black Theology*, ed. Cone and Wilmore, 1:71.

22. Cone, *A Black Theology of Liberation*, 126.

Chapter 25: Feminist Theology

1. Mary Daly, *The Church and the Second Sex: With a New Feminist Postchristian Introduction by the Author* (Boston: Beacon, 1975), 15.

2. Ibid., 221.

3. Mary Daly, *Beyond God the Father* (Boston: Beacon, 1973), 19.

4. Ibid., 10.

5. Mary Daly, *Gyn/ecology: The Metaethics of Radical Feminism* (Boston: Beacon, 1990), xlv.

6. Daly, *Church and the Second Sex*, 18.

7. Daly, *Gyn/ecology*, xxxviii.

8. Mary Daly, *Websters' First New Intergalactic Wickedary of the English Language* (Boston: Beacon, 1987), 304.

9. Mary Daly, quoted in Susan Bridle, "No Man's Land," *What Is Enlightenment?* (Fall–Winter 1999): 16.

10. Rosemary Radford Ruether, *Sexism and God-Talk: Toward a Feminist Theology* (Boston: Beacon, 1993), 116.

11. Ibid., 138.

12. Ibid., 23.

13. Ibid.

14. Ibid., 24.

15. Ibid., 114.

16. Rosemary Radford Ruether, *To Change the World: Christology and Cultural Criticism* (New York: Crossroad, 1989), 66.

17. Ibid., 68.

18. Elisabeth Schüssler Fiorenza, *Bread Not Stone: The Challenge of Feminist Biblical Interpretation* (Boston: Beacon, 1984), x.

Chapter 26: Evangelical Complementarianism and Egalitarianism

1. Wayne Grudem, *Systematic Theology: An Introduction to Biblical Doctrine* (Grand Rapids: Zondervan, 1994), 461.
2. Ibid., 465–66, emphasis original.
3. Richard B. Hays, *First Corinthians* (Louisville: Westminster John Knox, 1997), 131.

Chapter 27: Reformed Epistemology

1. Alvin Plantinga, "Reason and Belief in God," in *Faith and Rationality: Reason and Belief in God*, ed. Alvin Plantinga and Nicholas Wolterstorff (Notre Dame, IN: University of Notre Dame Press, 1991), 79.
2. Ibid.
3. Alvin Plantinga, *Warranted Christian Belief* (Oxford: Oxford University Press, 2000), 101.
4. Ibid.
5. James K. Beilby, *Epistemology as Theology: An Evaluation of Alvin Plantinga's Religious Epistemology* (Burlington, VT: Ashgate, 2005), 94–95.
6. Plantinga, *Warranted Christian Belief*, 251.
7. Ibid., 244 (cf. Calvin, *Institutes* 3.2.7).
8. Ibid., 293 (cf. Aquinas, *Summa contra Gentiles* 4.21–22).
9. Ibid., 245.
10. Ibid., 246.
11. Alvin Plantinga, *God, Freedom, and Evil* (Grand Rapids: Eerdmans, 1974), 29, 44–57.

Chapter 28: African Christology

1. John V. Taylor, *The Primal Vision: Christian Presence and African Religion* (London: SCM, 1963), 7.
2. John S. Pobee, "In Search of Christology in Africa: Some Considerations for Today," in *Exploring Afro-Christology*, ed. John S. Pobee (New York: Peter Lang, 1992), 10.
3. Timothy C. Tennent, *Theology in the Context of World Christianity: How the Global Church Is Influencing the Way We Think about and Discuss Theology* (Grand Rapids: Zondervan, 2007), 115.
4. John S. Mbiti, "Some African Concepts of Christology," in *Christ and the Younger Churches*, ed. Georg F. Vicedom (London: SPCK, 1972), 53.
5. Diane Stinton, *Jesus of Africa: Voices of Contemporary African Christology* (Maryknoll, NY: Orbis, 2004), 71.
6. Ibid., 71–72.
7. Ibid., 74.
8. Elizabeth Amoah and Mercy Amba Oduyoye, "The Christ for African Women," in *With Passion and Compassion: Third World Women Doing Theology*, ed. Virginia Fabella and Mercy Amba Oduyoye (Maryknoll, NY: Orbis, 1988), 39.
9. Charles Nyamiti, *Christ as Our Ancestor: Christology from an African Perspective* (Gweru, Zimbabwe: Mambo, 1984), 35.
10. Thomas Lawson, *Religions of Africa* (New York: Harper & Row, 1984), 63.

11. Kwame Bediako, *Christianity in Africa—The Renewal of a Non-Western Religion* (Maryknoll, NY: Orbis, 1995), 94.

12. Quoted in Nyamiti, *Christ as Our Ancestor*, 27.

13. Bediako, *Christianity in Africa*, 217.

14. Kwame Bediako, "The Doctrine of Christ and the Significance of Vernacular Terminology," *International Bulletin of Missionary Research* 22, no. 3 (1998): 110.

15. Nyamiti, *Christ as Our Ancestor*, 48.

16. Tennent, *Theology in the Context of World Christianity*, 126.

17. Bediako, *Christianity in Africa*, 217.

18. Ibid.

Chapter 29: Postmodern Theology

1. John Stephens and Robyn McCallum, *Retelling Stories, Framing Culture* (New York: Garland, 1998), 6.

2. Jean-François Lyotard, *The Postmodern Condition: A Report on Knowledge*, trans. Geoff Bennington and Brian Massumi (Minneapolis: University of Minnesota Press, 1984), xxiv.

3. John D. Caputo, *The Weakness of God: A Theology of the Event* (Bloomington, IN: Indiana University Press, 2006), 14.

4. Ibid., 1.

5. Ibid., 181.

6. Ibid., 44.

7. Jean-Luc Marion, *God without Being*, trans. Thomas A. Carlson (Chicago: University of Chicago Press, 1991), 210.

8. Ibid., 22.

9. Ibid., 48.

10. Ibid., 60.

11. Ibid., 40.

12. Caputo, *Weakness of God*, 4.

13. Ibid., 301.

14. Ibid., 61.

15. Ibid., 72.

16. Bernard of Clairvaux, *De consideratione* 7.16.

17. Duncan S. Ferguson, *Exploring the Spirituality of the World Religions: The Quest for Personal, Spiritual, and Social Transformation* (London: Continuum, 2010), 7.

18. Ibid., 8.

19. Ibid., 10.

Chapter 30: Open Theism

1. Gregory A. Boyd, *God of the Possible: A Biblical Introduction to the Open View of God* (Grand Rapids: Baker, 2000), 86.

2. Gregory A. Boyd, "The Open-Theism View," in *Divine Foreknowledge: Four Views*, ed. James K. Beilby and Paul R. Eddy (Downers Grove, IL: IVP, 2001), 17–18.

3. Ibid., 30.

4. Ibid., 39.

5. John Sanders, *The God Who Risks: A Theology of Providence* (Downers Grove, IL: IVP, 1998), 10.
6. Ibid., 169.
7. Ibid.
8. Ibid., 282.

Chapter 31: Philosophy of Religion and Analytic Theology

1. Alexander Vilenkin, *Many Worlds in One* (New York: Hill and Wang, 2006), 176.
2. Charles Darwin, *The Descent of Man and Selection in Relation to Sex*, 2nd ed. (New York: Appleton, 1909), 100.
3. Michael Ruse, *The Darwinian Paradigm* (London: Routledge, 1989), 268–69.
4. Walter Sinnott-Armstrong, "An Argument for Consequentialism," *Philosophical Perspectives* 6 (1992): 399.
5. Louise Antony, "Debate: Is God Necessary for Morality? Craig vs. Antony," University of Massachusetts (April 10, 2008), http://www.reasonablefaith.org/videos/debates/craig-vs-antony-university-of-massachusetts.
6. William Lane Craig, *The Only Wise God: The Compatibility of Divine Foreknowledge and Human Freedom* (Grand Rapids: Baker, 1987), 139.

Chapter 32: Chinese Eschatology

1. C. Peter Wagner, foreword to *The Coming Influence of China*, by Carl Lawrence and David Wang (Artesia, CA: Shannon, 2000), x.
2. Brother Yun, Peter Xu Yongze, and Enoch Wang, with Paul Hattaway, *Back to Jerusalem: Three Chinese House Church Leaders Share Their Vision to Complete the Great Commission* (Downers Grove, IL: IVP, 2003), 20.
3. Ibid.
4. David Aikman, *Jesus in Beijing: How Christianity Is Transforming China and Changing the Global Balance of Power* (Washington, DC: Regnery, 2003), 301.
5. Yun, Yongze, and Wang, *Back to Jerusalem*, 91.
6. Ibid., 57.
7. Timothy C. Tennent, *Theology in the Context of World Christianity: How the Global Church Is Influencing the Way We Think about and Discuss Theology* (Grand Rapids: Zondervan, 2007), 240.
8. Yun, Yongze, and Wang, *Back to Jerusalem*, 3.
9. Ibid., 70.
10. Ibid., 112.
11. Ibid., 57, 63.
12. Ibid., 70.
13. Carl Lawrence and David Wang, *The Coming Influence of China* (Artesia, CA: Shannon, 2000), 38.
14. Aikman, *Jesus in Beijing*, 138.

Chapter 33: Postliberal Theology

1. Hans W. Frei, *The Eclipse of Biblical Narrative: A Study in Eighteenth and Nineteenth Century Hermeneutics* (New Haven, CT: Yale University Press, 1974), 130.

2. Hans W. Frei, *The Identity of Jesus Christ: The Hermeneutical Bases of Dogmatic Theology* (Philadelphia: Fortress, 1975), 139–40.

3. Ibid., 145.

4. George A. Lindbeck, *The Nature of Doctrine: Religion and Theology in a Postliberal Age* (Louisville: Westminster John Knox, 1984), 16.

5. Ibid.

6. Ibid., 32.

7. Ibid., 128.

Chapter 34: Theology and the Arts

1. Jeremy Begbie, *Voicing Creation's Praise: Towards a Theology of the Arts* (London: T&T Clark, 1991), 200.

2. Jeremy Begbie, "Faithful Feelings: Music and Emotion in Worship," in *Resonant Witness: Conversations between Music and Theology*, ed. Jeremy Begbie and Steven R. Guthrie (Grand Rapids: Eerdmans, 2011), 323.

3. Ibid.

4. Ibid., 326.

5. Ibid., 328.

6. Ibid., 331; emphasis in original.

7. Ibid., 335.

8. Ibid., 336.

9. Ibid.

10. Ibid.

11. Ibid., 337.

12. Ibid.

13. Aquinas, *Summa theologiae* 2.1.9.1.

14. Ibid., 2.1.21.2.

15. Begbie, "Faithful Feelings," 352.

Chapter 35: A New Perspective on Paul and Justification

1. E. P. Sanders, *Paul and Palestinian Judaism: A Comparison of Patterns of Religion* (Minneapolis: Fortress, 1977), 75.

2. Ibid.

3. E. P. Sanders, *Paul, the Law, and the Jewish People* (Minneapolis: Fortress, 1983), 159.

4. Sanders, *Paul and Palestinian Judaism*, 463.

5. James D. G. Dunn, *Jesus, Paul, and the Law: Studies in Mark and Galatians* (Louisville: Westminster John Knox, 1990), 194.

6. Ibid.

7. Ibid., 198.

8. N. T. Wright, *What Saint Paul Really Said: Was Paul of Tarsus the Real Founder of Christianity?* (Grand Rapids: Eerdmans, 1997), 132–33.

9. N. T. Wright, *Justification: God's Plan and Paul's Vision* (Downers Grove, IL: IVP Academic, 2009), 121.

10. Ibid., 90.

11. Wright, *What Saint Paul Really Said*, 32–33.

12. Ibid., 94.

13. Ibid., 98.

14. Ibid., 132.

15. Wright, *Justification*, 251.

Chapter 36: Theological Interpretation of Scripture

1. Kevin J. Vanhoozer, "Introduction: What Is Theological Interpretation of the Bible?" in *Theological Interpretation of the New Testament: A Book-by-Book Survey*, gen. ed. Kevin J. Vanhoozer, and assoc. eds. Daniel J. Treier and N. T. Wright (Grand Rapids: Baker Academic, 2008), 15.

2. Ibid.

3. Ibid.

4. Ibid., 16.

5. Ibid.

6. Ibid., 16–17.

7. Ibid., 17.

8. Ibid., 19.

9. Ibid., 20, emphasis in original.

10. Ibid.

11. Ibid., 21, emphasis in original.

12. Ibid., 18.

13. Ibid., 22.

14. Ibid., 24.

Chapter 37: Evolutionary Creation

1. John H. Walton, *The Lost World of Genesis One: Ancient Cosmology and the Origins Debate* (Downers Grove, IL: IVP Academic, 2009), 22, 24.

2. Ibid., 44–45.

3. Ibid., 47–48.

4. Ibid., 54.

5. Ibid., 72–73.

6. Josephus, *Antiquities* 3.7.7 (180).

7. John H. Walton, *The Lost World of Adam and Eve: Genesis 2–3 and the Human Origins Debate* (Downers Grove, IL: IVP Academic, 2015), 117.

8. Ibid., 72.

9. Ibid., 79.

Chapter 38: Postconservative Theology

1. Roger E. Olson, *Reformed and Always Reforming: The Postconservative Approach to Evangelical Theology* (Grand Rapids: Baker Academic, 2007), 17.

2. Ibid.

3. Ibid., 55.

4. Ibid., 56.

5. Ibid., 59.
6. Ibid.
7. Ibid., 60.
8. Ibid.
9. Ibid., 61.
10. Stanley J. Grenz, *Revisioning Evangelical Theology: A Fresh Agenda for the 21st Century* (Downers Grove, IL: IVP Academic, 1993), 57.
11. Olson, *Reformed*, 64.
12. Ibid., 63.
13. Steven B. Sherman, *Revitalizing Theological Epistemology: Holistic Evangelical Approaches to the Knowledge of God*, Princeton Theological Monograph Series 83 (Eugene, OR: Pickwick, 2008), 9–10.

SUBJECT INDEX

SCRIPTURE INDEX

Contemporary Theology Video Lectures

Classical, Evangelical, Philosophical, and Global Perspectives

Kirk R. MacGregor

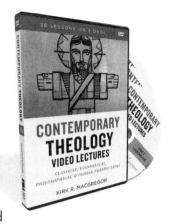

Contemporary Theology Video Lectures features 38 sessions (on 3DVDs) and provides a chronological survey of the major thinkers and schools of thought in modern theology. A companion to the textbook *Contemporary Theology: An Introduction*, these accessible and comprehensive sessions cover evangelical perspectives alongside mainline and liberal views, the influence of philosophy and the recent Christian philosophical renaissance on theology, global contributions, recent developments in exegetical theology, and the implications of theological shifts on ethics and church life.

These lectures are noteworthy for making complex ideas understandable and for tracing the landscape of modern theology in a well-organized and easy-to-follow manner. They are ideal for students, pastors, and independent learners who want to have an additional point of contact with the material from the main textbook on which they are based.

Available in stores and online!

ZONDERVAN®
.com

Luis de Molina

The Life and Theology of the Founder of Middle Knowledge

Kirk R. MacGregor

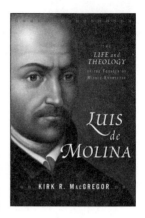

When Luis de Molina died in Madrid in 1600, he had every reason to believe he was about to be anathametized by Pope Clement VIII. The Protestant Reformation was splitting Europe, tribunals of the Inquisition met regularly in a dozen Spanish cities, and the Pope had launched a commission two years earlier to investigate Molina's writings.

Molina was eventually vindicated, though the decision came seven years after his death. In the centuries that followed Molina was relegated to relatively minor status in the history of theology until a renaissance of interest in recent years. His doctrine of God's "middle knowledge," in particular, has been appropriated by a number of current philosophers and theologians, with apologist William Lane Craig calling it "one of the most fruitful theological ideas ever conceived."

In *Luis de Molina: The Life and Theology of the Founder of Middle Knowledge*, author Kirk R. MacGregor outlines the main contours of Molina's subtle and far-reaching philosophical theology, covering his views on God's foreknowledge, salvation and predestination, poverty and obedience, and social justice. Drawing on writings of Molina never translated into English, MacGregor also provides insight into the experiences that shaped Molina, recounting the events of a life fully as dramatic as any of the Protestant Reformers.

With implications for topics as wide-ranging as biblical inerrancy, creation and evolution, the relationship between Christianity and world religions, the problem of evil, and quantum indeterminacy, Molina's thought remains as fresh and relevant as ever. Most significantly, perhaps, it continues to offer the possibility of a rapprochement between Calvinism and Arminianism, a view of salvation that fully upholds both God's predestination and human free will.

As the first full-length work ever published on Molina, Kirk MacGregor's *Luis de Molina* provides an accessible and insightful introduction for scholars, students, and armchair theologians alike.

Available in stores and online!